Human Factors Issues and the Impact of Technology on Society

Heather Lum
Embry–Riddle Aeronautical University, USA

A volume in the Advances in Human
and Social Aspects of Technology
(AHSAT) Book Series

Published in the United States of America by
 IGI Global
 Information Science Reference (an imprint of IGI Global)
 701 E. Chocolate Avenue
 Hershey PA, USA 17033
 Tel: 717-533-8845
 Fax: 717-533-8661
 E-mail: cust@igi-global.com
 Web site: http://www.igi-global.com

Library of Congress Cataloging-in-Publication Data

Names: Lum, Heather Christina, 1984- editor.
Title: Human factors issues and the impact of technology on society /
  Heather Lum, editor.
Description: Hershey PA : Information Science Reference, [2021] | Includes
  bibliographical references and index. | Summary: "This edited book
  addresses specific human factors issues associated with and related to
  technology use in society, offering a research perspective to advance
  readers understanding of how technology works, how we work, and how we
  work within the context of the technology we use"-- Provided by
  publisher.
Identifiers: LCCN 2021000188 (print) | LCCN 2021000189 (ebook) | ISBN
  9781799864530 (hardcover) | ISBN 9781799864547 (paperback) | ISBN
  9781799864554 (ebook)
Subjects: LCSH: Human engineering. | Technology--Social aspects. |
  Technological innovations--Social aspects.
Classification: LCC T59.7 .H8535 2021 (print) | LCC T59.7 (ebook) | DDC
  303.48/3--dc23
LC record available at https://lccn.loc.gov/2021000188
LC ebook record available at https://lccn.loc.gov/2021000189

This book is published in the IGI Global book series Advances in Human and Social Aspects of Technology (AHSAT) (ISSN: 2328-1316; eISSN: 2328-1324)

British Cataloguing in Publication Data
A Cataloguing in Publication record for this book is available from the British Library.

All work contributed to this book is new, previously-unpublished material.
The views expressed in this book are those of the authors, but not necessarily of the publisher.

For electronic access to this publication, please contact: eresources@igi-global.com.

Advances in Human and Social Aspects of Technology (AHSAT) Book Series

ISSN:2328-1316
EISSN:2328-1324

Editor-in-Chief: Mehdi Khosrow-Pour, D.B.A. Information Resources Management Association, USA

MISSION

In recent years, the societal impact of technology has been noted as we become increasingly more connected and are presented with more digital tools and devices. With the popularity of digital devices such as cell phones and tablets, it is crucial to consider the implications of our digital dependence and the presence of technology in our everyday lives.

The **Advances in Human and Social Aspects of Technology (AHSAT) Book Series** seeks to explore the ways in which society and human beings have been affected by technology and how the technological revolution has changed the way we conduct our lives as well as our behavior. The AHSAT book series aims to publish the most cutting-edge research on human behavior and interaction with technology and the ways in which the digital age is changing society.

COVERAGE

- Computer-Mediated Communication
- ICTs and human empowerment
- Human Rights and Digitization
- Activism and ICTs
- Cultural Influence of ICTs
- Technology and Freedom of Speech
- Digital Identity
- Public Access to ICTs
- Technology Adoption
- Cyber Bullying

IGI Global is currently accepting manuscripts for publication within this series. To submit a proposal for a volume in this series, please contact our Acquisition Editors at Acquisitions@igi-global.com or visit: http://www.igi-global.com/publish/.

Titles in this Series

For a list of additional titles in this series, please visit:
http://www.igi-global.com/book-series/advances-human-social-aspects-technology/37145

Ubiquitous Technologies for Human Development and Knowledge Management
Hakikur Rahman (Institute of Computer Management and Science, Bangladesh)
Information Science Reference • © 2021 • 396pp • H/C (ISBN: 9781799878445) • US $195.00

Technological Breakthroughs and Future Business Opportunities in Education, Health, and Outer Space
Angus Hooke (Australian Institute of Higher Education, Australia)
Business Science Reference • © 2021 • 353pp • H/C (ISBN: 9781799867722) • US $225.00

Technological Influences on Creativity and User Experience
Joshua Fairchild (Creighton University, USA)
Information Science Reference • © 2021 • 305pp • H/C (ISBN: 9781799843542) • US $195.00

Machine Law, Ethics, and Morality in the Age of Artificial Intelligence
Steven John Thompson (University of California, Davis, USA & University of Maryland Global Campus, USA)
Engineering Science Reference • © 2021 • 266pp • H/C (ISBN: 9781799848943) • US $295.00

Examining the Socio-Technical Impact of Smart Cities
Fenio Annansingh (York College, City University of New York, USA)
Information Science Reference • © 2021 • 231pp • H/C (ISBN: 9781799853268) • US $190.00

Human-Computer Interaction and Technology Integration in Modern Society
Hakikur Rahman (Institute of Computer Management and Science, Bangladesh)
Engineering Science Reference • © 2021 • 347pp • H/C (ISBN: 9781799858492) • US $195.00

For an entire list of titles in this series, please visit:
http://www.igi-global.com/book-series/advances-human-social-aspects-technology/37145

701 East Chocolate Avenue, Hershey, PA 17033, USA
Tel: 717-533-8845 x100 • Fax: 717-533-8661
E-Mail: cust@igi-global.com • www.igi-global.com

Table of Contents

Preface..xiv

Acknowledgment...xxi

Chapter 1
Pandemics, Preprints, and Praxis...1
    Michael R. Schwartz, WEAR Lab, USA
    Paul Oppold, University of Central Florida, USA

Chapter 2
Ethical Design of Social Technology: User Engagement and Attentional
Demands 20
    Fernando L. Montalvo, University of Central Florida, USA
    Michael Miuccio, University of Central Florida, USA
    Grace E. Waldfogle, University of Central Florida, USA

Chapter 3
Human Factors: An Authentic Learning Mobile Application Design Project
in a Higher Education and Industry Context...48
    Emily Cooney, Duquesne University, USA
    Nicole Martonik, Duquesne University, USA
    Lauren Kolber, Duquesne University, USA
    Emalee Sekely, Duquesne University, USA
    William J. Gibbs, Duquesne University, USA

Chapter 4

Augmented Reality: Panacea or Pandora's Box? 78
  Victoria L. Claypoole, Design Interactive, Inc., USA
  Clay D. Killingsworth, Design Interactive, Inc., USA
  Catherine A. Hodges, Design Interactive, Inc., USA
  Hannah K. Nye, Design Interactive, Inc., USA
  Larry A. Moralez, Design Interactive, Inc., USA
  Ernesto Ruiz, Design Interactive, Inc., USA
  Kay M. Stanney, Design Interactive, Inc., USA

Chapter 5

Strategic Implications of Organizational Culture, Knowledge, Learning
Organizations, and Innovation on Sustainable Organizations 109
  José G. Vargas-Hernández, University Center for Economic and
    Managerial Sciences, University of Guadalajara, Mexico
  Jorge Armando López-Lemus, Unibversidad de Guadajuato, Mexico

Chapter 6

The Utility of Neuro-Economics in the Services of ICT of the Exponential
SMEs of the Artisanal Industry of Women Entrepreneurs in Mexico 140
  Jovanna Nathalie Cervantes-Guzmán, University of Guadalajara,
    Mexico

Chapter 7

Facilitating the Adoption of Digital Health Technologies by Older Adults to
Support Their Health 164
  Maurita T. Harris, University of Illinois Urbana-Champaign, USA
  Wendy A. Rogers, University of Illinois Urbana-Champaign, USA

Chapter 8

Digital Mental Health Interventions: Impact and Considerations 180
  Christopher R Shelton, The Behrend College, Pennsylvania State
    University, Erie, USA
  Anitgoni Kotsiou, The Behrend College, Pennsylvania State University,
    Erie, USA
  Melanie D. Hetzel-Riggin, The Behrend College, Pennsylvania State
    University, Erie, USA

Chapter 9

Mariners or Machines: Who's at the Helm? Shifting Roles and
Responsibilities on Navy Warships...211
  Kimberly E. Culley, U.S. Submarine Force, USA

Chapter 10
Exploring Technology Tendencies and Their Impact on Human-Human

Interactions...222
    Heather C. Lum, Embry-Riddle Aeronautical University, USA

Compilation of References 239

Related References... 295

About the Contributors 325

Index.. 331

Detailed Table of Contents

Preface.. xiv

Acknowledgment xxi

Chapter 1
Pandemics, Preprints, and Praxis 1
> *Michael R. Schwartz, WEAR Lab, USA*
> *Paul Oppold, University of Central Florida, USA*

The speed and severity of the COVID-19 pandemic presents challenges not seen since the Spanish flu pandemic of 1918. Governments, healthcare providers, and industries are using all available resources to produce and distribute prevention and mitigation measures. This chapter examines the issues, challenges, and questions surrounding the use of wearable devices (e.g., Fitbit) in combating the COVID-19 pandemic. The implementation of wearables to prevent the spread of infection in the 2020 NBA Bubble is used as a case study of whether and how wearables should be used for detecting illnesses. The role of preprints and their influence on discourse about COVID-19 are also discussed in this chapter.

Chapter 2
Ethical Design of Social Technology: User Engagement and Attentional
Demands 20
> *Fernando L. Montalvo, University of Central Florida, USA*
> *Michael Miuccio, University of Central Florida, USA*
> *Grace E. Waldfogle, University of Central Florida, USA*

Social technology has become ubiquitous in everyday life. Developers of social technologies seek design elements and new technologies, such as machine learning algorithms, aimed at increasing user engagement. Increased user engagement with products or services is sought after by both companies, which benefit from increased sales and customers who desire technology which they are motivated to use. However, increased user engagement also results in increased demand on user attention. High demand on user attention results in problems for social technology users, including decreased task performance, decrements in working memory, increased anxiety, and more. Developers of social technology should take these negative effects on users into account when implementing new features into their products or services. This chapter proposes a framework for the ethical design of social technology, with a specific emphasis on the balance between user engagement and attentional demands on the user.

Chapter 3

Human Factors: An Authentic Learning Mobile Application Design Project in a Higher Education and Industry Context..48

    Emily Cooney, Duquesne University, USA
    Nicole Martonik, Duquesne University, USA
    Lauren Kolber, Duquesne University, USA
    Emalee Sekely, Duquesne University, USA
    William J. Gibbs, Duquesne University, USA

Human factors are integral to applied academic programs such as interaction design. In this chapter, the authors begin by reviewing precepts of authentic, "real-world" learning. From a human factors and interaction design viewpoint, they then describe an authentic learning project—a mobile application design—that was done by university students in collaboration with a leading global specialty retailer. Specifically, in terms of the project, the chapter reviews the following: 1) benefits and challenges of academic and industry collaborations; 2) human factors and interaction design processes, methods, and principles used throughout the authentic project; 3) anthropometric features of the project prototype and their implications for usability; 4) precepts of cognitive information processing (i.e., human attention, perception, and memory) and their importance for the design and usability of the project's interface; 5) insights and lessons learned about the use of authentic learning experiences in teaching human factors and interaction design.

Chapter 4

Augmented Reality: Panacea or Pandora's Box?..78

    Victoria L. Claypoole, Design Interactive, Inc., USA
    Clay D. Killingsworth, Design Interactive, Inc., USA
    Catherine A. Hodges, Design Interactive, Inc., USA
    Hannah K. Nye, Design Interactive, Inc., USA
    Larry A. Moralez, Design Interactive, Inc., USA
    Ernesto Ruiz, Design Interactive, Inc., USA
    Kay M. Stanney, Design Interactive, Inc., USA

Augmented reality technology holds great promise for extending and enhancing users' capabilities across numerous applications in both work and personal life. It would be easy to see AR, then, as a panacea, but thoughtful design is required if the benefits are to be realized without also realizing the nascent technology's great potential for harm. Current applications in commercial, military, and education and training settings are herein reviewed, along with consideration of potential future directions. This chapter also identifies hazards posed by poor design or haphazard application and provides recommendations and best practices for those engaged in the design of AR that seek to maximize the human utility of this rapidly maturing technology.

Chapter 5
Strategic Implications of Organizational Culture, Knowledge, Learning
Organizations, and Innovation on Sustainable Organizations 109

José G. Vargas-Hernández, University Center for Economic and
Managerial Sciences, University of Guadalajara, Mexico
Jorge Armando López-Lemus, Unibversidad de Guadajuato, Mexico

This study aims to analyze the strategic implications that the organizational culture has on organizational knowledge, learning, and innovation. It begins from the assumption that there is a direct and positive relationship between the organizational culture and knowledge, learning, and innovation in organizations. It also is assumed that organizational culture, knowledge, learning, and innovation are receptive to sustainable organizational practices. The method used is the appreciative inquiry as a collaborative dialogue based on the question of what is the best of and what might be that aims to design and implement innovations in sustainable organizational arrangements and processes. The theoretical framework is based on organizational cultural cognitivism theory and the theory of socio-ecological intergradation. It is concluded that sustainable organizations practices require the creation and development of an organizational culture supportive of knowledge, learning, and innovation practices.

Chapter 6
The Utility of Neuro-Economics in the Services of ICT of the Exponential
SMEs of the Artisanal Industry of Women Entrepreneurs in Mexico...............140

Jovanna Nathalie Cervantes-Guzmán, University of Guadalajara,
Mexico

The chapter explores the utility of neuroeconomics in decision making and behavior. Scientific knowledge will be advanced in the need for the application of neuroeconomics focused on one of the services of the information and communication technologies (ICT) of companies that is e-commerce of exponential artisanal SMEs of women entrepreneurs by developing a proposal for a business model to increase the possibility of growth of their companies at the level national and international level. The methodology used was deductive, exploratory, descriptive, correlational, and documentary. Neuroeconomics have the potential to explain the phenomena that are considered as a deviation from the prediction or behavioral bias of decision-making models in economic theory. The study up to this point is quantitative using primary and secondary sources for research.

Chapter 7
Facilitating the Adoption of Digital Health Technologies by Older Adults to
Support Their Health 164

    Maurita T. Harris, University of Illinois Urbana-Champaign, USA
    Wendy A. Rogers, University of Illinois Urbana-Champaign, USA

With over 50% of older adults in the United States managing at least one chronic condition, it is crucial to understand how to promote their self-management of positive health behaviors. Health interventions through digital health technologies are becoming more commonplace. Theoretical models related to health behavior change and technology acceptance can guide the design of these healthcare tools and lead to adoption by older adults to support their health. This chapter provides an overview of health behavior change and technology acceptance models to inform the development of digital health technology for older adults. This chapter illustrates the application of these models by describing two design personas that represent human factors designers. This chapter discusses the lack of inclusion of technology adoption and other long-term concepts and the need for further exploration that could inform understanding of technology integration into everyday health activities.

Chapter 8
Digital Mental Health Interventions: Impact and Considerations 180

    Christopher R Shelton, The Behrend College, Pennsylvania State
        University, Erie, USA
    Anitgoni Kotsiou, The Behrend College, Pennsylvania State University,
        Erie, USA
    Melanie D. Hetzel-Riggin, The Behrend College, Pennsylvania State
        University, Erie, USA

This chapter will provide a brief background on the need for digital mental health interventions given the high rates of mental health issues and the barriers to access quality care. Three main types of digital mental health interventions (internet-based interventions [IBIs], smartphone apps, and virtual and augmented reality [VR and AR, respectively]) will be discussed, followed by a consideration of the ethical and logistical issues surrounding digital mental health interventions. The chapter will then address issues related to content and design, user engagement, user contact, and formatting of the interventions. Finally, the chapter will end with a discussion of future directions.

Chapter 9

Mariners or Machines: Who's at the Helm? Shifting Roles and
Responsibilities on Navy Warships..211

Kimberly E. Culley, U.S. Submarine Force, USA

Building in layers of safety and sharpening the warfighting edge does not necessarily mean using technology more, but rather using it more effectively. Deftly applied automation can buy back time and cognitive resources for operators, decreasing the chances of human error, but technology also has the potential to become less of a tool and more of a crutch if operational fundamentals and basic seafaring skills are forsaken to automation. Operators must be able to rely on their own "sea sense," developed through experience and mentoring, and use technology to accomplish specific objectives rather than defer to automation as the default decision-maker. Maintaining the competitive warfighting edge requires cultivating skilled mariners who know how to fight a well-equipped ship; adding complexity to the system without accounting for the human element creates added risk and cutting-edge failure modes. Technology alone cannot make the ship safe, but when the operator lacks fundamental knowledge and experience, it can make the ship unsafe.

Chapter 10

Exploring Technology Tendencies and Their Impact on Human-Human
Interactions..222

Heather C. Lum, Embry-Riddle Aeronautical University, USA

Although traditionally researchers have focused on making robotics more user-friendly from a human perspective, a new theory has begun to take shape in which humans take on the perspective of a robotic entity. The following set of studies examined the concept of technomorphism defined as the attribution of technological characteristics to humans. This concept has been mentioned anecdotally and studied indirectly, but there is nothing currently available to tap into the various forms that technomorphism may take. Through the study of technomorphism, researchers have come slightly closer to the question of how technology is influencing our perceptions of what it means to be human. The findings from this work should help fuel the desire of others in the field to think about the potential influences of technomorphism during the design and implementation of new devices as well as in how technology may be related to how we perceive each other.

Compilation of References 239

Related References 295

About the Contributors 325

Index 331

Preface

This is a follow up to my first edited book entitled *Critical Issues Impacting Science, Technology, Society (STS) and Our Future* and further examines the role of technology on our society. The focus of this book is on specific human factors issues associated with and related to technology use in society. Human factors is the scientific discipline concerned with the understanding of interactions among humans and other elements of a system, and the profession that applies theory, principles, data, and other methods to design in order to optimize human well-being and overall system performance.

Technology has become ever more present in our society and has enabled such objects as smart phones, whole house systems, and even automated cars to be more relatable to the average person. People born between 1982 and 1998 have been surrounded by and use technology like no other generation in history, with college-aged students now experiencing their academic years more "wired in" than their predecessors (McBride & Nief, 2010). Similarly, technology and robotics companies are now beginning to utilize cutting edge equipment to turn humans into "super humans." For example, the Raytheon Sarcos created an exoskeleton, which allows a human user to increase his or her strength beyond normal human limits with minimal effort (Jacobsen, 2010). Exposure to this constant wave of technological devices may have caused a shift in our thinking from an organic view to a more technological one. Technology shapes our society in a multitude of ways. It has changed how we communicate with each other, both face to face as well as remotely. Businesses have been impacted equally by technology. Where would we be without the instant access to information via the Internet? The ability to send and receive information via email (over 294 billion sent every day or 2.8 million every second) has forever changed how we work and play (Tschabitscher, 2011). During the Covid-19 pandemic this past year, we have seen technology become a more important player in our everyday lives. From a complete shift to tele-commuting for work, purchasing food and supplies online and having them delivered without ever leaving your house, to the never ending Zoom meeting, technology, for good and bad, has enabled us to work, play, and live in a completely different way this year.

Given that modern Western society has instant access to nearly anything we can think of, even our perception of time is evolving. As one researcher at UC Berkeley explains, "Because of the ability to instantaneously respond to others, our perception of time has been altered. No longer do we feel like we have enough time in the day. Many find themselves spending their entire work time and even personal time replying to e-mails. Though data proves otherwise, we now feel like there is less than 24 hours in a day. When we are bored, we find ourselves spending our whole time chatting online. By the end of the day, we discover that we have spent hours on the internet (Meng, 2009, p. 1). With this influx of technology in our personal and professional lives, it is clear that we are fundamentally altering what is important to us as well as well as how we interact with each other. This book focuses on the role of and research by human factors professionals who are tackling societal issues as it pertains to society.

TARGET AUDIENCES

This book is geared toward human factors practitioners as they are conducting research, performing analyses, and creating better products and systems for users. It will also be for anyone who is interested in how technology has impacted the decisions we make as well as how human factors can be applied and help create better technological devices. Ultimately, the target audience are researchers in the field as well as the general public interested in what research and topics are being studied within the greater context of technology.

ORGANIZATION OF THE BOOK

Chapter 1. Pandemics, Preprints, and Praxis

The speed and severity of the COVID-19 pandemic presents challenges not seen since the Spanish flu pandemic of 1918. Governments, healthcare providers, and industries are using all available resources to produce and distribute prevention and mitigation measures. This chapter examines the issues, challenges, and questions surrounding the use of wearable devices (e.g., Fitbit) in combating the COVID-19 pandemic. The implementation of wearables to prevent the spread of infection in the 2020 NBA Bubble is used as a case study of whether and how wearables should be used for detecting illnesses. The role of preprints and their influence on discourse about Covid-19 are also discussed in this chapter.

Chapter 2. Ethical Design of Social Technology: User Engagement and Attentional Demands

Social technology has become ubiquitous in everyday life. Developers of social technologies seek design elements and new technologies, such as machine learning algorithms, aimed at increasing user engagement. Increased user engagement with products or services is sought after by both companies, which benefit from increased sales, and customers, who desire technology which they are motivated to use. However, increased user engagement also results in increased demand on user attention. High demand on user attention results in problems for social technology users, including decreased task performance, decrements in working memory, increased anxiety, and more. This chapter proposes a framework for the ethical design of social technology, with a specific emphasis on the balance between user engagement and attentional demands on the user.

Chapter 3. Human Factors: An Authentic Learning Mobile Application Design Project in a Higher Education and Industry Context

Human factors are integral to applied academic programs such as Interaction Design. In this chapter, the authors begin by reviewing precepts of authentic, "real-world" learning. Specifically, the chapter reviews the benefits and challenges of academic and industry collaborations, human factors and interaction design processes, methods, and principles used throughout the authentic project, anthropometric features of the project prototype and their implications for usability, precepts of cognitive information processing (i.e., human attention, perception, and memory, and insights and lessons learned about the use of authentic learning experiences in teaching human factors and interaction design.

Chapter 4. Augmented Reality: Panacea or Pandora's Box?

Augmented reality technology holds great promise for extending and enhancing users' capabilities across numerous applications in both work and personal life. It would be easy to see AR, then, as a panacea, but thoughtful design is required if the benefits are to be realized without also realizing the nascent technology's great potential for harm. Current applications in commercial, military, and education and training settings are herein reviewed, along with consideration of potential future directions. This chapter also identifies hazards posed by poor design or haphazard application and provides recommendations and best practices for those engaged in the design of AR that seek to maximize the human utility of this rapidly maturing technology.

Chapter 5. Strategic Implications of Organizational Culture, Knowledge, Learning Organizations, and Innovation on Sustainable Organizations

This chapter aims to analyze the strategic implications that the organizational culture has on organizational knowledge, learning and innovation. It begins from the assumption that there is a direct and positive relationship between the organizational culture and knowledge, learning and innovation in organizations. It also is assumed that organizational culture, knowledge, learning and innovation play a receptive to sustainable organizational practices. The method used is the appreciative inquiry as a collaborative dialogue based on the question of what is the best of and what might be that aims to design and implement innovations in sustainable organizational arrangements and processes. The theoretical framework is based on organizational cultural cognitivism theory and the theory of socio-ecological intergradation. It is concluded that sustainable organizations practices require the creation and development of an organizational culture supportive of knowledge, learning and innovation practices.

Chapter 6. The Utility of Neuro-Economics in the Services of ICT of the Exponential SMEs of the Artisanal Industry of Women Entrepreneurs in Mexico

The chapter is in illustration of the utility of neuroeconomics in decision making and behavior. Scientific knowledge will be advanced in the need for the application of neuroeconomics focused on one of the services of the information and communication technologies (ICT) of companies that is e-commerce of exponential artisanal SMEs of women entrepreneurs, by developing a proposal for a business model to increase the possibility of growth of their companies at the level national and international level. Neuroeconomics have the potential to explain the phenomena that are considered as a deviation from the prediction or behavioral bias of decision-making models in economic theory.

Chapter 7. Facilitating the Adoption of Digital Health Technologies by Older Adults to Support Their Health

With over 50% of older adults in the United States managing at least one chronic condition, it is crucial to understand how to promote their self-management of positive health behaviors. Health interventions through digital health technologies are becoming more commonplace. Theoretical models related to health behavior change and technology acceptance can guide the design of these healthcare tools and lead to adoption by older adults to support their health. This chapter provides an overview of health behavior change and technology acceptance models to inform the development of digital health technology for older adults. This chapter illustrates the application of these models by describing two design personas that represent human factors designers. This chapter discusses the lack of inclusion of technology adoption and other long-term concepts and the need for further exploration that could inform understanding of technology integration into everyday health activities.

Chapter 8. Digital Mental Health Interventions: Impact and Considerations

This chapter provides a brief background on the need for digital mental health interventions given the high rates of mental health issues and the barriers to access quality care. Three main types of digital mental health interventions (Internet-based interventions [IBIs], smartphone apps, and virtual and augmented reality [VR and AR, respectively]) were discussed, followed by a consideration of the ethical and logistical issues surrounding digital mental health interventions. The chapter then address issues related to content and design, user engagement, user contact, and formatting of the interventions. Finally, the chapter will end with a discussion of future directions.

Chapter 9. Mariners or Machines: Who's at the Helm? Shifting Roles and Responsibilities on Navy Warships

This chapter is a unique take on aspects of technology within a specific context; namely the role of technology within a navy warship. Building in layers of safety and sharpening the warfighting edge does not necessarily mean using technology more, but rather using it more effectively. Deftly applied automation can buy back time and cognitive resources for operators, decreasing the chances of human error, but technology also has the potential to become less of a tool and more of a crutch if operational fundamentals and basic seafaring skills are forsaken to automation. Operators must be able to rely on their own "sea sense," developed through experience and mentoring, and use technology to accomplish specific objectives rather than defer to automation as the default decision-maker. Maintaining the competitive warfighting edge requires cultivating skilled mariners who know how to fight a well-equipped ship; adding complexity to the system without accounting for the human element creates added risk and cutting-edge failure modes. Technology alone cannot make the ship safe, but when the operator lacks fundamental knowledge and experience, it can make the ship unsafe.

Chapter 10. Exploring Technology Tendencies and Their Impact on Human-Human Interactions

This chapter rounds out the book and is primarily concentrated on how technology is perceived by and influencing our human to human interactions. Although traditionally researchers have focused on making robotics more user-friendly from a human perspective, a new theory has begun to take shape in which humans take on the perspective of a robotic entity. The following set of studies examined the concept of technomorphism defined as the attribution of technological characteristics to humans. This concept has been mentioned anecdotally and studied indirectly, but there is nothing currently available to tap in to the various forms that technomorphism may take. Through the study of technomorphism, researchers have come slightly closer to the question of how technology is influencing our perceptions of what it means to be human. The findings from this work should help fuel the desire of others in the field to think about the potential influences of technomorphism during the design and implementation of new devices as well as in how technology may be related to how we perceive each other.

CONCLUSION

This topic is one that is only growing and is essential that we consider as technology becomes ever more present in our daily lives. This not only impacts us now but is something we need to consider for the future. It is also incredibly important for those in the human factors profession to consider the impact of technology for their work and for the users they are helping design for. Therefore, this has immense impact and is important to study from a research perspective in order to advance out understanding of how technology works, how we work, and how we work within the context of the technology we use.

REFERENCES

Jacobsen, S. (2010). *The exoskeleton's super technology*. Retrieved from: https://www.raytheon.com/newsroom/technology/rtn08_exoskeleton/

McBride, T., & Nief, R. (2010). *Beloit college mindset list, entering class on 2014*. Retrieved from https://www.beloit.edu/mindset/

Meng, J. (2009). *Living in internet time*. Retrieved from https://www.ocf.berkeley.edu/~jaimeng/techtime.html

Tschabitscher, H. (2011). *How many emails are sent every day?* Retrieved from http://www.radicati.com/

Acknowledgment

I would like to personally acknowledge and thank all of the authors for contributing their unique and thought provoking chapters to this book. I have thoroughly enjoyed reading your work and know that the readers will as well. The work you do serves as an important advancement, not only for the human factors community, but society as a whole.

Also, I would like to send a special thank you to all the reviewers who took the time to strengthen and improve the quality of this book through their comments and feedback. Reviewing is often a thankless job but I want you to know that both I as well as the chapter authors really appreciate your efforts!

Lastly, I would like to thank my cheerleader and support system, Scott Rispin. Things seem a little more possible with you standing next to me.

Heather Lum
Embry-Riddle Aeronautical University, USA

Chapter 1
Pandemics, Preprints, and Praxis

Michael R. Schwartz
WEAR Lab, USA

Paul Oppold
University of Central Florida, USA

ABSTRACT

The speed and severity of the COVID-19 pandemic presents challenges not seen since the Spanish flu pandemic of 1918. Governments, healthcare providers, and industries are using all available resources to produce and distribute prevention and mitigation measures. This chapter examines the issues, challenges, and questions surrounding the use of wearable devices (e.g., Fitbit) in combating the COVID-19 pandemic. The implementation of wearables to prevent the spread of infection in the 2020 NBA Bubble is used as a case study of whether and how wearables should be used for detecting illnesses. The role of preprints and their influence on discourse about COVID-19 are also discussed in this chapter.

INTRODUCTION

On June 28th, 2020 Johns Hopkins University reported ten million recorded cases of coronavirus disease 2019 (COVID-19) globally (Johns Hopkins, 2020; Treisman, 2020). At that time, there were more than 2.2 million instances of the disease and more than 126,000 deaths in the United States. Businesses shut down to protect customers and employees, healthcare systems scrambled to respond, and governments took steps to mitigate damage. The speed and severity of the COVID-19 pandemic

DOI: 10.4018/978-1-7998-6453-0.ch001

presents unique challenges in fields such as emergency medicine, logistics and shipping, education, and professional sports. Public health agencies are responding to meet the need for fast, reliable, and widespread testing. There is a global effort to develop and deploy vaccines for a disease that has many unknowns and few valid treatments. Industries, such as tourism and hospitality, are attempting to balance the safety risks of continuing operations during COVID-19 against the economic consequences of suspending business. Novel tools and techniques, including wearable technologies, are under investigation to mitigate the adverse consequences of global health pandemics to help people and businesses return to their pre-pandemic lifestyles. This chapter seeks to address the issues, policies, and practicalities of using wearable technologies to mitigate the adverse effects of pandemics. The use of wearables in the National Basketball Association's (NBA) "bubble" while finishing the 2019-2020 season is examined as a case study of how wearables can and whether they should be applied for the detection of illnesses. News outlets released articles that provided exposure for Oura. This led to increased sales as some consumers, believing the Oura ring and other wearable devices could detect the onset of COVID-19 earlier than other methods despite a body of evidence to support these claims, bought wearables. Oura has been scientifically validated for sleep tracking however, the only scientific evidence supporting the claim that wearables could detect the onset of COVID-19 came from anecdotal claims and scientific publications released as preprints. Preprints, the publication of research papers before undergoing peer review, have influenced the discourse in news media about Covid-19 and wearables. It is the aggregation of consumers reading news articles that cite preprints and high-profile cases, such as the NBA's use of Oura, that has led to premature adoption of wearables for purposes tangentially related to their intended use cases. Premature adoption of a device to assist in private and public health benefits may, at best, lead to beneficial outcomes; however, there is a significant likelihood that detrimental outcomes may occur instead. In the case of COVID-19, detrimental outcomes could include lifelong disability and death. Thus, it is imperative to understand how preprints, news media, and wearable device manufacturers influence adoption of wearable technologies for the mitigation of pandemics.

BACKGROUND

COVID-19 is caused by the SARS-CoV-2 virus (severe acute respiratory syndrome coronavirus 2), as named by the International Committee on Taxonomy of Viruses. As of December 5th, 2020, there have been over 66 million confirmed cases of COVID-19 globally and more than 1.5 million deaths according to the Johns Hopkins Coronavirus Resource Center (Johns Hopkins, 2020). The pandemic continues with no end in sight, save for the hope of a vaccine being produced, tested, and distributed in record time. Similar to the Spanish flu of 1918-1919, general precautions recommended by medical experts include physically distancing, wearing a multilayered mask over the mouth and nose, and frequently washing hands. Contemporary technologies have afforded people novel ways to seek medical help and diagnose and treat illnesses that people a century ago did not have. Videoconferencing technologies allow people to conduct telehealth appointments, computers afford the ability to construct, view, and disseminate advanced models of how diseases progress and may progress, and there is the possibility of diagnosing illnesses through data collected by wearable technologies.

Wearable devices, or wearables, include any worn or body-mounted tool or device (Baber, 2001). Baber's original definition includes head-mounted displays, smartwatches, bifocals, and shoes; however, we will use his revised definition for the remainder of this chapter. The term wearables is used to describe wearable computers, which are worn or body-mounted devices that must be charged regularly and collect, store, process, transmit, or transform data actively or passively. As Baber noted, wearable computers tend to follow the functions of their desktop counterparts and this has influenced the resulting designs. Advances in materials technology and electrical engineering are beginning to usher in a new design paradigm with more fashionable devices that may influence adoption; however, wearables remain constrained by consumer demand, economic forces, and technological possibilities (Schwartz, Oppold, & Hancock, 2019).

Wearable health monitoring devices seek to address the need for testing and tracing of individuals for public health purposes and monitoring physical distancing to reduce the spread of COVID-19 (Bian, Zhou, Bello, & Lukowicz, 2020). In the field of wearable technology, a clear distinction must be made between consumer-grade and clinical-grade devices (Jeong, Rogers, & Xu, 2020). Consumer-grade devices are not able to monitor health over time at a satisfactory rate to provide insight about illnesses, although, this may change as technologies continue to advance. Patches, rings, bracelets, and watches are currently in various stages of development, testing, or implementation to ameliorate some aspect of COVID-19 onset, spread, and severity. Wearable device manufacturers claim their products can perform some of the following functions: 1) monitor physiological data, such as body temperature and heart rate variability, 2) provide contact tracing information by recording who individuals have come into contact with, 3) measure the distance between individuals to ensure physical distancing is adhered to, and 4) warn users that they should not touch their face (D'Aurizio, Baldi, Paolocci, & Prattichizzo, 2020). Clinical-grade devices must undergo rigorous testing before claims can be made about their use. Consumer-grade devices do not have to meet the same validation standard (Schwartz, Oppold, & Hancock, 2019). The speed of development and deployment of non-FDA approved technologies is ideal for responding to threats that can spread exponentially, such as COVID-19; however, there exists an increased likelihood of a false sense of security, founded on false negatives, that can contribute to the spread of illnesses (Aguilar, Faust, Westafer, & Gutierrez, 2020; Kronbichler, Kresse, Yoon, Lee, Effenberger, & Shin, 2020). A high-profile case of applying wearables for pandemic mitigation was the 2020 NBA Bubble.

MAIN FOCUS OF THE CHAPTER

The National Basketball Association experienced a disruption to operations late in the 2019-2020 season due to the COVID-19 pandemic. Seeking to finish the season and recoup some of the seven billion dollars in annual revenue lost due to the league's emergency shutdown in March 2020, the NBA devised a plan to play an abbreviated version of its annual playoffs. The plan consisted of isolating players in a limited access area, known as a "bubble", to decrease the chances of players contracting and spreading COVID-19. The games were held at ESPN's Wide World of Sports Complex, part of the Walt Disney World resort near Orlando, Florida. Players had two wearable devices on them during their stay in Orlando: a Disney MagicBand and an Oura smart ring. The Disney MagicBand served as a hotel key, provided contact tracing, and was used at security checkpoints and for COVID-19 screenings (Clapp, 2020). The Oura smart ring measures pulse, movement, and body temperature via a sweet of onboard sensors (Koskimäki, Kinnunen, Rönkä, & Smarr, 2019). Oura claims the ring can predict the onset of COVID-19 related symptoms three days before symptoms appear with over 90% accuracy (WVU Medicine News, 2020). Researchers at West Virginia University (WVU) Medical Center and the WVU Rockefeller Neuroscience Institute created a mobile app containing a digital dashboard and a predictive algorithm that uses AI-guided models to predict the onset of COVID-19 related symptoms while patients are still asymptomatic. The smart ring, smart ring app, WVU's app, and the algorithm form a system that the researchers claim can be used to detect the onset of COVID-19 earlier and allow for infected individuals to be isolated sooner, thereby reducing the spread of the virus. Oura's app computes a 'readiness' score that indicates to the user if he or she should take a break or is clear to exercise with no restrictions (Kinnunen, Laakkonen, Kivela, Colley, Lahtela, Koskela, & Jurvelin, 2016). WVU's algorithm data mines the Oura data and translates data into COVID-19 related insights.

There are several issues with Oura and WVU's approach from a human factors perspective. How is readiness operationalized? Will recommendations from a readiness score be followed by professional athletes who are required to perform to their greatest ability every game? The Oura smart ring requires two mobile apps:

one to use the ring and another to provide COVID-19 related insights. The workload required to pair, much less use, a wearable device with an associated mobile app has been demonstrated to be enough of a barrier to prevent users from being able to adopt a wearable health monitoring device (Schwartz, Oppold, & Hancock, 2019). What is the workload of managing and interpreting insights from two apps for one function? The workload required to charge the battery of a wearable device presents another barrier to use (Brandao, 2016; Shih et al, 2015; Lazar, Koehler, Tanenbaum, & Nguyen, 2015). Numerous questions require investigation concerning the usability, compliance rate, effectiveness, and validity of using wearables for COVID-19 monitoring and mitigation.

Issues also exist regarding racial bias in health measurement (Sjoding, Dickson, Iwashyna, Gay, & Valley, 2020). Numerous wearable technologies, including the Oura ring, utilize photoplethysmography (PPG) to measure heart rate (Ogata, Sugiura, Osawa, & Imai, 2012). Measuring PPG requires shining a light on the skin; in most consumer-grade devices, this light is green. As blood travels under the skin's surface, variations in light intensity are collected to produce a measure of heart rate based on the reflection of light. Skin tone is determined by a natural pigment, melanin. Melanin is effective at absorbing visible light; thus, infrared light is recommended for measuring PPG (Gilchrest, Fitzpatrick, Anderson, & Parrish, 1977). Visible green light has been the predominant source of measuring heart rate in wearable devices, and there are racial inequities concerning the accuracy of wearable device data (Bickler, Feiner, & Severinghaus, 2005; Shcherbina, Mattsson, Waggott, Salisbury, Christle, Hastie, ... & Ashley, 2017). Over 80% of NBA players are people of color; therefore, using wearables outfitted with a green light sensor may produce inaccurate and unusable data (Tower, 2018). A further complication is presented by the likelihood of a professional athlete presenting with abnormal medical data (Shames, Bello, Schwartz, Homma, Patel, Garza, ... & Engel, 2020). The intersection of elevated melanin in the skin of people of color and presentation of abnormal physiological data in professional athletes means that wearable health monitoring is likely to be less accurate for athletes of color. Further complications arise if the skin is tattooed at the measurement site or if the device's algorithm was not tested on a diverse population. Tattoos may cause calcification of the skin at puncture sites that impede medical imaging (Homer, D'Orsi, & Sitzman, 1994). Furthermore, athletes perspire. Perspiration, tattoo ink, skin color, and density of skin tissue can all affect PPG readings. To overcome these artefacts, PPG signals must be detrended with a low pass filter for readings to be more accurate (Mohan, Nagarajan, & Das, 2016). It is unclear if consumer-grade health monitoring devices utilize detrending techniques. The Oura collects and interprets a user's baseline data and this may be enough to overcome the limitations of an individual presenting with data abnormal to a population; however, there are limitations with respect to the hardware and software in consumer-grade wearable devices and how these technologies are applied.

The 2020 NBA Bubble was in place from late July to October 11th, 2020. No cases of COVID-19 were recorded for the teams that participated, due in part to the precautionary measures put in place by the league (Pegher, 2020). The NBA developed a document that eventually contained more than one hundred pages of what every moment inside the Bubble would be like (Bontemps, 2020). Details about which activities athletes could partake in during their off time to the best way to sanitize basketballs and how to capture spit from referees' whistles were included (Pegher, 2020). Athletes had to wear one device, the Disney MagicBand, for accessing facilities on Disney property; however, two more wearables were optional for players. A worn proximity alarm notified players if they were standing within six feet of another person wearing a proximity alarm for more than five seconds. The alarm, an unnamed brand, was mandatory for league and team staff. The second player-optional device was a smart ring, the Oura ring. No figures exist for how many players opted to wear either the proximity alarm or the Oura ring. The NBA's success in preventing COVID-19 from entering the Bubble may be due, in part, to either or both of these wearable technologies; however, the impact of any single measure at preventing or limiting COVID-19 in the 2020 Bubble is impossible to tease out from the overall results. Less than two months later, the NBA announced an 8.8% positive COVID-19 test rate among the 546 athletes tested prior to the 2020-2021 season (NBA, 2020). The Bubble represented a 180 million dollar investment but resulted in 1.5 billion dollars in revenue that otherwise would have been lost (Beer, 2020). Negative press from COVID-19 infections may have affected the NBA's profits if any had occurred, although a decrease in revenue would be more likely to result from athletes being unable to participate in games and practices. Over one billion dollars is likely to be an incentive for any industry; however, what is certain is that a unique research opportunity was lost when implementation and compliance rates for following disease prevention protocols were not measured and reported.

Research is ongoing to determine whether wearable continuous glucose monitors may be able to play a role in infection risk assessment through analysis of body fluids. This capability, if it exists, may lead to more efficient evaluation and treatment of at-risk patients (; Lukas, Xu, Yu, & Gao, 2020). Remote monitoring of patients through wearable devices can reduce personal protective equipment (PPE) usage (Ehrhardt & Hirsch, 2020). PPE shortages are a major concern of healthcare systems while combatting COVID-19 (Mandrola, 2020). One approach seeking to circumvent the accuracy and measurement issues inherent in wrist-worn wearables is an on-body, skin-integrated sensor worn on the throat or thorax where respiratory biomarkers, such as coughing, are more likely to yield accurate information about respirational illnesses (Jeong et al., 2020). VitalConnect's chest-mounted patch measures heart and respiratory rates and pairs with a pulse oximeter used periodically and has been deployed in nursing homes, where a large percentage of COVID-19 deaths are occurring (Chan, Selvaraj, Ferdosi, & Narasimhan, 2013; McMichael, Currie, Clark, Pogosjans, Kay, Schwartz, ... & Duchin, 2020). All of these devices, however, require more validation before they can be relied upon for mitigation and detection of COVID-19.

Issues, Controversies, Problems

The preprint problem is exemplified by a Washington Post headline, "Wearable tech can spot coronavirus symptoms before you even realize you're sick" (Fowler, 2020). Covid-19 caused states to close high-risk business, such as gyms and concert venues, in March and the first reported case of the novel coronavirus in the U.S. occurred on January 20th, 2020. This timeline is too short for a specialized device to be developed for aiding the public in spotting the signs of Covid-19. The wearable mentioned in the Post article, the Oura ring, was developed before Covid-19 reached the U.S. and a novel application was developed for the existing hardware. However, software development also takes time. Physical and digital prototypes go through iterative design and development processes and while the process can be rushed, speed comes at the expense of quality (e.g., Cyberpunk 2077). Quality is paramount when developing an application for monitoring individual and public health during a pandemic.

The basis for the author's thesis rests on the initial findings of two research studies. Fowler mentions there are six studies investigating the utility of wearables for detecting Covid-19 but does not provide initial results from the other four or give the reader enough information to investigate further. The initial findings Fowler referenced were reported in preprint form. Preprints are scholarly works posted by researchers before the manuscripts have undergone peer review. Scientific research must be developed over time, much like hardware and software. Studies take months and even years to design, develop, pilot, collect and analyze data, interpret findings, and report the results. Peer review, the process of the scientific community evaluating research for its practical and applied merit, takes additional weeks and months. Preprints are a way for scientists and researchers to put their (unverified) findings into the world, thus making sure nobody else can gain credit for the work. No industry standard exists for preprints. Do "initial findings" contain the results of two study participants or 200? Work in progress papers have been presented at academic conferences for years. Why are preprints, which are posted online for anyone to view, necessary for researchers to make sure no one else receives credit for their work?

The preprint problem is magnified when journalists, who are also looking to not get scooped, take the initial findings and generate headlines that may be contradictory to the final, validated results. What happens if a study that is initially reported as a preprint is found to be invalid (note the difference between unverified and invalidated results)? Is the preprint pulled from the internet? Does the news media issue a retraction? Will future researchers who are looking to develop and test hypotheses be able to distinguish between a preprint and a peer reviewed study? Some article repositories are taking steps to address this issue by clearly labeling which articles are preprints, such as medRxiv (https://www.medrxiv.org/). The following cautionary statement is prominently displayed on medRxiv's homepage (emphasis medRxiv's):

Caution: Preprints are preliminary reports of work that have not been certified by peer review. They should not be relied on to guide clinical practice or health-related behavior and should not be reported in news media as established information.

This is a good first step; however, it is incumbent on journalists and news outlets to responsibly report information. For example, a reporter could state that research into using wearables to aid in early Covid-19 diagnoses is ongoing while also refraining from mentioning any features or capabilities of devices that have not yet been validated. To Fowler's credit, the article does go on to use words such as "could" or "may"; however, the article's headline uses the word "can". This is not an oversight. Articles at the Washington Post must be run by editors and, sometimes, the newspaper's legal department. There is big money here. Newspapers need headlines to drive subscriptions, tech startups need investment capital, and researchers need funding. The financial incentives reinforce the people involved until the echo chamber increases sales. This is driven by false and misleading statements from the researchers themselves, such as when speaking about the Oura ring's capabilities:

If we can provide insight into asymptomatic people who may be spreading the virus and help with earlier detection with this technology, it can inform better decision making, facilitate safety, and prioritize who gets testing and other health containment strategies,

-Dr. Ali Rezai, executive chair of the WVU Rockefeller Neuroscience Institute (Abbate, 2020)

The Oura ring, the device covered in the Post article, tracks health metrics, such as baseline body temperature, that may change as part of a set of symptoms people develop after contracting the Covid-19 virus. How then will wearables, and the Oura ring specifically, provide insights into *asymptomatic* individuals that constitute an estimated 40-45% of cases (Oran & Topol, 2020; Shakiba, Nazemipour, Heidarzadeh, & Mansournia, 2020)? There is evidence to indicate that even mild cases of Covid-19 may not manifest as fever, but rather as hyposmia or microsmia, a reduced ability to detect odors (Kim, Kim, Ra, Lee, Bae, Jung, & Kim, 2020). Another study found that fever was weakly associated with the presence of COVID-19 among children (King, Whitten, Bakal, & McAlister, 2020). It is unclear what percentage of Covid-19 cases are able to be identified by an Oura ring or similar device. Dr. Rezai uses the qualifier "if", but it is the responsibility of the medical and scientific community to call out false statements, especially statements that may lead to injury, illness, and loss of life. The news media disseminated Dr. Rezai's statement, not medRxiv's.

SOLUTIONS AND RECOMMENDATIONS

The results of the first Oura studies are promising and wearables, such as those produced by Oura, Fitbit and other manufacturers, may be a useful tool in the fight against infectious diseases; however, using these devices inappropriately or prematurely can have opposite and unintended effects (Smarr, Aschbacher, Fisher, Chowdhary, Dilchert, Puldon, ... & Mason, 2020). The danger exists when members of the public, spurred on by preprints that are reported in the press, believe the headlines and news stories constitute medical guidance. People may buy wearable health monitoring devices believing that the wearables will tell them when they are developing symptoms consistent with an illness. Research indicates almost half of people who get the coronavirus develop no symptoms and mild cases may develop symptoms that change health metrics not tracked by Oura, Fitbit, and Apple devices. People may make decisions about work, travel, recreation, and shopping activities based on a device that may not accurately indicate their medical condition. This belief may exist and help to perpetuate false positive rates. Maybe the Oura ring and similar devices can detect the symptoms of Covid-19 before most people would otherwise spot them, but we do not know yet. Validation takes time. A wearable already exists to protect individuals from Covid-19: *masks.*

The Journal of the American Medical Association has emphasized that coughing, shortness of breath, and fever are primary symptoms in a range of illnesses as indicated by both positive and false negative COVID-19 cases (Johns Hopkins Medicine, 2020; Kucirka, Lauer, Laeyendecker, Boon, & Lessler, 2020). Fevers and other symptoms are the manifestation of one possibility among a range of illnesses (e.g., H1N1, H7N3). Someone may test negative for COVID-19 yet have another potentially deadly illness. This highlights how wearables can help screen for a range of illnesses but can only serve as one tool in the toolbox of illness prevention and mitigation measures that are needed. One of the benefits touted by Oura is that someone could know if they needed a COVID-19 polymerase chain reaction (PCR) test sooner; however, receiving a PCR test too early may return a negative result because viruses take time to proliferate within the body and reach a detectable level of presence (Kucirka, Lauer, Laeyendecker, Boon, & Lessler, 2020). Current global shortages of PCR test reagents, required to isolate COVID-19's genetic material for testing, are further exacerbated by people seeking a COVID-19 test who do not need one. The purpose of this chapter is not to single the Oura ring out. The issues, challenges, and questions presented here apply to the entire class of consumer-grade wearable health monitoring devices. The Oura ring is the main device focused on in this chapter due to its application in the NBA Bubble, which drove brand recognition and influenced device adoption (Qermane & Mancha, 2020). Technological advances may obviate some of the industry's present issues; indeed, it would be beneficial if that is the case. Any technology must be applied in a context of proper use to maximize benefits and minimize harm.

Misinformation is a major issue for public health. Search engines and social media platforms are not well equipped to provide reliable, relevant, authoritative health information and the United States government has delivered conflicting, delayed messages (Donovan, 2020). Preprints do not benefit the general public when unverified information is spread online and in the news from seemingly trustworthy sources, the scientific and medical communities and major news outlets. Major harm may be done if the risk perception biases and social ethics of people are influenced by unvetted scientific and medical claims (Nielsen, Fletcher, Kalogeropoulos, & Simon, 2020). If preprints are here to stay, the medical and scientific communities need to develop a system for responsibly publicizing information and working with news outlets to accurately convey findings. MedRxiv's approach is a good start; a similar effort has not been seen in news media to date.

Over 360,000 deaths are attributed to COVID-19 in the United States. Any device or method that saves lives and prevents disease is worth investigating. However, medical guidance should not be implemented until validation studies have occurred. A novel coronavirus cough database (NoCoCoDa) is under development and is free to researchers (Cohen-McFarlane, Goubran, & Knoefel, 2020). The eventual goal is to implement audio monitoring of COVID-19 coughing in places such as continuing care facilities that will detect the distinct pathophysiology of coronavirus coughs (e.g., frequency, severity). Audio detection of respiratory issues, such as chronic obstructive pulmonary disorder, is diagnostically accurate and holds potential for coronavirus detection (Porter, Claxton, Brisbane, Bear, Wood, Peltonen, ... & Abeyratne, 2020). More research is required to validate the diagnostic accuracy of audio recording for the detection of coughing indicative of COVID-19.

Additional issues exist with regard to systemic social inequalities. Smartwatches and smart rings cost hundreds of dollars each. The impacts of Covid-19 have not been evenly distributed; communities of color and low-income communities have largely faced the brunt of the pandemic (Thakur, Lovinsky-Desir, Bime, Wisnivesky, & Celedón, 2020). Technologies that cost hundreds of dollars per person are not feasible for widespread deployment among people who cannot afford them. Population-level solutions exist that benefit communities as a whole and at scale are cheaper than solutions voluntarily implemented at an individual level. Wastewater monitoring systems are able to screen for multiple issues at once, such as pollution, illicit drug use, and disease spread (Nieuwenhuijse, Munnink, Phan, Munk, Venkatakrishnan, Aarestrup, ... & Koopmans, 2020; Yang, Kasprzyk-Hordern, Frost, Estrela, & Thomas, 2015). Front-end pooling of diagnostic samples is another possible solution; however, conflicting evidence is reported in this area of Covid-19 testing and more validation is required (Abid, Ferjani, El Moussi, Ferjani, Nasr, Landolsi, ... & Safer, 2020; Mallapaty, 2020). Solutions with lower accuracy and specificity levels than a PCR test, the current gold standard for COVID-19 testing, may find such solutions are good enough when stacked together (Reason, 2000; Roberts, 2019). Countries that implement multiple population-level public health safeguards are more likely to prevent or mitigate disease outbreaks. Wearable devices can be a useful tool in the arsenal of population-level safeguards, if implemented properly and the price point is similar to other solutions that scale. One route for wearable device manufacturers to pursue is U.S. Food and Drug Administration (FDA) approval. Continuous glucose monitors are one example of worn, FDA-approved devices that are covered by some healthcare plans in the United States, including Medicare (UAB Medicine, n.d.). One possibility, on a country-by-country basis, is that insurance may one day cover the cost of wearables for COVID-19 detection, thus saving money for insurers, clients, and healthcare systems.

CONCLUSION

Richard Evans (2005) notes in his book *Death in Hamburg: Society and Politics in the Cholera Years 1830-1910* that epidemics call the shots. Viral diseases are threats that spread silently, invisibly, and exponentially. A multilayered approach to disease prevention is necessary because if any one safeguard fails there are other layers to make up for holes in the defense (Griggs, 2020). Washing your hands does not completely protect you from inhaling viral particles and wearing a cloth mask provides some protection, if worn properly. Stack enough layers together, however, and you are safer than if you did not take precautionary measures or applied those measures inappropriately. A comparison can be made to driving a vehicle. Seatbelts, airbags, roll bars, and numerous other safety features are required to make driving as safe as possible. These measures must be applied appropriately (speed limits provide an indication of safe driving speeds) and used (seatbelts are ineffective if not worn) to keep drivers safe. The inappropriate application of technology, however, may do more harm than good. For an example, let us return to the driving scenario. While automobile manufacturers are making strides toward full self-driving (Level 5) vehicles, the reality of autonomous vehicles has yet to be realized. Many laws and regulations are in place about how, when, and where vehicles with partial and conditional autonomous driving capabilities can operate. Not following these laws can lead to injury and death (Sivak & Schoettle, 2015). Similar to keeping each other safe on the road, individuals and groups must apply multiple safeguards appropriately to keep each other safe in a pandemic. The analogy breaks down when one considers that viruses are invisible to the unaided eye and spread exponentially; however, this emphasizes the danger of not taking precautions against diseases and the necessity of applying multiple safeguards. If any time you drove you risked being struck by a vehicle you could not see and that collision could spread exponentially, contemporary transportation systems would be vastly different than the systems currently in place.

This is not to say that wearable devices, such as the Oura ring or Fitbit smartwatches, do not have a place in improving public health. Rather, their importance in the chain of systems that can be used to protect the public from diseases needs to be understood in order to be applied appropriately (Seshadri, Davies, Harlow, Hsu, Knighton, Walker, ... & Drummond, 2020). Fitbit and other wearable device companies collect population level statistics on their users. Hospitals can use anonymized data to monitor the virulence and spread of outbreaks while protecting users' privacy to prepare for influxes of patients more quickly. This would assist the healthcare system in flattening the curve. While no single user is protected from a disease by having a smartwatch or smart ring, society as a whole can benefit, and societies are made of individual people. Over 50 million American adults, approximately 16% of the population, have smartwatches (Heater, 2019). Combined with other population-level systems, wearable devices can assist with providing detection and tracing of viruses in a population. Scientific studies are beginning to delineate and validate how wearables can assist with Covid-19 detection; however, the science has not yet provided enough evidence for people to wager risking their lives on these devices. The NBA invested over one hundred million dollars to implement the 2020 Orlando Bubble, which made their return to play possible. Part of this cost went to food, housing, and travel; millions also went into a suite of protective layers that would prevent and mitigate the spread of COVID-19. The average person does not have access to these funds and will need to adjust their operations and expectations when operating during a pandemic; the NBA cannot be a baseline example. This information was not included the news article circulating last summer.

Consume critically. Carefully consider the claims made by the manufacturers of wearable technologies. Relying on an unvalidated, non-FDA approved device for disease prevention and detection may lead some people to have a false sense of security when their wearable does not indicate they may be ill when, in fact, they could be. This false sense of security could then lead to infecting others. It is possible that wearables, such as the Oura ring, could be part of a suite of tools and techniques to curb illnesses, but only when used appropriately. Device manufacturers can work with federal, state, and local governments to provide population-level monitoring of disease spread, which could help communities allocate healthcare resources more efficiently. The scientific community can more clearly indicate that preprints are not to be used for individual or organization-level health guidance, as medRxiv does. Scientists and researchers can choose to not cite preprints in their work, since the issue of what happens when a preprint is invalidated and retracted is still unclear. The point of why work-in-progress papers and technical reports are not sufficient for claiming credit for work has not been addressed. Work-in-progress papers are often submitted with clear gaps that need to be addressed before final submission to a journal, whereas preprints are posted online with the expectation that they are ready for submission to a journal. However, this does not address the issue of gaps in the research that may be exposed during the peer review process. The issue of whether researchers should use information reported in preprints as a foundation upon which to scaffold scientific theories also needs to be answered. What happens if unvalidated work is used as evidence in a court case? What about subsequent court cases that use the original case as precedent? We stand on the shoulders of giants, but without firm footing we risk regressing down a slippery slope.

There is no single solution for operating normally during a pandemic. Vaccines provide the greatest general protection; however, no vaccine is one hundred percent effective (Osterholm, Kelley, Sommer, & Belongia, 2012). Global health crises require a coordinated response between individuals and governments as there are no silver bullets. Wearable computers may one day be an additional layer in the battle against infectious diseases; however, the data do not yet support this conclusion. Applying a technology before the capabilities are vetted and implemented can lead to tragedy (e.g., Level 5 autonomous vehicles). Let us not forget the best and last line of defense we have against any threat: ourselves. Each layer of society plays its part. Wearable device manufacturers can present their products truthfully, scientists can ensure their work is peer reviewed before it is applied inappropriately, and consumers can think critically about the products they use. Understanding and implementing best practices now will benefit us during future pandemics.

REFERENCES

Abbate, E. (2020, June 17). Here's How the NBA's Coronavirus-Fighting Ring Might Help. *GQ*. https://www.gq.com/story/oura-ring-nba

Abid, S., Ferjani, S., El Moussi, A., Ferjani, A., Nasr, M., Landolsi, I., ... Safer, M. (2020). Assessment of sample pooling for SARS-CoV-2 molecular testing for screening of asymptomatic persons in Tunisia. *Diagnostic Microbiology and Infectious Disease*, *98*(3), 115125. doi:10.1016/j.diagmicrobio.2020.115125 PMID:32768876

Aguilar, J. B., Faust, J. S., Westafer, L. M., & Gutierrez, J. B. (2020). Investigating the impact of asymptomatic carriers on COVID-19 transmission. medRxiv. doi:10.1101/2020.03.18.20037994

Baber, C. (2001). Wearable computers: A human factors review. *International Journal of Human-Computer Interaction*, *13*(2), 123–145. doi:10.1207/S15327590IJHC1302_3

Barry, J. M. (2020). *The great influenza: The story of the deadliest pandemic in history*. Penguin UK.

Beer, T. (2020, Oct 20). Report: NBA's Bubble Prevented $1.5 Billion In Losses. *Forbes*. https://www.forbes.com/sites/tommybeer/2020/10/20/report-nbas-bubble-prevented-15-billion-in-losses/?sh=3215e3793823

Bian, S., Zhou, B., Bello, H., & Lukowicz, P. (2020, September). A wearable magnetic field-based proximity sensing system for monitoring COVID-19 social distancing. In *Proceedings of the 2020 International Symposium on Wearable Computers* (pp. 22-26). 10.1145/3410531.3414313

Bickler, P. E., Feiner, J. R., & Severinghaus, J. W. (2005). Effects of skin pigmentation on pulse oximeter accuracy at low saturation. *Anesthesiology: The Journal of the American Society of Anesthesiologists*, *102*(4), 715–719. doi:10.1097/00000542-200504000-00004 PMID:15791098

Bontemps, T. (2020, Jun 16). In documents, NBA details coronavirus testing protocols, including 2-week resting period for positive tests. *ESPN*. https://www.espn.com/nba/story/_/id/29321006/in-documents-nba-details-coronavirus-testing-process-orlando-campus-life

Chan, A. M., Selvaraj, N., Ferdosi, N., & Narasimhan, R. (2013, July). Wireless patch sensor for remote monitoring of heart rate, respiration, activity, and falls. In *2013 35th Annual international conference of the IEEE engineering in medicine and biology society (EMBC)* (pp. 6115-6118). IEEE. 10.1109/EMBC.2013.6610948

Clapp, M. (2020, Jun 18). NBA players can wear this Oura smart ring to monitor potential COVID-19 symptoms in Orlando. *The Comeback.* https://thecomeback.com/nba/nba-players-can-wear-this-oura-smart-ring-to-monitor-potential-covid-19-symptoms-in-orlando.html

Cohen-McFarlane, M., Goubran, R., & Knoefel, F. (2020). Novel coronavirus cough database: Nococoda. *IEEE Access: Practical Innovations, Open Solutions, 8,* 154087–154094. doi:10.1109/ACCESS.2020.3018028

D'Aurizio, N., Baldi, T. L., Paolocci, G., & Prattichizzo, D. (2020). Preventing Undesired Face-Touches with Wearable Devices and Haptic Feedback. *IEEE Access: Practical Innovations, Open Solutions, 8,* 139033–139043. doi:10.1109/ACCESS.2020.3012309

Donovan, J. (2020). *Concrete Recommendations for Cutting Through Misinformation During the COVID-19 Pandemic.* Academic Press.

Ehrhardt, N., & Hirsch, I. B. (2020). The Impact of COVID-19 on CGM Use in the Hospital. *Diabetes Care, 43*(11), 2628–2630. doi:10.2337/dci20-0046 PMID:32978180

Evans, R. J. (2005). *Death in Hamburg: society and politics in the cholera years.* Penguin Group USA.

Fowler, G. A. (2020 May 8). Wearable tech can spot coronavirus symptoms before you even realize you're sick. *The Washington Post.* https://www.washingtonpost.com/technology/2020/05/28/wearable-coronavirus-detect/

Griggs, M. B. (2020, Oct 31). A Swiss cheese approach to pandemic safety. *The Verge.* https://www.theverge.com/2020/10/31/21542207/swiss-cheese-infection-control-covid-19-antivirus

Heater, B. (2019, Feb 12). Sixteen percent of US adults own a smartwatch. *TechCrunch.* https://techcrunch.com/2019/02/12/sixteen-percent-of-u-s-adults-own-a-smartwatch/

Homer, M. J., D'Orsi, C. J., & Sitzman, S. B. (1994). Dermal calcifications in fixed orientation: The tattoo sign. *Radiology, 192*(1), 161–163. doi:10.1148/radiology.192.1.8208930 PMID:8208930

Jenner, E. (1801). *An inquiry into the causes and effects of the variolae vaccinae: a disease discovered in some of the western counties of England, particularly Gloucestershire, and known by the name of the cow pox.* Academic Press.

Jeong, H., Rogers, J., & Xu, S. (2020, July). Continuous on-body sensing for the COVID-19 pandemic: Gaps and opportunities. *Science Advances*. https://advances. sciencemag.org/content/early/2020/06/30/sciadv.abd4794

Jesty, R., & Williams, G. (2011). Who invented vaccination? *Malta Medical Journal*, *23*(2), 29–32.

Johns Hopkins. (2020). *Johns Hopkins Coronavirus Resource Center*. https:// coronavirus.jhu.edu/

Johns Hopkins Medicine. (2020, June 10). COVID-19 false negative test results if used too early. *ScienceDaily*. www.sciencedaily.com/releases/2020/06/200610094112.htm

Kim, G. U., Kim, M. J., Ra, S. H., Lee, J., Bae, S., Jung, J., & Kim, S. H. (2020). Clinical characteristics of asymptomatic and symptomatic patients with mild COVID-19. *Clinical Microbiology and Infection*, *26*(7), 948.e1–948.e3. doi:10.1016/j. cmi.2020.04.040 PMID:32360780

King, J. A., Whitten, T. A., Bakal, J. A., & McAlister, F. A. (2020). Symptoms associated with a positive result for a swab for SARS-CoV-2 infection among children in Alberta. *Canadian Medical Association Journal*, *193*(1), E1–E9. doi:10.1503/ cmaj.202065 PMID:33234533

Kinnunen, H., Laakkonen, H., Kivela, K., Colley, A., Lahtela, P., Koskela, M., & Jurvelin, H. (2016, Feb 23). *Method and system for assessing a readiness score of a user*. US patent 201562121425. https://patents.google.com/patent/WO2016135382A1

Koskimäki, H., Kinnunen, H., Rönkä, S., & Smarr, B. (2019, September). Following the heart: what does variation of resting heart rate tell about us as individuals and as a population. In *Adjunct Proceedings of the 2019 ACM International Joint Conference on Pervasive and Ubiquitous Computing and Proceedings of the 2019 ACM International Symposium on Wearable Computers* (pp. 1178-1181). 10.1145/3341162.3344836

Kronbichler, A., Kresse, D., Yoon, S., Lee, K. H., Effenberger, M., & Shin, J. I. (2020). Asymptomatic patients as a source of COVID-19 infections: A systematic review and meta-analysis. *International Journal of Infectious Diseases*, *98*, 180–186. doi:10.1016/j.ijid.2020.06.052 PMID:32562846

Kucirka, L. M., Lauer, S. A., Laeyendecker, O., Boon, D., & Lessler, J. (2020). Variation in false-negative rate of reverse transcriptase polymerase chain reaction– based SARS-CoV-2 tests by time since exposure. *Annals of Internal Medicine*, *173*(4), 262–267. doi:10.7326/M20-1495 PMID:32422057

Lukas, H., Xu, C., Yu, Y., & Gao, W. (2020). Emerging Telemedicine Tools for Remote COVID-19 Diagnosis, Monitoring, and Management. *ACS nano*.

Mandrola, J. (2020). CoViD-19 and PPE: Some of us will die because of the shortage. *Recenti Progressi in Medicina*, *111*(4), 183. PMID:32319434

McMichael, T. M., Currie, D. W., Clark, S., Pogosjans, S., Kay, M., Schwartz, N. G., Lewis, J., Baer, A., Kawakami, V., Lukoff, M. D., Ferro, J., Brostrom-Smith, C., Rea, T. D., Sayre, M. R., Riedo, F. X., Russell, D., Hiatt, B., Montgomery, P., Rao, A. K., ... Duchin, J. S. (2020). Epidemiology of Covid-19 in a long-term care facility in King County, Washington. *The New England Journal of Medicine*, *382*(21), 2005–2011. doi:10.1056/NEJMoa2005412 PMID:32220208

Mohan, P. M., Nagarajan, V., & Das, S. R. (2016, April). Stress measurement from wearable photoplethysmographic sensor using heart rate variability data. In *2016 International Conference on Communication and Signal Processing (ICCSP)* (pp. 1141-1144). IEEE. 10.1109/ICCSP.2016.7754331

NBA. (2020, Dec 2). *NBA and NBPA announce COVID-19 test results*. https://www.nba.com/news/nba-and-nbpa-announce-covid-19-test-results

Nielsen, R. K., Fletcher, R., Kalogeropoulos, A., & Simon, F. (2020). *Communications in the coronavirus crisis: lessons for the second wave. In Communications in the Coronavirus Crisis: Lessons for the Second Wave*. Reuters Institute for the Study of Journalism.

Nieuwenhuijse, D. F., Munnink, B. B. O., Phan, M. V., Munk, P., Venkatakrishnan, S., Aarestrup, F. M., ... Koopmans, M. P. (2020). Setting a baseline for global urban virome surveillance in sewage. *Scientific Reports*, *10*(1), 1–13. doi:10.103841598-020-69869-0 PMID:32792677

Oran, D. P., & Topol, E. J. (2020). Prevalence of Asymptomatic SARS-CoV-2 Infection: A Narrative Review. *Annals of Internal Medicine*.

Osterholm, M. T., Kelley, N. S., Sommer, A., & Belongia, E. A. (2012). Efficacy and effectiveness of influenza vaccines: A systematic review and meta-analysis. *The Lancet. Infectious Diseases*, *12*(1), 36–44. doi:10.1016/S1473-3099(11)70295-X PMID:22032844

Pegher, K. (2020, Oct 12). Coronavirus Today: The NBA's bubble worked. *Los Angeles Times*. https://www.latimes.com/science/newsletter/2020-10-12/coronavirus-today-nba-bubble-success-covid-lakers-coronavirus-today

Porter, P., Claxton, S., Brisbane, J., Bear, N., Wood, J., Peltonen, V., Della, P., Purdie, F., Smith, C., & Abeyratne, U. (2020). Diagnosing Chronic Obstructive Airway Disease on a Smartphone Using Patient-Reported Symptoms and Cough Analysis: Diagnostic Accuracy Study. *JMIR Formative Research, 4*(11), e24587. doi:10.2196/24587 PMID:33170129

Qermane, K., & Mancha, R. (2020). WHOOP, Inc.: Digital Entrepreneurship During the Covid-19 Pandemic. *Entrepreneurship Education and Pedagogy*, 2515127420975181.

Reason, J. (2000). Human error: Models and management. *BMJ (Clinical Research Ed.), 320*(7237), 768–770. doi:10.1136/bmj.320.7237.768 PMID:10720363

Roberts, S. (2020, Dec 5). The Swiss Cheese Model of Pandemic Defense. *New York Times.* https://www.nytimes.com/2020/12/05/health/coronavirus-swiss-cheese-infection-mackay.html

Schwartz, M., Oppold, P., & Hancock, P. A. (2019). Wearables and Workload. In Critical Issues Impacting Science, Technology, Society (STS), and Our Future (pp. 145-170). IGI Global. doi:10.4018/978-1-5225-7949-6.ch007

Seshadri, D. R., Davies, E. V., Harlow, E. R., Hsu, J. J., Knighton, S. C., Walker, T. A., Voos, J. E., & Drummond, C. K. (2020). Wearable sensors for COVID-19: A call to action to harness our digital infrastructure for remote patient monitoring and virtual assessments. *Frontiers in Digital Health, 2,* 8. doi:10.3389/fdgth.2020.00008

Shakiba, M., Nazemipour, M., Heidarzadeh, A., & Mansournia, M. A. (2020). Prevalence of asymptomatic COVID-19 infection using a seroepidemiological survey. *Epidemiology and Infection, 148,* 1–7. doi:10.1017/S0950268820002745 PMID:33183367

Shames, S., Bello, N. A., Schwartz, A., Homma, S., Patel, N., Garza, J., Kim, J. H., Goolsby, M., DiFiori, J. P., & Engel, D. J. (2020). Echocardiographic characterization of female professional basketball players in the US. *JAMA Cardiology, 5*(9), 991–998. doi:10.1001/jamacardio.2020.0988 PMID:32936269

Shcherbina, A., Mattsson, C. M., Waggott, D., Salisbury, H., Christle, J. W., Hastie, T., Wheeler, M., & Ashley, E. A. (2017). Accuracy in wrist-worn, sensor-based measurements of heart rate and energy expenditure in a diverse cohort. *Journal of Personalized Medicine, 7*(2), 3. doi:10.3390/jpm7020003 PMID:28538708

Shereen, M. A., Khan, S., Kazmi, A., Bashir, N., & Siddique, R. (2020). COVID-19 infection: Origin, transmission, and characteristics of human coronaviruses. *Journal of Advanced Research, 24,* 91–98. doi:10.1016/j.jare.2020.03.005 PMID:32257431

Sivak, M., & Schoettle, B. (2015). Road safety with self-driving vehicles: General limitations and road sharing with conventional vehicles. University of Michigan, Ann Arbor, Transportation Research Institute.

Sjoding, M. W., Dickson, R. P., Iwashyna, T. J., Gay, S. E., & Valley, T. S. (2020). Racial bias in pulse oximetry measurement. *The New England Journal of Medicine, 383*(25), 2477–2478. doi:10.1056/NEJMc2029240 PMID:33326721

Smarr, B. L., Aschbacher, K., Fisher, S. M., Chowdhary, A., Dilchert, S., Puldon, K., Rao, A., Hecht, F. M., & Mason, A. E. (2020). Feasibility of continuous fever monitoring using wearable devices. *Scientific Reports, 10*(1), 1–11. doi:10.103841598-020-78355-6 PMID:33318528

Thakur, N., Lovinsky-Desir, S., Bime, C., Wisnivesky, J. P., & Celedón, J. C. (2020). The Structural and Social Determinants of the Racial/Ethnic Disparities in the US COVID-19 Pandemic. What's Our Role? *American Journal of Respiratory and Critical Care Medicine, 202*(7), 943–949. doi:10.1164/rccm.202005-1523PP PMID:32677842

Tower, N. (2018, Dec 12). In an ethnic breakdown of sports, NBA takes lead for most diverse. *Global Sport Matters.* https://globalsportmatters.com/culture/2018/12/12/in-an-ethnic-breakdown-of-sports-nba-takes-lead-for-most-diverse/

Medicine, U. A. B. (n.d.). All About Continuous Glucose Monitors for People with Diabetes. *UAB Medicine News.* https://www.uabmedicine.org/-/all-about-continuous-glucose-monitors-for-people-with-diabetes

WVU Medicine News. (2020, May 28). WVU Rockefeller Neuroscience Institute announces capability to predict COVID-19 related symptoms up to three days in advance. *WVU Medicine.* https://wvumedicine.org/news/article/wvu-rockefeller-neuroscience-institute-announces-capability-to-predict-covid-19-related-symptoms-up-/

Vandenberg, O., Martiny, D., Rochas, O., van Belkum, A., & Kozlakidis, Z. (2020). Considerations for diagnostic COVID-19 tests. *Nature Reviews. Microbiology,* 1–13. PMID:33057203

Yang, Z., Kasprzyk-Hordern, B., Frost, C. G., Estrela, P., & Thomas, K. V. (2015). *Community sewage sensors for monitoring public health.* Academic Press.

Chapter 2

Ethical Design of Social Technology:
User Engagement and Attentional Demands

Fernando L. Montalvo

https://orcid.org/0000-0003-2277-3533
University of Central Florida, USA

Michael Miuccio
University of Central Florida, USA

Grace E. Waldfogle

https://orcid.org/0000-0002-8973-7193
University of Central Florida, USA

ABSTRACT

Social technology has become ubiquitous in everyday life. Developers of social technologies seek design elements and new technologies, such as machine learning algorithms, aimed at increasing user engagement. Increased user engagement with products or services is sought after by both companies, which benefit from increased sales and customers who desire technology which they are motivated to use. However, increased user engagement also results in increased demand on user attention. High demand on user attention results in problems for social technology users, including decreased task performance, decrements in working memory, increased anxiety, and more. Developers of social technology should take these negative effects on users into account when implementing new features into their products or services. This chapter proposes a framework for the ethical design of social technology, with a specific emphasis on the balance between user engagement and attentional demands on the user.

DOI: 10.4018/978-1-7998-6453-0.ch002

INTRODUCTION

Over the past two decades, social technologies, such as social networks, blogs, and smartphones, have permeated users' daily lives, altering consumer behavior, ways of living, and even cultural practices. Given that social technology design influences the behavior of not just the user, but also society at large (Bennett & Segerberg, 2012; De Reuver et al., 2016; Omamo et al., 2020), thorough consideration must be given to how ethical values are instilled in the technology itself by decision-makers, including human factors professionals, who design, develop, implement, and evaluate the products. Values of ethical importance differ from other values in that they are strongly focused on society and the user, and that they deal specifically with issues such as fairness, well-being, autonomy, virtue, trust, and justice (Friedman & Kahn, 2002). However, the ethical design of social technology is complicated by the social and technological environment, or sociotechnical system, in which it is situated. Simply put, ethical design of social technology is encumbered as a result of all the devices, services, and other technology that is often underlying the end user product. Behind this technology are equally complicated relationships among the technology, social forces, individual agency, corporate preferences, and more. Furthermore, given the recent advances in machine learning, algorithms may be self-modified or self-advanced in ways that are unknown even to the developers who designed the systems. This implies that the effects of these systems on the end user may not even be clear to developers unless some way to ensure system transparency is established. These challenges should be approached in deliberate and careful ways to ensure that a framework of the ethical design of social technology is in place as designers move forward with developing more advanced systems.

Social technology is a term that can be defined in multiple ways. In its primary sense, social technologies are those that help users connect with and manage a relationship network of other users of the same or associated technologies (Botin et al., 2017). Social networks, e-mail, and smartphones all provide the ability for us to interact with others or manage their contact information. More recently, social technology has been broadened to encompass technology that serves as a social actor in itself and with which we can interact in a social manner, such as virtual agents (Alexa, Siri, etc.) or social robots (Breazeal, 2002; Pereira et al., 2014). Social technologies leverage individuals' sociality motivation (Baumeister & Leary, 1995; Ryan & Deci, 2000) and social relationships to increase user engagement.

As a result of a push to increase user engagement through various methods, such as interruptive notifications, the current generation of social technologies present considerable risk to our ability to regulate our attention (e.g., Aranda & Baig, 2018; Yang & Gong, 2021). Machine learning algorithms in autonomous systems, such as those that help social media sites increase user engagement, are designed by software developers for a particular action (e.g., to discover patterns that can help identify posts that will increase user engagement among specific users). Through their design actions, the software developers have instilled corporate values into the algorithm (e.g., increased user screen times, increased advertising revenue, etc.). With its purpose designated, the algorithm uses its code to learn how to increase user engagement with little to no concern for any harmful effects it may have on the user. Although the human brain has evolved over millions of years and has sophisticated, though not fully understood (Mancas, 2016), mechanisms for the regulation of attention, it must now compete with this algorithm for the regulation of a user's attention. The algorithm continually learns which techniques (e.g., specific posts, intervals between types of posts, etc.) are likely to capture and maintain the user's attention firmly on a social media feed. If efficient enough, machine learning algorithms, such as the one in this example, raise an interesting question: Can artificial intelligence, machine learning, interruptive notifications, and other technological developments underlying social technologies outcompete our own brain's processes for the regulation of human attention? The answer, at least for short bursts of time, is probably yes. Machine learning learns a user's behavior, as well as their preferences and even latent patterns, leading to services and products that can potentially hijack a user's autonomy temporarily by outcompeting our own mental processes (Bryson & Winfield, 2017). Such technologies raise ethical alarms in regard to human welfare, autonomy, and more. Given their expertise at the intersection of cognitive processes, human behavior, and technology development and assessment, human factors professionals are well positioned to guide the intentional ethical design of social technologies.

While social technologies have opened up many positive opportunities, such as immediate access to information, improved communications with others, always-present entertainment, health data tracking, and even artificial social companionship, design issues and misuse of the technology present many risks. Some negative effects from social technology use, such as distracted driving, are well known, but other latent effects from these technologies can also interfere with other aspects of daily life and mental health. Social technology distractions are now a routine part of daily life (Furst et al., 2018; Hollis & Was, 2016; Horberry et al., 2019; Lawrence et al., 2017; Zarandona et al., 2019). The ability of social technology to tax the attentional capabilities of users stems from a combination of design features, user desires, corporate values, and societal developments. Smartphones, for example, have made a significant impact on our society, fundamentally becoming a key aspect of our daily lives (De Reuver et al., 2016; Kim et al., 2016; Park & Kaye, 2019; Wei, 2014). Driven by structural forces and societal norms, smartphone ownership is increasing at rapid rates in most areas of the world (Taylor & Silver, 2019). Competition among smartphone companies is high, and technology designers, including the human factors professionals embedded in technology development, work hard at implementing features that differentiate their products from others. Some of these features, such as notification lights, are designed to increase user engagement with the devices, which in turn increase user attentional demands.

Popular knowledge often presents the user as "in control" of the technology they are using, but technology can also exert its control on the user (Friedman & Kahn, 2002). For example, notifications from mobile devices can disrupt other tasks in which a student is engaging, even leading to changes in studying behavior and reduced learning efficiency (Rozgonjuk et al., 2019). Similarly, notifications can increase user engagement with services, such as news sites (Stroud et al., 2020). In these cases, the immediate behavior of the individual users is initiated by the technology. While there is an acceptable level of increase in user attentional demand, too much attention diverted toward a smartphone can decrease performance in other tasks (Rozgonjuk et al., 2018) or affect well-being (Sohn et al., 2019). This can have wider implications, including cognitive overload in critical decision-making workplace settings, such as healthcare environments (Cambier et al., 2020). Concerningly, our social technology is now so adept at pulling our attention toward it that we interact with our smartphones 76 times per day, on average (primarily to interact with social networks), leading to a total of 2,617 physical touches on a phone's user interface (Winnick, 2016). The present chapter focuses on reviewing the societal challenges presented by interruptive notifications, limited human attention, and the behavioral changes that result from social technology use, with the overarching aim of promoting the ethical design of future devices and services through a framework approach. Given the potential positive and negative consequences of increasingly demanding a user's attention, it is critical that human factor professionals understand the engagement needs and limits of users for the proper and ethical design of social technology.

USER ENGAGEMENT

User engagement is a quality of human–technology interaction that is desired by social technology providers and users alike. Successful user engagement relates to the ability to maintain a user's attention and interest in engaging with a technology or service (O'Brien & Toms, 2008). Balancing industry pressures, product design requirements, user needs, and values of ethical importance in design is difficult. User engagement is intrinsically linked to perceptions of good design and the development of a successful product or service. By incorporating features that increase user engagement, designers of social technology aim to meet individuals' motivational drives that move users toward engaging with a product. Whether designers improve the visual appeal of device displays, make virtual agent conversations feel more natural, or devise new methods to improve push notification effectiveness, the end goal is to increase users' desire to engage with their devices and services, which improves the financial bottom line for companies through increased sales, added subscribers, and increased visibility of marketing.

As shown in Figure 1, the technology industry is a highly competitive environment composed of hardware and software ecosystems that cater to multiple, and not always complementary, customers (Campbell-Kelly et al., 2015). In today's connected world, increasing user engagement can be a complex process involving multiple services, devices, and companies. In the fashion industry, for example, the number of social media followers, a measurement of brand engagement (Bitter & Grabner-Kräuter, 2013), is positively associated with increased retail sales (Schultz, 2016). Fashion companies must actively work at increasing customer engagement through good product design, a positive customer relations experience, product placement among social influencers (Casaló et al., 2018), and employing an effective communication strategy (Quijada et al., 2020). Although the end goal is to increase customer engagement with the brand, increasing user engagement with devices, social media services, and communication technologies is an important part of this process. Brands may choose to post regularly to social media platforms, such as Facebook and Instagram, in hopes of capturing user attention among a variety of competing posts. Given that social media platforms' main customers are advertisers, social media companies and marketing campaign service providers must work to guarantee a steady stream of engaged users to view the ads or posts. Social media companies employ techniques, such as user-data-generated algorithms (Camacho et al., 2020) and push notifications, to attempt to draw user attention toward their services (Manser, 2017). Notifications themselves are delivered through various mechanisms, such as ringtones and notification lights, which are developed by device manufacturers, such as Apple or Samsung. As such, the ecosystem seeking to increase user engagement is complex, with many actors having a vested financial need to capture user attention.

Figure 1. Social technology ecosystem showing interrelationships between major stakeholders

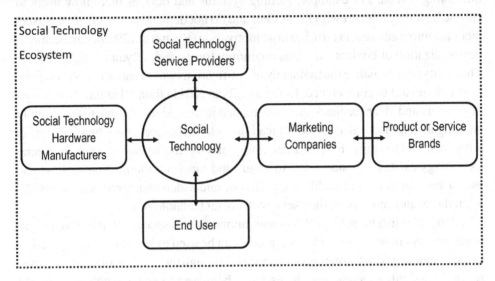

Users themselves prefer to use technology that delivers a heightened sense of personal involvement and meaning (Di Gangi & Wasko, 2016). Self-determination theory (SDT) provides a good framework from which to understand user needs and breaks down the underlying mechanisms that increase user engagement. SDT is a broad framework that examines human motivation and how social and cultural factors influence one's sense of volition (Deci & Ryan, 1985). This framework proposes three basic human motives: the need for autonomy, the need for competence, and the need for relatedness (Deci & Ryan, 1985, 2000; Ryan & Deci, 2000). Autonomy represents a basic desire for personal control or self-initiated behavior. An example of autonomy is providing users with the ability to choose the frequency of push notifications. Competence is a feeling or sense of mastery in what you are doing. For example, when users understand the user interface and feel competent in their ability to navigate a site, their need for competence has been fulfilled. Relatedness, also called the need for belonging, is one's need to feel cared for and/or connected with others. Given access to a user's real world and virtual social network of relationships, social technologies increase user engagement by notifying the user of their friends' posts, events, etc. These three motives can be experienced individually, all together, or as a combination of the two. If an individual is experiencing all three, they are self-determined, or intrinsically motivated, to pursue things that interest them. In relation to user experience, a balance of these motives would increase engagement and provide more meaningful interactions with the technology.

Research investigating self-determination theory with technology have found interesting results. For example, gaming systems and devices that allow users to choose how they interact with the system and do not demand actions from the users increase autonomy and, in turn, intrinsic motivation (Ryan et al., 2006). Furthermore, personalization of content increases autonomy for the user (Ryan & Rigby, 2018). The ability to personalize the frequency of notifications would entice users to that app or site. In regard to competence, Rigby and Ryan (2011) found that intuitive design of controls and clear feedback on performance increased user competence. Simply creating a clear user interface could lead users to feel competent when interacting with social technology. Finally, relatedness may be the easiest to explain. Social technology exists to connect users to others and form communication outlets. The use of interactions, such as likes, emoticons, and video chats, provides users the relatedness and connection they seek with social technologies.

Alongside other industry professionals, human factors specialists help develop and evaluate ways in which technology features can be used to increase user motivation toward engaging with technology or services. Through the addition of novel features, services, and other techniques, the user can be driven to engage with devices and services. For example, a notification earcon may pull a user from another task into using their smartphone and the application that generated the notification. Through aesthetic and sensory elements (high-quality audio, for example), additional novelty (new information through social media posts), feedback (push notifications), and maintenance of positive affect, among other elements, products and services can maintain user engagement. Recently, advanced algorithms attempt to keep the user engaged by timing the appearance if high-interest novelty when the user appears to be about to disengage based on past behavior. The goal of developers is to design devices and services effectively in order to attract user attention and maintain it for as long as possible.

Once a user disengages, the process to re-engage the user must begin anew. As such, there is a temporal aspect to user engagement consisting of a point of engagement, engagement period, disengagement, and re-engagement (O'Brien & Toms, 2008). Designing for user engagement requires a strong understanding of this temporal nature, as well as user preferences and catering to an individual user's engaged behavior. For example, given that too many notifications may lead a user to turn them off altogether, due to increased negative affect (disengagement), developers can adapt notification systems to adjust to individual users' tolerance levels (Braginsky, 2012), maintaining favorable user engagement intervals.

While it may appear on the surface that ever-increasing user engagement is beneficial for corporations, as well as users, who may be fulfilling an intrinsic desire to engage with the technology (Kim et al., 2016; Kim et al., 2013; O'Brien & Toms, 2008), the end result of the high demand for a user's attention can have both positive and negative consequences. User needs and desires are centered not simply on the social technology to which they are currently attending, but also on the sociotechnical ecosystem of the user. A person using a virtual agent, such as Alexa, in their kitchen may be attending to the device at the same time they are preparing a meal with multiple task steps and tools. As such, the user's needs are also encompassed in the requirements of other tasks around them. Similarly, other needs may be present, such as psychophysiological needs, which may include rest, eating, and sociality. Although this may seem outside the purview of user-centered design, the effects on rest patterns as a result of social technology engagement (Scott et al., 2019; Tandon et al., 2020) are just one indication of many that the impact of social technology goes beyond the immediate interaction. Excessive attentional demands from social technology can interfere negatively with the attentional and performance requirements of other tasks, as well as with the overall well-being of an individual.

CONCERNS ABOUT HUMAN FACTORS IN USER ENGAGEMENT

In both academic and research settings, human factors professionals use their expertise in human and system interaction to improve how technology meets the needs, abilities, and limitations of people (International Ergonomics Association, 2020). Given the systemic and multi-stakeholder nature of the field, human factors professionals work on the improvement of technology for both industry and user interests. Products or services that foster user engagement benefit both the industries that make the products, as well as the users who engage with them. However, when it comes to social technology, various concerns are raised due to excessive or distractive user engagement. Furthermore, given the hidden technologies involved in attracting user attention, such as advanced algorithms that constantly search for ways to increase user engagement (e.g., Zhang et al., 2018), users may not always be in control of their engagement with the technology.

Situations that can potentially harm users, such as the unfettered use of hidden algorithms to maintain user engagement, present the additional potential to hurt corporate image, financial performance, or business continuity (Delios, 2010). Human factors professionals are well versed in assessing and improving the well-being of the user in a human–system environment. Given this expertise, human factors as a field is well positioned to add values of ethical import to the development and implementation of technology in socially responsible industry (Dul et al., 2012). As proponents of user-centered design, human factors professionals should be familiar with some of the negative effects of excessive or distracting social technology use.

The pervasive and habitual use of social technology may cause changes in behavior and in cognitive impacts related to their use. In particular, much of the research on social technology has been conducted on smartphones, which are widely used (Taylor & Silver, 2019) and are a pervasive example of social technology. Unbeknownst to many users, smartphones may have a substantial impact on our attentional capacities. Recent research has shown that the mere presence of a smartphone significantly decreases performance on working memory tasks (Canale et al., 2019; Ward et al., 2017).

Smartphones also may affect attention via notifications. Notifications are commonly used in various applications and can indicate personally relevant information that can be highly distracting from the current focus of attention. Stothart and colleagues (2015) showed that receiving a smartphone notification significantly decreased performance in a sustained attention task when participants were not able to interact with their phone. They proposed that this may be due to notifications creating task-irrelevant thoughts. Ignoring a notification may be worse than engaging with it. However, even responding to a notification comes with its own costs in the form of resumption errors. Resumption errors, caused by resuming a task after a brief interruption, have been shown to be detrimental to performance (Cellier & Eyrolle, 1992; Monk, 2004; Brumby et al., 2013). Smartphone notifications are a frequent source of interruptions and can therefore lead to many resumption errors. Leiva and colleagues (2012) found smartphone notifications to be disruptive and able to quadruple the time needed to complete a task.

Studies of smartphone addiction have looked at how it relates to changes in brain structure and affective processes. Recently, research has started to explore smartphone addiction using neuroimaging. A magnetic resonance imaging study observed structural changes in the anterior insula and anterior cingulate cortex (Horvath et al., 2020). These changes mimic alterations of those who are addicted to substances and illustrate the importance of ethical consideration in design.

Interestingly, the presence of smartphones during one-on-one conversations drastically reduced the perceived quality of the interaction, as well as the empathetic connection (Misra et al., 2016). This lack of connection may, in part, contribute to the finding that depression and anxiety are significantly associated with smartphone addiction (Boumosleh & Jaalouk, 2017). Among a population of medical interns, those with higher depression and anxiety had an increase in phantom vibrations (Lin et al., 2013), which is the feeling of receiving a vibration notification when no notification was present. This suggests that a strong attachment is being developed to smartphones, especially under stressful situations. This attachment can have negative consequences when the smartphone is not nearby. For example, individuals who reported greater anxiety when separated from their smartphone showed greater deficits in working memory and inhibitory control than those with less separation anxiety (Hartanto & Yang, 2016).

Although situated in the user, these effects may be a symptom of a larger issue related to a nearly endless stream of media to consume via incoming notifications, applications, and the internet. This results in social technology users reporting being in a state of constant connectedness and alertness that has been referred to as online vigilance (Klimmt et al., 2017). Higher online vigilance was shown to be negatively correlated with mindfulness (Johannes et al., 2018) and overall well-being. While this shows a correlational relationship between smartphone awareness and well-being, a causal relationship was also observed with improvements to well-being when batching smartphone notifications to appear at specific times throughout the day (Fitz et al., 2019). This implies that design features that allow for the customization or personalization of notification delivery can potentially improve user well-being.

In addition to online vigilance, social technologies, such as smartphones, also encourage heavy media multitasking where individuals will engage in smartphone usage while watching television or completing school tasks, for example. Research has shown that media multitasking has negative effects on a wide array of cognitive functions, such as attention, working memory, long-term memory, and inhibitory control (for a review, see Uncapher & Wagner, 2018).

Social technology issues and attentional demands on individuals are many and make it a difficult topic to study. Continual behavioral and neurophysiological research will be needed as social technologies continue to develop and become more integrated in our daily lives. For instance, the recent popularity of at-home smart devices, such as Amazon's Echo, may also have cognitive effects that need to be examined. However, there is little research on these devices to date, with one study showing no effect on mental workload (Maier et al., 2019).

While many negative effects of smartphone use occur on the individual level, the widespread use of social technology also impacts society at large. The lack of transparency in the way that many algorithms work, the decisions they make, and how they influence users has recently become the subject of both political and ethical debate given the algorithms' wide-ranging societal effects (Buhmann et al., 2019). Recent documentaries, such as *The Social Dilemma*, show how the design decisions made by a handful of engineers can affect the thoughts and actions of billions of people (Girish, 2020). Institutes are established to help spread awareness of the dangers of social technology and propose a policy framework for lawmakers to adopt that will address structural imbalances between users and designers (Center for Humane Technology, 2020). Policies include holding industry accountable for manipulative design, increasing transparency, and educating users on potential harms of digital use. Human factors professionals help assess and educate industry, policy-makers, and users on the potential effects of technology on individuals or systems, as well as how these effects compound to have wide-ranging societal impacts, such as lost economic productivity (Jackson et al., 2003), higher accident rates (Horberry et al., 2019), or decision errors in healthcare settings (Fiorinelli et al., 2021).

Ethical Design of Social Technology

Values are desirable goals that guide action and are situated in a societal and not just individual frame (Fleischmann, 2013). Values are generally worth pursuing and good, but they are not necessarily so. The value of power is a good example; a dictatorship may value power, but it may not result in a positive and good experience for those under such a government. Similarly, in technology, a complex relationship of values may be present at all times. In nearly all companies, market and corporate values, such as increased sales or product quality, must be at the forefront of design in order for the product to be successful and the company to survive in a competitive environment. An algorithm designed to increase user engagement within a social network in order to generate increased advertising revenue is primarily catering to corporate and market values. Other values, however, are equally important in the development and implementation of products and services. An important design value in the human–computer interaction community is the concept of universal usability, or the goal that technology should cater to and be accessible to everyone (Shneiderman, 2000). This is a multifaceted value in that it strives to meet issues related to ease of use and functional design, while also addressing aspects such as fairness. Still other values, such as fun, well-being, privacy, modernity, and sustainability, may find their way into a single product or service as a result of corporate, developer, societal, or user desires. Although most of these may seem positive, they are not necessarily positive to everyone in the sociotechnical system. The increased drive for user engagement that results from corporate and market values certainly benefits advertisers, social media companies, and social technology developers, but its benefit to the user is not always so clear, with potentially serious negative effects to productivity, as well as mental and physical health. Compounded over time and individuals, excessive or interruptive user engagement can have a significant societal impact.

In these situations, emphasizing values of ethical importance is key. For developers of social technology, it is important to maintain a safe level of demand on users' attention. Human factors professionals have the skillset and knowledge to assess these demands and propose adjustments to products and services that improve user well-being while providing value to corporate stakeholders (Dul et al., 2012). Various methods, such as value-sensitive design (Friedman, 1996) or the implementation of ethical standards (Bryson & Winfield, 2017), have been proposed to help industries understand the potential ethical concerns related to their products and further ways in which the design could be guided in an ethical direction.

Of course, ethically driven design is challenging. Balancing positive user engagement with adequate demands on attention is difficult, given that companies need to cater to a multitude of stakeholders, such as their own ecosystem, app developers, advertisers, and the end user. Each of these agents has their own interests in the technology and their own values of ethical importance. Human factors professionals, along with other technology-development members, are often focused on usability features, as well as user experience elements that both attract consumers and increase user engagement (Kim, et al., 2013; O'Brien & Toms, 2008; Turner et al., 2017). However, usability, user experience, individuation, and pleasurable design elements are intrinsically linked, whether positively or negatively, with values of ethical importance (Friedman & Kahn, 2002). For instance, hedonomic design values seek to increase the pleasure from positive usage experiences while integrating individual-centered design (Hancock et al., 2005). Examples of hedonomic design elements may include vibrant user interfaces, higher-resolution cameras, and personalized notifications. Given that social technology influences human behavior, often in negative ways, designers of social devices and services need to consider which behaviors these hedonomic design features are promoting or influencing. A new feature in a personalized notification may provide a better user experience but result in further losses of productivity or increased anxiety for users. When these behaviors promote negative consequences, such as smartphone or social media addiction, corporate needs should be weighed against potential negative effects.

Social technology's behavioral and cognitive effects on the user often occur by design. Although research is currently in progress to determine the extent to which the drive for user engagement causes excessive demands on our attention, it is evident that an ethical turn is necessary to safeguard the user from the ever-increasing array of technological features designed to capture their attention.

FRAMEWORK FOR ETHICAL DESIGN

Social technology designers concerned about negatively affecting their users by instilling features that demand too much attention must strike a balance between industry needs for increased user engagement and the detrimental effects of increased attentional demands. Notification frequency, display color and intensity, scroll design, and customization should be moderated to draw less attentional demand from the user (Bhargava & Velasquez, 2020). Similarly, the very algorithms that can hijack a user's attention can be improved to assess the appropriate times in which a user can be interrupted, considerably lowering notification-generated workload (Okoshi et al., 2015). If done correctly, users can maintain engagement with technology-related services and products while reducing some of the negative impacts related to the products' attentional requirements. Social technology design should take into account both overt and latent risks that stem from excessive attentional demands at all stages of the process.

Figure 2 introduces our proposed framework for the ethical design of user engagement features in social technology, although the framework is certainly applicable to technology in general. The framework is composed of eight steps, as well as continual assessment to identify potential areas of concern before and after technology implementation. The conceptualization of the framework is grounded in fundamental characteristics of human factors: a systems approach, design driven, and a focus on performance and well-being (Dul et al., 2012). First, it takes a systems approach by considering that the development of technology happens in a multiple-stakeholder system. As such, human factors professionals must identify all stakeholders in the system, understand their motivations and values, and work to coherently implement these motivations and values into designs. It is design driven in that the framework follows a flow logical to human factors implementations in design. In this design frame, human factors professionals must not only help develop current technology using established knowledge, but also work at forecasting anticipated intended and unintended effects of the technology design and implementation (Woods & Decker, 2000). Consequently, human factors professionals must then eliminate bad design or unintended consequences by assessing, reassessing, and reworking design or service features. Human factors as a science provides the tools to: acquire the data, model use, predict effects, and design for improvement (Dul et al., 2012; Woods & Decker, 2000). Finally, it addresses performance and well-being by focusing on both the usefulness of the system to meet the needs of the primary stakeholders and the well-being of the user. The framework is also iterative in that knowledge generated through its use drives iterative design and adds to the human factors knowledgebase. The framework and examples of its application are described below.

Figure 2. Framework for the ethical design of user engagement features

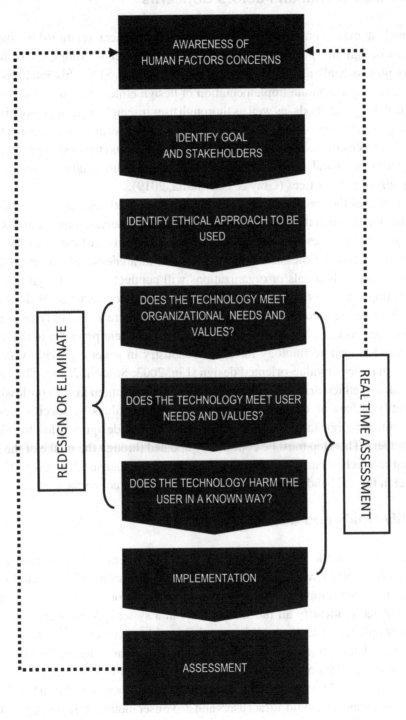

Awareness of Human Factors Concerns

Although it may seem like an intuitive cause-and-effect relationship, the link between design and potential negative effects on a user is complex. For human factors professionals as well as organizations, understanding this relationship is important. Any corporate implementation of design ethics must be informed both in ethical design methods, as well as thorough user research examining positive and negative implications of the chosen technology's usage. Awareness and education in applied ethics mediates the relationship between ethics and the design professional, strengthens individual practices by enhancing understanding, and helps instill ethics in organizational practices (Gray & Chivukula, 2019).

This step of the framework involves actors across both industry and academia, with the link between the two bridged through formal education mechanisms (e.g., employee education sessions, online training, professional certifications, continuing education, etc.) and professional societies. While awareness and education do not guarantee that individuals or organizations will conduct ethical design practices, they do improve the odds that a decision to adhere to or reject ethical design will be an informed and comprehensive one. Awareness here is not only centered in technological aspects, but also in ethical concerns. Current practices in the human factors and human–technology interaction industry in general provide very little training in ethics or value-oriented design (Liu, 2003; Shilton, 2018). This lack of knowledge in ethics-driven design limits the ability of human factors professionals to identify values of ethical importance, relate the values to specific designs, enact ethical design in their work, or promote ethical design's value to relevant stakeholders. This step must be continually updated through the intake of the latest relevant research, recurrent training, and feedback mechanisms that assess the end product in the wild and inform human factors or ethical concerns.

Identify Goals and Stakeholders

Given the user-centric perspective of the field, many human factors professionals give primary consideration to the user within the requirements presented by the organizations that employ them. However, a product- or service-centric view is better utilized to identify all the stakeholders in a system (Alexander, 2005). The ecosystem for social technology is complex, and important stakeholders may be difficult to identify from a user-centric perspective. Identifying all stakeholders is crucial to define the goals that must be met by the system.

Take, for example, a social media application, such as Facebook. From Facebook's perspective, features should attract users and drive user motivation to engage with the Facebook application or website. Users want an application that meets their needs, whether that be a sense of connection to other members of their social network or a source of general information, among other possibilities. Advertisers similarly have a vested interest in Facebook features, as these tools may help drive users to click on advertisements or view brand content. Commercial brands may potentially benefit from features if they help drive brand engagement through advertising or social media post conversions. To properly weigh values of ethical import with other corporate and user values, human factors professionals must have a good understanding of all system goals and stakeholders.

Identify the Ethical Approach to be Used

The specifics of ethical design approaches, such as value-sensitive design (Friedman, 1996), are extensive and cannot be covered in detail here. However, human factors professionals should be well versed in at least one ethical design methodology and should consistently use that ethical approach to design, rather than haphazardly attempting to incorporate ethics in design. Properly trained human factors professionals can serve as value advocates or as professionals in a design team whose role it is to promote ethical design and convert values of ethical design into technical specifications or processes (Fisher & Mahajan, 2010; Shilton & Anderson, 2017). Other proposals encourage the identification and usage of values levers, which are factors that promote ethical-values discussions within organizational and design settings (Shilton, 2013).

Ethical-value design should be implemented as an organizational value (Newman et al., 2017). In addition to proper ethical design approaches, another step in this direction is the identification of values of ethical importance that are related to the social technology created within an organization. In terms of user engagement, these values may include issues of human welfare (e.g., they do not cause negative changes in user behavior easily), trust (e.g., system transparency), or autonomy (e.g., allow the user to control the product or service as much as possible). Risk assessments must be conducted to identify which of these values are most concerning in the use of the technology and require design considerations. Additionally, given the complexity of the value ecosystem, values must be weighed against others to determine any competing values that could create a barrier to the implementation of ethical design or product development.

Ethical design discourse has been present in human–computer interaction for a considerable time (Friedman, 1996; Friedman & Kahn, 2002; Shilton, 2013; Wiener, 1953). As such, multiple methods have been developed to guide the values-oriented design of products. For example, the Ethical System Development Life Cycle (Spiekermann, 2015) proposes methods for incorporating ethical considerations into the engineering life cycle of a product. Other methods, such as value-sensitive design (Friedman, 1996), that help incorporate the value complexity of sociotechnical systems into development cycles have been evaluated and redeveloped over more than 20 years. However, while there is certainly generalizability in these methods, they must be structured to fit within the present organizational structure to reduce resistance and barriers to implementation. Ethical design professionals, such as value advocates, should ensure that the methods are implemented within existing company frameworks. This includes incorporating ethical design processes and positions within the hierarchical structure of the company to ensure accountability at every stage of the process.

Organizational or User Needs and Values

Once an ethical design approach has been identified, a key component of the design process is to test whether the product, feature, or service being designed can meet the need for which it was developed. Through user research, human factors professionals can assess the usefulness of a product, as well as its ability to meet design requirements. Some of these design needs may be requirements that a company must meet as a result of external influences. The ethical design ecosystem is not isolated within a company, as various organizations have proposed ethical design standards for various forms of technologies, some of which apply to the growing concerns related to privacy, human welfare, autonomy, and more in the social technology industry (Bryson & Winfield, 2017; Winfield, 2019).

User Well-Being

User well-being is a core tenet of the human factors field (Dul et al., 2012). The design process should incorporate continuous assessment to ensure that organizational and user needs are met, the technology does not affect user well-being, and ethical design is followed. One such method is real-time technology assessment (real-time TA), which seeks to map the sociotechnical system around technologies through stakeholder and dynamic assessment, identify unanticipated impacts of technology, find solutions, and develop design criteria to reduce negative effects from technology usage (Guston & Sarewitz, 2002). By implementing these kinds of assessments in the formal ethical design framework, value-oriented methods can be continually updated to have the greatest impact on the product development life cycle.

Any violation to stakeholder needs, values, or well-being should be assessed for risk and impact using ethics-oriented design practices. Human factors professionals can then assess whether the proper strategy is the redesign of technology (e.g., changing the frequency and batching of user notifications in social technology) or its elimination (e.g., eliminating notifications that fail to meet organizational or user needs) when a problem arises (e.g., excessive attentional demands).

Implementation and Assessment

The final stages of our framework are implementation and assessment. This includes the introduction of design elements in social technology and its market release. It should be noted that, in this implementation stage, ethical design should be adapted to the specific design goals of the technology being developed. In the context of social technology, three potentially useful relationships can exist between user engagement and attentional demand:

High User Engagement and Attentional Demand (e.g., continuous, non-adaptive interruptive notifications): Most current social media designs default to this classification with few adjustments for user needs. Users are continuously provided with notifications from all installed applications, attracting user attention and reengaging the user away from other tasks and toward the device. While this improves usability and user engagement, this can conflict with user attentional demands. Elements that use this design promote user engagement and high interactivity with the phone, while serving as a driving mechanism for some of the negative effects of social technology use described above. This level is appropriate for alarms, vigilance systems, and other technology that requires the user to remain engaged.

Low User Engagement and Attentional Demand (e.g., low to no notifications): Currently, some niche companies are designing phones that require low user engagement and attentional demand. These phones are offering limited features, allowing the user to remain disengaged from their phone. They are promoting their phones to individuals interested in minimizing the negative effects of smartphone usage. However, this also results in low levels of user engagement and limited social technology features.

Balanced User Engagement and Attentional Demand (e.g., batched and user-centric notifications): Designs in this classification category seek to maintain a moderate level of user engagement without a constant stream of auditory or visual display notifications, or seductive features that attract too much attention. Social technology design can seek to find a middle ground in order to satisfy most companies' need for user engagement and attentional demand while attenuating the negative effects on the user's affect and attention. An example of such a feature would be batched notifications, which provide information at a scheduled interval, decreasing demands on user attention (Okoshi, et al., 2015). While this seems to be the most desired relationship between engagement and attention, ethical designers should understand how other values may drive a need for greater demands on attention (such as in alerting or warning systems) or lower user engagement (such as with individuals looking to reduce their interactions with digital technologies).

These relationships between user engagement and attentional demands in product design are important to understand as a product is implemented, given that they affect the weight and impact that any ethical design methods will have on the final product.

Finally, implementation requires continual assessment, utilizing methods such as heuristic analysis, usability studies, engagement- vs. attention-oriented research, and more. Assessments can occur within the same organizations developing the technology, or externally, such as when academic departments examine the effects of specific elements of technology on cognition or perception. The results of these assessments should feed back into awareness and education, ethical design method development, and at any other points in the framework during which stakeholders need to make product decisions.

CONCLUSION

The above framework is meant to serve as a starting point for discussion and to raise awareness among human factors specialists of the impacts that technologies may have on users, as well as potential avenues for improvement. Although this may seem to be outside their immediate scope and training, human factors, user research, and design professionals should seek to be included in upper-management processes (especially as they relate to any processes affecting design) if they are to have leverage and input in the development of ethical design frameworks within corporations. Furthermore, human factors professionals are well positioned to understand the pervasive effects of technologies designed to increase user engagement by the end user. Given broad expertise in the engineering aspect of products and services, research methods, cognitive and perceptual processes, and user perspectives, human factors professionals can help instill ethical values into user engagement design.

It is clear that increasing user engagement with their products and services holds great value to social technology providers. However, this gain should not come at a considerable cost to the user. Although certainly not a new development, the advent of advanced and self-learning algorithms presents a unique challenge to safeguarding users given the lack of system transparency. Ignoring social technologies' increasing efficacy at engaging user attention promises to hurt the end user and polarize public opinion toward the industry. Ethical design discourse is not new, but it may finally be time for it to become a major driver of design values within social technology organizations.

REFERENCES

Alexander, I. F. (2005). A taxonomy of stakeholders: Human roles in system development. *International Journal of Technology and Human Interaction, 1*(1), 23–59. doi:10.4018/jthi.2005010102

Aranda, J. H., & Baig, S. (2018). Toward "JOMO": The joy of missing out and the freedom of disconnecting. In *Proceedings of the 20th International Conference on Human–Computer Interaction with Mobile Devices and Services.* Association for Computing Machinery. 10.1145/3229434.3229468

Baumeister, R. F., & Leary, M. R. (1995). The need to belong: Desire for interpersonal attachments as a fundamental human motivation. *Psychological Bulletin, 117*(3), 497–529. doi:10.1037/0033-2909.117.3.497 PMID:7777651

Bennett, W. L., & Segerberg, A. (2012). The logic of connective action: Digital media and the personalization of contentious politics. *Information Communication and Society, 15*(5), 739–768. doi:10.1080/1369118X.2012.670661

Bhargava, V. R., & Velasquez, M. (2020). Ethics of the attention economy: The problem of social media addiction. *Business Ethics Quarterly*, 1–39. doi:10.1017/beq.2020.32

Bitter, S., & Grabner-Kräuter, S. (2013). Customer engagement behavior: Interacting with companies and brands on Facebook. In S. Rosengren, M. Dahlén, & S. Okazaki (Eds.), Advances in advertising research (Vol. 4, pp. 3–17). Springer. doi:10.1007/978-3-658-02365-2_1

Botin, L., Bertelsen, P., & Nøhr, C. (2017). Sustainable and viable introduction of tele-technologies in healthcare: A partial two-sided market approach. In V. Vimarlund (Ed.), *E-health two-sided markets* (pp. 93–123). Elsevier., doi:10.1016/B978-0-12-805250-1.00008-3

Boumosleh, J. M., & Jaalouk, D. (2017). Depression, anxiety, and smartphone addiction in university students – A cross sectional study. *PLoS One, 12*(8), e0182239. Advance online publication. doi:10.1371/journal.pone.0182239 PMID:28777828

Braginsky, D. E. (2012). *Sending notifications to users based on users' notification tolerance levels.* U.S. Patent No. 20120239507A1. U.S. Patent and Trademark Office.

Breazeal, C. L. (2002). *Designing sociable robots.* MIT Press. doi:10.7551/mitpress/2376.001.0001

Brumby, D. P., Cox, A. L., Back, J., & Gould, S. J. (2013). Recovering from an interruption: Investigating speed–accuracy trade-offs in task resumption behavior. *Journal of Experimental Psychology. Applied, 19*(2), 95–107. doi:10.1037/a0032696 PMID:23795978

Bryson, J., & Winfield, A. (2017). Standardizing ethical design for artificial intelligence and autonomous systems. *Computer, 50*(5), 116–119. doi:10.1109/MC.2017.154

Buhmann, A., Paßmann, J., & Fieseler, C. (2019). Managing algorithmic accountability: Balancing reputational concerns, engagement strategies, and the potential of rational discourse. *Journal of Business Ethics, 163*(2), 265–280. doi:10.100710551-019-04226-4

Camacho, D., Luzón, M. V., & Cambria, E. (2020). New research methods & algorithms in social network analysis. *Future Generation Computer Systems, 114*, 290–293. doi:10.1016/j.future.2020.08.006

Cambier, R., Van Laethem, M., & Vlerick, P. (2020). Private life telepressure and workplace cognitive failure among hospital nurses: The moderating role of mobile phone presence. *Journal of Advanced Nursing, 76*(10), 2618–2626. doi:10.1111/jan.14496 PMID:32803902

Campbell-Kelly, M., Garcia-Swartz, D., Lam, R., & Yang, Y. (2015). Economic and business perspectives on smartphones as multi-sided platforms. *Telecommunications Policy, 39*(8), 717–734. doi:10.1016/j.telpol.2014.11.001

Canale, N., Vieno, A., Doro, M., Rosa Mineo, E., Marino, C., & Billieux, J. (2019). Emotion-related impulsivity moderates the cognitive interference effect of smartphone availability on working memory. *Scientific Reports, 9*(1), 1–10. doi:10.103841598-019-54911-7 PMID:31811205

Casaló, L. V., Flavián, C., & Ibáñez-Sánchez, S. (2018). Influencers on Instagram: Antecedents and consequences of opinion leadership. *Journal of Business Research, 117*, 510–519. doi:10.1016/j.jbusres.2018.07.005

Cellier, J.-M., & Eyrolle, H. (1992). Interference between switched tasks. *Ergonomics, 35*(1), 25–36. doi:10.1080/00140139208967795

Center for Humane Technology. (2020, October 8). *Potential policy reforms*. The Center for Humane Technology. https://www.humanetech.com/policy-reforms

De Reuver, M., Nikou, S., & Bouwman, H. (2016). Domestication of smartphones and mobile applications: A quantitative mixed-method study. *Mobile Media & Communication, 4*(3), 347–370. doi:10.1177/2050157916649989

Deci, E. L., & Ryan, R. M. (1985). *Intrinsic motivation and self-determination in human behavior.* doi:10.1007/978-1-4899-2271-7

Deci, E. L., & Ryan, R. M. (2000). The "what" and "why" of goal pursuits: Human needs and the self-determination of behavior. *Psychological Inquiry, 11*(4), 227–268. doi:10.1207/S15327965PLI1104_01

Delios, A. (2010). How can organizations be competitive but dare to care? *The Academy of Management Perspectives, 24*(3), 25–36. doi:10.5465/amp.24.3.25

Di Gangi, P. M., & Wasko, M. M. (2016). Social media engagement theory: Exploring the influence of user engagement on social media usage. *Journal of Organizational and End User Computing, 28*(2), 53–73. doi:10.4018/JOEUC.2016040104

Dul, J., Bruder, R., Buckle, P., Carayon, P., Falzon, P., Marras, W. S., Wilson, J. R., & van der Doelen, B. (2012). A strategy for human factors/ergonomics: Developing the discipline and profession. *Ergonomics, 55*(4), 377–395. doi:10.1080/00140139 .2012.661087 PMID:22332611

Fiorinelli, M., Di Mario, S., Surace, A., Mattei, M., Russo, C., Villa, G., Dionisi, S., Di Simone, E., Giannetta, N., & Di Muzio, M. (2021). Smartphone distraction during nursing care: Systematic literature review. *Applied Nursing Research, 151405,* 151405. Advance online publication. doi:10.1016/j.apnr.2021.151405 PMID:33745553

Fisher, E., & Mahajan, R. L. (2010). Embedding the humanities in engineering: Art, dialogue, and a laboratory. In M. E. Gorman (Ed.), *Trading zones and interactional expertise: Creating new kinds of collaboration* (pp. 209–230). MIT Press. doi:10.7551/ mitpress/9780262014724.003.0010

Fitz, N., Kushlev, K., Jagannathan, R., Lewis, T., Paliwal, D., & Ariely, D. (2019). Batching smartphone notifications can improve well-being. *Computers in Human Behavior, 101*(July), 84–94. doi:10.1016/j.chb.2019.07.016

Fleischmann, K. R. (2013). Information and human values. *Synthesis Lectures on Information Concepts, Retrieval, and Services, 5*(5), 1–99. doi:10.2200/ S00545ED1V01Y201310ICR031

Friedman, B. (1996). Value-sensitive design. *Interaction, 3*(6), 16–23. doi:10.1145/242485.242493

Friedman, B., & Kahn, P. H. Jr. (2002). Human values, ethics, and design. In A. Sears & J. A. Jacko (Eds.), *The human–computer interaction handbook* (pp. 1209–1233). CRC Press. doi:10.1201/9781410606723-48

Furst, R. T., Evans, D. N., & Roderick, N. M. (2018). Frequency of college student smartphone use: Impact on classroom homework assignments. *Journal of Technology in Behavioral Science*, *3*(2), 49–57. doi:10.100741347-017-0034-2

Girish, D. (2020, September 9). "The Social Dilemma" review: Unplug and run. *New York Times*. https://www.nytimes.com/2020/09/09/movies/the-social-dilemma-review.html

Gray, C. M., & Chivukula, S. S. (2019). Ethical mediation in UX practice. In *Proceedings of the 2019 CHI Conference on Human Factors in Computing Systems*. Association for Computing Machinery. 10.1145/3290605.3300408

Guston, D. H., & Sarewitz, D. (2002). Real-time technology assessment. *Technology in Society*, *24*(1–2), 93–109. doi:10.1016/S0160-791X(01)00047-1

Hancock, P. A., Pepe, A. A., & Murphy, L. L. (2005). Hedonomics: The power of positive and pleasurable ergonomics. *Ergonomics in Design*, *13*(1), 8–14. doi:10.1177/106480460501300104

Hartanto, A., & Yang, H. (2016). Is the smartphone a smart choice? The effect of smartphone separation on executive functions. *Computers in Human Behavior*, *64*, 329–336. doi:10.1016/j.chb.2016.07.002

Hollis, R. B., & Was, C. A. (2016). Mind wandering, control failures, and social media distractions in online learning. *Learning and Instruction*, *42*, 104–112. doi:10.1016/j.learninstruc.2016.01.007

Horberry, T., Osborne, R., & Young, K. (2019). Pedestrian smartphone distraction: Prevalence and potential severity. *Transportation Research Part F: Traffic Psychology and Behaviour*, *60*, 515–523. doi:10.1016/j.trf.2018.11.011

Horvath, J., Mundinger, C., Schmitgen, M. M., Wolf, N. D., Sambataro, F., Hirjak, D., Kubera, K. M., Koenig, J., & Christian Wolf, R. (2020). Structural and functional correlates of smartphone addiction. *Addictive Behaviors*, *105*(January), 106334. doi:10.1016/j.addbeh.2020.106334 PMID:32062336

International Ergonomics Association. (2020). *What is ergonomics?* https://iea.cc/what-is-ergonomics/

Jackson, T., Dawson, R., & Wilson, D. (2003). Reducing the effect of email interruptions on employees. *International Journal of Information Management, 23*(1), 55–65. doi:10.1016/S0268-4012(02)00068-3

Johannes, N., Veling, H., Dora, J., Meier, A., Reinecke, L., & Buijzen, M. (2018). Mind-wandering and mindfulness as mediators of the relationship between online vigilance and well-being. *Cyberpsychology, Behavior, and Social Networking, 21*(12), 761–767. doi:10.1089/cyber.2018.0373 PMID:30499683

Kim, Y., Kim, D. J., & Wachter, K. (2013). A study of mobile user engagement (MoEN): Engagement motivations, perceived value, satisfaction, and continued engagement intention. *Decision Support Systems, 56*, 361–370. doi:10.1016/j.dss.2013.07.002

Kim, Y., Wang, Y., & Oh, J. (2016). Digital media use and social engagement: How social media and smartphone use influence social activities of college students. *Cyberpsychology, Behavior, and Social Networking, 19*(4), 264–269. doi:10.1089/cyber.2015.0408 PMID:26991638

Klimmt, C., Hefner, D., Reinecke, L., Rieger, D., & Vorderer, P. (2017). The permanently online and permanently connected mind: Mapping the cognitive structures behind mobile internet use. In P. Vorderer, D. Hefner, L. Reinecke, & C. Klimmt (Eds.), *Permanently online, permanently connected* (pp. 18–28). Routledge. doi:10.4324/9781315276472-3

Lawrence, A. D., Kinney, T. B., O'Connell, M. S., & Delgado, K. M. (2017). Stop interrupting me! Examining the relationship between interruptions, test performance and reactions. *Personnel Assessment and Decisions, 3*(1), 2. doi:10.25035/pad.2017.002

Leiva, L. A., Bohmer, M., Gehring, S., & Křuger, A. (2012). Back to the app: The costs of mobile application interruptions. In *Proceedings of the 14th International Conference on Human Computer Interaction with Mobile Devices and Services*. Association for Computing Machinery. 10.1145/2371574.2371617

Lin, Y. H., Chen, C. Y., Li, P., & Lin, S. H. (2013). A dimensional approach to the phantom vibration and ringing syndrome during medical internship. *Journal of Psychiatric Research, 47*(9), 1254–1258. doi:10.1016/j.jpsychires.2013.05.023 PMID:23786911

Liu, Y. (2003). The aesthetic and the ethic dimensions of human factors and design. *Ergonomics, 46*(13–14), 1293–1305. doi:10.1080/0014013031000161088 PMID:14612320

Maier, T., Donghia, V., Chen, C., Menold, J., & McComb, C. (2019). Assessing the impact of cognitive assistants on mental workload in simple tasks. In *International Design Engineering Technical Conferences and Computers and Information in Engineering Conference* (Vol. 59278). American Society of Mechanical Engineers. 10.1115/DETC2019-97543

Mancas, M. (2016). What is attention? In M. Mancas, V. P. Ferrera, N. Riche, & J. G. Taylor (Eds.), *From human attention to computational attention: A multidisciplinary approach* (pp. 9–20). Springer. doi:10.1007/978-1-4939-3435-5_2

Manser, M. (2017). 7 mobile engagement statistics that show push notification ROI. *Medium*. https://airship.medium.com/7-mobile-engagement-statistics-that-show-push-notification-roi-f664409943a2

Misra, S., Cheng, L., Genevie, J., & Yuan, M. (2016). The iPhone effect: The quality of in-person social interactions in the presence of mobile devices. *Environment and Behavior*, 48(2), 275–298. doi:10.1177/0013916514539755

Monk, C. A. (2004). The effect of frequent versus infrequent interruptions on primary task resumption. *Proceedings of the Human Factors and Ergonomics Society Annual Meeting*, 48(3), 295–299. doi:10.1177/154193120404800304

Newman, A., Round, H., Bhattacharya, S., & Roy, A. (2017). Ethical climates in organizations: A review and research agenda. *Business Ethics Quarterly*, 27(4), 475–512. doi:10.1017/beq.2017.23

O'Brien, H., & Toms, E. G. (2008). What is user engagement? A conceptual framework for defining user engagement with technology. *Journal of the American Society for Information Science and Technology*, 59(6), 938–955. doi:10.1002/asi.20801

Okoshi, T., Ramos, J., Nozaki, H., Nakazawa, J., Dey, A. K., & Tokuda, H. (2015). Reducing users' perceived mental effort due to interruptive notifications in multi-device mobile environments. In *Proceedings of the 2015 ACM International Joint Conference on Pervasive and Ubiquitous Computing*. Association for Computing Machinery. 10.1145/2750858.2807517

Omamo, A. O., Rodrigues, A. J., & Muliaro, W. J. (2020). A system dynamics model of technology and society: In the context of a developing nation. *International Journal of System Dynamics Applications*, 9(2), 42–63. doi:10.4018/IJSDA.2020040103

Park, C. S., & Kaye, B. K. (2019). Smartphone and self-extension: Functionally, anthropomorphically, and ontologically extending self via the smartphone. *Mobile Media & Communication*, 7(2), 215–231. doi:10.1177/2050157918808327

Pereira, A., Prada, R., & Paiva, A. (2014). Improving social presence in human–agent interaction. In *Proceedings of the SIGCHI Conference on Human Factors in Computing Systems*. Association for Computing Machinery. 10.1145/2556288.2557180

Quijada, M. D. R. B., Arriaga, J. L. D. O., & Domingo, D. A. (2020). Insights into user engagement on social media. Findings from two fashion retailers. *Electronic Markets*. Advance online publication. doi:10.100712525-020-00429-0

Rigby, S., & Ryan, R. M. (2011). *Glued to games: How video games draw us in and hold us spellbound*. Praeger.

Rozgonjuk, D., Elhai, J. D., Ryan, T., & Scott, G. G. (2019). Fear of missing out is associated with disrupted activities from receiving smartphone notifications and surface learning in college students. *Computers & Education*, *140*, 103590. doi:10.1016/j.compedu.2019.05.016

Rozgonjuk, D., Kattago, M., & Täht, K. (2018). Social media use in lectures mediates the relationship between procrastination and problematic smartphone use. *Computers in Human Behavior*, *89*, 191–198. doi:10.1016/j.chb.2018.08.003

Ryan, R. M., & Deci, E. L. (2000). Self-determination theory and the facilitation of intrinsic motivation, social development, and well-being. *The American Psychologist*, *55*(1), 68–78. doi:10.1037/0003-066X.55.1.68 PMID:11392867

Ryan, R. M., & Rigby, C. S. (2018). *MIT handbook of gamification*. MIT Press.

Ryan, R. M., Rigby, C. S., & Przybylski, A. (2006). The motivational pull of video games: A self-determination theory approach. *Motivation and Emotion*, *30*(4), 344–360. doi:10.100711031-006-9051-8

Schultz, C. D. (2016). Insights from consumer interactions on a social networking site: Findings from six apparel retail brands. *Electronic Markets*, *26*(3), 203–217. doi:10.100712525-015-0209-7

Scott, H., Biello, S. M., & Woods, H. C. (2019). Identifying drivers for bedtime social media use despite sleep costs: The adolescent perspective. *Sleep Health*, *5*(6), 539–545. . doi:10.1016/j.sleh.2019.07.006 PMID:31523005

Shilton, K. (2013). Values levers: Building ethics into design. *Science, Technology & Human Values*, *38*(3), 374–397. doi:10.1177/0162243912436985

Shilton, K. (2018). Values and ethics in human-computer interaction. *Foundations and Trends in Human–Computer Interaction*, *12*(2), 1–53. doi:10.1561/1100000073

Shilton, K., & Anderson, S. (2017). Blended, not bossy: Ethics roles, responsibilities and expertise in design. *Interacting with Computers, 29*(1), 71–79. doi:10.1093/iwc/iww002

Shneiderman, B. (2000). Universal usability. *Communications of the ACM, 43*(5), 84–91. doi:10.1145/332833.332843

Sohn, S., Rees, P., Wildridge, B., Kalk, N. J., & Carter, B. (2019). Prevalence of problematic smartphone usage and associated mental health outcomes amongst children and young people: A systematic review, meta-analysis and GRADE of the evidence. *BMC Psychiatry, 19*(1), 1–10. doi:10.118612888-019-2350-x PMID:30606141

Spiekermann, S. (2015). *Ethical IT innovation: A value-based system design approach.* CRC Press. doi:10.1201/b19060

Stothart, C., Mitchum, A., & Yehnert, C. (2015). Supplemental material for the attentional cost of receiving a cell phone notification. *Journal of Experimental Psychology. Human Perception and Performance, 41*(4), 893–897. doi:10.1037/xhp0000100 PMID:26121498

Stroud, N. J., Peacock, C., & Curry, A. L. (2020). The effects of mobile push notifications on news consumption and learning. *Digital Journalism, 8*(1), 32–48. doi:10.1080/21670811.2019.1655462

Tandon, A., Kaur, P., Dhir, A., & Mäntymäki, M. (2020). Sleepless due to social media? Investigating problematic sleep due to social media and social media sleep hygiene. *Computers in Human Behavior, 113*, 106487. doi:10.1016/j.chb.2020.106487

Taylor, K., & Silver, L. (2019). *Smartphone ownership is growing rapidly around the world, but not always equally.* Pew Research Center. https://www.pewresearch.org/global/2019/02/05/smartphone-ownership-is-growing-rapidly-around-the-world-but-not-always-equally/

Turner, L. D., Allen, S. M., & Whitaker, R. M. (2017). Reachable but not receptive: Enhancing smartphone interruptibility prediction by modelling the extent of user engagement with notifications. *Pervasive and Mobile Computing, 40*, 480–494. doi:10.1016/j.pmcj.2017.01.011

Uncapher, M. R., & Wagner, A. D. (2018). Minds and brains of media multitaskers: Current findings and future directions. *Proceedings of the National Academy of Sciences of the United States of America, 115*(40), 9889–9896. doi:10.1073/pnas.1611612115 PMID:30275312

Ward, A. F., Duke, K., Gneezy, A., & Bos, M. W. (2017). Brain drain: The mere presence of one's own smartphone reduces available cognitive capacity. *Journal of the Association for Consumer Research*, 2(2), 140–154. doi:10.1086/691462

Wei, R. (2014). Texting, tweeting, and talking: Effects of smartphone use on engagement in civic discourse in China. *Mobile Media & Communication*, 2(1), 3–19. doi:10.1177/2050157913500668

Wiener, N. (1953). The machines as threat and promise. In P. Masani (Ed.), *Norbert Wiener: Collected works and commentaries* (Vol. 4, pp. 673–678). MIT Press.

Winfield, A. (2019). Ethical standards in robotics and AI. *Nature Electronics*, 2(2), 46–48. doi:10.103841928-019-0213-6

Winnick, M. (2016). *Putting a finger on our phone obsession. Mobile touches: A study on how humans use technology*. Dscout. https://blog.dscout.com/mobile-touches

Woods, D., & Dekker, S. (2000). Anticipating the effects of technological change: A new era of dynamics for human factors. *Theoretical Issues in Ergonomics Science*, 1(3), 272–282. doi:10.1080/14639220110037452

Yang, Q., & Gong, X. (2021). The engagement–addiction dilemma: An empirical evaluation of mobile user interface and mobile game affordance. *Internet Research*. Advance online publication. doi:10.1108/INTR-11-2020-0622

Zarandona, J., Cariñanos-Ayala, S., Cristóbal-Domínguez, E., Martín-Bezos, J., Yoldi-Mitxelena, A., & Cillero, I. H. (2019). With a smartphone in one's pocket: A descriptive cross-sectional study on smartphone use, distraction and restriction policies in nursing students. *Nurse Education Today*, 82, 67–73. doi:10.1016/j.nedt.2019.08.001 PMID:31445465

Zhang, F., Zhang, Y., Quin, L., Zhang, W., & Lin, X. (2018). Efficiently reinforcing social networks over user engagement and tie strength. In *IEEE 34th International Conference on Data Engineering (ICDE)*. IEEE. 10.1109/ICDE.2018.00057

Chapter 3
Human Factors:
An Authentic Learning Mobile Application Design Project in a Higher Education and Industry Context

Emily Cooney
Duquesne University, USA

Nicole Martonik
Duquesne University, USA

Lauren Kolber

Duquesne University, USA

Emalee Sekely
Duquesne University, USA

William J. Gibbs
Duquesne University, USA

ABSTRACT

Human factors are integral to applied academic programs such as interaction design. In this chapter, the authors begin by reviewing precepts of authentic, "real-world" learning. From a human factors and interaction design viewpoint, they then describe an authentic learning project—a mobile application design—that was done by university students in collaboration with a leading global specialty retailer. Specifically, in terms of the project, the chapter reviews the following: 1) benefits and challenges of academic and industry collaborations; 2) human factors and interaction design processes, methods, and principles used throughout the authentic project; 3) anthropometric features of the project prototype and their implications for usability; 4) precepts of cognitive information processing (i.e., human attention, perception, and memory) and their importance for the design and usability of the project's interface; 5) insights and lessons learned about the use of authentic learning experiences in teaching human factors and interaction design.

DOI: 10.4018/978-1-7998-6453-0.ch003

INTRODUCTION

In today's information society where technology is pervasive, college and university graduates face a workforce characterized by rapid innovation, new and emergent industry practices and methods, as well as ongoing technology development. These forces stimulate new ways of working and communicating and alter business models, workflows, and entire industries. Workers must be adaptive to the challenges of this dynamic environment and capable of thinking critically about and solving complex and ill-defined problems.

In higher education, an enduring challenge in many academic disciplines has been providing students "real-world" learning experiences that immerse students in collaborative contexts, so they deliberate and ultimately address authentic problems. Applied disciplines such as architecture and design, engineering, computer science, and business tend to emphasize the congruence between what is taught in the classroom and what is occurring in professional practice. As academic programs face increased competition for students due to demographic shifts, persistent and rapid technological innovations, among other things, authentic learning and the necessity of connecting the higher educational classroom with professional practice becomes even more highlighted.

Generally, traditional teaching and learning approaches in higher education tend to be of the objectivist epistemology - lecture, objective tests, and learning experiences that are more content-and instructor-centric than learner centered – and detached from "real-world", authentic problem-solving. Universities have been criticized for not adequately preparing students for today's highly dynamic workforce and information society as they continue to embody instructional approaches based on objectivist's assumptions (Alt, 2015).

Conversely, in today's information society, the workforce requires individuals to quickly adapt to changing work demands and unforeseen challenges, work collaboratively, think critically, make reasoned decisions, and resolve fluid and ill-defined problems (Huq & Gilbert, 2017; Lee & Hannafin, 2016). Teaching and learning based solely on behavioral and cognitivist-inspired approaches may be inadequate. While they may be appropriate for many learning situations and content, educators and researchers also advocate for instructional approaches reflective of a constructivists epistemology. In fact, Elander and Cronje (2016, p.390) found that of the courses they evaluated, all integrated both objectivist and constructivist principles and they noted that, "…learning tasks tend to be constructivist by nature while the provision of information tends towards direct instruction." From a constructivist perspective, teaching is a means of helping learners construct meaning by providing them authentic learning experiences and guiding them through the meaning-making process. Constructivists approaches to teaching and learning emphasize that learners be active rather than passive recipients of information; learners collaborate and cooperate with others to solve ill-defined, authentic problems; learning is scaffolded (i.e., support for learning); learning contexts are authentic and real-world; and the orientation is learner-centered rather than instructor-centered (Elander & Cronje, 2016; Lee & Hannafin, 2016; Jonassen, Peck, & Wilson, 1999; Jonassen, 1991). Central tenants of constructivism include: a) knowledge is constructed as learners interact with the environment, b) learning is a uniquely individualize process. The reality one constructs or comes to know is unique to that individual; c) the culture and community in which the learner exists influence the meaning or knowledge one constructs from an event; d) knowledge acquired by the learner in anchored in the contexts in which the learning event takes place; and e) the impetus for knowledge construction is rooted in dissonance between what one knows and what is observed in the environment (Marra, Jonassen, Palmer & Luft, 2014). Thus, authentic problem solving is ideally suited to promote high-order learning, as students reconcile the dissonance inherent in "real-life" problems.

Need for Authentic Learning Experience

Rooted in constructivism, authentic learning is associated with various instructional approaches (e.g., Project-based learning) that emphasize life-like contexts, real-world problems, higher-order thinking, and social dimensions of learning. Similarly, problem-based learning (PBL) is a methodology in which authentic problem solving is regarded as the foundation of learning. PBL originated in the mid-twentieth century from a dissatisfaction with conventional health science education that relied on instructor-centered lecture and memorization of decontextualized biomedical information. Early proponents of PBL insisted on developing clinical problem-solving skills of medical students to better prepare them for medical practice (Marra, Jonassen, Palmer & Luft, 2014). This aligns with today's educational goals, particularly in applied academic disciplines, that spotlight the need to develop student competency so they are prepared for professional life.

Interaction design is an applied design discipline concerned with "designing interactive products to support the way people communicate and interact in their everyday and working lives (Sharp, Rogers, & Preece, 2019, p. 9). Human factors is the study of human cognitive and physical abilities and limitations and the design of products and systems for human use (Stone, Chaparro, Keebler, Chaparro, & McConnell, 2018). The pursuit to understand the inherent influence human factors has on the designing of interactive products is central in interaction design. While interaction design and human factors have distinct vocabularies, traditions and methodological foundations, fundamentally they aim to ensure that products (e.g., physical devices, systems, environments) are useful, safe, and easy to use.

Authentic learning experience (constructivists approach) is particularly germane to academic programs that offer courses in applied subject areas such as interaction design, interactive media and design, user experience (UX) design, human computer interaction and human factors, where ultimately program curricula explore, to varying degrees, the intersection of or connection among humans, designed artifacts, and, to an increasing extent, technology (computation).

Discussing pedagogical approaches in teaching ergonomics and anthropometrics related to human-centric design, Wanberg, Caston and Bert (2019) note that pragmatic learning experiences better serve students, as theory by itself is insufficient for them to acquire working knowledge of a discipline. Pickens and Benden (2013) indicate that industry reports indicate that early-career human factors professionals often lacked practical knowledge and do not grasp the relevance of their learning to industry problems. To prepare new professionals for the mandates of human factors and related disciplines, "...their training should include practice in design, project management, working in interdisciplinary teams, and making persuasive arguments for human factors in all project phases. " (Rantanen, et al., 2013, p. 443) Educators in these disciplines should associate with industry in such a way that as industry changes curricular get updated (Rantanen & Moroney, 2012). Thus, the nature of human factors problems faced in industry and the approaches used to solve them can be reflected in the classroom. And despite the fact that such problems are often ill-structured and messy without a clear single solution, they are germane to classroom learning. When students do not engage in authentic learning experiences or do not practice their learning with real-world problems in an authentic context, their progression to human factors or related fields can be challenging (Sierra, Benne & Fisk, 2002).

In this chapter, the authors discuss precepts of human factors and interaction design to describe an authentic learning project - a mobile application design - that was done by university students in collaboration with a leading global specialty retailer. Specifically, they examine:

1. Benefits and challenges of academic and industry collaborations;
2. Human factors and interaction design processes, methods, and principles used throughout the authentic project;
3. Anthro/pometric features of the project prototype and their implications for usability;
4. Precepts of cognitive information processing (i.e., human attention, perception, and memory) and their importance for the design and usability of the project's interface;
5. Insights and lessons learned about the use of authentic learning experiences in teaching human factors and interaction design.

DESCRIPTION OF AUTHENTIC LEARNING PROJECT

In the fall semester of 2019, a leading global specialty retailer provided students in the Interactive Design program at Duquesne University (Interactive Design Studio course) a design challenge (project brief): design a smartphone application that alleviated known pain points within the in-store shopping experience associated with: a) product finding and browsing, b) product try on, and c) value maximization. These are authentic problems faced by many retailers who enable customers to augment shopping tasks with technology. Over a four-week period, student teams of 3-4 individuals created designs that they eventually presented to the retailer's UX team at the conclusion of the semester. What follows is a description of one team's project. Figure 1 depicts the process. The primary points of interaction with the retailer were at the beginning of the project and at the end.

Figure 1. Design process followed in project (Hartson & Pyla, 2012)

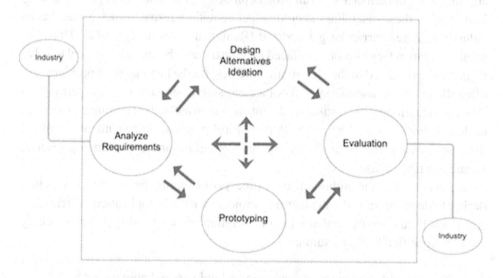

Employing a human-centered design approach, a team of three interaction design students designed a smartphone application with functionality to augment Product Finding and Browsing, Product Try On, and Value Maximization. The app the team designed could be used for online shopping as well as to augment tasks during in-store shopping. Specifically, to enhance customers' shopping experiences, the app included a "My Closet" space with three primary features:

1.   *Body profile* system helped customers with clothing fitting. Using an on-screen human model, users set body type and size requirements to ascertain clothing fit and personal preferences in terms of how the user desired their clothes to fit.

2.   *Outfit Creator* enabled users to identified clothing items, create outfit combinations, save outfits, and share them with friends.

3.   *Expense Planner* allows users to set spending limits. Once a limit was set, users could scan the barcode of in-store items and the app would allow them to determine if they can purchase items based on the determined amount and any store rewards the user had.

Description of Student Design Process: My Closet

This section describes the processes students (design team) took from researching the design opportunities presented to them in the retailer's project brief through to the development of a high-fidelity functioning prototype.

Design Research: Understanding the Issues

In the project brief, the global retailer stated that an outcome of the project would be a prototype application. The team conducted research to gain insights about customer behavior that could inform the design and focused its research on: a) how customers shop and their motives for shopping; specifically, how customers like to browse and locate products, b) how customers feel about trying on products, c) what customers find important when it comes to shopping for products, and d) how aware are customers of the retailer's values and rewards offerings. The team triangulated its research approach by using several data collection methods, customer survey, interviews, and contextual observations.

The survey presented 26 questions, mostly open-ended, to understand how customers prefer to shop (e.g., alone or with friends, in-store or online, their process when shopping, etc.) and to assess their familiarity with the retailer's shopping app and to rate their experience with it. In addition, the survey posed questions about customers' primary motivations for shopping, the most important factors that influence them when shopping for clothes, and new features that might be of interest to them on the retailer's app. The team conducted in-depth interviews with men and women in their mid-twenties. Interviews were conversational in nature to obtain more in-depth information about how customers shop (e.g., processes they use, etc.) and what they do and do not like about the shopping experience generally and with the retailer specifically. The team also visited the retailer's stores to make observations pertaining to how people shop and the activities they engage in while shopping in-store.

Participants

For the survey, a total of 52 people participated. While a majority (88.5%) of the participants were female, males (9.6%) also responded. Participants ages varied but most (50%) were between the ages of 20 and 25 (see Table 1). Geographically, most participants were from the Pittsburgh, Pennsylvania region and surrounding states (Ohio, Maryland, New Jersey, Virginia, and New York).

Table 1. Survey participants by years of age

Years of Age (n=52)	%
15-19	9.6%
20-25	50%
26-30	9.6%
31+	30.8%

Generally, findings highlighted clothing fit and cost as significant determinants in shopping. Most participants would use an app in-store if it made the shopping process easier, and they would be comfortable giving body measurements to an app to help with fitting. Data were also valuable in helping the team better understand how consumers think while shopping, their frustrations, and what they perceived was missing from the experience such as a) scanning tags to see sales or promotions, b) determining product availability, and c) seeing clothes on models with similar body types. In addition, from the survey and interview data, the team found that a) 83% of participants were interested in sizing preference (i.e., put in measurements and fit preferences to choose clothes), b) 69% showed interests in some form of "virtual try on," and c) 68% wanted scanning options if a product or size is unavailable in store.

Define: Implications of Research for Design

When analyzing data through several rounds of iteration, the team noted patterns from survey responses, commentary, and observations pertaining to shopping habits that seemed to be overarching among all participants and from which it made a list of main opportunities that needed to be addressed:

- Product Finding and Browsing
  - Getting items that aren't on the floor (in-store shopping)
  - Style clothes before buying
- Product Try On
  - Using body measurements to help find best fit
  - Using different size models and seeing the feel of fabrics
- Value Maximization
  - Staying within a budget
  - Offering available promotions/rewards

Design Ideation and Prototyping

Based on a summation of the research and it implications, the team designed three features (Body Profile, Outfit Creator, Expense Planner) for the app, each of which is discussed below.

Body Profile

The ideation process for the app design involved much iteration until the team settled on any design solution. One of the most challenging issues was having many big ideas but no plausible way of completing them. For instance, the team assumed it would be useful to create an augmented-reality, virtual try-on feature (e.g., for online shopping) by using the smartphone's camera and then layering images of clothes onto shopper's body virtually. However, for this project, the team felt it was not feasible to create an experience in which clothing images were layered realistically to fit over a shopper's body. The team felt that it would appear unrealistic, much like some filters available on social media platforms and it would not come close to replicating the experience of shopping in-store. Consequently, the team decided to create a Body Profile section (see Figure 2) that allows shoppers to input anthropometric measurements (e.g., height, body breadth and depth, hip breadth, shoulder breadth, and estimates of circumference and curvature) as well as fit preferences, and from which the app would tailor its clothing recommendations to the shopper's body shape and style choices. Body Profile helps to address the "product try on" pain point the global retailer presented in the project brief.

Figure 2. Body profile

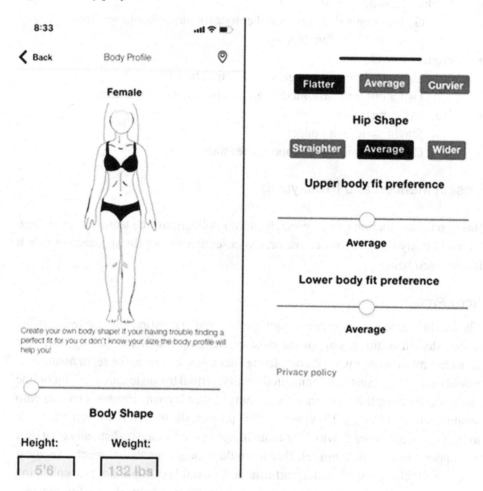

Outfit Creator

The Outfit Creator section of the app is designed to enable shoppers to: a) identify clothing items, b) create outfit combinations and save them within the app, and c) share these style creations among friends (see Figure 3). The team designed the Outfit Creator to implement a barcode scan for in-store use. When shoppers are in-store and see an item of interest, they scan its barcode to display the item and associated information. Shoppers can then instantly virtually mix-and-match the item with other clothes. They can also view the item on similar models based on the body profile preferences created with the Body Profile. This was an important feature to add because research showed that some customers were unfamiliar with the retailer's app or interacted with it infrequently, so the Outfit Creator offers them a personalized reason to utilize it while shopping in-store and online.

Figure 3. Outfit creator

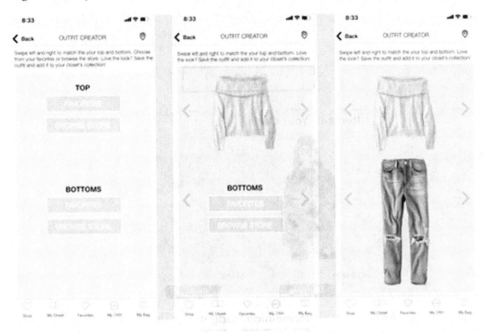

Expense Planner

The final step in the ideation process addressed the value maximization pain point presented in the project brief. The team intended to make the app useful in-store and out-of-store. From the research, shoppers, in terms of value maximation, were concerned with money they were spending and whether they could find promotions or rewards while shopping. The Expense Planner (see Figure 4) offers shoppers an easy way to make sure they stay within budget. Shoppers enter how much money they anticipate spending. While in the store, they scan the barcode of items of interest and the app calculates the budget while they shop. The Expense Planner also immediately presents promotions and sales upon scanning, and any loyalty program rewards connected to the shopper's profile are deducted. This feature helps make shoppers' experience more pain free because they do not need to think too hard about budget or make calculations when buying clothes.

Figure 4. Express planner

Prototyping the design was a challenging step of the process because the team formulated a lot of beneficial features, but they had to be incorporated into the retailer's existing app architecture that users would expect to easily navigate. Utilizing a prototyping tool, the team compiled all design component ideas into one cohesive My Closet feature, that was added to the main tab bar of the retailer's app interface. The My Closet landing screen allowed shoppers to choose to scan items and to access the Body Profile, Outfit Creator, or Expense Planner (see Figure 5). The team felt that these four main features presented a design solution that addressed all of the pain points the retailer presented in the project brief.

The team conducted user testing throughout the prototyping process. The team began usability testing on the retailer's app by giving users tasks and observing their interactions and processes of navigation, which helped to highlight areas necessitating design changes. During prototype development, the team perform user testing and interviewed users to gain additional insights about the functionally, usability, and perceived value of the features being designed. Finally, after the team had a functional prototype, more comprehensive user tests were performed, which proved essential in getting feedback about design features as well as what modification were still needed prior to presenting the proposed solutions to the retailer's UX team.

Presenting the Research and Design Prototype and Insights

Presenting the design research and prototype to the global retailer was a valuable experience for the student design team. It provided insight on how a global retailer's design team operates and the process it goes through when designing websites and apps. Meeting with them made clear that when designing, the focus is on the organizational and customer's vision and not the design team's vison – student team members were not designing for themselves. The student team had many interesting ideas, but they had to be integrated with the retailer's app and organizational brand and culture. Team members had to constantly step back and think, will this feature fit with the retailer and is it something the retailer would offer or use? This helped the team frame its work in the context of UX-interaction designers working for a specific retailer - not just UX-interaction design, in general. This revelation helped to condense ideas and gave focus to aspects that could make the retailer's app more usable, not only in stores but online as well.

Figure 5. My closet landing screen

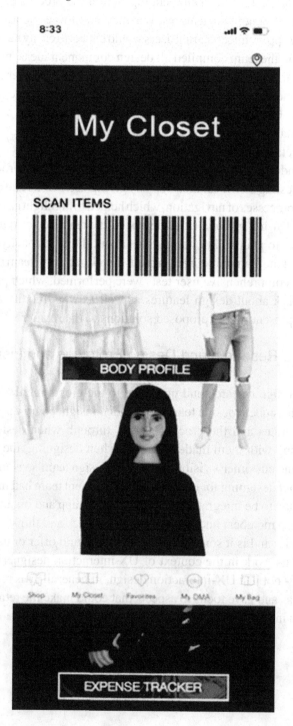

The team also learned the importance of feedback and user testing. In the early stages of creating prototypes team members shared design ideas and prototypes with users. They gave users tasks to complete with the prototypes, which gave them valuable insights about how users perceived and used design features. After testing, team members gathered and discussed all of the feedback, shared different perspectives, and then worked on refining the prototype. After presenting the design, the retailer's UX designers provided additional feedback on the research, design features, and prototype. From a student-designer perspective, the feedback was invaluable because it provided a professional UX-interaction design perspective about the things that worked and those things that needed improving. As student designers, the experience of working in a real-world, authentic setting with an actual interaction design and UX team within the industry was worthwhile educationally and professionally.

MY CLOSET, ELECTRONIC PERFORMANCE SUPPORT AND HUMAN FACTORS

The design of human-computer interactions and associated interfaces should be based on human dimensions, the cognitive, perceptual, and physical factors of users (Proctor, 2016). In this section the authors examine the My Closet project in terms of human factors, specifically decision-making, visual perception, and control coding.

Human Decision Making

A range of limitations, some of which are natural, and others imposed by situational or environmental factors, restrict human activity. Some common innate constraints that impact human performance are limits on perception and attention, cognitive processing speed, memory, and decision-making, and many of these can be overcome by properly designed performance support (Schaik, 2016). Most activities in which people take part such as communicating over distances, shopping, and traveling are aided or supported in some form. Support systems (e.g., calculators, software applications, computer technology, websites, etc.) augment human limitations (Johnson, 2014). While not all performance aids are electronic, Electronic Performance Support Systems (EPSS) have become important computer-based systems to enhance or extend performance for specific tasks, surmounting human and environment restrictions (Schaik, 2016). In fact, the purpose of many software applications and websites is to aid human decision-making. Johnson (2014, p. 175) offers guidelines for decision support applications and recommends that they: a) provide all options so people can compare and evaluate items; b) help people find alternatives - to expose users to unnoticed items or generate alternative on their choices; c) provide unbiased data; d) perform calculations. Do not required people to make calculations because they are not good at it, computers are; e) help people check assertions and assumptions by providing tools so they can keep their beliefs or notions in-check when decision-making. The student designed My Closet project is a support system to assist shoppers in a range of shopping activities, including decision-making and it's design reflects Johnson's guidelines.

Human Limitations and Decision-Making

In general, human decision-making is characterized as involving tasks in which an individual makes choices, often quickly and with limited available information, among a set of alternatives while being uncertain as to which choice is optimal (Stone, Chaparro, Keebler, Chaparro, & McConnell, 2018). When individuals are rationale or deliberate in choosing among alternatives, they partake in normative decision-making. Normative decision-making is not unlike the sort of decision processes used in scientific inquiry, financial forecasting, or medical diagnoses whereby alternatives and information are thoroughly analyzed to ascertain the optimal decision. However, cognitive science research suggests that constancy and rationality are not always traits of human decision-making and people often make subjective, irrational decisions (Johnson, 2014). Moreover, normative decision-making is cognitively demanding. For many everyday experiences such as shopping, the cognitive load imposed by normative decision-making is often too high. Instead, people frequently employ decision-making heuristics or mental shortcuts, such as eliminating choices by their characteristics (*eliminate by aspects*), deciding based on the information available (*availability heuristics*), and *satisficing*, which are less cognitively taxing and allow for speedy decision-making (Stone, et al., 2018). And this is where the My Closet features (Body Profile, Outfit Creator, and Expense Planner) act as electronic support system to aid decision-making or to help shoppers make choices easily and quickly.

For the My Closet project, the student-design team surveyed 52 shoppers about the processes they used during clothes shopping. Respondents' answers most frequently focused on topics related to decision-making, specifically about how they can make optimal choices or at least satisfactory choices when shopping. When shopping in-store and online, respondents want to, among other things, make choices about clothing by filtering items by prices, fabrics, and sizes; mix-and-match clothing alternatives, browse and assess individual items until discovering attractive clothing; and assessing choices by what is on sale. Respondents also indicated that fitting or entering measurements and clothing fit preferences to help select clothes was the most important factor for them. Shoppers use *eliminate by aspects* heuristics when the mix-and-match clothing items or evaluate attributes (e.g., price, size, style and fit preference, etc.) of alternatives and then no longer consider those alternatives with characteristics they find unattractive – features available in the Outfit Creator help shoppers do this. Shoppers use *availability heuristics* when their choices are influenced by information they recall or that is readily available to them at the time of decision making – such as feedback from friends, product availability, and sales, which are features of My Closet. And they *satisfice* or choose the most adequate alternative - not necessarily the best choice - when their ability to make an optimal choice is restricted, due to factors such as time constraints or limited information. A shopper may choose one item over another because the Expense Planner informs them of budget constraints.

The My Closet (Body Profile, Outfit Creator, and Expense Tracker) are intended as performance support for these types of decision-making heuristics. Using the Body Profile shoppers enter anthropometric measurements (e.g., height, body breadth and depth, hip breadth, shoulder breadth, and estimates of circumference and curvature) to generate a body profile that will help them identify accurate fit preferences for the brand. The profile can be saved and from which the app generates clothing recommendations. Based on fit preferences, shoppers can eliminate recommended items or save those of interest to the Closet for possible purchase, potentially reducing the cognitive load imposed as shoppers try to ascertain appropriate clothing choices based on fit preferences. The Outfit Creator helps shoppers easily select clothes and configure outfits while in-store or online shopping, thus allowing them to choose or eliminate items based on style preferences – also helping to alleviate decision-making complexity and cognitive load. A common decision-making scenario is as follows: in-store shoppers can scan the barcode of a shirt. The item displays in the Outfit Creator. To avoid trying on many different pairs of jeans, requiring mental and extensive physical effort, to locate a pair that match the shirt, the shopper can use the Outfit Creator interface to peruse jeans to find a matching pair, and then locate the pair in store, and try them on. Additionally, outfits can be shared so friends can weigh-in to help shoppers in making decisions.

With the Expense Tracker, shoppers can enter a shopping budget limit and while shopping it keeps track of the budget, providing them useful information to make purchase decisions. In addition, the Expense Tracker offers a Last-Minute Grabs section that provides product recommendations based on the remaining budget, many of which are on-sale items. These features provide valuable information to shoppers when making decisions within budgetary constraints, using *availability heuristics and satisficing*.

My Closet: Visual Perception and the Interface

The human visual system automatically imposes structure on visual information. Our visual perception tends to recognize objects in the world as whole shapes rather than separated or disparate pieces (Johnson, 2014). The Gestalt theory of perception offers a descriptive framework and guiding principles of visual perception that are relevant to the design of user interfaces. In the My Closet project, there are several features of the user interface that exploit these principles. The Outfit Creator screens, depicted in Figure 3 illustrates several of the perceptual features that student designers followed including proximity, similarity, continuity, and figure-ground. For example, people perceive items in a display that are in close proximity or items with similar visual features as related or grouped. Figure 6 depicts the top and bottom regions of the display. The separation (proximity) of the top and bottom regions suggests the regions are distinct or unrelated. The close proximity of items within a region suggests they are related or have a related purpose. Icons within each region have similar visual characteristics that further portend their similarity or relatedness. For instance, in the bottom tab bar, icons, while distinct, have similar size, type, color, and separation. These features, along with their proximity to one another, indicate they serve a related function and behave similarly.

Figure 6. Interface regions and visual perception

Figure 7. Interface: figure-ground

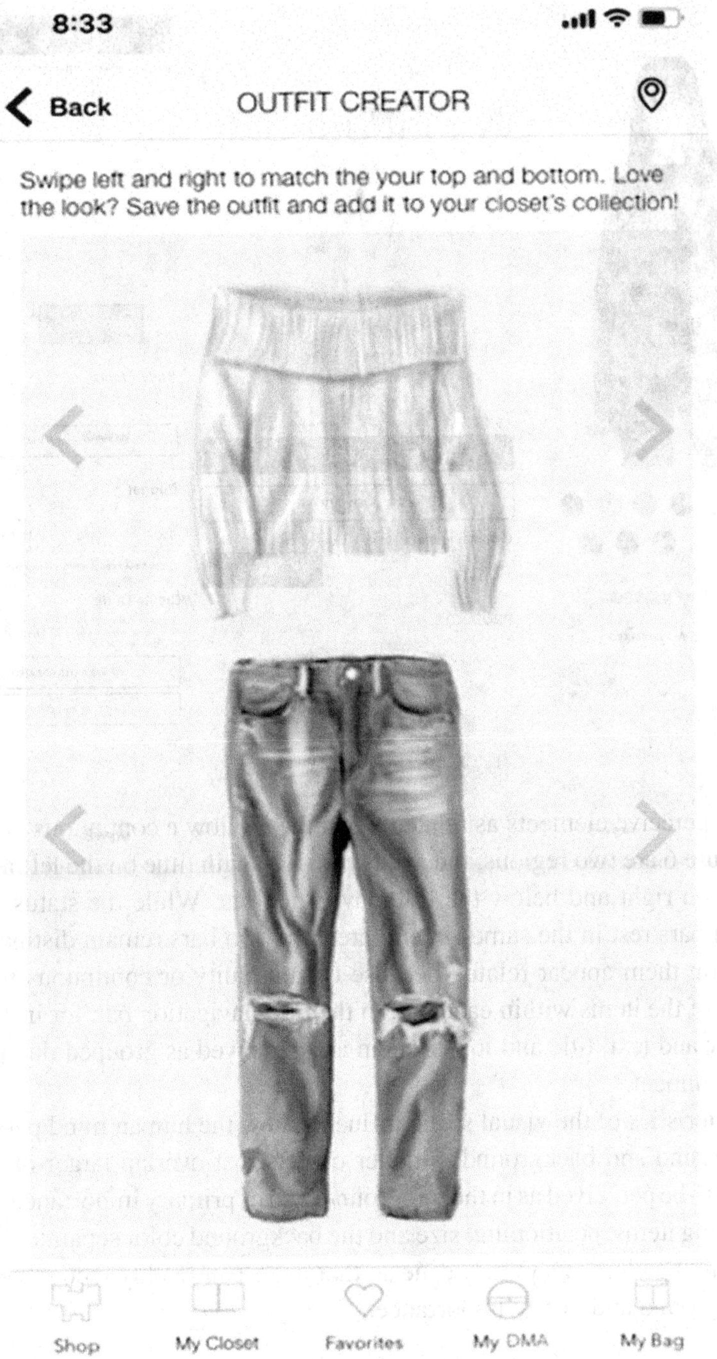

Figure 8. Control coding

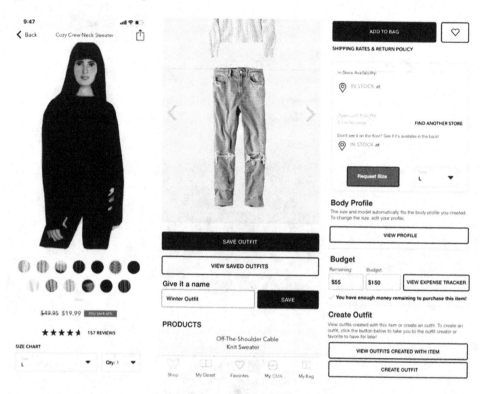

People perceive elements as related when they follow a continuous line. At the top of Figure 6 are two regions, the status bar (top) with time on the left and utility indicators on right and below the title-navigation bar. While the status and title-navigation bars rest in the same general area, the two bars remain distinct and the items within them appear related because of continuity or continuous horizontal alignment of the items within each bar. In the title-navigation bar, for instance, the back arrow and text, title and location pin are perceived as grouped due primarily to their alignment.

Characteristics of the visual scene influence how the human mind parses items into foreground and background. Smaller objects that overlap larger objects in a scene tend to be perceived as in the foreground, and of primary importance. In figure 7 the clothing items, positioning, size and the background color separate them from the surrounding elements in the scene so that users can readily recognize them as in the foreground and of key importance.

My Closet and Control Coding

"A key aspect of designing any control is making sure that the user knows what it does and is able to select the desired control when multiple controls are present" (Stone, et al., 2018, p. 112). Discriminating among controls becomes more challenging as the number of controls increases. This is particularly germane to smartphones that are essentially mobile computers with touchscreen displays that offer advanced input capabilities through gesture and other actions (Kim, Choeb, Choib, & Park, 2019). Affordance theory holds that the possibilities for action or affordances provided by a control should be unambiguous. Where possible, the control must convey its purpose and how it is to be use and its interaction modality should be consistent with the real-world (Ware, 2003; Norman, 2002).

Control coding can be used to help users distinguish controls by shape, texture, color, size, location, mode of operation, or by label (Stone, et al., 2018, p. 112). Figure 8 depicts coding techniques incorporated in the My Closet prototype including size, shape, location, color, and label. While not shown in the figure, the prototype included mode of operation coding given that some controls were discrete (e.g., toggle buttons) and others continuous (e.g., sliders to set body size in the Body Profile).

Controls and Smartphone Interactions

There were several nuisances the authors observed regarding control coding related to touchscreen displays. For example, labels can take time to read and may be occluded by the users' fingers when touching the display. The touch display surface inhibits the ability to discriminate by tactile sense (e.g., texture, shape) and mode of operation is metaphorical, as the interface simulates, albeit in a real way, the input operation. Soft rather than hard buttons are the prevailing means by which users invoke commands on smartphones interfaces, which is appropriate when users are stationary and not distracted by other situational impairments (Bragdon, Nelson, Li & Hinckley, 2011). As the name suggests, mobile devices are used when people are moving (e.g., walking) in a range of environmental settings that introduce a plethora of distractions, task demands or situational impairments, which can divide attention and impede the ability to interact with the device. The use of My Closet for some shopping tasks is complicated by the fact that when shopping people multitask. For instance, when a person is clothes shopping in-store, their attention is divided among multiple mental and physical tasks such as browsing for clothes, assessing clothing items, talking, carrying clothing or bags, etc. This limits the interactions they can have with a direct-touch smartphone application, as the application interface requires visual attention. Most likely, interacting with the interface and shopping tasks do not occur in parallel but rather sequentially as the cognitive and physical task demands (i.e., decision making, carrying bags, touching interface) require that attention be devote to only one task at the time. When the My Closet app is used in environments with situational impediments, there is likely to be a need to expand input vocabularies such as voice, eyes-free gestures, and other forms of interactions. Fruchard, Lecolinet and Chapuis (2020), for example, found using smartwatches and eyes-free gesture interactions suitable for interacting in various situational contexts. Similarly, Wong et al. (2020) investigated eye-free gestures (initiated by smartwatch bezel) on wearables and found that they offer potential for a variety of applications. One can envision a smartwatch interface to My Closet that allows shoppers to scan items with a smartwatch and because the watch does not need to be held, shoppers can issue eyes-free gestures on the watch (or voice commands, although people may be disinclined to use voice in public settings) to put the items in the Closet or Outfit Creator or to get pricing, sales, or availability information. A gesture, for instance, might be simply touching the watch bezel and then moving one's finger to make a short horizontal stroke and then a vertical stroke. Different types of strokes carry different meanings corresponding to interface commands that the user would learn, affording eyes-free interactions in specific situations. A shopper may even use an eyes-free gestures to send outfits to friends who can, along with the Outfits Creator, make recommendations. When the shopper is prepared, they can use the app to view choices or recommendations and then try on clothes while in-store shopping. It may even be plausible that shoppers can display outfit creations on store displays in dressing rooms or other private in-store spaces – and use eyes-free gestures on the watch to view outfits on store displays, eliminating the need to hold a smartphone.

CONCLUSION

Lessons Learned: Academic and Industry

In the Interactive Design Studio course students study human factors and their implication for interaction design. They learned primary and secondary design research methods and apply them when designing human-technology interaction and associated products. Students also gain understanding of the design lifecycle and related process models and corresponding phases, such as Analyze, Design, Evaluate, and Implementation and the Double Diamond process – Discover, Define, Develop, Deliver.

The ultimate purpose of the project presented in this chapter was to provide students an authentic learning experience in association with industry. Academic-industry collaborations can be beneficial on many levels. In terms of impact on the authentic learning experience for this course, the collaboration impacted two key areas: 1) Process – student teamwork process and 2) Project Authenticity.

Figure 9. Design process model (Hartson & Pyla, 2012)

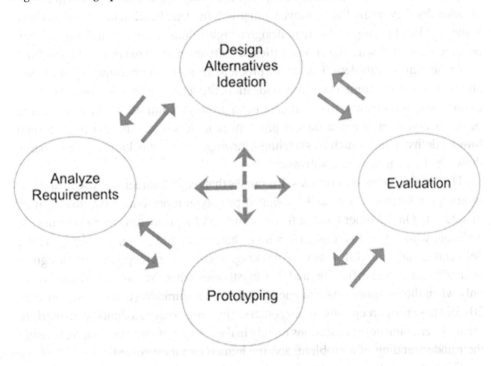

Figure 10. Common process adopted by novice design students

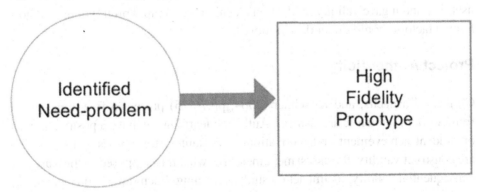

Process – Student Teamwork Processes

The course introduces students to various process models representing the interaction design life cycle. Figure 9 depicts the general phases of the process. It is not uncommon when presented a problem for which media software may be used to design a solution, students tend to adopt a process not unlike that depicted in Figure 10 whereby they immediately move from problem identification or what they think is the problem to using software to design a high-fidelity protype. In doing so, they become inundated with the complexities of software and visual design before fully understanding the problem. This can be problematic as it undercuts inquiry processes and de-empathizes human factors and ideation. Students can become locked in early to one idea, as their investment in creating a prototype inhibits additional ideation or discovery. Even when a design problem is understood, students often forego lower fidelity options such as sketching-drawings, paper mockups or whiteboards drawings in favor of media software.

This occurs for various reasons. In courses that require students to use media and prototyping software, a visually designed prototype represents a tangible artifact or solution. On the other hand, a full description of a problem is more abstruse. In addition, while in reality, design is a lot of hard work and designing is a strategic, deliberate, and thoughtful way of working, there is a perception that design is primarily about beautification and it is mysterious whereby a design comes about only when the designer gets a magical catalyst of inspiration (Dorst & Stolterman, 2015). These misperceptions, among others, can cause novice students particularly to regard interaction design solutions mainly in the context of media software, limiting their understanding of a problem, and the human factors involved.

The authors observed that throughout this academic-industry collaboration, the industry representatives focused primarily on processes, research, data, human behaviors and perception, usability, and ideas with little or no mention of visual designing or prototype fidelity. This help shift student perceptions about design and process, and where they should focus their efforts. It solidified ideas of process and usability and it gave validity to ideation techniques and rapid prototyping, and how human factors should direct design moves.

Project Authenticity

Gulikers, Bastiaens, and Kirschner (2004, pp.70-75) present a five-dimensional framework of authentic assessment. Authentic learning can have a positive impact on student achievement and motivation. Important factors in assessing learning are construct validity, the assessment measures what it is supposed to measure and consequential validity, its impact on student learning. Each dimension can vary in level of authenticity, but they provide a means to evaluate learning experiences. A summary of the dimensions is presented below.

Task: A real-world problem presented to students with pragmatic activities carried out in professional practice.

Physical Context: The tasks should be performed in such a way and in an environment so that students' knowledge, skills, and attitudes align with those in professional practice.

Social Context: The social interactions occurring during the tasks impact authenticity (e.g., often in professional practice people work in teams).

Criteria: What characteristics of the project are valued (e.g., what aspects of the project does the client value or find most interesting).

Standards: What is the degree of performance expected.

In this project students were assigned the following tasks: design a smartphone application that alleviated known pain points within the in-store shopping experience associated with: a) product finding and browsing, b) product try on, and c) value maximization. Based on the five-dimensional framework, in the author's view, the design challenge can be classified as authentic. Below is a mapping of the design challenge based on Gulikers, Bastiaens, and Kirschner's (2004) five-dimensional framework:

Task: Design a smartphone application for a global retailer constitutes an authentic task, as it is a similar, if not identical, task faced by the retailer. In fact, the retailer provided students the task because it was a challenge faced by its designers.

Physical and Social Context: Students interacted with design professionals and the majority of their work was done in teams and in spaces that afforded designing process. Thus, the physical and social contexts were quite real. However, a greater level of authenticity could be achieved if the interaction between the professional personnel increased throughout the project. As shown in Figure 1, industry personnel interacted with the course at the beginning and end of the project. In this case, greater interaction was prohibited, however, due to the professional designers' time and professional commitments.

Criteria: The fundamental criteria of the project related to known pain points within the in-store (and online) shopping experience associated with: a) product finding and browsing, b) product try on, and c) value maximization. At the same time, the professionals were expecting students to demonstrate a research process as well as a professionally developed documentation, presentation, and prototype.

Standard: There were multiple standards by which the project was judge (quality, depth of research, data analysis, human factors implications of design, etc.) but ultimately students were just based on the standards the retailers' design professionals experience in their daily work routines.

Table 2. Additional dimensions of authenticity

Characteristics	Dimensions of Authenticity
Project	
	Scope and scale
	Time-to-completion
	Severity level
	Fabricated-to-Authentic level (is the project fabricated or real)
Industry Personnel	
	Number of personnel
	Accessibility of personnel for project purposes
	Perceived value of investing in project
	Knowledge and expertise of human factors and design domains
Client or Organizational	
	Size
	Profile or Nature of business or organization
	Reputation
	Level of need

In classes, students generally get tested on human factors concepts (e.g., memory, perception, anthropometrics, etc.) and their implications in designing products or evaluating usability, among other things. This is important and useful to help them acquire declarative or factual knowledge, but it may be inadequate for learning procedural knowledge ("knowing how"). A student might understand principles and theory of human factors and interaction but be unable to use them adequately to address the types of problems faced by interaction designers and human factors practitioners. As a result, instructors assign projects, often with the intention to give students "real-world" experience with authentic problems. However, the authenticity of these projects can vary. In addition to the five-dimensional framework presented by Gilbert et el., Table 2 presents additional dimensions or factors, specifically regarding academic-industry collaborations, that influence authenticity. For instance, projects in which students work with a real "client" or organizations and that are of a wide scope and large scale will be more taxing in terms of resources, time, and impact and thus potentially more authentic compared to a small fabricated project. Moreover, when students work with organizations, the size and type of organization, number of personnel with whom students work, and their expertise are all factors impacting authenticity. In this project, students worked with a large global retailer with a reputation for design expertise. The organization had design departments with teams of design and human-computer-interaction (HCI) practitioners. These personnel were knowledge about the subject matter students were studying and thus could assess the work they completed with a high level of professional rigor, adding an even greater degree of authenticity.

Table 3. Project rubric

Project Assessment Rubric				
Project must show evidence of:				
	Needs improved	Satisfactory	Good	Excel
Design process				
Problem definition				
Research methods				
Data collection and analysis				
Requirement definition				
Ideation and prototyping				
Usability testing				
Artifacts-prototype				
Documentation-specifications				
Human factors				
Visual, tactical				
Auditory factors				
Attention, cognition				
Situational, environmental				
Decision making				
Physical, behavioral				
Anthropometric				
Team factors				
Cohesion				
Participation				
Engagement				
Professionalism				
Oral communications				
Written - documentation				
Timeliness				
Technical Competence				
Software, hardware				
Technical trends				

Preparing for future projects, the authors created a rubric (see Table 3) based on the activities in which took place during the project. The rubric reflects five dimensions: Design, Human factors, Professionalism, Team factors, and Technical competence. Based on the worked performed, these dimensions reflect primary areas on which students and instructors can focus their teaching and learning efforts.

REFERENCES

Alt, D. (2015). Assessing the contribution of a constructivist learning environment to academic self-efficacy in higher education. *Learning Environments Research*, *18*(1), 47–67. doi:10.100710984-015-9174-5

Bragdon, A., Nelson, E., Li, Y., & Hinckley, K. (2011). Experimental Analysis of Touch-Screen Gesture Designs in Mobile Environments. *CHI '11: Proceedings of the SIGCHI Conference on Human Factors in Computing Systems*, 403–412. 10.1145/1978942.1979000

Dorst, K., & Stolterman, E. (2015). *Frame Innovation: Create New Thinking by Design*. MIT Press. doi:10.7551/mitpress/10096.001.0001

Elander, K., & Cronje, J. (2016). Paradigms revisited: A quantitative investigation into a model to integrate objectivism and constructivism in instructional design. *Educational Technology Research and Development*, *64*(3), 389–405. doi:10.100711423-016-9424-y

Fruchard, B., Lecolinet, E., & Chapuis, O. (2020). Side-Crossing Menus: Enabling Large Sets of Gestures for Small Surfaces. *Proceedings of the ACM on Human-Computer Interaction, Association for Computing Machinery (ACM)*, *4*, 189:1 – 189:19. 10.1145/3427317

Gulikers, J. T., Bastiaens, T. J., & Kirschner, P. A. (2004). A five-dimensional framework for authentic assessment. *Educational Technology Research and Development*, *52*(3), 67–86. doi:10.1007/BF02504676

Hartson, R., & Pyla, P. S. (2012). *The UX book: Process and guidelines for ensuring a quality user experience*. Morgan Kaufman.

Huq, A., & Gilbert, D. (2017). All the world's a stage: Transforming entrepreneurship education through design thinking. *Education + Training*, *59*(2), 155–170. doi:10.1108/ET-12-2015-0111

Johnson, J. (2014). *Designing with the mind in mind: Simple guide to understanding user interface design guidelines*. Elsevier Science & Technology.

Jonassen, D. H. (1991). Objectivism versus constructivism: Do we need a new philosophical paradigm? *Educational Technology Research and Development*, *39*(3), 5–14. doi:10.1007/BF02296434

Jonassen, D. H., Peck, K. L., & Wilson, B. G. (1999). *Learning with technology: A constructivist perspective*. Prentice Hall.

Kim, H. K., Choe, M., Choi, Y., & Park, J. (2019). Does the Hand Anthropometric Dimension Influence Touch Interaction? *Journal of Computer Information Systems*, *59*(1), 85–96. doi:10.1080/08874417.2017.1305876

Lee, E., & Hannafin, M. J. (2016). A design framework for enhancing engagement in student-centered learning: Own it, learn it, and share it. *Educational Technology Research and Development*, *64*(4), 707–234. doi:10.100711423-015-9422-5

Marra, R., Jonassen, D. H., Palmer, B., & Luft, S. (2014). Why problem-based learning works: Theoretical foundations. *Journal on Excellence in College Teaching*, *25*(3&4), 221–238.

Norman, D. (2002). *The Design of Everyday Things*. Basic Books.

Pickens, A. W., & Benden, M. E. (2013). Curriculum Development for HF/E Graduate Students: Lessons Learned in an Ongoing Effort to Educate and Meet Industry Demands. *Proceedings of the Human Factors and Ergonomics Society Annual Meeting*, *57*(1), 452–456. doi:10.1177/1541931213571098

Proctor, R. W., & Vu, K.-P. L. (2016). Principles for Designing Interfaces Compatible With Human Information Processing. *International Journal of Human-Computer Interaction*, *32*(1), 2–22. doi:10.1080/10447318.2016.1105009

Rantanen, E. M., Colombo, D. J., Miller, S. M., Alexander, A. L., Lacson, F. C., & Andre, A. D. (2013). Practicing Relevant Skills in the Classroom: Advice From Experts in the Industry to Professors. *Proceedings of the Human Factors and Ergonomics Society Annual Meeting*, *57*(1), 443–446. doi:10.1177/1541931213571096

Rantanen, E. M., & Moroney, W. F. (2012). Employers' Expectations for Education and Skills of New Human Factors/Ergonomics Professionals. *Proceedings of the Human Factors and Ergonomics Society Annual Meeting*, *56*(1), 581–585. doi:10.1177/1071181312561121

Schaik, P. (2016). Chapter. In P. Barker (Ed.), Electronic Performance Support: Using Digital Technology to Enhance Human Ability (pp. 3–29). Taylor & Francis Group. doi:10.4324/9781315579047

Sharp, H., Rogers, Y., & Preece, J. (2019). *Interaction Design: Beyond Human-Computer Interaction*. John Wiley & Sons, Inc.

Sierra, E. A., Benne, M., & Fisk, A. D. (2002). It's a Zoo Out there: Teaching Human Factors in a Real—World Context. *Ergonomics in Design*, *10*(3), 6–10. doi:10.1177/106480460201000303

Stone, N., Chaparro, A., Keebler, J., Chaparro, B., & McConnell, D. (2018). *Introduction to Human Factors*. CRC Press., doi:10.1201/9781315153704

Wanberg, J., Caston, M., & Berthold, D. (2019). Ergonomics in Alternative Vehicle Design: Educating Students on the Practical Application of Anthropometric Data. *Ergonomics in Design*, *27*(3), 24–29. doi:10.1177/1064804618782615

Ware, C. (2003). Design as Applied Perception. In J. M. Carroll (Ed.), *Carroll, J. M. (2003). HCI Models, Theories, and Frameworks: Toward a Multidisciplinary Science* (pp. 11–26). Morgan Kaufmann Publishers. doi:10.1016/B978-155860808-5/50002-2

Wong, P. C., Zhu, K., Yang, X., & Fu, H. (2020). Exploring Eyes-Free Bezel-Initiated Swipe on Round Smartwatches. In *Proceedings of the 2020 CHI Conference on Human Factors in Computing Systems (CHI '20)*. Association for Computing Machinery. 10.1145/3313831.3376393

Key Terms and Definitions

Affordance: The design of the control (button, knob, etc.) informs users how to use it, such as a door handle affords the act of pulling.

Authentic Learning: Associated with various instructional approaches that emphasizes life-like contexts, real-world problems, higher-order thinking, and social dimensions of learning.

Constructivists Learning Approaches: Learning approaches that emphasize active engagement of learners and collaboration, learner-centered over instructor-directed learning, ill-defined real-world problem solving in authentic contexts.

Continuous Control: Type of control that provides choices along a continuum, such as a slider control used to set volume on an audio device.

Control Coding: Techniques use to help users distinguish controls such as by shape, texture, color, and size.

Discrete Controls: Type of control that provide limited choices (on/off), such as an on-off light switch.

Electronic Performance Support Systems (EPSS): Computer-based system intended to enhance or extend human performance for specific tasks.

Human Factors: The study of human cognitive and physical abilities and their implications for the design and use of products and systems.

Interaction Design: A design discipline concerned with the design of products and how people interact with them.

Objectivists Learning Approaches: Learning approaches primarily controlled by the instructor and typically characterized by lecture, objective tests, and learning experiences that are more content-and instructor-centric than learner centered.

Chapter 4
Augmented Reality:
Panacea or Pandora's Box?

Victoria L. Claypoole
Design Interactive, Inc., USA

Clay D. Killingsworth
Design Interactive, Inc., USA

Catherine A. Hodges
Design Interactive, Inc., USA

Hannah K. Nye
Design Interactive, Inc., USA

Larry A. Moralez
Design Interactive, Inc., USA

Ernesto Ruiz
Design Interactive, Inc., USA

Kay M. Stanney
iD https://orcid.org/0000-0003-2663-8662
Design Interactive, Inc., USA

ABSTRACT

Augmented reality technology holds great promise for extending and enhancing users' capabilities across numerous applications in both work and personal life. It would be easy to see AR, then, as a panacea, but thoughtful design is required if the benefits are to be realized without also realizing the nascent technology's great potential for harm. Current applications in commercial, military, and education and training settings are herein reviewed, along with consideration of potential future directions. This chapter also identifies hazards posed by poor design or haphazard application and provides recommendations and best practices for those engaged in the design of AR that seek to maximize the human utility of this rapidly maturing technology.

DOI: 10.4018/978-1-7998-6453-0.ch004

INTRODUCTION

Left in the care of a vessel beyond her comprehension, Pandora unleashed on the world all manner of evils and became the oft-invoked personification of the law of unintended consequences. That she did so with good intentions, seeking blessings for all humanity, makes hers an especially apt lesson for those engaged in shaping and applying emerging technologies. With each leap forward in immersive technological capability, such as augmented reality (AR), comes the promise of great reward alongside the potential for unexpected, unforeseen, and possibly harmful consequences. Like Pandora, we may find ourselves able to do – but unable to undo. Unlike Pandora, however, we are not condemned to ignorance, as our idiomatic "box" is of our own making and its contents at least partly predictable. Though we don't now and may never fully know the consequences of novel technologies and their applications, we have the luxury of time for planning and evaluation. With thoughtful design and measured implementation, we may be able to harness AR creations for greater good, reaping the benefits they afford while minimizing potential adverse impacts.

BACKGROUND

Augmented reality is an emerging immersive technology that allows people to view digital content superimposed on the physical world (Cabero & Barroso, 2016). In contrast to virtual reality (VR), which creates a self-contained world via which users are insulated from the real world, AR augments perception of the real world through digital, multisensory overlays (Milgram & Kishino, 1994). The rise of enterprise and consumer AR is as exciting as it is inevitable, and even now, in its early stages of adoption, AR has made a substantial impact in industrial, retail, and training sectors (Akçayır & Akçayır, 2017; Flavián et al., 2019). The applications are potentially limitless; for example, home mechanics may "see" as experts do, diagnosing and repairing complex automotive problems despite lacking experience. One can imagine a future in which every item purchased, and every trip taken are accompanied and guided by an augmented avatar. These are just a couple of the endless possibilities. The promise and utility of AR across a variety of applications is readily apparent, yet those adopting AR technology have an obligation to do so in a manner that maximizes benefits while minimizing risks and harm. The next section provides an overview of current AR applications in three main areas: commercial applications, education and training, and military uses, and considers challenges and complications that may lie ahead.

Commercial Applications

While AR commercial applications will predictably encompass a wide array of forms, for the purposes of this section applications in three burgeoning areas are reviewed: construction, maintenance, and retail.

Construction

The construction industry invests little in R&D, less than 1.0% of revenues, as compared to 3.5-4.5% for the automotive and aerospace sectors (Agarwal et al., 2016). This lack of investment has led to the industry being one of the least digitized, with little in the way of widely adopted technological innovations. This is particularly problematic because, while construction demand is rising worldwide, construction productivity is declining, with large projects going substantially over budget, overtime, understaffed, and ill-supported by digital tools and jobs performance aids (Spectar, 2019). Building Information Modelling (BIM) is a digital tool that has been adopted in the construction industry, with the promise of leveraging analytics to streamline construction processes, produce better estimates of project timelines, and reduce costs and errors (Wang et al., 2013). Yet, BIM has largely been relegated to the role of a representation and simulation tool, limiting its applications within actual construction sites. One potentially fruitful application of AR technologies within the construction industry is integration with BIM in a manner that takes into consideration the physical context of construction activities. This would allow for more contextualized and practical use of BIM within construction processes to reduce cost, time, and level of effort (Hou et al., 2013; Piroozfar et al., 2018).

AR applications in construction also have the potential to estimate, monitor, and potentially curb the carbon footprint of projects (Memarzadeh & Golparvar-Fard, 2012), increase safety by using AR in the field to keep worker's line of sight at the horizon instead of looking down at a mobile device when referencing information sources, thereby maintaining workers' situation awareness and helping them avoid dangers (Li et al., 2018), reduce risks such as by supporting discrepancy checking, provide inspectors with safety information pertinent to specific building locations as they conduct their evaluations (Yeh et al., 2012), and support determination of structural integrity after a natural disaster, such as earthquakes, by contextualizing stored information about a structure's original configuration (Dong et al., 2013; Kamat & El-Tawil, 2007). Other applications include visualizing the non-visible, such as by showing excavator operators where utility lines are buried (Behzadan et al., 2015; Talmaki et al., 2010), thereby reducing accident-associated costs and possible injuries or deaths (Fenais et al., 2020), and helping construction workers reach peak productivity on the job site by using AR to provide relevant information at the point-of-need (e.g., display pertinent information regarding a part, quality specifications, or installation instructions).

Panacea: AR technology has wide applicability within the construction industry and can be used to increase safety, minimize risks, streamline pre-construction design, expedite the building process, provide point-of-need job performance aids, and improve quality, thereby leading to substantial savings in the design, engineering, construction, and operations costs associated with construction projects.

Pandora's Box: AR technology adoption is arguably a tremendous lift for the construction industry, especially given the lack of digital infrastructure (e.g., digital information sources, etc.), technical standards, and paucity of tools to automatically generate digital assets. In addition, integration with existing platforms (e.g., ERP, IoT, etc.) will be essential to get AR applications quickly up and running. AR technology also imposes issues concerning design error liability, safety concerns on and off the construction site, data privacy issues, and intellectual property concerns (George & Ball, 2019). First, as AR can facilitate collaborative design, this could lead to multiple parties contributing to a singular design program file, and thus uncertainty regarding liability for design mistakes. Next, AR head worn displays (HWDs) have a narrow field-of-view and present vergence-accommodation conflicts that could distort visual perception and contribute to trips-and-falls and other safety concerns. Safety issues are compounded by the fact that no standard AR usage protocols are in place to help avoid such concerns. Further, AR products may be made available for use on a construction project and thus it will be important to disclaim liability for use by other parties. Data privacy issues also arise with AR use because confidential or proprietary information may be stored on these devices, and thus they are vulnerable to cybersecurity attacks that could threaten the security of sensitive information; these privacy issues are further exacerbated by a lack of regulation designating what is allowed and what is not in AR environments. Finally, with the myriad of potential users on a construction project, ownership rights of any intellectual property created through AR platform use should be carefully negotiated. Thus, as the construction industry adopts AR, they will likely encounter many complicated problems and challenges that must be carefully addressed in order to avoid unlocking the potential of Pandora's Box.

Maintenance

Within Industry 4.0, intelligent technologies are reconfiguring work, resulting in an evolution of requisite job skill requirements and associated worker roles and responsibilities (Accenture, 2018). For example, while maintenance workers formerly calibrated equipment on a weekly basis, today's workers are expected to calibrate but twice per month and, instead, collaborate with colleagues to install or troubleshoot complex equipment on a daily basis. Thus, an upskilling of the industrial sector is required, as through 2028 skill gaps are expected to leave ~2.4M positions unfilled and have an economic impact of ~$2.67T (Thomas et al., 2018). AR can help fill this gap by supporting apprentice operators at the point-of-need in quickly performing high-skilled tasks. AR technology also affords and is likely to engender instances of memory externalization, whereby a user's short- and long- term memory capacity is enhanced by AR point-of-need systems. AR systems are, of course, capable of serving such a basic memory-supporting function, but more advanced systems may be able to monitor user behavior and present reminders if, for example, a step in a procedure is missed. Further, coupling AR point-of-need support with artificial intelligence (AI) can result in adaptive solutions that provide the right information at the right time in the right format. This is a critically important step for AR applications to take, as a lack of feedback in existing AR-based maintenance platforms has likely contributed to slow adoption in the industrial sector (Siew et al., 2019). Thus, as workers engage with intelligent machines, AR can be used to augment and elevate human capabilities in a manner that is adaptive, innovative, and engaging, which could help overcome the "interest gap" in manufacturing jobs (Giffi et al., 2017).

In addition to upskilling, AR can support the manufacturing sector in keeping track of equipment maintenance, ensuring optimal productive capabilities, reducing costs associated with preventable equipment failure, and supporting consulting technical documents and manuals. All of these applications are likely to allow operators to visualize pertinent information hands-free at the point-of-need, which is expected to be a key element contributing to AR-derived productivity gains, accident prevention, and error reduction. Examples of such point-of-need AR support include real time monitoring of complex assembly lines and contextualized display of performance metrics; real-time job performance aids, including digitized and contextualized user manuals and operating flow charts (Deac et al., 2017); real-time monitoring of maintenance schedules and ability to order spare parts; support of warehouse logistics, such as finding the quickest route to specified items in order to enhance delivery efficiency (Glockner et al., 2014); as well as support of language barriers among workers through implementation of AR-based translation cues. Beyond enhancing operations, AR can support transferring knowledge and know-how from experienced technicians with deep institutional knowledge to operators who are being onboarded, thereby enhancing recruitment, training, and ultimately building and enhancing operators' knowledge of proper protocols and procedures (Claypoole, Stanney et al., 2020).

Panacea: AR-based maintenance applications promise to upskill workers, increase productivity, reduce repair time, increase first-time fix rates, decrease error rates, positively impact recruitment, training, and outcome performance, and transfer knowledge between experts and apprentices.

Pandora's Box: The content generation, safety concerns, data privacy issues, and intellectual property concerns noted for the construction industry above are also relevant to the industrial maintenance sector. In addition, integration with original equipment manufacturer (OEM) digital twins will be essential to enable AR solutions to close the loop between operator and system and optimize the synergies between them; yet, OEM digital twins are not yet widely available, standardized, or open-source (Bächle & Gregorzik, 2019). Further, a downside of using AR for memory externalization is that it may result in AR system dependency. This risk is not unique to AR, nor is the concern new. In fact, concern over potential deficits stemming from memory externalization date back at least as far as ancient Greece; Socrates raised the self-same issue with Phaedrus, arguing that writing would lead to forgetfulness in a learner's soul (Yunis, 2011). One may have heard similar arguments regarding the smartphone's ability to remember phone numbers, leading to a decrease in phone number memorization by users. However, like written documents, smartphones have been established as a reliable and accessible means of storing information far beyond phone numbers, as likely will AR systems become a rich source of operational information. The passive nature of AR-based maintenance solutions, where one-size-fits-all static instructions and guidance cues are given to users, can limit the beneficial nature of support information and reduce the overall effectiveness of augmented feedback; thus, undergoing the heavy lift to develop AI-driven adaptive AR content is likely requisite for more widespread, high utility adoption (Siew et al., 2019).

Retail

Personalized shopping is the expectation today, where consumers can see, engage with, and create unique products by customizing them to meet their preferences. Consumers want to "select a product type—be it a pair of pants, a car, or a dining room table—and then interactively dial and swipe their way to achieve the perfect dimensions, color, and style of whatever they are looking for" (Cook et al., 2020, p.2). In 2020, nearly 50% of retailers plan to deploy augmented or virtual reality shopping experiences, with this paradigm eventually becoming the standard shopping experience. For example, BMW's ARKit allows potential shoppers to customize the inside of a car with their personal choices (Strange, 2017). Home goods and hardware retailers are offering customers the ability to see how a product, for instance a piece of patio furniture, will fit in their desired location (Allison, 2018). Similarly, retailers have AR applications that allow consumers to see how well a product would fit or look. For example, Nike has an app that helps shoppers find their shoe size by pointing their phone camera at their feet (McKinnon, 2020). Once a product is purchased, some retailers are now incorporating AR functions to aid in operation of or familiarization with their products. AR can guide consumers through unboxing, installation, product introduction, documentation, operations, and troubleshooting (Churchill, 2020). This AR-delivered support infrastructure can translate into a superior consumer experience, while alleviating pressure on service operations. For example, TechSee's Virtual Technician uses AR to instruct consumers on how to set-up and connect a wide variety of electronic devices, from a modem to a coffee machine (Shaham, 2020).

Panacea: AR technology can transform the retail and customer experience by supporting initial customer engagement and purchase, onboarding, setup, troubleshooting, and regular maintenance. In general, returns on investment in AR technology in the retail space have been demonstrated through increased conversion, reduced return rates, and enhanced brand recognition (Gaioshko, 2017).

Pandora's Box: A lack of regulation could cause problems in the retail space, as with AR one's likeness and personal possessions become digitized. This could certainly result in these applications crossing "the creepy line," as their users should have no 'reasonable expectation' of privacy (Warzel, 2014). Thus, the "incongruity between the availability of digital information about individuals and the opacity of the purposes, uses, and intentions of those accessing such information" (Tene & Polonetsky, 2014, p. 71) could be disastrous. As they become increasingly personalized, retail applications could manipulate consumers' thinking and buying habits to the benefit of the retailor but to the detriment of the consumer. For example, "try before you buy" options for clothing could be hacked, with clothes being scantly overlaid on an imposter's nude body superimposed on a consumer's face and, in turn, spread online, thereby damaging one's reputation (Bilyk, 2020). AR could also be used to hijack accounts via surveillance and data mining schemes that slightly manipulate and overlay AR content (e.g., ad stacking fraud schemes), creating an even bigger identity theft challenge than the one already threatening consumers today. AR retail applications must thus carefully consider hacking and security threats that could cross the line of what an ordinary user would find unacceptable.

Education and Training Applications

Augmented reality fosters experiential, immersive learning, which captures and directs attention and engages learners in hands-on activities, thereby leading to faster and deeper learning, with retention rates far out-performing conventional didactic learning methods (Adedokun-Shittu et al., 2020; Bacca et al., 2014; Bujak et al., 2013; Santos et al., 2014; Wu et al., 2013). AR has been demonstrated to enhance the learning of physical geography, with improved performance and retention (Adedokun-Shittu et al., 2020), to visualize abstract and difficult to comprehend concepts, such as mathematics, and make them easier to grasp (Bujak et al., 2013), and to support discovery learning, such as learning in a science museum, with demonstrated cognitive gains when AR scaffolds are used (Yoon et al., 2012).The potential to contextualize the learning experience, coupled with a medium that is more conducive to interactive pedagogical approaches, is expected to result in improved learning outcomes across a variety of fields and learning modalities (Gerup et al., 2020). Such contextualized learning, which embeds learners into relevant learning environments, increases the likelihood that learned knowledge and skills will transfer to the real world (Bransford et al., 2000). However, successful transfer may also depend heavily on the degree of declarative and procedural knowledge the student possesses prior to learning in context. Thus, a user centered approach to the design of AR training systems is crucial.

Augmented reality also affords possibilities for embodied learning, which is a method of education that encourages bodily interaction and personal experience to enhance learning outcomes (Radu & Antle, 2017; Wen & Looi, 2019). This approach draws inspiration from research in embodied cognition, which suggests a deep continuity between mind and body such that cognition itself is highly dependent on the features of the agent's physical body (Shapiro, 2014). Previous research has shown that integrating one's body into the learning process has a significant positive impact on learning (de Nooijer et al., 2013; Skulmowski & Rey, 2018; Stieff et al., 2016; Toumpaniari et al., 2015; Vallée-Tourangeau et al., 2016). Novel embodied learning paradigms implemented in AR have been shown to produce significant learning gains (Johnson-Glenberg et al., 2014; Johnson-Glenberg et al., 2016; Lindgren et al., 2016). Designers should thus attempt to leverage AR training systems in a way that encourages the learner to interact within a relevant environment, enacting task-specific gestures while repeatedly carry out psychomotor tasks.

Augmented reality training at the point-of-need aims to bring support as close to the real-world task as possible. AR technologies have a unique advantage in that they can support virtually any task, anywhere, and are uniquely enabling for tasks that require procedural and psychomotor learning. This is in stark contrast to traditional information sources, such as central kiosks, that often force workers to seek support away from the workplace with no opportunity to put newly learned material to immediate use. Stolovitch and Keeps (2011) showed that the impact of learning can be almost non-existent when carried out away from the workplace and without an opportunity to put newly learned skills to use. This may result from the fact that the learner has not had a chance to embed the new behavior into memory. Here is where AR technologies can further support learning, affording opportunities to use newly acquired knowledge and skills with a volume of repetition constrained only by time. Embedding and supporting learning at the point-of-need couples context-relevant learning with direct feedback by bringing it as close to the task to be performed as possible, resulting in behavioral modification that may not be achievable via traditional learning methods.

One educational -area that has seen considerable success in implementing AR is that of medical training (Ferrer-Torregrosa et al., 2015; Ferrer-Torregrosa et al., 2016; Küçük et al., 2016; Léger et al., 2017; Léger et al., 2018). Life-like simulations can be carried out using AR content overlaid on a manikin, providing health care professionals with realistic scenarios to hone their skills without the need for costly special-purpose manikins or patient actors. Incorporating AR in surgical training has reduced time spent performing operations while improving the precision of the procedure (Kersten-Oertel et al., 2013), yielded positive outcomes when training for tumor resections (Abhari et al., 2015), improved vascular access procedures (Jeon et al., 2014; Robinson et al., 2014), produced improvements when teaching ophthalmoscopy (Leitritz et al., 2014; Rai et al., 2017), decreased time to identify spatial layout of organs in surgical settings (Pelanis et al., 2020), and improved outcome measures when conducting ultrasound-guided lumbar punctures (Keri et al., 2015). In general, AR training solutions are particularly well-suited to foster learning of skills needed when dealing with today's intelligent systems, such as complex reasoning, critical thinking, creativity and socio-emotional intelligence (Accenture, 2018). As AR technologies continue to improve and incorporate higher-fidelity elements, such as haptic controls and feedback, it is likely that the noted learning and retention improvements will continue to expand.

Panacea: Use of AR for education and training can be highly engaging and experiential, which could substantially increase learning and knowledge retention.

Pandora's Box: Few AR educational applications adopt a pedagogical approach or incorporate instructional strategies (Radianti et al., 2020; Saltan & Arslan, 2016), likely because of a lack of guidelines for how best to integrate AR with learning theories (Santos et al., 2014) and a paucity of models to characterize the factors that maximize the use of AR to assist and guide toward learning outcomes (Radu, 2012), which could limit training efficacy. For example, novice learners deal with high levels of extraneous processing and thus if students are presented with large amounts of augmented information during initial learning, without carefully designed techniques to direct attention, they are likely to experience cognitive overload, thereby hindering learning gains (Claypoole, Brawand et al., 2020). Further, integration of AR into traditional learning methods may be costly, challenging, and met with general resistance (Lee, 2012).

While thoughtfully designed AR training applications have great potential, poor design could lead to many adverse outcomes. One of the most salient of these relates to safety. While AR affords increased safety for training dangerous tasks and in dangerous environments, poorly designed training paradigms could lead to negative transfer of training in the real world. A substantial gap between a learner's perceived competence and their actual ability, especially if an ineffective training paradigm has both inflated the former and reduced the latter, poses risk of serious injury or death. The training effectiveness of AR training systems should thus be iteratively evaluated prior to deployment to ensure reliable, positive training transfer.

Military Applications

Augmented reality solutions are gaining traction in military training (Venero et al., 2012; Yeh & Wickens, 2001), vehicle operations (Livingston et al., 2011), and maintenance (Claypoole, Killingsworth et al., 2020). For example, AR can be used to display realities of the battlefield and augment it with high-stakes annotation information, such as by displaying animated terrain for military intervention planning, training large-scale combat scenarios, and simulating real-time enemy actions. The Tactical Augmented Reality (TAR, 2020) is one such solution. TAR provides sensor mapping, navigation, and 3D surface models to support enhanced operational maneuver and fires as well as wireless links to share information among squad members, such as positions of allied and enemy forces and tactical images. Further, AR has long been used in the (non-spatialized) HUDs used by fighter pilots to display information relevant to aircraft operation in the periphery of the pilot's vision. The spatialized AR displays available today may prove similarly useful to pilots and are being considered for use to enhance decision making, such as by presenting information that is obscured either by the structure of the aircraft or by environmental conditions, as well as to support initial pilot qualification, dogfighting, refueling, and maneuvering through use of virtually overlaid aircraft and other visual cues displayed in an airborne pilot's helmet (Underwood, 2020). Land navigation and geography-related tactics have also been trained via AR displays overlaid on physical sandboxes that model specific geographic locations (Goldberg et al., 2017), as have Tactical Combat Casualty Care (TCCC) skills (Stanney, Moralez et al., 2020).

AR military solutions hold promise as a tool for managing information and potentially reducing cognitive demands, leading to better situational awareness and other desirable outcomes (Brandão & Pinho, 2017; Mao & Chen, 2020). Maintenance activities can also be supported by AR, including step-by-step contextualized job performance aids and remote assistance of military equipment maintenance (Claypoole, Killingsworth et al., 2020). Moreover, AR holds the promise of providing real-time operational support to the warfighter, enabling them to capture faults and anomalies during vehicle and aircraft inspection and providing AR-based historical records. AR can even support the dissemination of expert tribal knowledge through the capture of first-person media related to step-wise processes (Claypoole, Killingsworth et al., 2020).

Panacea: Augmented reality has broad applicability in the military, from use in flight or vehicle simulation and training as a cost-effective and low risk alternative to live training, to battlefield combat simulation to support military intervention planning that provides competitive advantage, to TCCC response training to save lives on the battlefield, to procedural guidance and remote maintenance support to manage and sustain military assets more effectively, and more. These AR applications can support the military in innovating and advancing to remain ahead of the worthiest adversaries.

Pandora's Box: Augmented reality solutions must be designed effectively to realize their potential. If AR solutions are poorly adapted to military applications, such as those that may present too much information to users, when combined with the cognitive demand of monitoring the stressful environment associated with military operations for threats may result in limited or faulty situational awareness (Karlsson, 2015; Livingston et al., 2011). As AR has no formal standards to guide its application, such complications are highly probable (Ullo et al., 2019). This lack of standards is complicated by the fact that AR is often meant to be employed adaptively, 'on condition,' rather than based on pre-set protocols or standards and thus traditional information sources (e.g., training or maintenance manuals) lose effectiveness in guiding AR system design. Thus, AR systems for military applications face significant challenges associated with high information demands, chaotic and unpredictable conditions, and baseline stress levels on the battlefield, making the design of military-specific adaptive AR systems challenging, with the consequences of poor design immense.

One general safety concern for all AR applications, especially those associated with long duration exposure, is that of cybersickness – a form of motion sickness unique to immersive technologies (Stanney, Lawson et al., 2020). Cybersickness can be mitigated by carefully strategizing exposure durations and break schedules. Novel methods of evaluating user sickness in real-time could also be developed to prompt users to take breaks before adverse symptoms arise. Future improvements in HWD technology aim to wholly eliminate the risk of cybersickness, but additional safety problems during use may remain. For example, if digital objects rendered in AR systems occlude a user's view, they may collide with an object in the real environment. Developers should be mindful of the characteristics of intended users' physical environment, especially potential hazards, and the ways in which digitally rendered objects may occlude the real world. A safety bounding box that generates digitally rendered boundaries when the user nears a real-world object could mitigate this risk (Stanney, Nye et al., 2020).

In summary, AR technology has a plethora of potential benefits, including increased safety, minimized risks, streamlined planning processes, expedited production process, increased productivity, improved point-of-need job performance aids, improved remote support, improved quality, positively impacted recruitment, training, and outcome performance, increased learning and knowledge retention, improved transfer of knowledge between experts and apprentices, and improved user experience. However, due to a lack of standards and pedagogy to guide design of AR applications, paucity of tools to automatically generate adaptive digital assets and content, non-standard digital infrastructures, difficulty in integrating with existing platforms (e.g., OEM digital twins, ERP, IoT, learning management systems, etc.), and lack of usage protocols and regulatory guidelines, adoption of AR technology is expected to be a tremendous lift. Thus, a focus on providing design guidelines and pedagogy could be a first step in preventing Pandora's Box from being unlocked as AR experiences mass adoption.

HOW TO DESIGN FOR AR – BEST PRACTICES AND RECOMMENDATIONS

Simply put, designing for AR is exciting. It is hard to blame designers for feeling tempted to fill a user's field of view with futuristic and aesthetic user interaction (UI) paradigms. Indeed, when AR is depicted in movies, TV shows, and video games, that is often what we see. However, while AR should in fact be igniting highly creative UI transformation, currently the AR user experience is replete with traditional tangible graphical user interfaces (GUIs). Thus, Oren (1990) would suggest, AR is squarely in the "incunabular" stage, where old forms persist that, while familiar, are not particularly well-suited to the AR medium. Arguably, it is time for designers to catch up with the huge leaps AR hardware has undergone in the past half-decade by developing AR UI such that it is personalized, adaptive, anticipatory, context aware, implicit, and ultimately invisible. Yet, while discussion of moving from "interface" to "ambient intelligence," where an omnipresent technological infrastructure is hidden from end-users and smoothly integrated into everyday objects and the surrounding environment, has been envisioned for decades (Olson et al., 2015), it has yet to be achieved. In the meantime, the provision of basic guidelines derived from perception, cognition, and learning sciences can support creation of highly functional AR UI designs. This section aims to take a first step towards realizing such guidelines by providing recommended best practices for designing functional, usable, useful, and engaging AR applications.

Avoid Information Overload

With tangible UI as the current design paradigm of choice for AR, it is critically important to consider the information demands imposed by potentially cluttering and visually distracting interface objects, such as menus, windows, and icons. By considering the information processing capacity of users, the chance of information overload from these overlaid objects can be reduced. This involves anticipating the timing and coordination of augmented information presentation and adopting a minimalistic design approach, such as through use of context-aware tangible UI designs that appropriately appear and disappear given the task at hand and use of voice and gaze interaction to avoid the need for explicit UI commands whenever possible. Additionally, the interpretation of human pose and gesture to deduce user actions and automatically trigger supportive UI responses can reduce information overload.

Design for Different Environments

Environment has always been an important human-centered design consideration, but it becomes even more critical when the system begins to invade users' real-world spaces. The following environmental factors must be considered to make effective use of AR:

Brightness

Are the intended users of the system outside or inside? How bright is the room they are working in? The light level of a user's working area can dramatically impact their ability to see AR system elements. Since luminosity plays such a critical role, it is essential that high-contrast UI elements be used. In some cases, the brightness of a user's working area may mean no currently available augmented reality headset is appropriate, and a handheld device should be used instead.

Ambient Noise Level

The ambient noise level of the intended working area can drastically impact the suitability of a given system design. Each modality of information delivery has its own strengths and weaknesses that must be weighed. Compared to text, auditory cues can be more subtle and diegetic, but these can become wholly unusable if the environment is sufficiently loud. Visual cues are more obvious than auditory cues, but place demands on the pre-frontal cortex, the area of the brain that is associated with working memory (Gazzaley et al., 2007). For instances in which the user's environment is noisy, designers should rely more on visual cues to deliver critical information and use auditory cues only in supporting roles.

Space

The dimensions of the space users work within constrain their augmented environment. Users may be students in a classroom environment at risk for encroaching on other students' space. Or, they might be inspection technicians, evaluating surface corrosion on an aircraft with a 40-foot wingspan. They could also be oil field operators, performing a complicated shutdown procedure distributed across a labyrinthine complex. To better understand how to design for these drastically different environments, we should first consider Cutting and Vishton's (1995) definition of the three types of space in XR environments: personal space, action space, and vista space. Personal space is defined as "the zone immediately surrounding the observer's head, generally within arm's reach and slightly beyond". It's in this zone that users complete most of their tasks. Action space is the zone in which the user may interact with objects or people and radiates outward 30 meters from the user. Contextualized markers to which the user may travel are one example of a UI element found in action space. The last type of space, vista space, is defined as 30 to 100 meters from the user. Vista space is reserved for landmarks, or UI elements that can help orient the user in their augmented environment. The degree to which these zones should be used is directly impacted by the user's environment. For students in a classroom, systems should be designed with focus on their personal spaces, with action space used sparingly. The inspection technician will still complete most tasks in their personal space, but their action space can be used to aid navigation. For the oil field operator, vista space should be utilized to provide landmarks they can use to orient themselves in the maze of pipes.

Design for Engagement

Engagement is a principal goal for those who design AR systems. By providing users with naturalistic spatial cues, AR already has an advantage in providing superior immersion, and therefore engagement, over traditional 2D displays (Ragan et al., 2010). Even so, engagement is not guaranteed. Usability is a key factor in whether a person remains engaged with a system (O'Brien & Toms, 2008); avoid design inconsistencies and test out usability issues that could break immersion. To increase engagement with an AR system, users' intrinsic motivation should be promoted by providing them with meaningful information and feedback throughout their experience (O'Brien & Toms, 2008). In addition to intrinsic motivation, flow can also be supported through AR design. Flow is achieved through a delicate balance between the skill of the user and the difficulty of the task (Csikszentmihalyi, 1990). By making augmented systems adaptive to adequately challenge the skill of the user, engagement can be increased, and the user provided with an active sense of control. Fostering embodying interaction and allowing users to manipulate objects in their space in a natural and realistic way can support both intrinsic motivation (Erbas & Demirer, 2019; Khan et al., 2019; Saadon et al., 2020) and flow (Chen, 2020; Ibáñez et al., 2014).

Design for Naturalistic Interactions

In the real environment, we intuitively understand the constraints and affordances of objects we may interact with. The cues that allow us to understand how to interact with these objects are not easily replicated in an augmented reality environment. Consider a glass of water on your desk; the reflected light and shadows cast by the glass tell you its approximate position. If you intend to pick up the glass, information like its size and the amount of water inside allow you to anticipate the force needed to lift it. Faithfully replicating this simple interaction in AR is currently beyond our technological capabilities. On the one hand, virtual worlds are the stuff of magic; their greatest strength is that they are free from the constraints of the real world. But by the same token they are also alien, unbounded by the rules that shape how we understand and interact with our surroundings. The lack of constraints can induce uncertainty in the mind of the user. Though presently limited by the hardware, interactions in AR should be designed to model the real world as completely as possible in conjunction with additional multi-modal cues. Naturalistic interactions can be achieved in several ways. First, hand gestures should be extremely simple while balancing fidelity. For example, low fidelity, high simplicity gestures maybe be easier to learn and use over high fidelity, low simplicity gestures for object manipulation tasks (Aliprantis et al., 2019). Second, the use of whole-body movement interactions (e.g., physically walking) should be designed with moderate fidelity to reduce physical fatigue (Rogers et al., 2019). Moderate fidelity could be instantiated with auditory and visual cues that emulate waking without physically requiring the user to move. Third, AR should simulate realistic physics of 3D objects, such as visually simulating weight by incorporating colliders (a component that defines the shape and physical properties of a 3D object; for a review of colliders, see Unity Technologies, 2020) on 3D objects. For example, a ball made of steel should not bounce when dropped, but a ball made of rubber should. Additionally, a raycast (a digital line drawn from a defined starting point that interacts with colliders) can be incorporated on 3D objects to simulate weight (e.g., small bend for light objects versus increased bend for heavier objects; XR Association, 2019). Finally, for behaviors difficult to replicate in AR, perceptual illusions should be used as a substitution (e.g., using haptics to simulate grabbing a 3D model; Rogers et al., 2019). Perceptual illusions, or sensory substitutions, can simulate missing senses with an additional cue from another sensory system. For example, the sound of wind rushing can create the sense of movement even though a user may be stationary. Perceptual illusions not only increase simulation fidelity but can also decrease the cost of development (Debarba et al., 2018; Nilsson, 2018; Storms, 2002).

Consider Use of Spatial Audio

Audio within AR applications can completely change the experience for a user. Just as in films and video games, well-designed audio can create an immersive, emotional experience in AR. AR in particular has the opportunity to provide a soundscape, an audio experience that provides location-based audio sources that react to the space around them. For example, echoes can become louder when a user speaks nearer to a wall (Garay-Cortes & Uribe-Quevedo, 2016). Likewise, an object that falls on concrete will make a different sound than one that falls on grass. These audio cues help the user understand the properties of objects and their location, which aids in world building and immersion. Spatial audio can be achieved by correlating sound with an object or location; audio sources should originate in the corresponding direction to improve presence by producing binaural hearing (Witmer & Singer, 1998). Additionally, spatial-audio should provide realistic volume levels that mimic the real world – the sound of a person talking from five feet away and the sound of a person talking from 20 feet away should sound different and should have lifelike fall-off curves.

Avoid Adverse Psychophysiological Effects

AR is still a novel technology, and while its psychophysiological effects have been under investigation (Riva et al., 2016), much remains unknown. HWDs present unique constraints for users that are not encountered when designing for 2D displays. Featuring prominently among these considerations is the risk of cybersickness. At least 20% of the population - and perhaps as much as 80% - may experience cybersickness symptoms during or after engaging in some immersive medium (Stanney et al., 2003). Though well-documented in relatively immersive technology-naïve participants using virtual reality (VR) for limited durations – typically less than a day, often only a couple of hours – the long-term effects of cybersickness are unknown. Whether habituation occurs with regular use, as with sailors getting their "sea legs", will have sizeable consequences for users. It seems likely that optical see-through AR will induce cybersickness less readily than VR, given the smaller proportion of the visual information users perceive which is simulated, but most research to date has not discriminated among the various species of immersion, and AR-specific risks have yet to be fully characterized (Hughes et al., 2020). If AR is widely adopted in the enterprise for training and operational support systems, individuals psychologically or physiologically unable to endure significant AR exposure could be at a disadvantage for career growth or be excluded entirely from fields that become dependent on regular AR use. While some individuals may be biologically precluded from using AR in any capacity, understanding and actively mitigating the risk factors for cybersickness is imperative if designers are to ensure that these novel capabilities make life and work more enjoyable and more productive for more people.

IMPLICATIONS OF WIDESPREAD ADOPTION

Social and economic ramifications of AR design also merit consideration when designing in this space. In the modern attention- and information-based economy of freeware (e.g., Google, free mobile apps), as well as in the broader consumer-driven economy, omnipresent advertising is the rule. This aggressive advertising has traditionally been limited largely to the internet and public, physical spaces. However, in-roads have recently been made into operating systems and user interfaces – for example, advertisements embedded in Microsoft Windows menus and Samsung smartphone notifications – such that users' attention may be solicited in a space previously considered offline (Warren, 2017; Weinbach, 2020). With ubiquitous, always-on consumer AR, no space either physical or perceptual would be truly unmarketable. A not-too-distant future can be conceived in which advertisements no longer need to draw attention but can instead be suddenly superimposed on the visual field of HWD users. Worse still is the potential for advertising revenue subsidizing the upfront cost of acquiring the hardware; should AR headsets become as integral to daily life as smartphones are presently, a business model could thrive which steeply discounts the purchase price of HWD's at the cost of selling users' data and serving more frequent or intrusive advertisements. Always-on gaze tracking could allow such advertising to lock the HWD function being used so that the user can only proceed once the user has visually fixated the relevant display for an amount of time. AR HWDs have the potential to decrease the cost of accessing extra-cranial information, decreasing separation between mind and machine and becoming functional extensions of their users' cognitive capabilities, but this exciting possibility comes with great potential for exploitation.

Widespread consumer adoption of AR hardware will undoubtedly have substantial impacts on social norms as well. Most or all of these are, however, unlikely to be truly novel changes, instead representing the extension of existing trends. Among the most likely changes affect norms surrounding privacy and anonymity. Cameras are currently more ubiquitous than ever before thanks to near-universal adoption of the smartphone: More than 80% of adults in the United States now own a smartphone capable of picture and video capture (Pew Research Center, 2019). However, the normalization of consumer AR would represent a change perhaps greater even than the smartphone. The front-facing camera is an integral part of full-featured AR devices; simpler heads-up displays impose no such requirement, but if the environment is to be augmented it must be monitored. This may appear a trivial difference from smartphones, which largely have two or more cameras apiece, but the difference lies in accessibility. It can no longer be assumed that any conversation between two people is, to some degree, private if at least one party is using an AR headset. With AR HWD's, every user's point of view has the potential to be recorded at all times. If the AR HWD is online, via wireless internet or cellular connection, this effectively guarantees that the user's field of view is accessible to any interested third party.

CONCLUSION

While the promise of AR and its widespread application are immense, implementation of this technology should first and foremost present an improvement over what an individual can achieve unaided, and do so without adverse consequences. AR holds great promise for enhancing users' wellbeing and increasing task productivity, efficacy, and efficiency. Translated into a job performance aid, a domain expert's knowledge may be leveraged by countless other less experienced professionals. AR-enhanced training may allow the training of skills to be largely automated in much the same way that online learning allows the automation of knowledge transfer. Access to the keen perceptual skills and procedural knowledge of domain experts need not be constrained by geography if both parties have access to well-designed AR systems. All of these advancements hold great promise for their direct beneficiaries and, by extension, society writ large. The great potential, however, comes with potential risk should adoption be done unsystematically.

Just as when considering a particular use case for AR designers must ask themselves "Why AR?", so is it more generally the duty of AR designers to be continually asking "How could this be abused?" One of the most critical competencies for citizens of the modern world is the ability to parse reliable and useful information from a torrent of noise. The very devices that afford the greatest potential for enabling users to achieve this end – presently smartphones and, eventually, AR devices – are also the most credible threat to their ability to do so. Mishandled, AR is unlikely to provide a net benefit; actively exploited, it is certain not only to fail to deliver on its great promise but to deprecate even more basic competencies and quality of life. Designers of AR hardware and software are opening an idiomatic box whose contents, once out, cannot be put back. Unlike Pandora, the contents of our box are not wholly beyond our control. It is thus the duty of those in this field to design with unintended consequences in mind and carefully craft these systems to guard against them. The attention of users is a finite resource of great personal value to the individual and great monetary value to others. As a conceptual successor to the smartphone, consumer AR stands to either correct or exacerbate the induced malaise which so often accompanies maladaptive use of smartphones. Careless design – building what can be built with no consideration to what should be built – is unlikely to produce a net positive outcome.

The advent of reliable, ubiquitous eye tracking capabilities as incorporated into AR HWDs marks a further incursion into the private life of the individual. In this respect, as in many others noted here, this is not truly novel but rather a continuation of trends made apparent by the widespread adoption of smartphones. User data collected by smartphones includes such previously private information as the daily travel routine, frequency of visiting various stores or locations outside the home, and common contacts. The necessity of a front-facing camera for operational AR HWDs extends the possibility of tracing common contacts from merely those reached by calling or messaging services to include those face-to-face interactions. Inferring the thoughts and intentions of a particular user is limited at present to several degrees of abstractive inference; AR HWDs afford a similar sort of mindreading with at least one fewer degrees of inference. Concatenating gaze tracking with location data provides the ability to discern the user's interest as a function of their present environment. Uniting gaze tracking and imaging from the front-facing camera could yield even more granular insight. With an always-online device, the user's moment-to-moment locus of attention would be accessible at all times. The utility of these functions – gaze tracking, personal data collections, etc. – must be weighed against the potential for collection, use, and abuse by third parties. The simplest solution for all capabilities which might be abused to the detriment of the end user is also the least desirable: Omit, or at least deprecate, the function in question. However, this is analogous to leaving Pandora's box closed; while we may remove the risk, we also ensure that none of the potential benefit is realized. It is thus imperative that those engaged in the design of AR hardware and software remain keenly aware of the risk posed to the user and proactively design to mitigate it. Thus, while AR has tremendous potential to provide seamless, rich user interactions that enhance experiences in the real world, it is critical to understand users' goals, contexts, needs, and abilities to create successful, effective, and value-added AR applications.

REFERENCES

Abhari, K., Baxter, J. S. H., Chen, E. C. S., Khan, A. R., Peters, T. M., de Ribaupierre, S., & Eagleson, R. (2015). Training for Planning Tumour Resection: Augmented Reality and Human Factors. *IEEE Transactions on Biomedical Engineering*, 62(6), 1466–1477. doi:10.1109/TBME.2014.2385874 PMID:25546854

Accenture. (2018). *It's learning. Just not as we know it: How to accelerate skills acquisition in the age of intelligent technologies*. G20 Young Entrepreneurs' Alliance. https://www.accenture.com/_acnmedia/thought-leadership-assets/pdf/accenture-education-and-technology-skills-research.pdf

Adedokun-Shittu, N. A., Ajani, A. H., Nuhu, K. M., & Shitu, A. J. K. (2020). Augmented reality instructional tool in enhancing geography learners' academic performance and retention in Osun state Nigeria. *Education and Information Technologies*, 25(4), 3021–3033. doi:10.100710639-020-10099-2

Agarwal, R., Chandrasekaran, S., & Sridhar, M. (2016, October). The digital future of construction. In *Voices*. McKinsey Global Institute. https://www.globalinfrastructureinitiative.com/sites/default/files/pdf/The-digital-future-of-construction-Oct-2016.pdf

Akçayır, M., & Akçayır, G. (2017). Advantages and challenges associated with augmented reality for education: A systematic review of the literature. *Educational Research Review*, 20, 1–11. doi:10.1016/j.edurev.2016.11.002

Aliprantis, J., Konstantakis, M., Nikopoulou, R., Mylonas, P., & Caridakis, G. (2019). Natural Interaction in Augmented Reality Context. VIPERC@IRCDL 2019.

Allison, A. (2018, March 20). *Virtually view Lowe's spring collection in your backyard*. Lowe's Corporate. https://corporate.lowes.com/newsroom/stories/fresh-thinking/virtually-view-lowes-spring-collection-your-backyard

Association, X. R. (2019). *XR primer 1.0: A starter guide for developers*. https://xra.org/wp-content/uploads/rs-xr-primer-1.0-01.pdf

Bacca, J., Baldiris, S., Fabregat, R., & Graf, S. (2014). Augmented reality trends in education: A systematic review of research and applications. *Journal of Educational Technology & Society*, 17(4), 133–149.

Bächle, K., & Gregorzik, S. (2019). Digital twins in industrial applications: Requirements to a comprehensive data model. *Industrial Internet Consortium Journal of Innovation*. https://www.iiconsortium.org/news/joi-articles/2019-November-JoI-Digital-Twins-in-Industrial-Applications.pdf

Behzadan, A. H., Dong, S., & Kamat, V. R. (2015). Augmented reality visualization: A review of civil infrastructure system applications. *Advanced Engineering Informatics*, *29*(2), 252–267. doi:10.1016/j.aei.2015.03.005

Bilyk, V. (2020). Augmented reality issues: What you need to know. *The App Solutions Development Blog*. https://theappsolutions.com/blog/development/augmented-reality-challenges/

Brandão, W. L., & Pinho, M. S. (2017). Using augmented reality to improve dismounted operators' situation awareness. *2017 IEEE Virtual Reality (VR)*, 297–298. doi:10.1109/VR.2017.7892294

Bransford, J. D., Brown, A. L., & Cocking, R. R. (2000). *How people learn* (Vol. 11). National Academy Press.

Bujak, K. R., Radu, I., Catrambone, R., MacIntyre, B., Zheng, R., & Golubski, G. (2013). A psychological perspective on augmented reality in the mathematics classroom. *Computers & Education*, *68*, 536–544. doi:10.1016/j.compedu.2013.02.017

Cabero, J., & Barroso, J. (2016). The educational possibilities of Augmented Reality. *New Approaches in Educational Research*, *5*(1), 44–50. doi:10.7821/naer.2016.1.140

Chen, C.-H. (2020). Impacts of augmented reality and a digital game on students' science learning with reflection prompts in multimedia learning. *Educational Technology Research and Development*, *68*(6), 3057–3076. doi:10.100711423-020-09834-w

Churchill, L. (2020, March 9*). The nightmare after Christmas: 'Tis the season for augmented reality for retailers*. TechSee: Intelligent Visual Assistance. https://techsee.me/blog/augmented-reality-for-retailers/

Claypoole, V., Brawand, N. P., Padron, C. K., Miller, C. A., Archer, J. L., Hughes, C. L., Horner, C. K., Riley, J. M., Fidopiastis, C. M., & Stanney, K. M. (2020). Unified Pedagogical FRamework ON Training in eXtended Reality (UPFRONT-XR). *International Journal of Artificial Intelligence in Education*.

Claypoole, V. L., Killingsworth, C. D., Hodges, C. A., Riley, J. M., & Stanney, K. M. (2020, in preparation). Multimodal interactions within augmented reality operational support tools for shipboard maintenance. In V. G. Duffy, M. R. Lehto, Y. Yih, & R. W. Proctor (Eds.), Human-Automation Interaction: Manufacturing, Services and UX. Springer ACES Book Series (ACES-Automation, Collaboration and E-Services).

Claypoole, V. L., Stanney, K. M., Padron, C. K., & Perez, R. (2020). Enhancing Naval enterprise readiness through augmented reality knowledge extraction. *Proceedings of the Interservice/Industry Training, Simulation, and Education Conference (I/ITSEC) Annual Meeting.*

Cook, A. V., Ohri, L., Kusumoto, L., Reynolds, C., & Schwertzel, E. (2020, January 10). *Augmented shopping: the quiet revolution.* Deloitte Insights. https://www2.deloitte.com/us/en/insights/topics/emerging-technologies/augmented-shopping-3d-technology-retail.html

Csikszentmihalyi, M. (1990). *Flow: The psychology of optimal experience.* Harper & Row.

Cutting, J. E., & Vishton, P. M. (1995). Perceiving layout and knowing distances: The integration, relative potency, and contextual use of different information about depth. In W. Epstein & S. Rogers (Eds.), Handbook of perception and cognition: Vol. 5. Perception of space and motion (pp. 69-117). Academic Press.

de Nooijer, J. A., van Gog, T., Paas, F., & Zwaan, R. A. (2013). Effects of imitating gestures during encoding or during retrieval of novel verbs on children's test performance. *Acta Psychologica, 144*(1), 173–179. doi:10.1016/j.actpsy.2013.05.013 PMID:23820099

Deac, C. N., Deac, G. C., Popa, C. L., Ghinea, M., & Cotet, C. E. (2017). Using augmented reality in smart manufacturing. In B. Katalinic (Ed.), *DAAAM Proceedings* (1st ed., Vol. 1, pp. 0727–0732). DAAAM International Vienna. 10.2507/28th.daaam.proceedings.102

Debarba, H. G., Boulic, R., Salomon, R., Blanke, O., & Herbelin, B. (2018). Self-attribution of distorted reaching movements in immersive virtual reality. *Computers & Graphics, 76,* 142–152. doi:10.1016/j.cag.2018.09.001

Dong, S., Feng, C., & Kamat, V. R. (2013). Sensitivity analysis of augmented reality-assisted building damage reconnaissance using virtual prototyping. *Automation in Construction, 33,* 24–36. doi:10.1016/j.autcon.2012.09.005

Erbas, C., & Demirer, V. (2019). The effects of augmented reality on students' academic achievement and motivation in a biology course. *Journal of Computer Assisted Learning, 35*(3), 450–458. doi:10.1111/jcal.12350

Fenais, A. S., Ariaratnam, S. T., Ayer, S. K., & Smilovsky, N. (2020). A review of augmented reality applied to underground construction. *Journal of Information Technology in Construction, 25,* 308–324. doi:10.36680/j.itcon.2020.018

Ferrer-Torregrosa, J., Jiménez-Rodríguez, M. Á., Torralba-Estelles, J., Garzón-Farinós, F., Pérez-Bermejo, M., & Fernández-Ehrling, N. (2016). Distance learning ects and flipped classroom in the anatomy learning: Comparative study of the use of augmented reality, video and notes. *BMC Medical Education, 16*(1), 230. doi:10.118612909-016-0757-3 PMID:27581521

Ferrer-Torregrosa, J., Torralba, J., Jimenez, M. A., García, S., & Barcia, J. M. (2015). ARBOOK: Development and Assessment of a Tool Based on Augmented Reality for Anatomy. *Journal of Science Education and Technology, 24*(1), 119–124. doi:10.100710956-014-9526-4

Flavián, C., Ibáñez-Sánchez, S., & Orús, C. (2019). The impact of virtual, augmented and mixed reality technologies on the customer experience. *Journal of Business Research, 100*, 547–560. doi:10.1016/j.jbusres.2018.10.050

Gaioshko, D. (2017). *10 ways how augmented reality can help retailers*. Retail Dive. https://www.retaildive.com/ex/mobilecommercedaily/10-ways-how-augmented-reality-can-help-retailers

Garay-Cortes, J., & Uribe-Quevedo, A. (2016). Location-based augmented reality game to engage students in discovering institutional landmarks. *2016 7th International Conference on Information, Intelligence, Systems Applications (IISA)*, 1–4. 10.1109/IISA.2016.7785433

Gazzaley, A., Rissman, J., Cooney, J., Rutman, A., Seibert, T., Clapp, W., & D'Esposito, M. (2007). Functional Interactions between Prefrontal and Visual Association Cortex Contribute to Top-Down Modulation of Visual Processing. *Cerebral Cortex (New York, N.Y.), 17*(suppl_1), i125–i135. doi:10.1093/cercor/bhm113 PMID:17725995

George, M. K., & Ball, K. (2019, July 2). Legal Risks Of Virtual And Augmented Reality On The Construction Site. *Mondaq*. https://www.mondaq.com/unitedstates/construction-planning/820886/legal-risks-of-virtual-and-augmented-reality-on-the-construction-site

Gerup, J., Soerensen, C. B., & Dieckmann, P. (2020). Augmented reality and mixed reality for healthcare education beyond surgery: An integrative review. *International Journal of Medical Education, 11*, 1–18. doi:10.5116/ijme.5e01.eb1a PMID:31955150

Giffi, C., Rodriguez, M. D., & Mondal, S. (2017). *A look ahead: How modern manufacturers can create positive perceptions with the US public*. Deloitte Center for Industry Insights. https://www2.deloitte.com/us/en/pages/manufacturing/articles/public-perception-of-the-manufacturing-industry.html

Glockner, H., Jannek, K., Mahn, J., & Theis, B. (2014). *Augmented Reality in Logistics: Changing the way we see logistics—A DHL perspective.* DHL Customer Solutions & Innovation. https://www.dhl.com/content/dam/downloads/g0/about_us/logistics_insights/csi_augmented_reality_report_290414.pdf

Goldberg, B., Davis, F., Riley, J. M., & Boyce, M. W. (2017). Adaptive Training Across Simulations in Support of a Crawl-Walk-Run Model of Interaction. In D. D. Schmorrow & C. M. Fidopiastis (Eds.), *Augmented Cognition. Enhancing Cognition and Behavior in Complex Human Environments* (pp. 116–130). Springer International Publishing. doi:10.1007/978-3-319-58625-0_8

Hou, L., Wang, X., & Truijens, M. (2013). Using Augmented Reality to Facilitate Piping Assembly: An Experiment-Based Evaluation. *Journal of Computing in Civil Engineering, 29*(1), 05014007. Advance online publication. doi:10.1061/(ASCE)CP.1943-5487.0000344

Hughes, C. L., Bailey, P. S., Ruiz, E., Fidopiastis, C. M., Taranta, N. R., & Stanney, K. M. (2020. (Manuscript submitted for publication). The psychometrics of cybersickness in augmented reality. *Frontiers in Virtual Reality: Virtual Reality in Industry.*

Ibáñez, M. B., Di Serio, Á., Villarán, D., & Kloos, C. D. (2014). Experimenting with electromagnetism using augmented reality: Impact on flow student experience and educational effectiveness. *Computers & Education, 71,* 1–13. doi:10.1016/j.compedu.2013.09.004

Jeon, Y., Choi, S., & Kim, H. (2014). Evaluation of a simplified augmented reality device for ultrasound-guided vascular access in a vascular phantom. *Journal of Clinical Anesthesia, 26*(6), 485–489. doi:10.1016/j.jclinane.2014.02.010 PMID:25204510

Johnson-Glenberg, M. C., Birchfield, D. A., Tolentino, L., & Koziupa, T. (2014). Collaborative embodied learning in mixed reality motion-capture environments: Two science studies. *Journal of Educational Psychology, 106*(1), 86–104. doi:10.1037/a0034008

Johnson-Glenberg, M. C., Megowan-Romanowicz, C., Birchfield, D. A., & Savio-Ramos, C. (2016). Effects of embodied learning and digital platform on the retention of physics content: Centripetal force. *Frontiers in Psychology, 7,* 1819. doi:10.3389/fpsyg.2016.01819 PMID:27933009

Kamat, V. R., & El-Tawil, S. (2007). Evaluation of Augmented Reality for Rapid Assessment of Earthquake-Induced Building Damage. *Journal of Computing in Civil Engineering, 21*(5), 303–310. doi:10.1061/(ASCE)0887-3801(2007)21:5(303)

Karlsson, M. (2015). *Challenges of designing augmented reality for military use.* https://www.diva-portal.org/smash/get/diva2:823544/FULLTEXT01.pdf

Keri, Z., Sydor, D., Ungi, T., Holden, M. S., McGraw, R., Mousavi, P., Borschneck, D. P., Fichtinger, G., & Jaeger, M. (2015). Computerized training system for ultrasound-guided lumbar puncture on abnormal spine models: A randomized controlled trial. *Canadian Journal of Anaesthesia / Journal Canadien D'anesthesie, 62*(7), 777–784. doi:10.100712630-015-0367-2

Kersten-Oertel, M., Jannin, P., & Collins, D. L. (2013). The state of the art of visualization in mixed reality image guided surgery. *Computerized Medical Imaging and Graphics, 37*(2), 98–112. doi:10.1016/j.compmedimag.2013.01.009 PMID:23490236

Khan, T., Johnston, K., & Ophoff, J. (2019). The Impact of an Augmented Reality Application on Learning Motivation of Students. *Advances in Human-Computer Interaction, 2019*, 1–14. doi:10.1155/2019/7208494

Küçük, S., Kapakin, S., & Göktaş, Y. (2016). Learning anatomy via mobile augmented reality: Effects on achievement and cognitive load. *Anatomical Sciences Education, 9*(5), 411–421. doi:10.1002/ase.1603 PMID:26950521

Lee, K. (2012). Augmented Reality in Education and Training. *TechTrends, 56*(2), 13–21. doi:10.100711528-012-0559-3

Léger, É., Drouin, S., Collins, D. L., Popa, T., & Kersten-Oertel, M. (2017). Quantifying attention shifts in augmented reality image-guided neurosurgery. *Healthcare Technology Letters, 4*(5), 188–192. doi:10.1049/htl.2017.0062 PMID:29184663

Léger, É., Reyes, J., Drouin, S., Collins, D. L., Popa, T., & Kersten-Oertel, M. (2018). Gesture-based registration correction using a mobile augmented reality image-guided neurosurgery system. *Healthcare Technology Letters, 5*(5), 137–142. doi:10.1049/htl.2018.5063 PMID:30800320

Leitritz, M. A., Ziemssen, F., Suesskind, D., Partsch, M., Voykov, B., Bartz-Schmidt, K. U., & Szurman, G. B. (2014). Critical evaluation of the usability of augmented reality ophthalmoscopy for the training of inexperienced examiners. *Retina (Philadelphia, Pa.), 34*(4), 785–791. doi:10.1097/IAE.0b013e3182a2e75d PMID:24670999

Li, X., Yi, W., Chi, H.-L., Wang, X., & Chan, A. P. C. (2018). A critical review of virtual and augmented reality (VR/AR) applications in construction safety. *Automation in Construction, 86*, 150–162. doi:10.1016/j.autcon.2017.11.003

Lindgren, R., Tscholl, M., Wang, S., & Johnson, E. (2016). Enhancing learning and engagement through embodied interaction within a mixed reality simulation. *Computers & Education*, *95*, 174–187. doi:10.1016/j.compedu.2016.01.001

Livingston, M. A., Rosenblum, L. J., Brown, D. G., Schmidt, G. S., Julier, S. J., Baillot, Y., & Maassel, P. (2011). Military applications of augmented reality. In *Handbook of Augmented Reality* (pp. 671–706). Springer. doi:10.1007/978-1-4614-0064-6_31

Mao, C.-C., & Chen, F.-Y. (2020). Augmented Reality and 3-D Visualization Effects to Enhance Battlefield Situational Awareness. In T. Ahram, R. Taiar, S. Colson, & A. Choplin (Eds.), *Human Interaction and Emerging Technologies* (pp. 303–309). Springer International Publishing. doi:10.1007/978-3-030-25629-6_47

McKinnon, T. (2020, May 8). *10 of the Best Augmented Reality (AR) Shopping Apps to Try Today*. Indigo9Digital. https://www.indigo9digital.com/blog/how-six-leading-retailers-use-augmented-reality-apps-to-disrupt-the-shopping-experience

Memarzadeh, M., & Golparvar-Fard, M. (2012). *Monitoring and Visualization of Building Construction Embodied Carbon Footprint Using DnAR-N-Dimensional Augmented Reality Models*. doi:10.1061/9780784412329.134

Milgram, P., & Kishino, F. (1994). A taxonomy of mixed reality visual displays. *IEICE Transactions on Information and Systems*, *77*(12), 1321–1329.

Nilsson, N. C. (2018). Perceptual Illusions and Distortions in Virtual Reality. In N. Lee (Ed.), *Encyclopedia of Computer Graphics and Games*. Springer. doi:10.1007/978-3-319-08234-9_245-1

O'Brien, H. L., & Toms, E. G. (2008). What is user engagement? A Conceptual Framework for defining user engagement with technology. *Journal of the American Society for Information Science and Technology*, *59*(6), 938–955. doi:10.1002/asi.20801

Olson, N., Nolin, J., & Nelhans, G. (2015). Semantic web, ubiquitous computing, or internet of things? A macro-analysis of scholarly publications. *The Journal of Documentation*, *71*(5), 884–916. doi:10.1108/JD-03-2013-0033

Oren, T. (1990). Designing a new medium. In B. Laurel (Ed.), *The Art of Human-Computer Interface Design* (pp. 467–479). Addison-Wesley.

Pelanis, E., Kumar, R. P., Aghayan, D. L., Palomar, R., Fretland, Å. A., Brun, H., Elle, O. J., & Edwin, B. (2020). Use of mixed reality for improved spatial understanding of liver anatomy. *Minimally Invasive Therapy & Allied Technologies*, *29*(3), 154–160. doi:10.1080/13645706.2019.1616558 PMID:31116053

Pew Research Center. (2019). *Demographics of Mobile Device Ownership and Adoption in the United States*. https://www.pewresearch.org/internet/fact-sheet/mobile/

Piroozfar, D. P. (2018, July). *The application of Augmented Reality (AR) in the Architecture Engineering and Construction (AEC) industry*. International Conference on Construction in the 21st Century (CITC-10), Colombo, Sri Lanka.

Radianti, J., Majchrzak, T. A., Fromm, J., & Wohlgenannt, I. (2020). A systematic review of immersive virtual reality applications for higher education: Design elements, lessons learned, and research agenda. *Computers & Education, 147*, 103778. doi:10.1016/j.compedu.2019.103778

Radu, I. (2012). Why should my students use AR? A comparative review of the educational impacts of augmented-reality. *IEEE International Symposium on Mixed and Augmented Reality (ISMAR)*, 313–314. 10.1109/ISMAR.2012.6402590

Radu, I., & Antle, A. (2017). Embodied learning mechanics and their relationship to usability of handheld augmented reality. *IEEE Virtual Reality Workshop on K-12 Embodied Learning through Virtual Augmented Reality (KELVAR)*, 1–5. 10.1109/KELVAR.2017.7961561

Ragan, E. D., Sowndararajan, A., Kopper, R., & Bowman, D. A. (2010). The effects of higher levels of immersion on procedure memorization performance and implications for educational virtual environments. *Presence (Cambridge, Mass.)*, *19*(6), 527–543. doi:10.1162/pres_a_00016

Rai, A. S., Rai, A. S., Mavrikakis, E., & Lam, W. C. (2017). Teaching binocular indirect ophthalmoscopy to novice residents using an augmented reality simulator. *Canadian Journal of Ophthalmology, Journal Canadien D'ophtalmologie, 52*(5), 430–434. doi:10.1016/j.jcjo.2017.02.015 PMID:28985799

Riva, G., Baños, R. M., Botella, C., Mantovani, F., & Gaggioli, A. (2016). Transforming Experience: The Potential of Augmented Reality and Virtual Reality for Enhancing Personal and Clinical Change. *Frontiers in Psychiatry, 7*, 164. doi:10.3389/fpsyt.2016.00164 PMID:27746747

Robinson, A. R., Gravenstein, N., Cooper, L. A., Lizdas, D., Luria, I., & Lampotang, S. (2014). A mixed-reality part-task trainer for subclavian venous access. *Simulation in Healthcare: Journal of the Society for Simulation in Healthcare, 9*(1), 56–64. doi:10.1097/SIH.0b013e31829b3fb3 PMID:24310163

Rogers, K., Funke, J., Frommel, J., Stamm, S., & Weber, M. (2019). Exploring Interaction Fidelity in Virtual Reality: Object Manipulation and Whole-Body Movements. *Proceedings of the 2019 CHI Conference on Human Factors in Computing Systems*, 1–14. 10.1145/3290605.3300644

Saadon, N. F. S. M., Ahmad, I., Hanapi, A. N. C. P., & Che, H. (2020). The Implementation of Augmented Reality in Increasing Student Motivation: Systematic Literature Review. *IOP Conference Series. Materials Science and Engineering, 854*, 012043. doi:10.1088/1757-899X/854/1/012043

Saltan, F., & Arslan, O. (2016). The use of augmented reality in formal education: A scoping review. *Eurasia Journal of Mathematics, Science and Technology Education, 13*(2), 503–520. doi:10.12973/eurasia.2017.00628a

Santos, M. E. C., Chen, A., Taketomi, T., Yamamoto, G., Miyazaki, J., & Kato, H. (2014). Augmented reality learning experiences: Survey of prototype design and evaluation. *IEEE Transactions on Learning Technologies, 7*(1), 38–56. doi:10.1109/TLT.2013.37

Shaham, H. (2020). *Augmented reality instruction manual: The perfect user manual?* TechSee: Intelligent Virtual Assistance. https://techsee.me/blog/augmented-reality-instruction-manual/

Shapiro, L. (Ed.). (2014). *The Routledge handbook of embodied cognition.* Routledge. doi:10.4324/9781315775845

Siew, C. Y., Ong, S. K., & Nee, A. Y. C. (2019). A practical augmented reality-assisted maintenance system framework for adaptive user support. *Robotics and Computer-integrated Manufacturing, 59*, 115–129. doi:10.1016/j.rcim.2019.03.010

Skulmowski, A., & Rey, G. D. (2018). Embodied learning: Introducing a taxonomy based on bodily engagement and task integration. *Cognitive Research: Principles and Implications, 3*(1), 6. doi:10.118641235-018-0092-9 PMID:29541685

Spectar. (2019). *Optimizing construction with augmented reality: how augmented reality is shaping the smart job site of tomorrow.* https://cdn2.hubspot.net/hubfs/4905971/SpectarWhitepaper.pdf

Stanney, K. M., Hale, K. S., Nahmens, I., & Kennedy, R. S. (2003). What to expect from immersive virtual environment exposure: Influences of gender, body mass index, and past experience. *Human Factors, 45*(3), 504–520. doi:10.1518/hfes.45.3.504.27254 PMID:14702999

Stanney, K. M., Lawson, B. D., Rokers, B., Dennison, M., Fidopiastis, C., Stoffregen, T., Weech, S., & Fulvio, J. M. (2020). Identifying causes of and solutions for cybersickness in immersive technology: Reformulation of a research and development agenda. *International Journal of Human-Computer Interaction, 36*(19), 1783–1803. doi:10.1080/10447318.2020.1828535

Stanney, K. M., Moralez, L., Archer, J., Brawand, N. P., Martin, E., & Fidopiastis, C. M. (2020. (Manuscript submitted for publication). Performance gains from adaptive extended reality training fueled by artificial intelligence. *Journal of Defense Modeling and Simulation.*

Stanney, K. M., Nye, H., Haddad, S., Padron, C. K., Hale, K. S., & Cohn, J. V. (2020, in press). eXtended reality environments. In G. Salvendy & W. Karwowski (Eds.), Handbook of human factors and ergonomics (5th ed.). New York: John Wiley.

Stieff, M., Lira, M. E., & Scopelitis, S. A. (2016). Gesture supports spatial thinking in STEM. *Cognition and Instruction, 34*(2), 80–99. doi:10.1080/07370008.2016.1145122

Stolovitch, H. D., & Keeps, E. (2011). *Telling ain't training.* American Society for Training and Development.

Storms, R. L. (2002). Auditory-visual cross-modality interaction and illusions. In K. M. Stanney (Ed.), *Handbook of Virtual Environments: Design, Implementation, and Applications* (pp. 455–470). Lawrence Erlbaum Associates.

Strange, A. (2017, December 6). *BMW Uses ARKit to Let You Customize Your New Car in iOS.* Next Reality. https://mobile-ar.reality.news/news/bmw-uses-arkit-let-you-customize-your-new-car-ios-0181532/

Talmaki, S. A., Dong, S., & Kamat, V. R. (2010). *Geospatial Databases and Augmented Reality Visualization for Improving Safety in Urban Excavation Operations.* doi:10.1061/41109(373)10

TAR. (2020). Tactical augmented reality. http://www.tacticalaugmentedreality.com

Technologies, U. (2020). *Unity Manual: Colliders.* Retrieved October 28, 2020, from https://docs.unity3d.com/Manual/CollidersOverview.html

Tene, O., & Polonetsky, J. (2014). A theory of creepy: Technology, privacy and shifting social norms. *Yale Journal of Law and Technology, 16*(1), 59–102. https://yjolt.org/sites/default/files/theory_of_creepy_1_0.pdf

Thomas, R., Bhat, R., Khan, A., & Devan, P. (2018). Deloitte and The Manufacturing Institute skills gap and future of work study. *Deloitte Insights.* https://www. themanufacturinginstitute.org/wp-content/uploads/2020/03/MI-Deloitte-skills-gap-Future-of-Workforce-study-2018.pdf

Toumpaniari, K., Loyens, S., Mavilidi, M.-F., & Paas, F. (2015). Preschool Children's Foreign Language Vocabulary Learning by Embodying Words Through Physical Activity and Gesturing. *Educational Psychology Review*, 27(3), 445–456. doi:10.100710648-015-9316-4

Ullo, S. L., Piedimonte, P., Leccese, F., & De Francesco, E. (2019). A step toward the standardization of maintenance and training services in C4I military systems with Mixed Reality application. *Measurement*, *138*, 149–156. doi:10.1016/j. measurement.2019.02.036

Underwood, K. (2020, April 1). Augmented reality goes airborne. *Signal.* https:// www.afcea.org/content/augmented-reality-goes-airborne

Vallée-Tourangeau, F., Sirota, M., & Vallée-Tourangeau, G. (2016). Interactivity mitigates the impact of working memory depletion on mental arithmetic performance. *Cognitive Research: Principles and Implications*, *1*(1), 26. doi:10.118641235-016-0027-2 PMID:28180177

Venero, P., Rowe, A., & Boyer, J. (2012). Using Augmented Reality to Help Maintain Persistent Stare of a Moving Target inn an Urban Environment. *Proceedings of the Human Factors and Ergonomics Society Annual Meeting*, 56(1), 2575–2579. doi:10.1177/1071181312561535

Wang, X., Love, P. E. D., Kim, M. J., Park, C.-S., Sing, C.-P., & Hou, L. (2013). A conceptual framework for integrating building information modeling with augmented reality. *Automation in Construction*, *34*, 37–44. doi:10.1016/j.autcon.2012.10.012

Warren, T. (2017, March 17). *Microsoft is infesting Windows 10 with annoying ads.* The Verge. https://www.theverge.com/2017/3/17/14956540/microsoft-windows-10-ads-taskbar-file-explorer

Warzel, C. (2014, January 17). *How Google leapfrogged the creepy line.* Buzz Feed News. https://www.buzzfeednews.com/article/charliewarzel/how-google-leapfrogged-the-creepy-line

Weinbach, M. (2020, July 4). *Ads are taking over Samsung's Galaxy smartphones— And it needs to stop.* Android Police. https://www.androidpolice.com/2020/07/04/ ads-are-taking-over-samsungs-galaxy-smartphones-and-im-fed-up/

Wen, Y., & Looi, C.-K. (2019). Review of Augmented Reality in Education: Situated Learning with Digital and Non-digital Resources. In P. Díaz, A. Ioannou, K. K. Bhagat, & J. M. Spector (Eds.), *Learning in a Digital World: Perspective on Interactive Technologies for Formal and Informal Education* (pp. 179–193). Springer. doi:10.1007/978-981-13-8265-9_9

Witmer, B., & Singer, M. (1998). Measuring presence in virtual environments: A presence questionnaire. *Presence (Cambridge, Mass.), 7*(3), 225–240. doi:10.1162/105474698565686

Wu, H.-K., Lee, S. W.-Y., Chang, H.-Y., & Liang, J.-C. (2013). Current status, opportunities and challenges of augmented reality in education. *Computers & Education, 62*, 41–49. doi:10.1016/j.compedu.2012.10.024

Yeh, K.-C., Tsai, M.-H., & Kang, S.-C. (2012). On-Site Building Information Retrieval by Using Projection-Based Augmented Reality. *Journal of Computing in Civil Engineering, 26*(3), 342–355. doi:10.1061/(ASCE)CP.1943-5487.0000156

Yeh, M., & Wickens, C. D. (2001). Display signaling in augmented reality: Effects of cue reliability and image realism on attention allocation and trust calibration. *Human Factors, 43*(3), 355–365. doi:10.1518/001872001775898269 PMID:11866192

Yoon, S. A., Elinich, K., Wang, J., Steinmeier, C., & Tucker, S. (2012). Using augmented reality and knowledge-building scaffolds to improve learning in a science museum. *Computer-Supported Collaborative Learning, 7*(4), 519–541. doi:10.100711412-012-9156-x

Yunis, H. (Ed.). (2011). *Plato: Phaedrus.* Cambridge University Press.

Chapter 5
Strategic Implications of Organizational Culture, Knowledge, Learning Organizations, and Innovation on Sustainable Organizations

José G. Vargas-Hernández

iD https://orcid.org/0000-0003-0938-4197

University Center for Economic and Managerial Sciences, University of Guadalajara, Mexico

Jorge Armando López-Lemus
Unibversidad de Guadajuato, Mexico

ABSTRACT

This study aims to analyze the strategic implications that the organizational culture has on organizational knowledge, learning, and innovation. It begins from the assumption that there is a direct and positive relationship between the organizational culture and knowledge, learning, and innovation in organizations. It also is assumed that organizational culture, knowledge, learning, and innovation are receptive to sustainable organizational practices. The method used is the appreciative inquiry as a collaborative dialogue based on the question of what is the best of and what might be that aims to design and implement innovations in sustainable organizational arrangements and processes. The theoretical framework is based on organizational cultural cognitivism theory and the theory of socio-ecological intergradation. It is concluded that sustainable organizations practices require the creation and development of an organizational culture supportive of knowledge, learning, and innovation practices.

DOI: 10.4018/978-1-7998-6453-0.ch005

INTRODUCTION

Corporate and organizational culture plays a receptive role to sustainable organizational practices leading to economic growth and efficiency, social inclusion and justice, and environmental sustainability. Organizational development is a workplace-oriented process integrating knowledge generation, representation, communication and sharing, learning and training management, and structuring regulations in achieving results. There is a relationship between the worker's involvement and workplace learning of new sustainable organizational development initiatives and processes. Sustainable organizational development is a pervasive philosophy globally subscribed to the commitment that organizations have to meet the needs of the current generation while not compromising the ability to meet their own needs of future generations.

Appreciative inquiry is a collaborative dialogue based on the question of what is the best of and what might be that aims to explore, discover, understand, analyze and implement innovations in organizational arrangements and processes.

Old economy-based traditional organizations are transforming rapidly into new development paths with more informal and creative organizations identified with new economy organizations, more collaborative and participative organizational cultures. Individuals and society that acknowledge the relevance that natural resources, the bio ecosystem, and the environment have for human development, get involved in organizational practices of conservation, maintenance, and enhancement of environmentally sustainable development. These practices require the creation and development of an organizational culture supportive of knowledge, learning, and innovation practices.

The study begins by analyzing the components and features of the organizational development to continue with the analysis of knowledge transferal, the characteristics and elements of any learning organization, and organizational innovation. Finally, the study intends to present a strategic approach to these issues and the concluding remarks.

ORGANIZATIONAL CULTURE

Culture is the set of shared values, vision, assumptions, beliefs and norms, which govern organizational policies and people (Bandura, 2002). Organizational culture is a shared understanding and learned way of perceiving, thinking, and feeling about problems that are transmitted to members of the organization (Dicle and Okan, 2015). Organizational cultures structure, control and govern individual behaviors through values, rules, norms, and operating procedures.

Organizational cultural cognitivism theory sustains that the focus of learning, power, and control is the individual who promotes organizational culture and learning coherence (Tomasello, 2010; Thakker and Durrant, 2011). The theory of socio-ecological intergradation using a theory-building approach mimics natural ecosystems to contribute to the development of sustainable supply chain activities and practices. Socio-ecology intergradation gradually merges the social and ecological system to shift the focus from global to more regional and local supply chain connected operations.

The resource-based and the knowledge-based views supported by human resource practices, information technology capabilities, environment, and organizational culture are issues that have a direct effect on sustainable organizational performance. Human resource management and organizational culture are sources of competitive advantage that make valuable contributions to organizational sustainable development effectiveness. Human resources management practices are related to sustainable organizational development performance although the technology-based staff development may have not significant contributions.

An organizational sustainable system supports a structure to attract and retain human talent and facilitates an organizational culture to promote greening. Organizational green behavior and green culture may promote motivation and incentives for green practices in designing renewable and efficient-energy products and processes (Gupta, 2008). Personnel motivation and opportunities for feedback support effective management performance and organizational goals leading to maximizing the achievement of sustainable organizational development. Green training and development motivate and engage human resources to cultivate a sustainable organizational culture, build competencies, value the organizational environment and solve problems related.

Creation of organizational core competencies as a strategy to enable sustainable organizational development and growth, organizations must identify people and match with positions for more personalized career development, giving them more specific guidance y expert support in organizational culture and conflict management. Expert and process-oriented are two approaches validated by theory most used in different contexts to raise the organizational capacity on consulting the organizations in organizational development. To develop the organizational capacity is required to determine the best approach in consulting the organizations taking into consideration the contextual variables, although the most used is the expert role (Boonstra & Elving, 2009).

Green values teaching and inculcation for the organizational greening is a supportive task of leader involvement (Siebenhüner and Arnold, 2007) which demands competencies and environment-friendly culture and behaviors (Rimanoczy and Pearson, 2010). Green human resource development and training improve awareness and knowledge, build positive and proactive attitudes and develop a culture of competencies toward organizational environmental issues management (Zoogah, 2011). Organizational environment green behaviors can be promoted by implementing managerial tools to create and develop a culture, such as the use of financial incentives, green compensation, and reward system (Phillips, 2007; Liebowitz, 2010).

Environmental performance in Mexican organizations is positively related to employee empowerment (Daily et al. 2012) forming eco-entrepreneurs, motivated, skilled, and ecologically oriented to become involved in greening the organization and environmental activities by organizing natural, human and financial resources to develop a green-oriented culture and add value to organizational outcomes (Renwick et al.,2013).

Educating, developing, and training the workforce on sustainable organizational development for utilizing the knowledge and skills in processes, as well as involvement in organizational ethics, governance, transparency, accountability, and compliance, etc., are relevant issues and concerns for organizational culture and management change. Environmental training has effects on sustainable development (Ji et al., 2011), the implementation of an environmental management system, and the development of an environmentally oriented organizational culture (Teixeira et al., 2012). The organizational culture has an impact on organizational sustainable development.

Organizational culture focuses on the development of workforce cohesion and motivation through the core values of the organization. A diverse workforce may use its competencies to reach the best organizational culture despite that the focus, reasons, and execution may vary regarding the resources and how they are used to achieve sustainable organizational development and growth (Bianchi, 2012). The overall organizational culture is tied to the development of the workforce and teamwork through motivating them and focusing on instilling a sense of identity and cohesion amongst the individuals involved to create leadership. Leadership styles influence the development of organizational structure and culture and foster knowledge (Alsabbagh and Khalil, 2016).

Organizational vision and culture must be led by leadership to inspire and guide all the empowered workers to excel in their practices and activities framed by a clear code of conduct in ethical, environmental, and safety issues and concerns. Workers use their energies to use their whole self at their work (Moxley 2000, p. 12). Career development for the workers aligned to the vision and incorporated into the values of the organizational culture creates a bond between the organization and workers supported by the motivation to attain the organizational goals. A factor for generating organizational sustainable development and growth is the operationalization of the organizational vision and structure while the individual role in a work organization is in guiding through the work environment

Individual reputation in the organization can be enhanced with the provision of the right education and knowledge to conduct organizational growth through the transfer of knowledge, organizational culture and leadership development, team building activities, etc. All these results of organizational communication have an impact on the development of strategic competencies and the creation of organizational competitive advantages. Human resources embed sustainability into the organizational culture to align the vision, values, mission, leadership, and strategies to long-term sustainable economic, social, and environmental results.

The core values of sustainable organizational developments are embedded in the organizational culture to be developed into processes and procedures. The embedded organizational culture within sustainable organizational strategies shapes the sustainability vision and strategy to be implemented for the sustainable organizational development system aligning all the stakeholders involved. The organizational development process might be complex and turbulent and to avoid the risk of losing touch with the real world (Patton 1997, 26-29), it is recommended an independent internal evaluator to prevent potential bias (Sonnichsen 2000; Love 1991).

However, the involvement of all stakeholders in these actions contributes to the creation of an organizational culture oriented towards more organizational citizenship behaviors in favor of the environment. Appropriate governance mechanisms encourage all the stakeholders involved in the organization to create a culture, value and engage sustainability practices, and ensures organizational representation of critical functions.

The organization can create, develop and maintain the organizational culture giving purpose and a sense of identity while working in a cohesive team to improve the environment. The organizational culture requires the management and staff involvement to provide a sense of identity, leadership, and reputation, to support innovation, digitalization, environmental sustainability, sustainable organizational growth. Proportions of distribution of workers by demographic indicators referring to majorities and minorities, affect and are affected by the organizational culture in terms of stereotypes, bias, etc.

A sustainable work system allows both personal and professional development to workers building on individual and organizational sustainable development. A sustainable work system processes foster two-way communication and dialogue aimed to improve other organizational factors such as meaningfulness, comprehensibility, and manageability of post-bureaucratic and contemporary work creating the conditions needed for individual and organizational sustainable development (Heckscher, 1994).

A strong organizational culture, management of an organizational brand, analysis of the situation to formulate relevant ideas and backup innovation, and possession of core competencies and capabilities such as niche strategic management of brand reputation, have a direct link to organizational sustainable development and growth. Organizational culture facilitates organizational citizenship behaviors that promote organizational sustainable development (Angelis, 2016). Institutional rules and regulations, organizational culture, procedures, and routines, etc., are an example of obstacles to fulfill the gender gap equality programs for more resilient sustainable organizational development.

The organizational culture must be innovated, involved, and engaged in a code of conduct framed by freedom and guidance. Organizational innovation may have severe intertwined management, institutional setting problems, and environmental constraints causing negative operational changes and lack of collaboration influencing the organizational culture.

KNOWLEDGE TRANSFERAL

The organizational capability to facilitate and integrate the knowledge-creation of value in the structure, motivation, and communication processes leads to sustainable organizational development and growth. Organizations enable the development and enhancement of the organizational knowledge to provide the factors within motivation, communication, cohesion, organizational structure, and behavior.

Organizational knowledge is the main factor that contributes to organizational long-term core competencies which in turn have a high impact on long-term sustainable organizational development and growth. Knowledge human resources development and their retention (Belle, 2016) in organizational learning improve the culture, values, resources, capabilities, processes, mechanisms, etc., becomes a priority of cultural cognitivism in organizational sustainable development (XiaomiAn and Wang, 2010; Csikszentmihalyi, 2015).

Organizational cognition can contribute to improving the computational capacity for organizational knowledge management, problem-solving, and decision-making processes supported by the organizational demands and goals (Moon et al., 2017; Staats and Gino 2013). Cognitive factors have an impact on organizational knowledge assets aimed to change sustainable organizational development (Attwell, 2010) in a motivating environment (Birmingham, 2015) requiring self-actualization (Adcock, 2012).

Organizational knowledge is challenged by the cognitive dissonance theory by exploiting accommodation and assimilation processes at the individual knowledge level by introducing and accepting new organizational behaviors (Adcock, 2012).

Knowledge-based (KBV) and resource-based (RBV) theories support the notion that human resources are equally relevant that other organizational resources. Human resource management practices have a relationship with sustainable organizational development innovation and performance. The resource-based theory and knowledge-based theory argue that organizational human resources are equally relevant that other organizational resources to incorporate innovative processes in attaining sustainable organizational development performance.

The human capital theory and Drucker's knowledge-worker productivity theory sustain that the knowledge of individuals in an organization is an asset (Wong, 2012; Adcock, 2012). Investments in human resources development with an emphasis on knowledge and innovation-based organizations are crucial in dynamic organizational environments to achieve sustainable organizational development performance.

Knowledge-based organizations under the analysis of knowledge-based theory sustain that knowledge innovation has an impact on sustainable organizational development performance leading to the creation of by-products of knowledge capabilities contributing to and organizational competitive advantage, stability, employee satisfaction, etc. Knowledge-based innovation from the perspective of resource-based view as a mediator for human resource management practices is a key resource for competitive advantage and sustainable organizational development (Lopez-Cabrales, Pérez-Luño, and Cabrera 2009).

The value theory is based on the knowledge obtained from executed projects as a factor that affects the organizational ability to sustain development and growth (Chinta & Kloppenborg's 2010). Organizational knowledge as a tool enables long-term value creation by establishing the sustainable core competencies keeping up with innovation to be created and managed should be differentiating between the organizational and social values to take action leading to sustainable organizational development and growth.

Sustainable human resources management practices should be engaged in sharing intra-organization information and knowledge to attain goals, create value and competitive advantage. The use of an organizational communication system enables the exchange and sharing of knowledge and common experiences amongst individuals and groups which leads to organizational effectiveness and sets the foundations for organizational development (Tucker et al., 1996). Organizational communication develops the knowledge required by tasks within the adequate policies creating a community in the organization (Elving, 2005).

Organizational communication allows individuals to share their knowledge and experiences leading to manage its tacit knowledge (Tucker et al., 1996) developed towards the creation of a sustainable organizational competitive advantage (Osterloh & Frey, 2000). The creation of organizational knowledge with the involvement of all the stakeholders holds value through a brand name identified with the potential benefits (Tauber, 1981; Broniarczyk & Alba, 1994) associated with the constructed identity and the connected values such as trust (Keller, 1987).

Organizational knowledge can be created, maintained, and efficiently transferred through consistent communication across all aspects, structures, and hierarchies. Organizations are developing new tools for more viable and efficient organizational communication channels that enable the transferal of knowledge and deliver a sense of efficiency and overall development to all the involved individuals within the organization (Haslam, 1997). Development of open communication channels across all the organizational levels focusing on communicating the purpose of developing sustainable core values and to transfer and disseminate the knowledge.

The organization's value knowledge is maintained through communication and an organizational structure and tied to core competencies that enable sustainable organizational development and growth which can be realized if produces more value and benefits (Bianchi, 2012). Organizational communication is prevalent to maintain the sense of an organizational community while still involved with other external communities and develop the networks to facilitate the knowledge transferal with the support of teams.

The organization strives to communicate consistently to transfer knowledge, values, and skills to the workforce regarding the processes while maintaining the organizational standards. Sustainable organizational development and growth are connected by the ability to transfer knowledge that creates value and enables the development of core competencies. Consistent transferal of organizational knowledge for sustainable development enables to development of a connection to the overall organizational health and personal development for each one of the workforce, allowing them to communicate with freedom and independence and becoming more motivated.

Organizational development encompasses the core competencies enabling to enhance them and manage the benefits of long-term organizational knowledge. The results delivered by an intervention of organizational development are measured in terms of exchange and transfer of organizational knowledge and the impact on individual and organizational performance in terms of the achievement of the goals.

Any organizational development intervention must promote more than supporting the status quo and accomplish a change to renew it. The organizational sustainable development intervention to be fully tailor-made to the organization's developmental needs starting from the current organization's climate and perceived training needs in managerial needs to create and develop an organizational culture where the agendas, purposes, and meanings are shared in explicit organizational knowledge involving all the stakeholders (Choo 2000, Järvinen & Poikela 2001).

Organizational knowledge provided by the aptitude and ability to develop projects adds value to the skills and process within the sustainable organizational core competencies (Chinta & Kloppenborg, 2010). Organizational development is a change process that creates and improves the knowledge and skills of all the stakeholders giving them opportunities to be included.

The organizational stakeholders' behaviors need to be properly developed by the organizational structure, knowledge management and the standardization of benefits (Holbrook & Hirschman, 1982) should be clear to the workforce to enable the organization to maintain sustainable development and growth. Rotation of the workforce through different organizational practices allows one to gain a broad knowledge of the operations and functions of the organization.

Ambidextrous organizations pursue exploration and exploitation of knowledge applied to developmental activities within the organizational structure. Organizational structure and behavior is an emerging theory in some industrial sectors linked to the concepts of power, opportunities, and proportions with delimiting factors (Kanter 2008). Position power changes benefit organizational development by giving individuals opportunities in a wider range of organizational knowledge in new projects and exposure through the stages to other people in other areas and functions in the organization and value their potentials (Kanter, 2008). Organizational knowledge needs to be shared through all hierarchical levels in all issues and aspects to deliver the improvements and tied to personalized career path plans too much personal motivation, interests, and capabilities.

The motivation of all the workforce enables the organizational team and leadership development to further improve as it develops the creation and transference of knowledge, learning, processes, practices, and performance. Motivation and communication of the organizational team focused on the development of individuals involved with a commitment of knowledge and expertise to continuing growth deliver the organizational performance.

Managerial balance of performance leads to sustainable organizational growth through the continual creation of knowledge and development of standardized competencies. The organizational capability to attain and apply knowledge obtained from projects to create value through the improvement of the process used to accomplish the projects leads to sustainable growth (Chinta & Kloppenborg, 2010; Bianchi, 2012). The creation of knowledge combined with experiences of members as an organizational competence creates value to achieve overall and long-term sustainable growth (Bianchi, 2012; Tucker et al., 1996; Chinta & Kloppenborg, 2010). Continual organizational knowledge development enables sustainable value creation to develop sustainable organizational development and growth.

Organizational change requires information and knowledge based on the performance to design an action plan of intervention to innovate processes, to motivate the need to work cohesively, and transfer new knowledge and skills to improve performance. Organizational change must move and transform organizations from consuming to regenerative and upskilling work and resources to have positive results on the individual and organizational sustainable development. Organizational workforce cohesion should focus on the organization´s needs and vision related to the individual´s competencies and knowledge, creating motivation and working as a team with a sense of pride in continual growth and developing expertise.

A motivational program may enable the transferal of organizational knowledge and learning (Osterloh & Frey, 2000) which are considered as intangible competencies to function in a cohesive unit with abilities and skills of the workforce to enable organizational development. In this logic, the tangible competencies are the tangible resources (Schmiedinger et al., 2005). Transferal of organizational knowledge conducted through sharing experiences by the communication system (Tucker, Meyer & Westerman, 1996) in the organizational structure leads to the sustainability of an organization (Roberts & O'Reilly, 1974).

Individuals seek personal development at the workplace having a job that offers this to commit skills, knowledge, and abilities to the organization which in turn seeks organizational development through the commitment and efforts to achieve the higher performance output. Organizational knowledge exchange to improve the processes of sustainable organizational strategic development advancement in structures, strategies and policies, motivation, communication, and leadership processes, promotes organizational development effectiveness and performance (Cummings & Worley, 2014).

Organizational development focuses on the need to exchange knowledge and learning with an emphasis on individual and social elements within the organization about concepts such as organizational and work design, group dynamics, leadership, etc. (Cummings & Worley, 2014). Organizational knowledge exchange to improve the processes of sustainable organizational strategic development advancement in structures, strategies and policies, motivation, communication, and leadership processes, promotes organizational development effectiveness and performance (Cummings & Worley, 2014).

Organizational design converging with knowledge accumulation based on the principle of self-organization account for measuring the performance of tacit knowledge in a sustainable learning organization model.

The workforce needs to be in a constant transfer of knowledge through experiential and educational practices to advance their development to gain a broader understanding of processes aligned with the goals, philosophy, culture, and outcomes of the organization. The organization needs to expand the expertise and broad knowledge within the workforce by providing education and training, communicating results, and engaging them in the process of achieving the best results and outcomes, enhancing the organizational growth. Education and training try elements necessary to develop individual and team-based organizational knowledge, developing common interests across de hierarchical levels to achieve organizational development and growth.

Organizational climate enables organizations the continuous development of a cycle of knowledge transferal through communication among the workers (Elving, 2005). A continuous cycle of organizational communication patterns encompasses a continuous interpersonal relationship to enable transferal of knowledge to develop teams aimed to develop sustainable core competitive advantages as a managerial strategy that leads to sustainable organizational development and growth (Roberts & O'Reilly; Postmes, 2003; Tucker et al., 1996). Organizations engaged in long-lasting relationships and dialogue with workers creates corporate branding and foster sustainable organizational development (Aggerholm, Anderson & Thomsen, 2011).

Transferal of knowledge through organizational communication contributes to develop and manage sustainable competitive advantages (Tucker et al., 1996). Communication patterns enable knowledge transferal which is crucial for the creation, development, and management of organizational core competencies and their overall success (Roberts & O'Reilly, 1974; Tucker et al., 1996).

Sustainable organizational health and growth hinge on communication to enable the transferal of knowledge, skills, and competencies, as well as the community cohesion that contributes to innovation and sustainable organizational development. Organizations should develop balanced organizational communication and climate programs enable to the structure of individual behaviors in organizations enable to provide opportunities to enhance knowledge and learning, shape organizational structure, and motivate organizational behaviors (Kanter, 2008).

Feedback is a mechanism for acquiring awareness, information, and knowledge supporting, self-correcting, and ensuring sustainability to organizational development.

LEARNING ORGANIZATIONS

Organizational learning deals with the complexities and uncertainties of sustainable organizational development efforts (Bovaird, 2007). Organizational development involves the implementation, support, and design of organizational modifications. Organizational learning for integration of environmental sustainability practices contributes to building a holistic green organization (Kerr, 2006; Siebenhüner and Arnold, 2007). A holistic and constructivist approach to organizational development by principles is based on standards and regulations workplace-oriented, adapted, and systematically structured on an organizational learning and knowledge management systems. However, the development initiative processes are complex, uncertain, and ambiguous, relying more on ongoing continuous learning processes and evaluation of outcomes.

Sustainability is a fundamental learning principle applied to the sustainable circular learning cycle in the concept of the sustainable learning organization. The greening of the organizations requires support from top-management support for mutual organizational learning to identify the crucial factors and the integration of green activities, practices, and efforts to promote environmentally sustainable organizational behaviors. Top management and project management of the organization are the key players for any initiative on organizational sustainable development.

An interpretive model sustains that organizational learning is a source of cognitive and psychological empowerment of workers for developing their technological and managerial capabilities, involving them in decision-making processes and practices (Rahimian et al., 2014, Thomas and Velthouse, 1990). The learning components have an impact on organizational innovation (Sedighi 2016).

The cognitive learning factors have an impact on the organizational cognition, knowledge, and learning management system aimed to improve the effectiveness of sustainable organizational development in any learning organization (Marshall, 2007). Organizational cognition is a systemic discipline concerned with organizational collective learning based on multidisciplinary research (Alhabeeb and Rowley, 2017; Atwood et al., 2010; Belle, 2016) aimed to organize the components of human resources, structure, design, technology, culture, and social networks. Organizational sustainable development has managerial research implications for specific environmental and green issues (Commission on Environment and Development 1987; Brundtlandt in Hoverstadt and Bowling, 2005; Baumgartner and Korhonen, 2010; Becker, 2010; Patra, 2009).

The cognitive components of learning, knowledge, and structure are very significant factors and contribute with a positive impact towards organizational sustainable development. Organizational cognitive, learning, and culture elements are factors that have an impact on Organizational sustainable development. Organizational cognitive factors, behavioral, leadership styles, organizational structure social, and contextual elements are relevant for the organizational learning tacit and explicit knowledge and sustainable development.

The organizational cognitive, knowledge and learning perspectives are influenced by factors such as organizational culture, leadership, knowledge, training, and development, empowerment, organizational structure and strategy, performance (Alalwan et al., 2016; Adcock, 2012; Coetzer et al., 2017). Trait leadership and organizational cognition theories argue that the cognitive domain is an ability of supportive leadership (Mumford et al., 2016; Dicle and Okan, 2015) that encourages organizational collaborative learning between internal and external environments (Atwood et al., 2010).

Organizational learning and entrepreneurial activities are related to the individual and team. Organizational learning is an individual and organizational dynamic process extending from intuition, interpretation, integration, and institutionalization of organizational change (Crossan et al.,1999). There is a positive relationship between the dimension of organizational learning and entrepreneurship (Aghajani et al. 2015). Learning organization has a relationship with entrepreneurial performance

(Safamansh et al. 2015). Organizational learning capacity has an impact on innovation performance (Gomez and Wojahn 2017).

Organizational change is defined in terms of learning. A learning organization may induce a change of learning processes with creativity and innovation as an organizational existential value in a flexible and cohesive structure with the lowest cost and waste of resources (Kouhkan & Mousavi 2015, Gomez & Wojahn 2017, Safamansh et al. 2015, and Hoveida 2007). Creativity has a relationship with a learning organization. Less formal and more organic organizational structure promotes more democratic values and organizational learning (Martínez-Leon and Martínez-García, 2011).

Learning and knowledge processes take into account the individual, group, and organizational capabilities and performance (Saadat and Saadat, 2016). The grouping arrangements within the line organization structure can limit organizational mutual learning, knowledge management, and idea exchange. The process of organizational learning increases the self-esteem of the involved individuals when gaining experience to achieve their goals (Gomez & Wojahn 2017, Kouhkan & Mousavi 2015, Aghajani et al. 2015, Sedighi 2016, Ehsani Ghodsi & Seyed Abbaszadeh 2012, and Hoveida 2007).

The organizational structure has an impact on the workforce development based on usage of knowledge, communication channels, motivation, and cohesion considered as the foundations of core competencies (Han et al. 2010 and Hill & Bowen's (1997). The organic organizational structure is more sustainable providing more organizational learning integrating knowledge in less formal and centralized ways, modularized and combined in processes (Tran and Tian, 2013). A learning organization changes in attitude to favor collective learning to achieve organizational growth and development (Alvani, 2008).

The learning approach to sustainable development requires that project owners get more involved as the leader, sponsor, mentor, and critic by development changes (Van de Ven et al., 2000). Individual and organizational differences have to be turned into benefits to find the common ground for a greater sense of active and shared responsibilities to improve individual and organizational learning and development.

Sustainable organizational development change must take into account the quality work and the continuous organizational learning processes adapted to the new institutional reality and organizational memory (Pfeffer and Sutton 2000) from emerging thinking and activity levels most suited to the specific current situation.

Institutionalization of strategic change and renewal of sustainable organizational development practices is part of the organization's memory based on founded on organizational learning starting with the steering and guiding the organizational operations and practices (Crossan et al., 1999). Learning institutions identified with higher education institutions that provide educational and academic services which are the basis to similar abilities, functions, and relationships to become learning organizations whether they are capable to promote and have an impact with organizational innovation.

Appropriate encouragement to continue change to create a learning organization with the institutionalization of a strong organizational culture to facilitate knowledge sharing through communication fosters creativity and innovation. Institutionalizing strong organizational culture with horizontal structures to facilitate information, communication, and knowledge sharing flows are required to create an innovative and creative learning organization. Organizations need to create and develop knowledge and learning units with capabilities to collect information and provide feedback and support sustainable organizational development (Patton 1998).

The information and knowledge explosion involving information and communication technologies is leading to shorter innovation cycles, continuous individual and organizational learning and knowledge systems, and sustainable organizational development. Innovative employees should be attracted to the organization and retained. Implementation of an organizational learning and knowledge system including project principles results in specific experiences related to the standard for management systems, such as the strategies and objectives formulated on customer-based requirements, definition of management, resources, optimization, and support processes focused on the optimization and fulfillment of organizations.

Organizational development initiatives play a role in engaging workers by tapping into their efforts for sustainability practices while promoting trust, loyalty, and confidence, as well as formalizing knowledge sharing and learning to create organizational responsiveness to internal and external factors. Loyal workers to their organization make them staying at the workplace and are committed to develop individuals, improve quality of performance and upgrade programs through learning and knowledge infrastructures (Kouhkan & Mousavi 2015; Hoveida 2007).

Organizational learning culture development enhances the acquisition, interpretation, and distribution of tacit and explicit organizational knowledge (Mehrabi et al., 2013). The explicit organizational knowledge must be systematically structured and documented including all the relevant information on need-oriented processes, procedures, regulations, etc., aimed to promote and improve sustainable organizational development. Organizational learning and knowledge culture help to be reused to support organizational living-learning environments (Bandura, 2002).

Organizational learning from the best practices will continuously innovate involving the workforce in better opportunities of development created at all levels, engaging, increasing commitment and responsibility.

The rational planning models for managing organizational development and change has some limitations which are being addressed by the perspective of process and learning model on organizational change viewed as an open process of learning and adaptation (March 1981; Beer et al., 1990; Brulin and Svensson, 2012), or as organizational development (Bennis et al., 1985). Sustainable organizational development is a component of procedural and organizational adaptability and maturity. Planned organizational change is conceptualized as managed learning (Schein, 1996).

Organizational development planning is supported by knowledge, learning, and change mechanism. In sustainable organizational development, planning to emerge knowledge, learning, and change dimensions despite that they are not the values, assumptions, strategies, and objectives (Friedman et al, 1987). Organizations use to have a high workload of current work processes that may be reduced by targeting the organizational resources to make more rational and efficient use.

Managerialism is an approach to public sector organizations that have rapidly adopted other trends such as learning organizations, strategic human resource and knowledge management (Wiig, 2002) practices in operational task management aimed to achieve sustainable wellbeing and performance and to promote organizational sustainable development.

Evaluations have an impact in assessing the theory of change promoted by learning programs that lead to sustainable organizational development. The organizational process evaluation to use systematic feedback should be conducted within a comprehensive framework supported by an organizational sustainable development intervention aimed to enhance organizational capacity building.

Ongoing evaluations aimed to confirm expectations need to focus more on long-term results of sustainability activities rather than on short-term effects questioning action patterns that trigger developmental learning (Schein, 1996; Ellström, 2001). Organizational internal self-evaluation and applied formative development active evaluation are needed (Patton 1997, 104 106) as being used and improvement-oriented to be implemented for organizational sustainability development (Patton, 1998, 225).

ORGANIZATIONAL INNOVATION

Organizational innovation is an advantageous attribute since the industrial revolution for those organizations that accept new ideas generated within or appropriated from somewhere else, developed and implemented to develop a competitive advantage, to create value, and attain benefits.

Organizational innovation means using knowledge, tools, practices, and manpower to achieve specific goals through non-recurring strategies. Innovative organizations develop a creative environment where all the stakeholders involved can find the motivation to generate new ideas. More of the environmental constraints in a complex system and institutional setting are posed by the institution of the market (Hirschhorn 1988) which helps to understand the limits of organizational innovation priorities. Organizations incorporate innovative practices and processes leading to sustainable organizational innovation performance. Organizational innovation improves corporate practices, methods, organizational coordination instruments, and management strategies through structural changes.

Organizational innovations are dependent on the psychological structures of humans involved in organizations (Vansina, 1998) which may be understood in simplistic approaches that do not consider other variables such as participation of workers in the organizational change and innovation. The organization has specific operating conditions to become learning organizations and their potential impacts on organizational innovation.

Organizational innovation mediates between human resource management practices sustainable organizational development performance, which is related to organizational knowledge and environmental sustainability. Human resource management practices are defined as the policies and practices relevant to perform the routines of all personnel for sustainable organizational development performance mediated by organizational innovation (Foss and Lyngsie 2011). Human resources management development enhances organizational innovation emphasizing motivation to encourage competencies which improves the sustainable organizational development outcomes performance.

Organizational innovation and effective performance management are resources to achieve measures of goals in organizational sustainable development performance. The new innovative organizational working mechanisms have effects on the organizational dynamics and are contributing more than the old practices to sustainable organizational development performance.

The components of the learning organization have a relationship with innovation (Kouhkan and Mousavi 2015). The components of learning organizations have a significant direct impact on transparency, empowerment and leadership, teamwork, experimentation, reward, etc., and organizational innovation leading to the improvement of organizational performance. Organizational innovation is supported by its core competencies and contributes to create and develop a competitive advantage leading to continuing growth (Egbu, 2004). Organizational learning and leadership are factors that promote the use of innovative methods to improve organizational sustainable development (Danish et al., 2015). Leadership abilities are required to influence learning activities to improve the work processes which results in efficiency and organizational sustainable development.

Increasing the organizational ability to deal with emerging environmental needs, demands and changes at the different levels is dependent on the organizational capabilities to innovate, transform and renovate through arrangements of flexible collaboration and relationships of cooperation while the workers are internally committed to the sustainable organizational development.

An organizational change and innovation processes founded on participation need to create an internal commitment, responsibility, and empowerment of all the involved workers and stakeholders of the organization (Argyris 1998) in organizational practices where the means fit the ends of an organizational sustainable development.

The organizational context is considered a mediating construct of organizational innovation. The academic and research environment influences organizational innovation and economic, social, cultural, and environmental development (Simao, 2016). Interactive action research is a continuous, joint learning process between the participants and researchers. Organizational resources and infrastructure development are relevant elements to create knowledge and innovativeness in dynamic organizational environments in achieving sustainable organizational performance and development.

The public sector R&D organization in the fields of welfare and health recognize the professionalization of human resources as the most important element to promote ongoing internal organizational sustainable development and organizational learning management (Sharp 2001) through action-oriented as well as outcome-oriented projects (Geertshuis et al. 2002). Transformation of public organizations in a public sector R&D organization operating in the fields of health and welfare is supported on organizational sustainable development and organizational learning management through internal processes.

Human resource management and staff development influence organizational innovation working mechanisms playing a mediating role for sustainable organizational development performance. Working with innovative mechanisms and improved human resources practices more engaged with staff development are more open to organizational dynamics and more innovation change.

Implementation of human resource management and organizational innovation practices are critical factors to benefit organizations to achieve sustainable organizational development performance. The organizational human resource development and innovation practices promote creativity and productivity that have a positive relationship to sustainable organizational development performance outcomes. Human capital development is a relevant factor of staffing creativity assuring high standard employees and organizations.

Sustainable organizational development performance is based on the execution of action plans resulting in the positioning of products and services. Organizational human resources practices and organizational innovation are relevant to organizational strategic management aim to attaining sustainable organizational development and performance (Barney, 1991) leading to organizational economic development, working dynamics, and firm competitiveness.

Systematic customer and worker involvement in sustainable organizational development in the workplace innovation help to learn about its needs and the potential sources of knowledge for change and innovation. Workers that bring innovation to the organizations have knowledge, skills, and expertise in close relationship with the application of staff development techniques, leading to creativity. This close relationship between organizational innovation and staff development influences knowledge, process, and product innovation.

Knowledge innovation is related to organizational innovation, processes, new products, and services innovation and development leading to organizational development innovation and sustainable organizational development performance. Organizational knowledge has a close relationship with organizational innovation which begins by recruiting, creating, and developing human talent in innovative teams and networks for sustainable organizational development.

Organizational values and competencies emphasize the collective teamwork formed by diverse groups of individuals having cohesion that have to improve unique competencies and set the performance standards. Group problem solving and teamwork affect the support on organizational innovation.

Organizational knowledge-based innovation has an intervening effect between human resources management practices and their relationships with sustainable organizational development and performance. Organizational knowledge innovation supported by the resources-based theory mediates resources for product and service development outcomes creating sustainable competitive advantage. Innovation and involvement in the sustainable development of structure, leadership, and tools innovation lead to brand reputation and business opportunities for sustainable organizational growth.

The organizational management structure not meeting the requirements is leading to low results and efficiency in the economic system. The development of the economic organizational structures requires high institutional quality constantly adapting to technical and social innovations. Boons and Lüdeke-Freund (2013) find that sustainable innovation research neglects how organizations combine value proposition and chain in a financial and business model in the contexts of sustainable organizational, technological and social innovations and propose normative requirements.

Self-organization processes require new intellectual knowledge creatively applied in horizontal cooperation through synergetic processes of a dissipative system between organizations leading to a new development in innovative goods and services and contributing to the growth of the economic system.

Organizational innovation distinguishes between new and old organizational knowledge practices. New ideas that are created, developed, and implemented in the organization spans execution and determination for knowledge, processes, and product development (Damanpour 1996). Organizational change requires information and knowledge based on the performance to design an action plan of intervention to innovate processes, motivate the need to work cohesively, and transfer new knowledge and skills to improve performance.

The staff development based on extensive training based on knowledge, skills, and experience has a positive effect on organizational innovation.

The consistently organizational innovation through small and incremental changes of its processes contribute to the individual and team development and growth to achieve the goals. New and improved organizational and administrative practices, products, and processes innovation are resource mechanisms based on learning and knowledge to benefit employee satisfaction, organizational stability, to create value, and to attain the organizational advantage and performance (Chowhan 2016; Zehir, Üzmez, and Yıldız 2016).

Organizational change and innovation are required to overcome the difficulties to promote changes in values, business models, procedures, leadership, entrepreneurial strategies, and abilities to adapt (Moore & Manring, 2009). Organizations have to adapt continuously to changes and innovations in business models, promote entrepreneurial strategies to achieve the goals (Moore & Manring, 2009).

Knowledge, product, and process innovation positively influence sustainable organizational development performance mediated by organizational innovation (Volberda, Van Den Bosch, and Heij, 2013) influenced by human resource management practices (Tsang and Zahra 2008). Organizations accomplish sustainability by encouraging organizational knowledge, product and processes innovation, and pursuing human resources development.

STRATEGIC ANALYSYS

Strategy plays a relevant role in organizational learning and knowledge which have a significant impact on organizational sustainable development by guiding the organizational activities by the changing internal and external environment and technological changes. Organizational change is also studied from the learning perspective for strategy (Beer et al., 1990; Mintzberg, 1994). Organizational sustainable strategies and policies consider continues organizational learning, training, and development of human resources demanded organizational strategic continuous change to meet the requirements of the external environment (Crossan and Berdrow, 2011; Morais--Storz and Nguyen, 2017) which need continuous information gathering and processing (Pietrzak and Paliszkiewicz, 2013).

Organizational strategies must focus on organizational sustainable development considering the strategies for organizational leadership to foster organizational learning (Goodyear et al., 2014). Strategies of organizational structure aim to be more flexible and humanistic enable to empower the workers who in turn have an impact on organizational learning and development (Ahadi, 2011; Martínez-Leon and Martínez-García, 2011).

The institutional setting of organizational sustainable development change corresponds to organizational learning processes and the institutionalization of structures, processes, and strategies of transformation. Identifying emerging sustainability trends and learning sustainable development competencies must be the outcome of a collaboration strategy between all the involved stakeholders including local communities and NGOs.

Organizational knowledge enables management to develop strategies and policies to tackle the challenges and to maintain control over its practices and procedures (Hill & Bowen 1997). Bianchi (2016) proposes a conceptual, theoretical, and methodological framework on organizational policy to assess and manage organizational sustainable development performance.

Organizational learning and culture strategies harmonize organizational culture and its impact on organizational sustainable development (Jahmurataj, 2015, Danish et al., 2015; Martin, 2014). Knowledge and skills development as a core competency of the organization being its workforce can focus on a strategy of longevity through continuous innovation.

Although the relationship between organizational strategies and organizational learning is not very clear (Hotho et al., 2015), both seem to be moderated and mediated by the support of leadership, organizational culture, structure, and technology (Goodyear et al., 2014) since they are related to activities carried out and linked to the organizational goals. Leadership commitment and a sense of belonging with capabilities affect organizational creativity and innovation. A motivation and reward system with an experimentation component affects the organizational ability to innovate.

Evaluating the outcomes of the goals set, organizational strategies can be adjusted depending upon the internal and external environmental changes in such a way that this practice has strong links with organizational learning, knowledge management, and sustainable organizational development.

CONCLUSION

There are strategic implications that the organizational culture has on organizational transfer of knowledge, learning organizations, and organizational innovation. Organizational sustainable development must be supported by organizational culture, organizational knowledge, and learning management to conduct organizational change interventions and should be a focal goal in its strategic organizational development planning. Organizations need to develop a culture of organizational learning and knowledge sharing management to enhance the organizational competitive advantage and performance leading to improve organizational sustainable development.

The components of the learning organization have a direct impact on organizational innovation. Organizational knowledge transfer creates a competitive advantage as resources of learning organizations have an effect on change organizational culture towards a more oriented organizational innovation.

Learning organization and organizational innovation are two components of organizations needed to develop a transparent vision of organizational change to all the stakeholders increasing their commitment and accountability and accelerating and improve their goals. Organizations must adapt and implement management systems and well-structured regulations in learning and knowledge systems based on the constructivist theory and supported by information technology, involving all the stakeholders in knowledge sharing to improve the corporate learning culture in the workplace for securing sustainable organizational development.

Organizational leadership must provide the appropriate motivational, spiritual and material rewards to creative and innovative ideas as well as the empowerment of individuals and teams through applied knowledge sharing, development, increase of intellectual capital, training, and staffing creativity and innovation. Appropriate motivational rewards, fair promotion, and pay systems are factors that stimulate organizational creativity and innovation.

Networking contributes to linking cooperation to facilitate learning, knowledge, and innovation, share resources, and economic, technical, and social solutions increasing the potential for the implementation y coordination of sustainable organizational development initiatives. Organizational development leads to resources consumption in consuming work while in regenerative work, resources become regenerated and grow, thus creating a foundation for individual and organizational sustainable development (Docherty et al., 2002). Individuals and organizations can sustainably develop creating resources to deal with future challenges.

REFERENCES

Adcock, A. (2012). Cognitive dissonance in the learning processes. *Encycl. Sci. Learning,* 588–590.

Aggerholm, H. K., Anderson, S. E., & Thomsen, C. (2011). Conceptualising employer branding in sustainable organizations. *Corporate Communication: An International Journal, 16*(2), 105–123. doi:10.1108/13563281111141642

Aghajani, H. A., Samadi Mirakalei, H., & Samadi Myrkalei, H. (2015). The relationship between entrepreneurship and characteristics of a learning organization. *Management Efficiency, 35*(9), 39-64.

Alalwan, A. A., Dwivedi, Y. K., Rana, N. P., & Williams, M. D. (2016). Consumer adoption of mobile banking in Jordan: Examining the role of usefulness, ease of use, perceived risk and self-efficacy. *Journal of Enterprise Information Management, 29*(1), 118–139. doi:10.1108/JEIM-04-2015-0035

Alhabeeb, A., & Rowley, J. (2017). Critical success factors for eLearning in Saudi Arabian universities. *International Journal of Educational Management, 31*(2), 131–147. doi:10.1108/IJEM-01-2016-0006

Alsabbagh, M., & Khalil, A. H. (2016). The impact of leadership styles on organizational learning (an empirical study on the education sector in Damascus city). *International Journal of Academic Research in Business & Social Sciences, 6*(5), 197–217. doi:10.6007/IJARBSS/v6-i5/2126

Alvani, S. M. (2008). *Public Administration*. Ney Publications.

Angelis, C. T. (2016). The impact of national culture and knowledge management on governmental intelligence. *Journal of Modelling in Management, 11*(1), 240–268. doi:10.1108/JM2-08-2014-0069

Argyris, C. (1998). Organizational behavior: Production of knowledge for action in the world of practice. In J. McKelvey & M. Neufeld (Eds.), *Industrial relations at the dawn of the new millennium* (pp. 54–61). New York State School of Industrial and Labor Relations.

Attwell, G. (2010). Work-based mobile learning environments: Contributing to a socio-cultural ecology of mobile learning. *International Journal of Mobile and Blended Learning, 2*(4), 19–34. doi:10.4018/jmbl.2010100102

Atwood, M. A., Mora, J. W., & Kaplan, A. W. (2010). Learning to lead: Evaluating leadership and organizational learning. *Leadership and Organization Development Journal, 31*(7), 576–595. doi:10.1108/01437731011079637

Bandura, A. (2002). Social cognitive theory in cultural context. *Applied Psychology, 51*(2), 269–290. doi:10.1111/1464-0597.00092

Barney, J. (1991). Firm resources and sustained competitive advantage. *Journal of Management, 17*(1), 99–120. doi:10.1177/014920639101700108

Baumgartner, R. J., & Korhonen, J. (2010). Strategic thinking for sustainable development. International Sustainable Development Research Society, 18, 71-75.

Becker, J. (2010). Use of backcasting to integrate indicators with principles of sustainability. *International Journal of Sustainable Development World, 17*(3), 189–197. doi:10.1080/13504501003726974

Beer, M., Eisenstat, R. A., & Spector, B. (1990). *The Critical Path to Corporate Renewal.* Harvard Business School Press.

Belle, S. (2016). Organizational Learning? Look Again. *The Learning Organization, 23*(5), 332–341. doi:10.1108/TLO-01-2016-0007

Bennis, W., Benne, K., & Chin, R. (1985). *The Planning of Change.* International Thompson Publishing.

Bianchi, C. (2012). Enhancing performance management and sustainable organizational growth through system-dynamics modelling. In *Systemic management for intelligent organizations* (pp. 143–161). Springer Berlin Heidelberg. doi:10.1007/978-3-642-29244-6_8

Bianchi, C. (2016). Fostering Sustainable Organizational Development Through Dynamic Performance Management. In *Dynamic Performance Management. System Dynamics for Performance Management* (Vol. 1). Springer. doi:10.1007/978-3-319-31845-5_3

Birmingham, U. o. (2015). *Learning Theories, Stages and Styles.* University of Birmingham.

Boons, F., & Lüdeke-Freund, F. (2013). Business models for sustainable innovation: State-of-the-art and steps towards a research agenda. *Journal of Cleaner Production, 45*(April), 9–19. doi:10.1016/j.jclepro.2012.07.007

Boonstra, J. J., & Elving, W. J. L. (2009) Veranderen als kunstje, kunde of kunst. In Communicatiemanagement in praktisch perspectief. Assen: Van Gorcum. Blz.

Bovaird, T. (2007). Beyond engagement and participation: User and community coproduction of public services. *Public Administration Review, 67*(5), 846–860. doi:10.1111/j.1540-6210.2007.00773.x

Broniarczyk, S. M., & Alba, J. W. (1994). The importance of the brand in brand extension. *JMR, Journal of Marketing Research, 31*(2), 214–228. doi:10.1177/002224379403100206

Brulin, G., & Svensson, L. (2012). *Managing Sustainable Development Programmes: A Learning Approach to Change.* Gower Publishing.

Chinta, R., & Kloppenborg, T. J. (2010). Projects and processes for sustainable organizational growth. *S.A.M. Advanced Management Journal, 75*(2), 22.

Choo, Chun Wei (2001). Knowing Organization as Learning Organization. *Education + Training, 43*(4/5), 197-205.

Chowhan, J. (2016). Unpacking the black box: Understanding the relation-ship between strategy, HRM practices, innovation and organizational performance. *Human Resource Management Journal, 26*(2), 112–133. doi:10.1111/1748-8583.12097

Coetzer, A., Kock, H., & Wallo, A. (2017). Distinctive characteristics of small businesses assites for informal learning. *Human Resource Development Review*, 18–32.

Commission on Environment and Development. (1987). *World Commission on Environment and Development* (Brundtland Report). Available from: http://www.ace.mmu.ac.uk/ eae/Sustainability/Older/Brundtland_Report.html

Crossan, M., Lane, H. W., & White, R. E. (1999). An organizational learning framework: From intuition to institution. *Academy of Management Review, 24*(3), 522–537. doi:10.5465/amr.1999.2202135

Crossan, M. M., & Berdrow, I. (2011). Organizational learning and strategic renewal. *Strategic Management Journal, 24*(11), 1087–1105. doi:10.1002mj.342

Csikszentmihalyi, M., (2015). Society, culture, and person: a systems view of creativity. *Syst. Model Creativity, 47*–61.

Cummings, T. G., & Worley, C. G. (2014). *Organization development and change.* Cengage Learning.

Daily, B. F., Bishop, J. W., & Massoud, J. A. (2012). The role of training and empowerment in environmental performance: A study of the Mexican maquiladora industry. *International Journal of Operations & Production Management, 32*(5).

Damanpour, F. (1996). Organizational Complexity and Innovation Developing and Testing Multiple Contingency Models. *Management Science, 42*, 693–716.

Danish, R. Q., Munir, Y., Kausar, A., Jabbar, M., & Munawar, N. (2015). Impact of change, culture and organizational politics on organizational learning. *Rev. Contemp. Bus.Res, 3*(1), 115–126.

Dicle, Ü., & Okan, R.Y. (2015). The relationship between organizational structure andorganizational learning in Turkish automotive R&D companies. *Int. J. Manag. Stud. Res.*, 62–71.

Docherty, P., Forslin, J., Shani, A. B., & Kira, M. (2002) Emerging Work Systems: From Intensive to Sustainable? In Creating Sustainable Work Systems: Perspectives and Practices. London: Routledge.

Egbu, C. O. (2004). Managing knowledge and intellectual capital for improved organizational innovations in the construction industry: An examination of critical success factors. *Engineering, Construction, and Architectural Management, 11*(5), 301–315. doi:10.1108/09699980410558494

Ehsani Ghods, H., & Sayed Abbas Zadeh, M. M. (2012). Relationship between learning organization with creativity and innovation, a high school teacher and colleges. *Journal-Research New Approaches in Educational Administration. Islamic Azad University of Shiraz, 4,* 12–21.

Ellström, P.-E. (2001). Integrating learning and work: Conceptual issues and critical conditions. *Human Resource Development Quarterly, 12*(4), 421–435.

Elving, W. J. (2005). The role of communication in organisational change. *Corporate Communications, 10*(2), 129–138. doi:10.1108/13563280510596943

Foss, N. J., & Lyngsie, J. (2011). *The Emerging Strategic Entrepreneurship Field: Origins.* Academic Press.

Friedman, S., Scholink, E., & Cocking, R. (1987). *Blue prints for thinking: The role of planning in cognitive development.* CambriDge Univ. Press.

Geertshuis, S., Holmes, M., Geertshuis, H., Clancy, D., & Bristol, A. (2002). Evaluation of workplace learning. *Journal of Workplace Learning, 14*(1), 11–18.

Gomes, G., & Wojahn, R. M. (2017). Organizational learning capability, innovation and performance. *Revista ADM, 52,* 163–175.

Goodyear, M., Ames-Oliver, K., & Russell, K. (2014). *Organizational Strategies for Fostering a Culture of Learning.* University of Kansas.

Gupta, A. (2008). Earth on fire: Implications for corporate responsibility. *American Journal of Business, 23*(1), 3–4.

Han, S. H., Kim, D. Y., Jang, H. S., & Choi, S. (2010). Strategies for contractors to sustain growth in the global construction market. *Habitat International, 34*(1), 1–10. doi:10.1016/j.habitatint.2009.04.003

Han, Y. J., Nunes, J. C., & Dreze, X. (2010). Signaling status *with* luxury goods: *The* role *of* brand prominence. *Journal of Marketing, 74*(4), 15–30. doi:10.1509/jmkg.74.4.015

Haslam, S. A. (1997). Stereotyping and social influence: Foundations of stereotype consensus. In R. Spears, P. J. Oakes, N. Ellemers, & S. A. Haslam (Eds.), *The social psychology of stereotyping and group life* (pp. 119–143). Blackwell.

Heckscher, Ch. (1994). *Defining the post-bureaucratic type*. Sage.

Hill, R. C., & Bowen, P. A. (1997). Sustainable construction: Principles and a framework for attainment. *Construction Management and Economics, 15*(3), 223–239. doi:10.1080/014461997372971

Hirschhorn, L. (1988). *The workplace within: Psychodynamics of organizational life*. The Mit Press. doi:10.7551/mitpress/7306.001.0001

Holbrook, M. B., & Hirschman, E. C. (1982). The experiential aspects of consumption: Consumer fantasies, feelings, and fun. *The Journal of Consumer Research, 9*(2), 132–140. doi:10.1086/208906

Hotho, J.J., & Lyles, M.A. (2015). The mutual impact of global strategy and organizational learning: current themes and future directions. *Glob. Strat. J.*, 85–112.

Hoveida, R. (2007). *Investigating the relationship between learning the components of the organization and improving the quality of education the door* (Master's thesis). Governmental Universities of Isfahan Province and Presentation of Student University Model, University of Isfahan.

Hoverstadt, P., & Bowling, D. (2005). Organisational Viability as a factor in Sustainable. *International Journal of Technology Management and Sustainable Development, 4*(2), 131–146.

Jahmurataj, V. (2015). Impact of Culture on Organizational Development: Case Study Kosovo. *Academic Journal of Interdisciplinary Studies, 4*(2), 206–210. doi:10.5901/ajis.2015.v4n2s1p206

Järvinen, A., & Poikela, E. (2001). Modelling Reflective and Contextual Learning at Work. *Journal of Workplace Learning, 13*(7/8), 282-289.

Ji, L., Huang, J., Liu, Z., Zhu, H., & Cai, Z. (2011). The effects of employee training on the relationship between environmental attitude and firms' performance in sustainable development. *International Journal of Human Resource Management, 23*(14), 2995–3008. doi:10.1080/09585192.2011.637072

Kanter, R. M. (2008). *Men and women of the corporation: New edition*. Basic Books.

Keller, K. L. (1987). Memory factors in advertising: The effect of advertising retrieval cues on brand evaluations. *The Journal of Consumer Research, 14*(3), 316–333. doi:10.1086/209116

Kerr, I.R. (2006). Leadership strategies for sustainable SME operation. *Business Strategy and the Environment, 15*(1), 30-39.

Kouhkan, A., & Mousavi, S. A. (2015). Review the relationship between the components of the organization Learner and Organizational innovation) Case study: (FreeUniversity of Mazandaran) *First International Conference on Economics, Management, Accounting, Social Sciences.*

Liebowitz, J. (2010). The role of HR in achieving a sustainability culture. *Journal of Sustainable Development, 3*(4), 50-57.

Lopez-Cabrales, A., Pérez-Luño, A., & Cabrera, R.V. (2009). Knowledge as amediator between HRM practices and innovative activity. *Hum Resour Manage., 48*(4), 485–503. doi: 48:4113 doi:10.1002/hrm.v

Love, A. (1991). *Internal evaluation. Building organizations from within.* Sage.

March, J. G. (1981). Footnotes to organizational change. *Administrative Science Quarterly, 26*(4), 563–577. doi:10.2307/2392340

Marshall, N. (2007). Cognitive and practice-based theories of organisational knowing andlearning: incompatible or complementary? In *Proceedings of OLKC Learning Fusion.* University of Brighton.

Martínez-Leon, I. M., & Martínez-García, J. A. (2011). The influence of organizationalstructure on organizational learning. *International Journal of Manpower, 32*(5), 537–566. doi:10.1108/01437721111158198

Mehrabi, J., Soltani, I., Alemzadeh, M., & Jadidi, M. (2013). Explaining the relationship between organizational structure and dimensions of learning organizations (case study: Education organization in Boroojerd county and the related departments). *International Journal of Academic Research in Business & Social Sciences*, 116–129.

Mintzberg, H. (1994). *The Rise and Fall of Strategic Planning: Reconceiving Roles for Planning, Plans, Planners.* The Free Press.

Moon, H., Ruona, W., & Valentine, T. (2017). Organizational strategic learning capability: Exploring the dimensions. *European Journal of Training and Development, 41*(3), 222–240. doi:10.1108/EJTD-08-2016-0061

Moore, S. B., & Manring, S. L. (2009). Strategy development in small and medium sized enterprises for sustainability and increased value creation. *Journal of Cleaner Production, 17*(2), 276–282. doi:10.1016/j.jclepro.2008.06.004

Morais-Storz, M., & Nguyen, N. (2017). The role of unlearning in metamorphosis and strategic resilience. *The Learning Organization, 24*(2), 93–106. doi:10.1108/ TLO-12-2016-0091

Mumford, M. D., Michelle, E., Higgs, T. C., & McIntosh, T. (2017). Cognitive skills and leadership performance: The nine critical skills. *The Leadership Quarterly, 28*(1), 24–39. doi:10.1016/j.leaqua.2016.10.012

Osterloh, M., & Frey, B. S. (2000). Motivation, knowledge transfer, and organizational forms. *Organization Science, 11*(5), 538–550. doi:10.1287/orsc.11.5.538.15204

Patra, R. (2008). Vaastu Shastra: Towards sustainable development. *Sustainable Development Journal, 17*(4), 244–256. doi:10.1002d.388

Patton, M. (1997). *Utilization-focused Evaluation*. Sage.

Patton, M. (1998). Discovering Process Use. *Evaluation, 4*(2), 225-233.

Pfeffer, J. (2010). Building sustainable organizations: The human factor. *The Academy of Management Perspectives, 24*(1), 34–45.

Phillips, L. (2007). Go green to gain the edge over rivals. *People Management*, p. 9. Available at: www2.cipd.co.uk/pm/peoplemanagement/b/weblog/ archive/2013/01/29/ gogreentogaintheedgeoverrivals-2007-08.aspx

Pietrzak, M., & Paliszkiewicz, J. (2013). *Framework of Strategic Learning: the PDCA Cycle*. Warsaw University of Life Sciences.

Postmes, T. (2003). A social identity approach to communication in organizations. *Social Identity at Work: Developing Theory for Organizational Practice, 81*, 191-203.

Rahimian, H., Zamaneh, M. P., Ahmadpour, M., & Piri, M. (2014). A study of the relationship between empowerment and organizational learning among employees of gas transmission company. *J. Life Sci. Biomed, 4*(6), 550–556.

Renwick, D., Redman, T., & Maguire, S. (2013). Green human resource management: A review, process model, and research agenda. *International Journal of Management Reviews, 15*(1), 1–14. doi:10.1111/j.1468-2370.2011.00328.x

Rimanoczy, I., & Pearson, T. (2010). Role of HR in the new world of sustainability. *Industrial and Commercial Training, 42*(1), 11–17. doi:10.1108/00197851011013661

Roberts, K. H., & O'Reilly, C. A. (1974). Failures in upward communication in organizations: Three possible culprits. *Academy of Management Journal, 17*(2), 205–215.

Saadat, V., & Saadat, Z. (2016). Organizational learning as a key role of organizational success. *Procedia: Social and Behavioral Sciences, 230*(12), 219–225. doi:10.1016/j.sbspro.2016.09.028

Schein, E. (1996). Kurt Lewin's Change Theory in the field and in the classroom: Notes toward a model of managed learning. *Systems Practice, 9*(1), 27–47. doi:10.1007/BF02173417

Schmiedinger, B., Valentin, K., & Stephan, E. (2005). Competence based business development-organizational competencies as basis for successful companies. *Journal of Universal Knowledge Management, 1*, 13–20.

Sedighi, M. (2016). Application of word co-occurrence analysis method in mapping of the scientific fields (case study: The field of Informetrics). *Computer Science. Library Review*. Advance online publication. doi:10.1108/LR-07-2015-0075

Sharp, C. (2001). *Evaluation of Organizational learning intervention and Communities of Practice*. Paper presented in Australasian Evaluation Society Conference, Canberra.

Siebenhüner, B., & Arnold, M. (2007). Organizational learning to manage sustainable development. *Business Strategy and the Environment, 16*(5), 339–353. doi:10.1002/bse.579

Simao, L. B. (2016). External relationships in the organizational innovation. *RAI Revista de Administração e Inovação, 13*(3), 156–165. doi:10.1016/j.rai.2016.06.002

Sonnichsen, R. (2000). *High Impact Internal Evaluation. A Practitioner's Guide to Evaluating and Consulting Inside Organizations*. Sage. doi:10.4135/9781483328485

Tauber, E. M. (1981). Brand franchise extension: New product benefits from existing brand names. *Business Horizons, 24*(2), 36–41. doi:10.1016/0007-6813(81)90144-0

Teixeira, A. A., Jabbour, C. J. C., & de Sousa Jabbour, A. B. L. (2012). Relationship between green management and environmental training in companies located in Brazil: A theoretical framework and case studies. *International Journal of Production Economics, 140*(1), 318–329. doi:10.1016/j.ijpe.2012.01.009

Thakker, D. R. (2011). Culture and cognitive theory: Toward a reformulation. *Cult. Cog. Psychopathol, 3*, 53–71.

Thomas, K. W., & Velthouse, B. A. (1990). Cognitive elements of empowerment: An "interpretive" model of intrinsic task motivation. *Academy of Management Review, 15*(4), 666–681.

Tomasello, M. (2010). *Culture and Cognitive Development*. Institute of Evolutionary Anthropology.

Tran, Q., & Tian, Y. (2013). Organizational structure: Influencing factors and impact on a firm. *Am. J. Ind. Bus. Manag, 3*(02), 229–236. doi:10.4236/ajibm.2013.32028

Tucker, M. L., Meyer, G. D., & Westerman, J. W. (1996). Organizational communication: Development of internal strategic competitive advantage. *The Journal of Business Communication, 33*(1), 51-69.

Van de Ven, A. H., Angle, H. L., & Poole, M. S. (Eds.). (2000). *Research on the Management of Innovation: The Minnesota Studies*. Oxford University Press.

Vansina, L. (1988). The general manager and organizational leadership. In M. Lambrechts (Ed.), *Corporate revival: Managing into the nineties*. University Press.

Volberda, H. W., Van Den Bosch, F. A., & Heij, C. V. (2013). Management innovation: Management as fertile ground for innovation. *European Management Review, 10*(1), 1–15. doi:10.1111/emre.12007

Wiig, K. (2002). Knowledge management in Public Administration. *Journal of Knowledge Management, 6*(3), 224-239.

Wong, P. S. (2012). *Drucker's Knowledge-Worker Productivity Theory: A Practitioner's Approach to Integrating Organisational Work Processes with Drucker's Six Major Factors Determining Knowledge-Worker Productivity*. Southern Cross University.

Xiaomi, A., & Wang, W. (2010). Knowledge management technologies and applications: a literature review. IEEE, 138–144.

Zehir, C., Üzmez, A., & Yıldız, H. (2016). The effect of SHRM practices on innovation performance: The mediating role of global capabilities. *Procedia: Social and Behavioral Sciences, 235*, 797–806. doi:10.1016/j.sbspro.2016.11.088

Zoogah, D. B. (2011). The dynamics of green HRM behaviors: a cognitive social information processing approach, *Zeitschrift Für Personalforschung/German Journal of Research in Human Resource Management, 25*(2), 117-139.

KEY TERMS AND DEFINITIONS

Innovation: Is to use knowledge to build a new one.

Knowledge Transfer: Knowledge transfer (TC) is the set of activities aimed at the dissemination of knowledge, experience, and skills in order to facilitate the use, application and exploitation of knowledge and R&D capabilities of the university outside the scope academic by other institutions.

Learning Organizations: Is one that facilitates learning for all its members, sharing information globally and undergoing continuous transformation in itself. The learning company changes the culture of the company, whatever its activity or structure.

Organizational Culture: It is the set of beliefs, habits, values, attitudes and traditions of the members of a company.

Sustainable Organizational Development: Sustainable organizational development focuses on value creation, environmental management, environmentally friendly production systems and the formation of human capital, social responsibility is linked to transparency, dialogue with stakeholders and care for the environment and the social inclusion.

Strategy: It is the direction or orientation that is given to the internal resources of an organization depending on the demands of its environment and surroundings to develop a competitive advantage that allows it to survive, lead, etc.

Chapter 6

The Utility of Neuro-Economics in the Services of ICT of the Exponential SMEs of the Artisanal Industry of Women Entrepreneurs in Mexico

Jovanna Nathalie Cervantes-Guzmán
University of Guadalajara, Mexico

ABSTRACT

The chapter explores the utility of neuroeconomics in decision making and behavior. Scientific knowledge will be advanced in the need for the application of neuroeconomics focused on one of the services of the information and communication technologies (ICT) of companies that is e-commerce of exponential artisanal SMEs of women entrepreneurs by developing a proposal for a business model to increase the possibility of growth of their companies at the level national and international level. The methodology used was deductive, exploratory, descriptive, correlational, and documentary. Neuroeconomics have the potential to explain the phenomena that are considered as a deviation from the prediction or behavioral bias of decision-making models in economic theory. The study up to this point is quantitative using primary and secondary sources for research.

DOI: 10.4018/978-1-7998-6453-0.ch006

INTRODUCTION

Neuroeconomics is an emerging discipline that combines the findings and modeling tools of neuroscience, psychology and economics to explain the behavior of human choice (Glimcher, 2003).

The aspects in neuroeconomics that propose a new significant episode of change, according to Glimcher and Rustichini (2004) are:

- Integration of behavioral work carried out by economists, psychologists and neuroscientists, for the development of a unified theory of the choice of behavior.
- Technological advances that allow us to look at the brain will eventually replace the simple mathematical ideas of economics with more detailed neuronal descriptions.

Within the framework of the above considerations, SMEs in Mexico constitute 95% of established companies and contribute 23% to Gross Internal Product, but they have a series of problems that cause 75% to close their operations after 2 years in the market (INEGI, 2010), and its chance of success is on average from 25% to 30% below the world average that is 40% (Fernández, 2010). It is appropriate to highlight that 47% directed by the female gender, contributing 37% of GIP, also contribute 70% of GIP and allocate 70% of their income to the community and family (González, 2016). Despite this, Latin America has the highest rate of business failure run by women. In Mexico alone, 2.2 million formal companies 17.63% are directed by the female gender, in addition, that 50% have a profit of less than $ 50,000 USD compared to 25% of the companies that operate men (Power & Magnoni, 2010).

According to the United Nations Educational, Scientific and Cultural Organization (UNESCO, 2001), it states that the artisanal sector has a predominant role in economic development and the fight against poverty, but they lack a long way to go to achieve its maximum potential in generating employment and income to achieve greater economic growth in developing countries. The artisanal sector has great untapped potential in e-commerce that can generate a greater amount of income and jobs that produce a social and economic impact on entrepreneurs worldwide and especially women (Foote, 2015).

The objective in the research using neuroeconomics, a model proposal focused on understanding consumer decision-making on one of the services of the information and communication technologies of companies focus in electronic commerce of exponential artisanal SMEs of women entrepreneurs will be developed.

BACKGROUND

Statement of the Problem

According to the International Telecommunication Union (2015), internet is used by 43.3% of the world's population, which corresponds to 3,200 million Internet users. Companies use ICT as a new channel for the dissemination of products and/or services, appearing a second group of ICT services formed by the electronic commerce which is a mode of remote purchases through a network of telecommunication's that has increased its potential by adapting people with new technologies. The way in which internet has increased its penetration in the online market has caused changes in the way in which business interacts with consumers, developing e-commerce causing companies to increase the total number of sales and an increase in online retail interactions of consumers (VanderMeer, et al, 2001). The number of digital buyers worldwide is rapidly expanding from 1,32 billion in 2014 to 1,66 billion in 2017 and is expected to increase to 2,14 billion in 2021 (Statista, 2018). What translates into an increase in electronic sales of retailers globally from 2014 in 1.336 billion dollars to 2,290 billion dollars in 2017 and an increase in 4,479 billion dollars is forecast for 2021 (Statistica, 2018). With a participation in retail e-commerce 2016 in the Asia and the Pacific regions with 12.1%, Eastern Europe with 8.3%, North America with 8.1%, Central and Eastern Europe with 3.4% and Latin America with 1.9% (Statista, 2018).

The increase in online shopping has transformed the internet into a powerful force, being a tool that has a great influence on consumer behavior (McGaughey & Mason, 1998), modified the way the individual acquires a product by the large amount of information that it provides, making it easier for the potential client to evaluate the products and services of different suppliers, which modifies the traditional buying behavior (Koufaris, 2003). Because it allows the purchase through crossed channels, this together with the development of technological characteristics such as the search for information, the evaluation of the different alternatives offered and the realization of the purchase (Constantinides, 2004).

In order to increase the number of consumers and their conversion rate, it is necessary to understand online consumer behavior to improve their shopping experience and satisfaction (Zhang, et al, 2011). Consumer behavior in the traditional market is different from its purchasing behavior in electronic commerce, with the information of this limited and poorly studied (Denis, et al, 2009) in terms of making the purchase decision (Brynjolfsson, et al, 2010) being the void of literature that focuses on this research. Increasing theoretical knowledge in the decision-making process in this area is crucial, and this can be explored by developing a new behavior model (Rickwood & White, 2009).

Electronic commerce offers great potential for the expansion of companes to international markets by intensifying the sales power by creating a new distribution channel to reach new customers, develop their own marketing strategies and produce new business opportunities (Colvee 2013). In addition, e-commerce is a powerful tool that allows SMEs to move faster in the development phases by positioning the company in the world market (Hussain, 2013). The proper management of electronic commerce will allow artisanal SMEs to increase their competitiveness (Aragon & Rubio, 2005) in a sector where, despite their significant participation and their annual growth rate of over 4%, they have not been able to increase it (FONART, 2009).

One of the big problems for the integration of SMEs in e-commerce is to achieve efficiency in electronic platforms due to ignorance of customer behavior in decision making (Sacristan, 2013).

In the context of the above considerations, SMEs in Mexico constitute 95% of established companies and contribute 23% to GIP, but they have a series of problems that cause 75% to close their operations after 2 years in the market (INEGI, 2009), and its chance of success is on average from 25% to 30% below the world average which is 40% (Fernández, 2010). At the international level, the percentage of survival and the half-life of SMEs is similar in countries such as Spain, where more than 70% does not exceed 4 years of life and 80% of SMEs fail within the first 5 years, in the United States of America 30% of SMEs do not reach the third year and have an average life of 6 years and in the underdeveloped countries only the first 3 years of life survive between 50% and 75%.

Artisanal SMEs are a great engine of the economy where 47% are directed by the female gender, contributing 37% of GIP, they also allocate 70% of their income to the community and the family unlike men who contribute only between 30% and 40% (González, 2016). Despite this, Latin America has the highest rate of business failures managed by women. In Mexico, only 2,2 million formal companies 17.63% are directed by the female gender, in addition, that 50% have a profit of less than $ 50,000 USD against 25% of the companies that operate men (Power & Magnoni, 2010) .

The artisanal sector is a global creative economy, which represents what can be exemplified as a country that would symbolize the fourth largest economy and labor force in the world according to the Inter-American Development Bank (IDB). It is a global industry that generates revenues of $ 34 billion per year, and only developing countries provide 64% of global exports. According to the United Nations Organization for Education, Science and Culture (UNESCO, 2001), it states that the artisanal sector has a predominant role in economic development and in the fight against poverty. In addition, preferences in market consumption are changing because they care about the origin of the product, which they produce and how it was manufactured, changing their preferences for mass-produced products at hand, the only one of its kind and independent design (INDEGO Africa, 2016). They have a long way to go to achieve their full potential in employment and income generation to achieve greater economic growth in developing countries.

Justification

The artisanal sector has great untapped potential in electronic commerce that can generate a greater amount of income and jobs that produce a social and economic impact on entrepreneurs around the world and especially women (Foote, 2015). This can be achieved through the use of neuroeconomics, which is an emerging discipline that combines the findings and tools of modeling neuroscience, psychology and economics to explain the behavior of human choice; neuroscience provides tools to answer questions of economic models that cannot be explained; and economics contributes to neuroscience decision models to examine the mechanisms of communication between brain circuits (Glimcher, 2003).

Scientific knowledge will be advanced in the need for the application of neuroeconomics in the e-commerce of exponential artisanal SMEs of women entrepreneurs, having the potential to explain the phenomena that are considered as deviation from the prediction or behavioral bias of the models of decision making to achieve the increase of its market on a larger scale and its growth regardless of its size and location.

The study will be designed with the theme of women entrepreneurs of exponential artisanal SMEs certified internationally by the NGO "Women Owned". First, it will conduct a survey of young millennials that are 80% of the people who buy in e-commerce. The results will allow to improve electronic commerce through neuroeconomics techniques to increase the possibility of growing their businesses nationally and internationally.

The variables of the research were formed by the review of literature based on PhD thesis and an article focused on neuro-correlation in decision-making, the online consumer decision-making process, the intention to purchase the consumer in the online purchasing environment, neuroeconomic studies in decision-making and the role of emotions in decision-making through a cognitive approach to neuroeconomics.

MAIN FOCUS OF THE CHAPTER

Matrix of Operationalization of the Variables

Theme	General objective	General research question	Specific objectives	Research questions	Variables	Hypothesis	Methodological analysis
Proposal for the utility of neuro-economics in the services of ICT of the exponential SMES of the artisanal industry of women entrepreneurs in Mexico.	Develop a proposal for a theoretical model that evaluated the behavior in the decision making of the consumer in e-commerce of exponential Mexican artisanal SMEs directed by women entrepreneurs	How can we develop a theoretical model that evaluated behavior in the decision making of the consumer in the e-Commerce of exponential Mexican artisanal SMEs run by women entrepreneurs?	Examine the factors that expose the relationship between decision making and consumer behavior in e-commerce	What are the factors that expose the relationship between decision making and consumer behavior in e-commerce?	Characteristics of the website	The characteristics of the website have a positive relationship with the intention to purchase	Descriptive and inferential statistics
			Expose the economic context of artisanal SMEs and the challenges of gender equity in developing countries	How is the economic context of artisanal SMEs and the challenges of gender equity in developing countries?	ConsumerConsumer	characteristicscharacteristics have a positive relationship with the intention to purchase	Descriptive and inferential statistics
			Analyze from a quantitative perspective the point of view of millennial consumer, their behavior for decision-making in the e-commerce of exponential Mexican artisanal SMEs directed by enterprising women	How is a millennial consumer point of view from a quantitative perspective, their behavior for decision making in the e-commerce of exponential Mexican artisanal SMEs directed by enterprising women?	Characteristics of the brand	The characteristics of the brand have a positive relationship with the intention to purchase	Descriptive and inferential statistics
					Purchase intention		Statistics inferential

Source: Own elaboration

LITERATURE REVIEW

Artisanal SMEs in the Economic Context of the Countries

According to the United Nations Educational, Scientific and Cultural Organization (UNESCO), artisanal products have characteristics that define them as their usefulness, esthetic a, artistic, creative, link to culture, decoration, functionality, traditional, symbolic and significantly social (Etienne-Nugue, 2009).

Artisanal SMEs in Developing Countries

After agriculture, the artisanal sector is the second employer in developing countries, mostly made up of women who perform traditional handicrafts to obtain economic resources. These countries have a competitive advantage because of their cultural traditions, artisanal skills and specialized raw materials (Foote, 2015).

The artisanal sector is a global creative economy, it can be exemplified by representing it as a country that would symbolize the fourth largest economy and labor force in the world according to the Inter-American Development Bank (IDB). It is a global industry that generates revenues of $ 34 billion a year, with only developing countries providing 64% of exports worldwide. According to the United Nations Educational, Scientific and Cultural Organization (UNESCO, 2001), it states that the artisanal sector has a predominant role in economic development and the fight against poverty. In addition, preferences in market consumption are changing because they care about the origin of the product, who made it and how it was manufactured, changing their preferences for mass-produced products to the handmade, the only one of its kind and independent design (INDEGO AFRICA, 2016).

Handcrafts SMEs in Mexico

In Mexico, handicrafts are the main economic-cultural item in terms of production, the generation of renumbered work with 43% dedicated to the manufacture of handicrafts, and a total cultural expenditure of 37.7%, is an industry which generates 122 million pesos, which is represented in terms of a GIP 1.3 higher than that of agriculture (INEGI, 2012).

In the current economic context caused by the economic crisis and unemployment, the relevance of artisanal SMEs that produce garments, household goods and objects with various uses has increased (Sandoval & Guerra, 2010). These productions are integrated by the various fields of human, cultural, social, educational and economic development, the latter being the development of a business (Hernández-Girón, et al, 2007).

Challenges of Gender Equity in the Business World

Companies that have greater gender equity increase their results causing higher levels of growth and performance; this paradigm shift according to the report on the Principles of Empowerment of Women in Businesses published by the UN Women (2016) are:

- Women are key economic agents that produce prosperity, employment, innovation and are an engine of development. The greater the number of women belonging to the Economically Active Population (EAP) the economy increases because it leads to greater social mobility with benefit in the family, community and society.
- There is a positive correlation between business activity and GIP growth. Productivity in Latin America and the Caribbean could increase by 25% if female entrepreneurship is supported.
- The use of female talent would produce benefits for companies such as creativity, efficiency and business efficiency, and improvement of business management.
- Companies with a greater presence of women tend to develop corporate social responsibility and diversity schemes in philanthropic work, which leads to an improvement in the brand image, customer loyalty, recruitment of professional talent, and increased productivity.

In countries where there is a greater number of women entrepreneurs there is greater economic growth, in contrast to countries where it is restricted there is a stagnant economy, there is also an impact on the social environment (UNIDO, 2011). In spite of this, there are currently twice as much male as female entrepreneurship (Reynolds, et al, 2002).

The female gender decides to undertake to obtain their own income, develop an innovative idea, move up in their work careers, flexibility between work, family (Heller, 2010) and by necessity this being a factor that has a direct relationship between the level of development and the business development rate generating a correlation between the developing countries that have a higher rate as opposed to the more developed countries have a lower rate showing a concordance between the levels of low economic remuneration and the creation of a company developed by women (ECLAC, 2004).

Entrepreneurs from Developing Countries

Research in emerging countries by the National Foundation for Women Business Owners (NFWBO) found that women who own business have common characteristics regardless of the business, its establishment, administration, operation, and goals differs from that of the male gender since they are aimed at owning small businesses, making decisions based on diverse criteria, higher priority to quality of life instead of increasing business income, investments controlled by the lack of support for part of the institutions to obtain credit, limited capital, and mainly seek to reconcile the different aspects of their life; in contrast to their counterparts that focus on financial and economic aspects oriented towards profitability. They have similar problems for the growth of their companies, having common needs to achieve this as access to information, training, technological assistance and access to national and international markets.

The contribution of women in the economy of Latin America and the Caribbean had an increase of 35% in 1980 to 53% in 2007 promoting economic growth, financial security in the family, increase in consumption capacity and reduction in poverty of the region (Pages & Piras, 2010).

Despite the increase in female labor participation, this continues to have several problems, according to the World Economic Forum (WEF) according to the report on the Global Gender Gap 2016 that gender equality in economic activity and Labor will be possible in 170 years (Hernández, 2016). Similarly, the 2009 report indicates that the gender gaps with the greatest degree of relevance in Latin America and the Caribbean are in the sub-indices of economic and political participation.

The gender gap in the business sector increases in developing countries, these being the majority of the countries in the Latin American and Caribbean region, where only 22% of women work independently (Hellen, 2010).

SMEs that are led by 51% by women entrepreneurs generate an important contribution to the economy representing 31% to 38%, which constitutes 8 to 10 million, in formal SMEs in developing countries. Female entrepreneurship is composed of micro-sized SMEs 32% to 39%, small size 30% to 36%, medium-sized 17% to 21% (Shukla, 2011).

Despite these figures, according to a study by McKinsey of the IFC (2011), women-led businesses are restricted in their growth path with a reduction in their per capita income growth rate by 0.1 - 0.3 percentage points.

Entrepreneurship in Mexico

Mexico where the economic participation of women is only 43% compared to 78% of men. Despite constituting 51.2% of people enrolled in postgraduates, only 29% have leadership positions in companies, 23% in intermediate positions and 5% in board of directors. They have a salary gap with respect to the same work performed by the male gender from 15% to 20% and in leadership positions up to 40% (UN Women, 2016).

According to the 2016 State Competitiveness Index composed of a statewide survey of 32,000 people, a sum was added to the weights of each indicator at the state level, defined as the normalized values from 2001 to 2014 multiplied by the weight of each indicator. The indicator that had an increase of 160 in its weight and has remained constant until 2014 was the index of labor informality between women and men. The indicator of economically active women only increased in their weight 60 staying relatively equal until 2014. The wage equity indicator had an increase of 30 in their weight and has only increased 30 until 2014.

Also, according to the World Economic Report Forum (2017) worldwide it can be seen that there was a stagnation in the progress of the global index of gender equity, but in contrast in Mexico this had a decrease

THEORETICAL FRAMEWORK

The success of a company in e-commerce depends on various factors that are classified in 3 main categories:

1. Characteristics of the website
2. Characteristics of the consumer
3. Characteristics of the brand

Characteristics of the Website

They are integrated by the attributes of the website that have an influence on the consumer's intention to purchase. These include:

Aesthetic Appearance

In the online shopping environment, visual elements can be used through the use of images, videos and other interactive features (Kim, et al, 2005). Being considered aesthetic appearance as a positive sensory experience that being the element that has a greater influence on the emotional experience of the consumer (Nasermoadeli, et al, 2013).

The aesthetic appeal on websites directly influences the internal affective state causing a sense of connection through images (Wang, et al, 2011).

Experience Flow

It is defined by Kim, Suh & Lee (2013) as consumer behavior in the interaction of man and computer. That is, your attention is totally focused on the activity you are doing online. This state of immersion is integrated by emotional and cognitive factors, and its interrelation with the flow components necessary to have skills and controls to interact with the website (Rose, et al, 2012).

Consumer Characteristics

In addition to the computer factors, the specific characteristics of the consumer also influence the decision of online purchases through the attitude towards the website (Hausman & Siekpe, 2009). Cowart & Goldsmith (2007) mention that the intention to participate in purchases through the internet is related to the styles in the decision making of consumers, where the objectives of the consumer are the drivers that allow him to experience the pleasure of acquired assets (Balaji, et al, 2007).

One of the factors that affect consumer decision-making is gender, this was demonstrated in a study conducted by Hui & Wan (2007) who evaluated the purchase of clothes online, discovering that in the female gender there is a certain degree of uncertainty due to the lack of satisfaction caused by the experience of buying the product that was generated physically by trying on clothes, generating a lower degree of cognitive and affective attitudes in the intention to buy online unlike men. For the male gender where interactivity has a positive impact, a friendly interface, and sufficient information in web design, which leads to a faster purchase decision (Ganguly, et al, 2010).

Likewise, the consumer culture has a vital role in decision-making in e-commerce, for the mitigation of its effects the design of the website must allow simple navigation, greater interactivity and have the necessary information to facilitate the purchase decision (Cowart & Goldsmith, 2007). For example, trust has a great value for the consumer in the West (Chen, et al, 2012).

Behavior

In consumer behavior, the emotional state related to enjoyment has a relationship similar to pleasure and excitement (Penz & Hogg, 2011). Enjoying purchases has an important impact on the flow status of buyers, generating an intention to revisit the websites (Kim, et al, 2013), exposing a direct relationship between flow and affection (Novak, et al, 2000) .

When a decision is made, the emotional and cognitive state of an individual guides him to the evaluation of the perceived risks and benefits of the decision that leads him to a final decision, later said process works as a feedback mechanism that will affect future decisions (Gutnik, et al, 2006).

Both emotional systems for decision making are integrated by:

- The analytical system is defined by Epstein (1994) as the involvement of conscious cognitive process that uses various algorithms and normative rules to generate logical behaviors that are oriented to reason.

- The experiential system being conceptualized by Slovic, Finucane, Peters & MacGregor (2004) as the use of past experiences, associations related to emotion when making decisions, taking into account to a greater extent the unconscious process than the conscious one.

Emotions have an influence on decision making, it also has indirect effects on the behavior of the individual through the implicit configuration of cognitive representations and this has positive or negative effects depending on the type of emotion such as anger, fear, happiness or the pleasure (Forgas, 2001).

Characteristics of the Brand

The intention to make an online purchase depends on the characteristics of the brand and the type of goods offered on the website, those that present a greater ease for sale online are the search products compared to the goods of experience (Moon, et al, 2008). The characteristics also influence the presentation in the former, which can lead to positive consumer participation in online purchases (Won Jeong, et al, 2009). In addition, offering sensory information generates pleasure and a positive perspective on consumers (Lian & Lin, 2008).

Products and Attributes of the Company

The purchase decision of consumers is faster when they have enough product and company information (Davidson, et al, 2000), showing a directly proportional relationship between the attitude of the buying behavior with the level of information of the good (Chiou, 2000).

In the purchase intention when a consumer acquires products via online, the predictive factor that has a greater relevance is the search for information, in addition to having an impact on the perceived risk of behavior, increasing their tendency to buy the product (Nowlis & McCabe, 2000; Phau & Poon, 2000).

Perceived Utility

Perceived utility is defined as the degree to which a person believes that using a particular system will accelerate their personal growth and improve performance in their work (Davis, 1989).

It is one of the factors with a greater degree of relevance in behavior when a decision is made and is related to convenience and ease of use (Davis, Bagozzi & Warshaw, 1989).

METHODOLOGY

Based on the needs of the study based on the information obtained from research files, the methodology used in the work was as follows:

- Documentary research. The research is documentary, depending on what was proposed by Pasteur (2013) uses documents, collects information, analyzes and presents results. It was used in the study in order to collect the documents that may be essential to understand and contextualize the study.
- Correlational Research. Allows to relate the variables of the problem in a particular context (Baptista, et al, 2010). One of its main characteristics is that it allows examining the relationship between the variables looking for their association but it is not necessary to find their causal relationships (Bernal, 2010).
- Quantitative Approach It is defined by Tamayo (2010) as the measurement of the variables and their relationship through a verification to test the hypothesis and validate their theories, offering the possibility of having a broader approach to women in developing countries.

The instrument of the present investigation is a questionnaire, it is integrated by the variable characteristics of the web page, which was carried out through the information adapted from the thesis investigations of: Anen (2007), Karimi (2003) and Cheung (2015).

The second variable characteristics of the consumer, was generated with the information adapted from the thesis research of: Anen (2007), Karimi (2003), Gutnik, Forogh, Yoskowitz & Patel (2005), and Rohan (2013).

The third variable characteristics of the brand, was carried out with the information adapted from the thesis research of: Anen (2007), Karimi (2003) and Leelayouthayotin (2004). (See figure 1)

Analysis of Research and Results

The reliability of the design of the data collection instrument was verified through a reliability analysis in the SPSS software calculating the Cronbach Alpha where the items measure the same construct and are highly correlated (Castañeda, at el, 2010). Of the elements analyzed, a reliability of 83.0% was obtained, which is considered high according to the classification of Anastasi & Urbina (1998) (See Appendix 1).

Figure 1. Proposed model
Source: Own elaboration

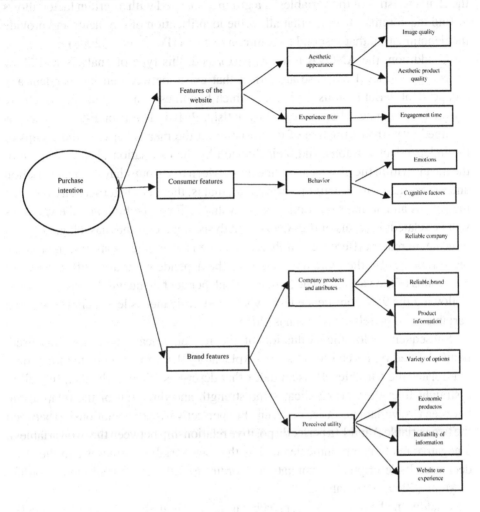

In addition, the Kaiser-Meyer-Olkin (KMO) test was performed for the Analysis of the components with Varimax rotation that between closer to 1 has the value obtained implies that the relationship between the variables is high (Benavente, et al, 2011). The value of KMO is 0.807 which is considered remarkable. Likewise, the Bartlett sphericity test was carried out, where, if it is less than 0.05, it is accepted as a null hypothesis so that the factor analysis can be applied (ibid, 2011). Its significance is 0.000, so factor analysis can be applied. (See Appendix 2)

For the evaluation of the applicability of the questionnaire, it begins with the factor analysis with varimax rotation defined as the simplicity of a factor by the variance of the squares of its factor loads in the observable variables (Pérez, et al,

2004), this is for the interpretation of the factors in a faster way, because examining the characteristics of the variables of a group associated with a certain factor allows to find the common features that allow the identification of the factor and provide the denomination that respond to common features (Pérez, et al, 2004)

In addition, the ANOVA test was performed, this type of analysis will allow measuring the level of cause and effect that exists between an independent and a dependent variable, thus explaining which hypotheses are tested and which are rejected (Hernández, Fernández and Baptista, 2010). The F or F-test statistic is obtained from the estimation of the variation of the means between the groups of the independent variables and their division by the estimation of the variation of the means within the groups, if the means between the groups have a great variation and the average within a group varies little, that is, there is a heterogeneity between the groups and an internal similarity, the value of F will be high and the variables will be related; in terms of the ANOVA analysis of a factor that has a higher F will indicate a greater difference and therefore there is a stronger relationship between the variables, also the more the average of the dependent variable differs between the groups of the variables The higher the independent value will be the value of F. Following the 95% confidence level when its significance is less than 0.05 the two variables will be related (Cárdenas, 2015).

Subsequently, for the evaluation of the model, linear regression was used, being defined by Pérez (2011) as the explanatory determination of the functional that relates the variables. R^2 is an index that describes whether the data fit well in a straight line; Pearson r indicates the strength and direction of the relationship between two variables, varies between -1 (a perfectly negative relationship between the two variables) and 1 (a perfectly positive relationship between the two variables), a negative relationship, indicates that as that one variable increases and the other decreases. Its descriptive interpretation according to Gilford (1954) adapted according to Mejía (2009): (See table 2)

In addition, the Beta coefficient (standardized) was analyzed, which indicates the explanatory hierarchy of the independent variables based on the explanatory weight in relation to the dependent variable. Having a significance of less than 0.05, it is assumed that 95% confidence of the independent variables contribute significantly to the model. The Beta coefficient (not standardized) indicates for each unit that the independent variable increases as the dependent variable increases (Santana, sf).

Finally, to analyze the relationship between the different variables for testing the hypothesis, a non-parametric analysis was carried out using the Kruskal Wallis test. It was used to test the hypotheses when exposing if there is a difference between the medians, when the value of the probability associated with the statistic is above the level of significance of 5% or 0.05 the null hypothesis is accepted when the theoretical value exceeds statistical. (Reidl, at el, 2010). (See table 3, 4 and 5)

Table 2. Pearson's descriptive interpretation r

Value	Range	Descriptive interpretation of the correlation.
r	<20	Slightly insignificant
r	0.21 - 0.40	Low. Defined but low
r	0.41 - 0.70	Moderate, substantial
r	0.71 - 0.90	Marked, high
r	0.90 - 1.00	Very high, very significant

Source: Guilford (1954). Adaptation Mejía (2009)

Table 3. Independent variable analysis

Dimension	Confidence interval 95%	Cronbach's alpha	KMO	Barlett test
Web page characteristics	The intervals are represented by normal distribution. The confidence interval for the averages are quite robust and not very sensitive to the violation of the assumption	0.704	0.765	0.000
Consumer characteristics	The intervals are represented by normal distribution. The confidence interval for the averages are quite robust and not very sensitive to the violation of the assumption	0.828	0.781	0.000
Brand characteristics	The intervals are represented by normal distribution. The confidence interval for the averages are quite robust and not very sensitive to the violation of the assumption	0.753	0.803	0.000

Source: Own elaboration

Table 4. Simple

regression Simple regression			
	1	2	3
Tests	Website	features Consumer	characteristics Brand characteristics
Value P e 95% Confidence	Interval 95.0% confidence intervals for the average: 0.0 +/- 0.198422 [-0.198422.0.198422		
Constant	- 1.10	- 0.01	- 8.39
B	0.599 ***	0.351 ***	0.750 ***
ANOVA (F)	17,526 ***	16,082 ***	20,842 ***
R2	71.1%	94%	85.9%
Pearson r	0.843	0.969	0.927

Source: Own elaboration

Table 5. Multiple

regression Multiple regression			
	1	2	3
Tests	Website	features Consumer	characteristicsbrand
Constant	-1.51		
B	0.221 ***	0.154 ***	0.887 ***
ANOVA (F)	69.547 ***		
R2	77.1%		
Pearson r	0.878		
Kruskal Wallis	89.2%	90.4%	90.3%

Source: Own elaboration

FUTURE RESEARCH DIRECTIONS

In this article the use of any neuroscience technique was not involved, which cannot fully illustrate this particular aspect of the model regarding our current study.

Within the limitations of the thesis are that it is not a parametric statistic, because to perform a parametric analysis it must start from the following assumptions:

1. The population distribution of the dependent variable is normal: the universe has a normal distribution.
2. The level of measurement of the dependent variable is interval or ratio.

3.   When two or more populations are studied, they have a homogeneous variance: the populations in question have a similar dispersion in their distributions.

Parametric statistics need to meet four requirements to apply:

1.   The dependent variable must be distributed normally or very similar.
2.   The homogeneity of the variances when comparing groups should have the same dispersion with respect to the average of the dependent variable.
3.   Assignment and random selection of groups (completely random sampling)
4.   The dependent variable is measured at the interval or ratio level (Reidl, et al, 2010).

CONCLUSION

Neuroeconomics can provide the enrichment of specific economic models with the option of neuro-psychological penetration.

It is necessary to implement in the e-commerce consumers of the exponential SMEs of the artisanal industry the knowledge of the discipline of neuroeconomics because the brain activity represents ¾ of the decisions taken, likewise each process involves the neurons that influence a particular behavior, In addition, the network of neural connections in the brain changes as the person acquires knowledge and experience. Therefore, neuroeconomics plays an important role in achieving the objective of better operational efficiency to accelerate market reactions and increase consumer expectations

REFERENCES

Anen, C. (2007). *Neural correlates of economic and moral decision-making* (Tesis doctoral).

Balaji, S., Babu, M. M., & Aravind, L. (2007). Interplay between network structures, regulatory modes and sensing mechanisms of transcription factors in the transcriptional regulatory network of E. coli. *Journal of Molecular Biology*, *372*(4), 1108–1122. doi:10.1016/j.jmb.2007.06.084 PMID:17706247

Baptista, P., Fernández, C., & Hernández, R. (2006). *Metodología de la investigación* (6th ed.). Editorial McGraw Hill.

Baptista, P., Fernández, R., & Sampieri, C. (2010). *Metodología de la investigación*. Editorial Mc Graw Hill.

Brynjolfsson, E., Dick, A., & Smith, M. (2010). A nearly perfect market? *Quantitative Marketing and Economics*, 8(1), 1-33.

CEPAL. (2004). Novena conferencia regional sobre la mujer de América Latina y El Caribe. *Consenso de México*.

Chen, T., Drennan, J., & Andrews, L. (2012). Experience sharing. *Journal of Marketing Management*, 28(13-14), 1535–1552. doi:10.1080/0267257X.2012.736876

Cheung, J. (2015). *Exploring Consumers' Experiential Responses and Shopping Intentions toward Visual User-Generated Content in Online Shopping Environments* (PhD Thesis). The University of Manchester, Manchester, UK.

Chiou, J. (2000). Antecedents and Moderators of Behavioral Intention:Differences between US and Taiwanese Students. *Genetic, Social, and General Psychology Monographs*, 126(1), 105–124. PMID:10713903

Constantinides, E. (2004) Influencing the online consumer's behavior: The Web experience. *Internet Research*, 14(2), 111-126.

Cowart, K. O., & Goldsmith, R. E. (2007). The influence of consumer decision-making styles on online apparel consumption by college students. *International Journal of Consumer Studies*, 31(6), 639–647. doi:10.1111/j.1470-6431.2007.00615.x

Davidson, R. J., Jackson, D. C., & Kalin, N. H. (2000). Emotion, plasticity, context, and regulation: Perspectives from affective neuroscience. *Psychological Bulletin, Vol*, 126(6), 890–909. doi:10.1037/0033-2909.126.6.890 PMID:11107881

Davis, F. (1989). Perceived Usefulness, Perceived Ease of Use, and User Acceptance of Information Technology. *Management Information Systems Quarterly*, 13(3), 319–339. doi:10.2307/249008

Davis, F., Bagozzi, R., & Warshaw, P. (1989). User Acceptance of Computer Technology: A Comparison of Two Theoretical Models. *Management Science*, 35(8), 982–1003. doi:10.1287/mnsc.35.8.982

Epstein, S. (1994). Integration of the cognitive and the psychodynamic unconscious. *The American Psychologist*, 49(8), 709–724. doi:10.1037/0003-066X.49.8.709 PMID:8092614

Etienne-Nugue, J. (2009). *Hablame de las artesanias*. UNESCO.

FONART. (2009). *Manual de Diferenciación entre Artesania y Manualidad*. Recovered from https://www.fonart.gob.mx/web/pdf/DO/mdma.pdf

Foote, W. (September 29, 2015). Tapping the potential of the artisan economy. *Forbes*. Recovered from https://www.forbes.com/sites/willyfoote/2015/09/29/tapping-the-potential-of-the- worlds-fourth-largest-economy/#3ea27e3f1aa2

Forgas, J. P. (Ed.). (2001). *Feeling and thinking: The role of affect in social cognition*. Cambridge University Press.

Glimcher, P. (2003). *Decisions, Uncertainty and the Brain: The Science of Neuroeconomics*. The MIT Press. doi:10.7551/mitpress/2302.001.0001

Glimcher, P. W., & Rustichini, A. (2004). Neuroeconomics: The Consilience of Brain and Decision. *Science*, *306*(5695), 447–452. doi:10.1126cience.1102566 PMID:15486291

González, M. (2016). 31% del PIB nacional es aportado por mujeres empresarias. *Informa BTL*. Recovered from https://www.informabtl.com/31-del-pib-nacional-es-aportado-por-mujeres-empresarias/

Gutnik, L., Forogh, A., Yoskowitz, N., & Patel, V. (2006). The role of emotions in decision making: a cognitive neuroeconomic approach towards understanding sexual risk behavior. *Journal of Biomedical Information*. doi:10.1016/j.jbi.2006.03.002

Hausman, A., & Siekpe, J. (2009). The effect of web interface features on consumer online purchase intentions. *Journal of Business Research*, *62*(1), 5–13. doi:10.1016/j.jbusres.2008.01.018

Heller, L. (2010). Mujeres emprendedoras en América Latina y el Caribe: realidades, obstáculos y desafíos. Santiago de Chile: United Nations.

Hernández-Girón, J., Yexcas, M., & Domínguez-Hernández, M. (2007). Factores de éxito en los negocios de artesanía en México. *Estudios Gerenciales*, *23*(104), 77–99. doi:10.1016/S0123-5923(07)70018-9

Hussain, A. (2013). El potencial del comercio electrónico: oportunidades para las PYME de los países en desarrollo. *Revista del centro de comercio internacional*. Recovered from http://www10.iadb.org/intal/intalcdi/PE/2014/14253.pdf

Indego Africa. (2016). How the artisan sector can change the world. *ONE*. Recovered from https://www.one.org/us/2016/05/13/how-the-artisan-sector-can-change-the-world/

INEGI. (2009). *Censo Económico*. Micro, pequeña, mediana y gran empresa. Recovered from https://www.inegi.org.mx/est/contenidos/espanol/proyectos/censos/ce2009/default.asp?s=est&c=14220

INEGI. (2012). *Conociendo México*. Análisis de la demografía de los establecimientos 2012. Recovered from http://buscador.inegi.org.mx/search?tx=analisis+de+la+demografia+de+los+establecimientos&q=analisis+de+la+demografia+de+los +establecimientos&site=sitioINEGI_collection&client=INEGI_Default&proxystylesheet=INEGI_Default&getfield

International Telecommunication Union. (2015). Measuring the Information Society Report. Ginebra: ITU.

Karimi, S. (2013). *A purchase decision-making process model of online consumers and its influential factor a cross sector analysis* (PhD thesis). Manchester Business School.

Kim, H., Suh, K., & Lee, U. (2013). Effects of collaborative online shopping on shopping experience through social and relational perspectives. *Information & Management, 50*(4), 169–180. doi:10.1016/j.im.2013.02.003

Kim, J., Park, J., Kim, J., & Park, J. (2005). A consumer shopping channel extension model: Attitude shift toward the online store. *Journal of Fashion Marketing and Management, 9*(1), 106–121. doi:10.1108/13612020510586433

Leelayouthayotin, L. (2004). *Factors influencing online purchase intention: the case of health food consumers in Thailand* (PhD thesis). Universidad Southern Queensland, Australia.

McGaughey, R., & Mason, K. (1998). The Internet as a marketing tool. *Journal of Marketing Theory and Practice, 6*(6), 1–11. doi:10.1080/10696679.1998.11501800

Moon, B.J. (2004). Consumer adoption of the internet as an information search and product purchase channel: some research hypotheses. *International Journal of Internet Marketing and Advertising, 1*(1), 104-118.

Nasermoadeli, A., Ling, K. C., & Severi, E. (2013). Exploring the Relationship between Social Environment and Customer Experience. *Asian Social Science, 9*(1), 130–141.

Nowlis, S., & McCabe, D. (2000). The effect of the inability to touch merchandise on the likelihood of choosing products online. In *American Marketing Association. Conference Proceedings.* (Vol. 11, p. 308). American Marketing Association.

Pasteur, L. (2013). *Características y diferencias de la investigación documental, de campo y experimental*. Formación de competencias para la investigación.

Penz, E., & Hogg, M. (2011). The role of mixed emotions in consumer behaviour: Investigating ambivalence in consumers' experiences of approach-avoidance conflicts in online and offline settings. *European Journal of Marketing, 45*(1/2), 104–132. doi:10.1108/03090561111095612

Phau, I., & Poon, S. (2000). Factors influencing the types of products and services purchased over the Internet. *Internet Research, 10*(2), 102–113. doi:10.1108/10662240010322894

Powers, J., & Magnoni, B. (2010). *Dueña de tu propia empresa: identificación, análisis y superación de las limitaciones a las pequeñas empresas de las mujeres en América Latina y el Caribe*. Fondo Multilateral de Inversiones, BID.

Reidl, L., Cuevas, C., & López, R. (2010). *Métodos de Investigación en Psicología*. Universidad Nacional Autónoma de México. Recovered from https://www.rua.unam.mx/objeto/7987/metodos-de-investigacion-en-psicologia

Rickwood, C., and White, L. (2009). Pre-purchase decision-making for a complex service: retirement planning. *Journal of Services Marketing, 23*(3), 145-153.

Rohan, D. (2013). *Neuroeconomic Studies on Personality and Decision-Making* (Tesis doctoral). The University of Minnesota.

Rose, S., Clark, M., Samouel, P., & Hair, N. (2012). Online Customer Experience in e-Retailing: An empirical model of Antecedents and Outcomes. *Journal of Retailing, 88*(2), 308–322. doi:10.1016/j.jretai.2012.03.001

Sacristan, J. (2013). La pyme tiene problema para lanzar su e-commerce. *El economista*. Recovered from https://www.eleconomista.es/catalunya/noticias/4766122/04/13/La-pyme-tiene- problemas-para-lanzar-su-ecommerce.html

Sandoval, E., & Guerra, E. (2010). *Migrantes e indígenas: acceso a la información en comunidades virtuales interculturales*. Recuperado de www.eumed.net/libros/2010b/684/

Shukla, M. (2011). *Entrepreneurship and small business management*. Kitab Mahal.

Slovic, P., Finucane, M. L., Peters, E., & MacGregor, D. G. (2004). Risk as analysis and risk as feelings: Some thoughts about affect, reason, risk, and rationality. *Risk Analysis, 24*(2), 311–322. doi:10.1111/j.0272-4332.2004.00433.x PMID:15078302

Statista. (2018). *E-commerce share of total global retail sales in 2016, by region.* The Statistics Portal. Recovered from https://www.statista.com/statistics/239300/number-of-online-buyers-in-selected-countries/

Statista. (2018). *Number of digital buyers worldwide from 2014 to 2021 (in billions).* The Statistics Portal. Recovered from https://www.statista.com/statistics/251666/number-of-digital-buyers-worldwide/

Statista. (2018). *Retail e-commerce sales worldwide from 2014 to 2021 (in billions US dollars).* The Statistics Portal. Recovered from https://www.statista.com/statistics/379046/worldwide-retail-e-commerce-sales/

UNESCO. (2001). *Artesanías creadoras.* París: Unesco, Sección de Artesanías y Diseño.

United Nations Industrial Development Organisation (UNIDO). (2001). *Women Entrepreneurship Development in Selected African Countries.* Working Paper No. 7, United Nations Industrial Development Organisation.

VanderMeer, D., Dutta, K., & Datta, A. (2012). A Cost-Based Database Request Distribution Technique for Online e-Commerce Applications. *Management Information Systems Quarterly, 36*(2), 479–507. doi:10.2307/41703464

Wang, Y., Minor, M., & Wei, J. (2011). Aesthetics and the online shopping environment: Understanding consumer responses. *Journal of Retailing, 87*(1), 46–58. doi:10.1016/j.jretai.2010.09.002

WeConnect International. (n.d.). *Prospere como mujer empresaria.* Recovered from https://weconnectinternational.org

Won Jeong, S., Fiore, A., Niehm, L., & Lorenz, F. (2009). The role of experiential value in online shopping: The impacts of product presentation on consumer responses towards an apparel web site. *Internet Research, 19*(1), 105–124. doi:10.1108/10662240910927858

Zhang, T., Agarwal, R., & Lucas, H. (2011). The value of IT-enabled retailer learning: personalized product recommendations and customer store loyalty in electronic markets. *MIS Quarterly, 35*(4), 859.

APPENDIX 1

Table 6. Cronbach's alpha

Cronbach's alpha	No. of elements
.870	55

Source: Own elaboration with SPSS

APPENDIX 2

Table 7. Cronbach's alpha

Kaiser-Meyer-Olkin measure of adequacy of Sampling		.807
	Aprox. Chi-cuadrado	6885.926
Bartlett's sphericity test	gl	1485
	Sig.	.000

Source: Own elaboration with SPSS

Chapter 7

Facilitating the Adoption of Digital Health Technologies by Older Adults to Support Their Health

Maurita T. Harris
University of Illinois Urbana-Champaign, USA

Wendy A. Rogers
University of Illinois Urbana-Champaign, USA

ABSTRACT

With over 50% of older adults in the United States managing at least one chronic condition, it is crucial to understand how to promote their self-management of positive health behaviors. Health interventions through digital health technologies are becoming more commonplace. Theoretical models related to health behavior change and technology acceptance can guide the design of these healthcare tools and lead to adoption by older adults to support their health. This chapter provides an overview of health behavior change and technology acceptance models to inform the development of digital health technology for older adults. This chapter illustrates the application of these models by describing two design personas that represent human factors designers. This chapter discusses the lack of inclusion of technology adoption and other long-term concepts and the need for further exploration that could inform understanding of technology integration into everyday health activities.

DOI: 10.4018/978-1-7998-6453-0.ch007

INTRODUCTION

In 2019, the world population included 703 million people aged 65 years or over; by 2050 this number is projected to double (United Nations, 2019). With this increase, there will be more people managing chronic health conditions, namely, "conditions that last 1 year or more and require ongoing medical attention or limit activities of daily living or both" (Centers for Disease Control and Prevention, 2020). Approximately 80% of older adults have at least one chronic condition, and 77% have at least two (National Council on Aging, n.d.). Factors contributing to acquiring a chronic condition lie within one's health behaviors, such as diet and physical activity. Health behaviors are "actions taken by individuals that affect health or mortality" (Short & Mollborn, 2015; p. 2) and should be considered broadly to ensure that the various aspects of aging are considered (Ziegelmann & Knoll, 2015). Consequently, supporting health self-management of chronic conditions reduces healthcare costs and improves health outcomes (Bodenheimer et al., 2002; Wheeler et al., 2003). Technology interventions that can support health self-management are promising.

Use of Technology by Older Adults for Health

Technology tools can support older adults in self-managing their health. In contrast to popular stereotypes, older adults are not afraid to use technology (Mitzner et al., 2010). The use of healthcare technology by older adults is well-illustrated by a recent report from the Pew Research Center (Vogels, 2019). The report focused on data from adults born between 1945 to 1996 and technology use across generations. Vogels (2019) reported that 25% of adults over age 50 used a smartphone to get health information and track health, 21% used a tablet to get health information, and 7% used a tablet to track health. Although they tended not to be early adopters, 23% bought smartphones, 10% bought tablets, 7% bought wearable devices, and 1% bought home health and safety devices. This illustrates that older adults are buying technologies, and some are using technologies to manage their health.

Design of Digital Health Technology

Some health interventions incorporate behavior change models and digital health technologies to support the user in making a behavior change. Ronquillo and colleagues (2020) defined digital health technology as "the use of information and communications technologies in medicine and other health professions to manage illnesses and health risks and promote wellness. Digital health has a broad scope and includes the use of wearable devices, mobile health, telehealth, health information technology, and telemedicine." Digital health technology, like any technology, can support a behavior change by simplifying the task the user is completing (Mohr et al., 2014). Additional benefits of digital health technologies include improving healthcare access, lowering healthcare costs, and providing more personalized health care for patients (Ronquillo et al., 2020). The most used digital health interventions that focused on behavior change are mobile phone applications, text messaging, and the internet (Taj et al., 2019).

This chapter aims to emphasize the value of considering health behavior change models and technology acceptance models to design digital health technology for older adults. We first review the literature and introduce common models of health behavior change and technology acceptance. To illustrate the application of these theoretical models, we examine two design personas, Beatrice, and Trav, who represent human factors designers working with digital health technologies. These design personas are presented in Figure 1.

Beatrice is a user experience designer at a start-up company. She completed a competitive analysis of other companies that focus on self-monitoring wearable devices for those with hypertension and found that older adults rarely use these devices. To develop a foundation and set the start-up apart from well-established companies, Beatrice is interested in understanding what models and theories in the literature can inform her about what would make an older adult interested in using their wearable devices.

Trav is a lead human factors researcher at a large-scale company focusing on designing an integrated health system, including a mobile application and a portal, on supporting health self-management and transitions from surgery to home rehabilitation. With the integrated health system development, Trav aims to accommodate multiple stakeholders' needs, including healthcare providers, older adults, family members, and care partners. Given that there are different groups of people interacting with the health system (including older adults), Trav is interested in understanding the best possible ways to accommodate each group's needs and capabilities.

Neither Beatrice nor Trav have specific experience designing for older adults. They will first have to understand more about older adults' capabilities and limitations and be sure to include them in the design process (supported by insights from Boot et al., 2020, Czaja et al., 2019, and McLaughlin & Pak, 2020).

INSIGHTS FROM HEALTH BEHAVIOR CHANGE MODELS

There are multiple models in the literature that focus specifically on health behavior change. These models provide a useful template in health behavior interventions where the goal is to influence the acceptance of positive behaviors. Two categories of models are presented here: continuum and stage models (Schwarzer, 2011). Continuum models illustrate a linear route to action, where the predictors within the model end with intentions leading to the behavior (Schwarzer, 2011). Stage models focus on matching an individual to a qualitative stage in an intervention (Schwarzer & Luszczynska, 2008). Knowing the difference between these types of models allows designers to support users' goals and help them perceive digital health technology's usefulness. In the next section, we will review some common health behavior change models used in the literature.

Standard Models of Health Behavior Change

The Health Belief Model (HBM) was one of the original models developed to explain health behavior (Rosenstock, 1974). It consists of nine predictors, divided into three sections. The first section is individual perceptions, namely, perceived susceptibility and perceived seriousness. The second section is modifying factors, which are demographic variables (e.g., age), socio-psychological variables (e.g., peer and reference group pressure), structural variables (knowledge about the disease), perceived threat, and cues to action (e.g., advice from others). The third section, the likelihood of action, includes perceived benefits, perceived behavior, and the likelihood of taking recommended preventive health action.

The Theory of Reasoned Action (Fishbein & Ajzen, 1975) was developed to understand one's intentions to behave and consisted of attitudes and subjective norms. Later, the Theory of Planned Behavior was developed as an extension and included perceived behavioral control to explain actions not under volitional control, which is one's ability to decide to perform a behavior (Ajzen, 1991). This extension resulted in three predictors affecting intentions, namely, attitudes, subjective norm, and perceived behavioral control.

The Transtheoretical Model of Health Behavior Change posited that an individual goes through six stages of change with the support of ten processes of change (Prochaska & Velicer, 1997). The six stages are pre-contemplation, contemplation, preparation, action, maintenance, and termination. In other words, the stages range from them not intending or thinking about doing the behavior to terminating the behavior. The ten processes are consciousness-raising, dramatic relief, environmental reevaluation, self-reevaluation, self-liberation, counterconditioning, stimulus control, contingency management, and helping relationships.

Lastly, the Health Action Process Approach explained health behaviors by including other behaviors (e.g., Social Cognitive Theory; Schwarzer, 1999) and includes two phases: a motivation phase and a volition phase. The motivation phase, choosing which action to take, includes risk perception, outcome expectancies, and self-efficacy. The volition phase, planning the behavior and acting, consists of the initiative, maintenance, and recovery.

Of the models described, the Health Belief Model, the Theory of Reasoned Action, and the Theory of Planned Behavior are considered continuum health behavior change models. Each model includes similar predictors, which all lead to the likelihood or the intentions of doing a specific behavior. However, some aspects set them apart. For example, the Health Belief Model focuses on both the health condition and the individual, whereas the Theory of Reasoned Action and the Theory of Planned Behavior focus more on the individual. These models also do not focus on behavior variance, which results in an intention-behavior gap where the individual may intend to do a behavior but does not.

Unlike the continuum models, the Transtheoretical Model of Health Behavior Change is a stage model, allowing the individual to be matched to a specific stage leading to its outcome. Lastly, the Health Action Process Approach model consists of two stages with aspects of a continuum model. The purpose of incorporating the two is to overcome the intention-behavior gap. Understanding the differences between the health behavior change models and the type of models (i.e., continuum and stage) is useful for developing digital health technologies because it allows for diverse methods.

Use Case Illustrations

In our examples, Beatrice and Trav are designing digital health technologies that are geared towards health self-management. After reviewing the literature, they each decide on a model that best suits their needs. Beatrice decided to look more into Health Belief Model because it included sections that would help her understand older adults, hypertension, and possible ways to advertise to older adults. To understand the different predictors, she developed a design brief using the Health Belief Model as a template, which contained information on the goal population, statistics on older adults and hypertension, information surrounding hypertension (e.g., consequences), examples to target this population, and benefits and barriers to self-monitoring one's health with a wearable device (see Figure 2). With this brief, she was able to refine the target group that the start-up company was going to aim for by focusing on older adults who are most susceptible but did not see the severity of having hypertension.

With his focus on developing an integrated health system that accommodates multiple stakeholders, Trav is concerned about incorporating the various behaviors and stages that the different groups of people may be in at a time. Trav is interested in using the Transtheoretical Model of Health Behavior Change given its individualistic focus on specific stages an individual can be in at any given time and processes that can influence moving to the next stage. Trav's team decided that each stage will represent a stage that an individual may be in when using the integrated health system (see Figure 3). Trav's design goal for the integrated health system is to develop a design that is welcoming for those who have not used the system (i.e., pre-contemplation), through to those who are aiming to continue to do the health behavior (i.e., maintenance stage).

INSIGHTS FROM TECHNOLOGY ACCEPTANCE MODELS

Health behavior interventions, including digital health technologies, must consider how technology acceptance models can inform the intervention. Technology acceptance models include predictors that lead to the acceptance of a range of technologies (e.g., information technologies and gerontechnology). Although health behavior change models include predictors that will support the behavior change, technology acceptance models consider predictors that might help with the uptake of technology. To some extent, we know attitudes lead to behavior intentions, leading to acceptance of the behavior within health behavior change models (Venkatesh et al., 2003). The same is true for technology acceptance models because their origins derived from the Theory of Planned Behavior.

Standard Models of Technology Acceptance

The Technology Acceptance Model (TAM; Davis, 1989), informed by Theory of Planned Behavior, is a foundational model for modern technology acceptance models. TAM consisted of three predictors that led to technology acceptance: perceived usefulness, perceived ease of use, and subjective norm (i.e., important persons believe that the individual should or should not do the behavior).

The Unified Theory of Acceptance and Use of Technology (UTAUT) integrated TAM and seven other models across health behavior, psychology, and technology acceptance to develop a theory that explains acceptance (Venkatesh et al., 2003). UTAUT consists of four predictors and four moderators. The four predictors are performance expectancy, effort expectancy, social influence, and facilitating conditions. Compared to TAM, UTAUT contained the same three predictors but with different names and included facilitating conditions. The four moderators included in UTAUT were gender, age, experience, and voluntariness of use. In UTAUT, age was the sole moderator that moderated all of the key relationships between the four predictors and behavioral intention and use behavior outcomes. In 2012, Venkatesh and colleagues (2012) extended UTAUT by incorporating habit, hedonic motivation, and price value to develop UTAUT2.

To better understand the role that age plays in technology acceptance, Chen and Chan (2014) developed the Senior Technology Acceptance Model (STAM). Their goal was to understand the predictors associated with the acceptance, specifically technology usage of gerontechnology (e.g., technologies that increase independent living and social participation) among older adults in Hong Kong (Chen & Chan, 2014). STAM differed from other technology acceptance models by adding older adults' age-related health and ability characteristics. Overall, age-related health and ability characteristics predicted technology usage in ways that previous models did not consider. For example, age was negatively associated with perceived ease of use.

With the current models of health behavior change and technology acceptance, there is a lack of unification within and between the fields, with various terms standing for the same thing (Taj et al., 2019). For example, within the technology acceptance models, perceived usefulness and performance expectancy are similar in definitions. However, many of the predictors in the individual models would be defined as attitudes (see Figure 4).

Use Case Illustrations

To understand the acceptance of digital health technologies, Beatrice and Trav are interested in how the different technology acceptance models can be applied to understand what they should do next with their digital health technologies. After refining the target population, Beatrice decided that STAM would be most informative because it was developed specifically to understand older adults' acceptance of various technologies (see Figure 5). STAM enabled Beatrice to continue focusing on the different facets of older adults (e.g., commonalities of age-related conditions), which is not explicitly stated in other technology acceptance models (e.g., cognitive ability).

After reviewing at each stage in the Transtheoretical Model of Health Behavior Change, Trav decided that UTAUT2 would be more useful due to the addition of hedonic motivation and price value. Trav believes that these two predictors should be considered because both predictors may be important at any possible stage the user is in at any given time. To ensure that the integrated health system is designed to include older adults, Trav's team conducted a needs assessment to understand what features older adults would need to perceive the integrated health system as useful, pleasurable to use, and easy to use during the transition. With this information, Trav's team took the predictors in UTAUT2 into consideration during the integrated system development (see Figure 6).

TECHNOLOGY ADOPTION AND OWNERSHIP

Technology adoption tends to be left out of the conversation regarding technology acceptance. Technology adoption is the *long-term integration* of technology into one's everyday activities. The adoption of digital health technologies empowers the user to take control of their health and reap the positive benefits that the technology can have on their health (e.g., more personalized healthcare). To understand the adoption of technology to support healthy behaviors, it is important to recognize that ownership and adoption are not interchangeable terms. People may own the technology but not incorporate it into their everyday activities (Magsamen-Conrad & Dillon, 2020).

Long-term concepts are not incorporated in technology acceptance models that would help understand adoption, such as habit formation and maintenance. Habit formation may be a better signal for predicting if someone will complete the behavior than intentions (Wood & Neal, 2016) due to the intention-behavior gap (Schwarzer, 2011). For example, a potential user may see the wearable device that Beatrice is developing and conclude that they intend to buy it to use but never do so. Maintenance is included as a stage in the Transtheoretical Model of Health Behavior Change. However, it has not been incorporated into the technology acceptance models. Maintenance is where the user is preventing relapse and continuing the behavior. These are just examples of long-term concepts that should be considered when aiming to understand digital health technology adoption.

CONCLUSION

With Beatrice and Trav's design personas, we illustrated how different theoretical models can be applied to influence the development of digital health technologies and inform design decisions. These examples show the real value in understanding these different models for developing digital health technology. This approach will inform the technology lifecycle (e.g., design to dissemination) as well as the adoption of everyday technology by the user.

Beatrice and Trav defined their population and predictors to develop better digital health technologies with the incorporation of both health behavior change and technology acceptance models. The incorporation of both types of models is not new. Ahadzadeh and colleagues (2015) integrated the health belief model and the technology acceptance model for understanding how both models affect internet usage for health-related purposes. Combining the two models predicted the usage of the internet, and the behavior was proactive compared to reactive. The TAM predictors have a mediating role in the influence of health consciousness. With a "no size fits all" mentality, it is vital to consider the age-related differences and health behaviors that older adults can engage in when developing health behavior change interventions. This is especially important for health technologies intended to support behavior change.

Health technology must fit the user's needs across the lifespan. Incorporating lifespan theories in the design process will support understanding one's self-awareness, perceptions of aging, and understanding of how life changes affect health (Ziegelmann & Knoll, 2015). Examples of lifespan theories are the Socioemotional Selectivity Theory (SST; Carstensen, Isaacowitz, & Charles. 1999) and the Selective Optimization with Compensation model (SOC; Baltes & Baltes, 1990).

In this chapter, standard health behavior change and technology acceptance models were described in terms of continuum compared to stage models. The continuum models focused on the linear path to the behavior, and the stage models focused on associating a stage to the individual. Understanding differences among the models provides insights for design of digital health technologies. For example, perceived ease of use and perceived usefulness are common among the technology acceptance models; however, predictors related to sociability are different from each of the models discussed. Regardless of which model is selected, the models provide a template to follow that can guide the design process. The resultant products will help the users reach their goal of health self-management.

REFERENCES

Ahadzadeh, A. S., Pahlevan Sharif, S., Ong, F. S., & Khong, K. W. (2015). Integrating Health Belief Model and Technology Acceptance Model: An Investigation of Health-Related Internet Use. *Journal of Medical Internet Research, 17*(2), e45. doi:10.2196/jmir.3564 PMID:25700481

Ajzen, I. (1991). The theory of planned behavior. *Organizational Behavior and Human Decision Processes, 50*(2), 179–211. doi:10.1016/0749-5978(91)90020-T

Baltes, P. B., & Baltes, M. M. (1990). Psychological perspectives on successful aging: The model of selective optimization with compensation. In P. B. Baltes & M. M. Baltes (Eds.), *Successful Aging* (pp. 1–34). Cambridge University Press. doi:10.1017/CBO9780511665684.003

Bodenheimer, T., Lorig, K., Holman, H., & Grumbach, K. (2002). Patient self-management of chronic disease in primary care. *Journal of the American Medical Association, 288*(19), 2469–2475. doi:10.1001/jama.288.19.2469 PMID:12435261

Boot, W. R., Charness, N., Czaja, S. J., & Rogers, W. A. (2020). *Designing for Older Adults: Case Studies, Methods, and Tools* (1st ed.). CRC Press. doi:10.1201/b22187

Carstensen, L., Isaacowitz, D., & Charles, S. (1999). Taking time seriously: A theory of socioemotional selectivity. *The American Psychologist, 54*(3), 165–181. doi:10.1037/0003-066X.54.3.165 PMID:10199217

Centers for Disease Control and Prevention. (2020). *About Chronic Diseases*. https://www.cdc.gov/chronicdisease/about/index.htm#:~:text=Chronic%20diseases%20are%20defined%20broadly,disability%20in%20the%20United%20States

Chen, K., & Chan, A. H. S. (2014). Gerontechnology acceptance by elderly Hong Kong Chinese: A senior technology acceptance model (STAM). *Ergonomics, 57*(5), 635–652. doi:10.1080/00140139.2014.895855 PMID:24655221

Czaja, S. J., Boot, W. R., Charness, N., & Rogers, W. A. (2019). *Designing for Older Adults: Principles and Creative Human Factors Approaches* (3rd ed.). CRC Press. doi:10.1201/b22189

Davis, F. D. (1989). Perceived usefulness, perceived ease of use, and user acceptance of information technology. *MIS Quarterly, 13*(3), 319–340. doi:10.2307/249008

Fishbein, M., & Ajzen, I. (1977). *Belief, attitude, intention, and behavior: An introduction to theory and research*. Addison-Wesley.

Lally, P., & Gardner, B. (2013). Promoting habit formation. *Health Psychology Review, 7*(sup1), S137–S158. doi:10.1080/17437199.2011.603640

Levy, B. R., & Myers, L. M. (2004). Preventive health behaviors influenced by self-perceptions of aging. *Preventive Medicine, 39*(3), 625–629. doi:10.1016/j.ypmed.2004.02.029 PMID:15313104

Magsamen-Conrad, K., & Dillon, J. M. (2020). Mobile technology adoption across the lifespan: A mixed methods investigation to clarify adoption stages, and the influence of diffusion attributes. *Computers in Human Behavior, 112*(106456), 106456. Advance online publication. doi:10.1016/j.chb.2020.106456 PMID:32834465

McLaughlin, A. C., & Pak, R. (2020). *Designing displays for older adults* (2nd ed.). CRC Press., doi:10.1201/9780429439674

Mitzner, T. L., Boron, J. B., Fausset, C. B., Adams, A. E., Charness, N., Czaja, S. J., Dijkstra, K., Fisk, A. D., Rogers, W. A., & Sharit, J. (2010). Older adults talk technology: Technology usage and attitudes. *Computers in Human Behavior, 26*(6), 1710–1721. doi:10.1016/j.chb.2010.06.020 PMID:20967133

Mohr, D. C., Schueller, S. M., Montague, E., Burns, M. N., & Rashidi, P. (2014). The behavioral intervention technology model: An integrated conceptual and technological framework for eHealth and mHealth interventions. *Journal of Medical Internet Research*, *16*(6), e146. doi:10.2196/jmir.3077 PMID:24905070

National Council on Aging. (n.d.). *Healthy Aging Facts*. https://www.ncoa.org/news/resources-for-reporters/get-the-facts/healthy-aging-facts/

Prochaska, J. O., & Velicer, W. F. (1997). The transtheoretical model of health behavior change. *American Journal of Health Promotion*, *12*(1), 38–48. doi:10.4278/0890-1171-12.1.38 PMID:10170434

Ronquillo, Y., Meyers, A., & Korvek, S. J. (2020). Digital health. In *StatPearls*. StatPearls Publishing. https://www.ncbi.nlm.nih.gov/books/NBK470260/

Rosenstock, I. M. (1974). The health belief model and preventive health behavior. *Health Education Monographs*, *2*(4), 354–386. doi:10.1177/109019817400200405

Schwarzer, R. (1999). Self-regulatory processes in the adoption and maintenance of health behaviors. *Journal of Health Psychology*, *4*(2), 115–127. doi:10.1177/135910539900400208 PMID:22021474

Schwarzer, R. (2011). *Health Behavior Change*. Oxford University Press., doi:10.1093/oxfordhb/9780195342819.013.0024

Schwarzer, R., & Luszczynska, A. (2008). How to Overcome Health-Compromising Behaviors: The Health Action Process Approach. *European Psychologist*, *13*(2), 141–151. doi:10.1027/1016-9040.13.2.141

Short, S. E., & Mollborn, S. (2015). Social determinants and health behaviors: Conceptual frames and empirical advances. *Current Opinion in Psychology*, *5*, 78–84. doi:10.1016/j.copsyc.2015.05.002 PMID:26213711

Taj, F., Klein, M. C. A., & van Halteren, A. (2019). Digital health behavior change technology: Bibliometric and scoping review of two decades of research. *JMIR mHealth and uHealth*, *7*(12), e13311. doi:10.2196/13311 PMID:31833836

United Nations, Department of Economic and Social Affairs, Population Division. (2019). *World Population Ageing 2019: Highlights* (ST/ESA/SER.A/430). Author.

Venkatesh, V., Morris, M. G., Davis, G. B., & Davis, F. D. (2003). User acceptance of information technology: Toward a unified view. *MIS Quarterly, 27*(3), 425–478. doi:10.2307/30036540

Venkatesh, V., Thong, J. Y. L., & Xu, X. (2012). Consumer acceptance and use of information technology: Extending the unified theory of acceptance and use of technology. *MIS Quarterly, 36*(1), 157–178. doi:10.2307/41410412

Vogels, E. A. (2019). *Millennials stand out for their technology use, but older generations also embrace digital life.* https://www.pewresearch.org/fact-tank/2019/09/09/us-generations-technology-use/

Wheeler, J. R., Janz, N. K., & Dodge, J. A. (2003). Can a disease self-management program reduce healthcare costs? The case of older women with heart disease. *Medical Care, 41*, 706–715. doi:10.1097/01.MLR.0000065128.72148.D7 PMID:12773836

Wood, W., & Neal, D. T. (2016). Healthy through habit: Interventions for initiating & maintaining health behavior change. *Behavioral Science & Policy, 2*(1), 71–83. doi:10.1353/bsp.2016.0008

Ziegelmann, J. P., & Knoll, N. (2015). Future directions in the study of health behavior among older adults. *Gerontology, 61*(5), 469–476. doi:10.1159/000369857 PMID:25660128

APPENDIX

Figure 1.

Beatrice and Trav design personas

Name: Beatrice
Age: 26
Job: User experience designer at a start-up company focusing on developing health self-monitoring wearable devices for hypertension.

Goal: To ensure the wearable health devices include components that empower older adults to want to engage with their wearable devices, which will lead to more self-monitoring of their health.

Name: Trav
Age: 27
Job: Human factors research lead at a large-scale company focusing on designing an integrated health system, including a mobile application and a portal, on supporting health self-management and transitions from surgery to home rehabilitation.

Goal: To support the design of a system designed to accommodate multiple stakeholders' needs, including healthcare providers, older adults, family members, and care partners.

Figure 2.

Example of Health Belief Model stages for a self-monitoring wearable device

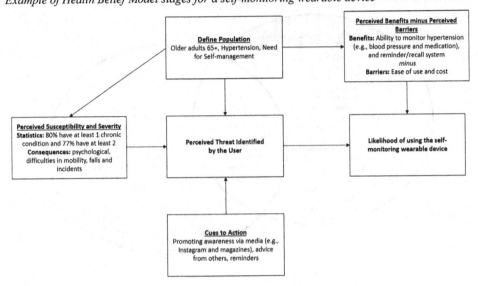

Figure 3.

Example of user stages in an integrated health system for home rehabilitation

Figure 4.

Predictors of behavior from health behavior change and technology acceptance models

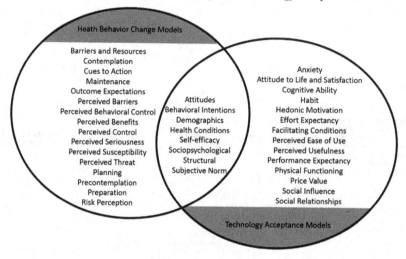

Figure 5.

The utilization of STAM in the development of a self-monitoring wearable device

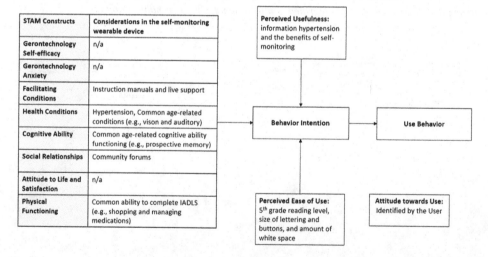

Figure 6.

The utilization of UTAUT2 in the development of an integrated health system

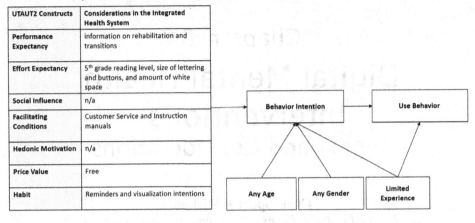

UTAUT2 Constructs	Considerations in the Integrated Health System
Performance Expectancy	information on rehabilitation and transitions
Effort Expectancy	5th grade reading level, size of lettering and buttons, and amount of white space
Social Influence	n/a
Facilitating Conditions	Customer Service and Instruction manuals
Hedonic Motivation	n/a
Price Value	Free
Habit	Reminders and visualization intentions

Chapter 8
Digital Mental Health Interventions:
Impact and Considerations

Christopher R Shelton
The Behrend College, Pennsylvania State University, Erie, USA

Anitgoni Kotsiou
The Behrend College, Pennsylvania State University, Erie, USA

Melanie D. Hetzel-Riggin
ⓘD https://orcid.org/0000-0001-7302-0676
The Behrend College, Pennsylvania State University, Erie, USA

ABSTRACT

This chapter will provide a brief background on the need for digital mental health interventions given the high rates of mental health issues and the barriers to access quality care. Three main types of digital mental health interventions (internet-based interventions [IBIs], smartphone apps, and virtual and augmented reality [VR and AR, respectively]) will be discussed, followed by a consideration of the ethical and logistical issues surrounding digital mental health interventions. The chapter will then address issues related to content and design, user engagement, user contact, and formatting of the interventions. Finally, the chapter will end with a discussion of future directions.

DOI: 10.4018/978-1-7998-6453-0.ch008

INTRODUCTION

Advancements in computers, technology, and the internet have led to rapid changes in mental health interventions. One growing field of study and practice in mental health treatment is the use of digital mental health interventions for psychological issues (Mora et al., 2008; Proudfoot et al., 2011; Wantland et al., 2004). With the increase of Internet and technology use for psychological purposes, both the research evidence and the use of telehealth has risen sharply (Ben-Zeev, 2020; Maheu & Gordon, 2000; Wantland et al., 2004).

According to data provided by the World Health Organization (WHO; Kessler et al., 2009), mental health disorders occur commonly across the world. In the United States alone, the lifetime prevalence rate of any type of mental health disorder is 47.4% (Kessler et al., 2009); similar rates are demonstrated across the globe (GBD Disease and Injury Incidence and Prevalence Collaborators, 2017). Wang et al. (2007) indicated that most people suffering from mental illness around the world do not receive treatment. While both younger and older populations tend to avoid mental health treatment, data reveal that emerging adults (i.e., 18-25 years old) have the highest rates of any mental health illness in comparison to all other adult populations; at the same time, emerging adults receive the lowest rate of mental health treatment compared to all other adult populations (Substance Abuse and Mental Health Services Administration, 2017). Overall, a vast expansion of treatment availability needs to occur (Wang et al., 2007). However, several barriers to treatment exist, such as affordability, accessibility, and availability of treatments or providers, as well as stigma associated with mental health. Addressing mental health needs using technology offers a way to reduce these barriers (Andersson & Titov, 2014; Boggs et al., 2014; Spek et al., 2007; Schueller et al., 2019; Wang et al., 2007).

As of 2018, 89% of adults use the internet and 77% of adults in the United States own a smartphone (Pew Research Center, 2017). Many digital or technological interventions and services have been created to assist with addressing mental health needs. Multiple practitioners developed these services to provide easy access to information and intervention-based programs to individuals who seek immediate attention (Cugelman et al., 2011).

Considering the COVID-19 pandemic, the desire for and use of digital mental health interventions has skyrocketed (Ben-Zeev, 2020; Torous et al., 2020). The COVID-19 pandemic has increased the need for mental health services to be provided via telehealth, as restrictions were put in place that would prohibit physical proximity between providers and consumers. Phone and videoconference are the methods most used and reported to be as acceptable, feasible, and effective as in-person delivery (Gloff et al., 2015; Osenbach et al., 2013). However, given the high rates of mental health concerns, significant barriers to care, and technological advances that have occurred in recent years, digital mental health interventions are becoming more common and effective. Three main types of digital mental health interventions (Internet-based interventions [IBIs], smartphone apps, and virtual and augmented reality [VR and AR, respectively]), have shown promise in treatment outcomes and accessibility.

DIGITAL MENTAL HEALTH INTERVENTIONS

Internet-Based Interventions

Internet-based interventions (IBIs), as set forth by Andersson and Titov (2014), encompass, "treatments that are mainly delivered via the Internet with at least some therapeutic tasks delegated to the computer" (p. 4). Internet-based interventions have proven to be quite effective across a wide range of psychological domains. Effective IBIs exist for treatment of a broad range of anxiety related issues (Andersson et al., 2005; Titov et al., 2010), as well as more specifically for severe health anxiety (Hedman et al., 2015), social anxiety disorder (SAD; Dagööa et al., 2014), phobias (Andersson et al., 2013; Kok et al., 2014), and panic disorder (PD; Klein et al., 2006; Ruwaard et al., 2010). Moreover, effective IBIs also exist for treating depression (Ruwaard et al., 2009; Williams & Andrews, 2013), comorbid depression and anxiety (Andersson et al., 2007; Arnberg et al., 2014), and even postnatal depression (O'Mahen et al., 2013). Internet-based interventions have also proven effective for treatment of posttraumatic stress disorder (PTSD) (Amstadter et al., 2009; Klein et al., 2009), alcoholism (Postel et al., 2005), chronic pain (Böing, 2014), and weight loss (Tate et al., 2001). It should be noted that this is not an exhaustive list of issues that IBIs have proven effective in treating; rather, it is simply meant to illustrate the breadth of areas in which IBIs are effective.

IBIs have been developed based on numerous psychological theories, including cognitive behavioral therapy (iCBT; Dagööa et al., 2014; Donker et al. 2013; Johansson et al., 2013; Kaltenthaler et al., 2006; Titov, 2007), behavioral activation (BA; Ly et al., 2014; O'Mahen et al., 2013), acceptance and commitment therapy (ACT; Böing, 2014), interpersonal therapy (Dagööa et al., 2014; Donker et al., 2013), psychodynamic therapy (Johansson et al., 2013), mindfulness-based therapy (Ly et al., 2014), problem-solving therapy (Johansson & Andersson, 2012), and transdiagnostic therapy (Titov, et al., 2010; Titov et al., 2011). IBIs using an integrative approach that use parts of several treatment modalities have also been developed, such as BA combined with ACT (Carlbring et al., 2013), mindfulness-based cognitive therapy (Beck et al., 2014), and transdiagnostic CBT (Newby et al., 2014). Another integrative

IBI combines elements of many treatment modalities, such as, BA, mindfulness and acceptance, and social skills training (Meyer et al., 2009).

IBIs have shown to be cost-effective (Blanchard, 2011; Hedman et al., 2011; Hedman et al., 2014), as well as clinically efficacious (Barak et al., 2008; Hedman et al., 2014; Proudfoot, 2004). Further, IBIs have the added benefit of flexibility; allowing clients to start immediately, work around their schedules, and work at the pace they desire (Boggs et al., 2014; Spek, et al., 2007). Moreover, IBIs allow clinicians to monitor a client's progress and outcomes in an IBI, as well as their overall safety, and are less prone to therapist drift (Andersson & Titov, 2014). Qualitative research by King et al. (2006) found that adolescent participants reported several stigma-related advantages offered by IBIs, including being able to avoid possible negative reactions from clinicians that they might encounter in face-to-face (F2F) treatments, as well as feeling less exposed emotionally. Lintvedt and colleagues (2008) found that among college students who self-reported a need for help, only a third sought help from traditional F2F mental health services. They concluded that an IBI (MoodGYM; Australian National University, 2015) was an effective way of reaching those students who needed help but did not seek out more traditional therapeutic treatment. Finally, studies have also shown that IBIs can be used by general practitioners with the same results as if the treatment had occurred with a psychologist (Pier et al., 2008; Shandley et al., 2008). Overall, while there is a large divide between mental health services that are needed and those that are offered (Kazdin, 2017; Postel et al., 2008), IBIs can help to begin to bridge that gap by educating individuals on mental health issues, reducing stigmas, and perhaps most importantly, simply increasing access to treatments (Farrell & McKinnon, 2003).

Smartphone Apps

Smartphones have been evaluated to integrate mental health services through technology (Luxton et al., 2011). Given that almost 80% of the world's population has access to mobile phones and the Internet, it is not surprising that thousands of mental health apps have been developed and are available for smartphone users. The increased use of smartphones globally has made smartphone apps more accessible for use in mental health care (Anthes, 2016). Many of these mental health apps are being recommended by health care providers and educational systems (Melcher & Torous, 2020; Mordecia et al., 2021).

Digital applications can be downloaded and used to monitor, record, and in some cases modify mental health, such as providing location-based services to alert users to the nearest mental health clinic; providing self-help mantras and guided meditations; and tracking mood ratings based on self-report (Luxton et al, 2011). Other newer applications addressing health needs through automated technology include such things as fitness watches automatically alerting users with feedback regarding different health concerns (e.g., having an elevated heartrate and the benefits of taking a deep breath to help depress the elevated heartrate). Further, smartphone applications were developed specifically to address mental health concerns stemming from the pandemic, such as symptoms of anxiety and depression (Kotsiou et al., 2021), while existing ones published updates with features relevant to COVID-19.

Smartphone apps can provide significant support for F2F interventions, increasing the overall effectiveness of treatment. Ivanova et al. (2016) found that the use of a smartphone app was able to compensate for the lack of clinician services for a wait-list control group when compared to evidence-based treatment for anxiety. In a random clinical trial of the smartphone app 'SuperBetter', users showed greater reductions in depressive symptoms than control participants (Roepke et al., 2015). The version of the app that addressed general mental health was as effective if not more effective than the specific cognitive strategies.

In a meta-analysis of smartphone apps for depression, Firth et al. (2017a) reported that smartphone apps were moderately more effective than no intervention in reducing depressive symptoms across 18 studies. Smartphone apps were also slightly more effective than other active interventions, especially when paired with other F2F or digital interventions. Similarly, Firth and colleagues (2017b) conducted a meta-analysis on nine randomized controlled trials of effectiveness of mental health apps on anxiety symptoms. Compared to control conditions, smartphone apps led to a small to moderate reduction in anxiety symptoms compared to control conditions, although there was significant variation across the studies. Further analysis demonstrated that apps that targeted general mental health and those that were integrated with other treatments led to the greatest benefit. Taken together, the results of the meta-analyses suggest that mental health apps can be a promising tool to reduce depression and anxiety.

Lagan et al. (2021) provided an overview of the state of available mental health apps currently available in iOS and Android stores. Of the 278 mental health apps that were available on both platforms, the most common functionality features identified were journaling, mood tracking, psychoeducation, mindfulness, and breathing techniques. Unfortunately, only a third of the apps were updated regularly, and many of them did not have strong levels of security. Metrics regarding effectiveness and engagement were also poor for most of the apps. Similarly, Larsen et al. (2019) reported that while 64% of the apps they found that claimed they were effective in addressing mental health issues, only three of the apps referenced published literature to support their claims. Larsen et al. (2016) also reported that while some apps provide best practice interventions, few provide truly comprehensive interventions and some even provide harmful content. In addition, research has demonstrated that app store ratings were not indicative of usability, clinical utility, or effectiveness

(Singh et al., 2016). Therefore, while smartphone apps can be useful treatment additions, the current state of mental health apps available to consumers are not as safe, comprehensive, and effective as we need them to be (Huckvale et al., 2020; Longyear & Kushlev, 2021).

Virtual/Augmented Reality

Virtual reality (VR) technology allows for the creation of electronic and interactive environments very similar to the real world. The computer-generated worlds can simulate reality with a high degree of precision, in part, because they involve visual, auditory, and tactile sensory information (Bastiaens et al., 2014). As the technology progresses, significant advances have been made towards using VR for therapeutic purposes. There are certain characteristics that render this technology a unique and valuable tool for mental health intervention.

Authenticity is the most basic advantage of VR in therapeutic settings. Theoretical or practical knowledge learnt through the authentic environment that VR can provide is more likely to be transferable and applicable to real life than imaginal experiences (Bastiaens et al., 2014). Skill competence can also be achieved easier and faster through VR than other modes of therapy (Deiman & Bastiaens, 2010; Wood & Reefke, 2010). The learning environment in VR settings is likely to provide a more realistic setting, which may increase the generalizability of learned skills, due, in part, to the high resemblance to real-life tasks capable of being introduced within VR environments (Bastiaens et al., 2014; Gulikers et al., 2005). A second unique advantage of VR is the depth of immersion the learner experiences, which allows for greater learning capacity (Bastiaens et al., 2014). All the senses that are involved when an individual uses VR (i.e., visual, auditory, and tactile) result in significant immersion within the virtual environment at both psychological and perceptual level.

Augmented reality (AR) technology takes a step forward from VR by augmenting real world environments with digital, computer generated visual or auditory content (e.g., trying on virtual eyeglass frames, playing Pokemon Go) (Chantzi et al., 2013; Hofmann & Mosemghvdlishvili, 2014). Much like VR, AR has been used in the military, engineering, medical training, and navigation (GPS) among other fields (Hofmann & Mosemghvdlishvili, 2014). In education, the use of AR has been shown to be very beneficial for learners. Studies demonstrate potential relations with AR use and improved long-term memory (Vincenzi et al., 2003), collaboration (Morrison et al., 2009), and physical task performance (Tang, Owen, Biocca, & Mou, 2003), while it has been shown to be slightly more effective in student motivation (Kaufmann & Dünser, 2007). Within the mental health field, AR technology has been effective in interactional and situational training with developmentally disabled individuals (Kim, 2013) and in assisting with exposure therapy, which is commonly used in the treatment of phobias (Breton-Lopez et al., 2010; Juan et al., 2005). More specifically regarding phobia treatment, the findings of a recent metanalysis (Suso-Ribera et al., 2019) demonstrate that VR exposure therapy, AR exposure therapy, and F2F exposure therapy were equally effective in reducing fear.

VR can be particularly helpful with treating mental health disorders that are related with social interactions, social skills, and fears. Individuals dealing with disorders within the anxiety spectrum, such as phobias, social anxiety, panic attacks, OCD, or PTSD, may find VR assisted psychotherapy very helpful and effective (Opriş, Pintea, et al., 2012). VR can also prove to be effective with individuals experiencing symptoms present in psychoses, substance abuse, and eating disorders (Freeman et al., 2017; Valmaggia et al., 2016). The authenticity and physicality of VR exposes individuals to environments otherwise inaccessible to them (Rizzo & Kim, 2005), allowing therapists to assist clients in learning appropriate and healthy skills needed to cope with their disorder that can transfer to real life situations (Freeman et al., 2017).

Besides development and implementation of treatment, VR has potential uses in assessment, diagnosis, identification of symptom triggers, formation of predictive and causal factors, and determination of key environmental elements (Freeman et al., 2017). Progress in VR and AR technology in the mental health field is astonishing, and advanced hardware and software continues to be developed. However, VR and AR technology is still far from being easily accessible to most mental health service providers and researchers. As a result, there is significant gap in our understanding of the true impact VR and AR technology may have on addressing mental health issues globally (Freeman et al., 2017).

Ethical Concerns Regarding Guidelines and Standards

Of particular concern, due to the rise in use of digital interventions, are ethical codes used to guide these interventions. Currently, several different guiding bodies, such as the American Psychological Association, American Counseling Association, the National Board of Certified Counselors, and the National Association of Social Workers, have updated ethical guidelines to directly reflect the use of digital interventions by practitioners (Rummell & Joyce, 2010). Midkiff and Joseph Wyatt (2008), note that while there have been improvements in bridging the gap between face-to-face treatment and digital interventions, much remains. Moreover, it is up to licensing boards and academics to help shape the future of digital mental health interventions. While detailing all the ethical and legal issues confronting digital interventions is beyond the scope of this paper, some of the more relevant issues are examined below.

Competence across several different domains is crucial in providing good treatment to a client, as well as the overall success of a digital intervention. First and foremost, as with F2F treatment, a clinician must be competent in offering the specific type of treatment, as well as familiar with the empirical literature pertaining to the treatment offered. It is the responsibility of the clinician to ensure that evidence-based treatments are provided to clients (Fisher & Fried, 2003; Midkiff et al., 2008). Therefore, if treatment for a disorder using digital interventions is not effective, or if the research into the effectiveness is still in progress, it is the responsibility of the clinician to report this to potential clients and to offer other evidence-based treatments or referrals to such treatments as an alternative.

When developing or providing digital interventions, a few additional issues involving competence arise (Fitzgerald et al., 2010). For instance, being able to verbally communicate your thoughts and ideas to a client is important in a F2F clinical setting. However, when providing services through digital interventions it is also important to be skilled at written communication, as this could be the primary form of contact. Further, many visual elements typically incorporated while conducting F2F assessments or diagnoses are lost using digital interventions. The ability to note a client's demeanor, hygiene, affect, and other visual elements is often difficult with digital interventions. Even if the digital intervention is being conducted using a video medium, a clinician must be cognizant of the fact that their ability to gather this information may still be limited (Childress, 2000; Midkiff & Joseph Wyatt, 2008; Rummell & Joyce, 2010).

Moreover, a clinician embarking on the path of digital interventions needs to be very competent in the realm of computer technology and security. Computer technology is a field that is changing rapidly. As a result, it is crucial that a clinician providing digital interventions be very comfortable with the technological means utilized to provide the treatment. They should have a comprehensive knowledge of working with video chat software, chat rooms, emailing, and any other technological methods used to provide service (Midkiff & Joseph Wyatt, 2008; Rummell & Joyce, 2010).

One drawback of digital interventions is the ever-present challenge of maintaining security of all data (Bennett et al., 2010; Coventry & Branley, 2018). Like the rapid advance of computer technology, computer security is also expanding and there has been a rapid increase in the number of hacking incidents in recent years (McLeod & Dolezel, 2018). Therefore, one must be intimately familiar with technological advances to ensure the privacy of their clients. Digital interventions must take precautions to use secure means of communication, as well as ensure that all data stores are encrypted to prevent accidental or nefarious leaks of information (Midkiff & Joseph Wyatt, 2008).

Beyond that, digital interventions face other problems common to F2F treatments as well. As with F2F treatment, digital interventions need to take into greater consideration how cultural considerations may factor into the effectiveness of the treatment (Mohr et al., 2014; Yellowlees et al., 2008). Of further concern is the inconsistency in research on clinician attitudes regarding digital interventions (Bucci et al., 2019; Gun et al., 2011; Mora et al., 2008; Stallard et al., 2010; Vigerland et al., 2014; Whitfield & Williams, 2004). Lastly, there is likely to be a risk of negative effects of treatment on clients. Yet, as noted by Rozental et al. (2014), there was not a consensus on how to best measure this occurrence in digital interventions.

Other important ethical considerations that clinicians wishing to conduct digital interventions should acquaint themselves with include avoidance of harm, informed consent, privacy and confidentiality, legal issues, liability, rules governing public statements, advertising, testimonials, fees, and undeclared conflicts of interest (Childress, 2000; Fitzgerald et al., 2010; Martinengo et al., 2019; Perle et al., 2011; Zack, 2008). One issue with the rise in research and application of digital mental health intervention is the lack of guidelines and standards to help this new field grow (Barak et al., 2009; Batterham et al., 2019; Proudfoot et al., 2011). For example, there are several different terms used to represent online mental health treatment, such as computer-mediated interventions, cybertherapy, eHealth, Internet psychotherapy, and webcounseling (Barak et al., 2009; Rummell & Joyce, 2010). As a result, there is a lack of clarity in the field, which causes issues for consumers and researchers alike. For that reason, researchers have worked towards setting up guidelines meant to standardize the field (Andersson, 2009; Barak et al., 2009; Proudfoot et al., 2011; Torous et al., 2019).

SOLUTIONS AND RECOMMENDATIONS

Content and Design

Several different elements work together to create appropriate overall content and design. Items to consider include appearance (color usage, layout, organization, and screen size), burdens placed on the user (difficulty of use and length of intervention), content (needs to be clear, accurate, and simple), delivery (animations, audio, illustrations, text, video, vignettes, and testimonials), message (source and style), and participation (interaction and reinforcement; Ritterband et al., 2009). Although research is limited, it has been suggested that a need exists for examining content and design related factors further to determine what value they may add to the digital mental health intervention (Ritterband et al., 2006).

Ease of login and navigation, useful and accurate information, consistent content updates, and being able to self-monitor progress made toward goal were all important factors affecting extended visits and revisits for adults (Brouwer et al., 2008; Schneider, van Osch, & de Vries, 2012a). Further, according to a systematic review examining not just mental health but physical health digital interventions, on average they lasted

10 weeks, were setup in a modular fashion, included interactive elements, received updates once a week, and were used by clients once a week (Kelders et al., 2012). Furthermore, the results indicated that digital mental health interventions were more likely to use tunneling (directed guidance through the intervention material) than those used for lifestyle change or chronic conditions. In contrast, digital mental health interventions were the least likely to use reduction (simplifying complex concepts or behaviors into easily understood steps) or self-monitoring (allowing participants to keep track of their own progress towards goals).

In addition, results demonstrate that elements such as interactivity (Barak et al., 2008; Brouwer et al., 2011; Rini et al., 2014; Ritterband et al., 2006), use of audio and graphic elements (Ritterband et al., 2006), consistent updates to the website (Brouwer et al., 2011) and the use of tunneling (Crutzen et al., 2012) have the potential to increase the effectiveness of a digital mental health intervention. Further, a review by Barak et al. (2008), suggests that both synchronous communication (live communication through chat, webcam, or other means) and asynchronous communication (communications that are not live, such as email and forums) with participants can be effective.

Engagement

Factors related to user engagement with digital mental health interventions have been studied in several groups (Borghouts et al., 2021). Povey et al. (2016) conducted qualitative focus groups regarding the acceptability of digital mental health interventions. The researchers reported that user engagement and acceptability of interventions was related to three areas. First, app characteristics played a role in user engagement and acceptability of the app. Specifically, content, ease of use, security features (such as password protection), level of personal information sharing, accessibility, and graphics were identified as areas of importance for consumers. Second, personal factors (such as literacy, language, technological ability, self-awareness about one's mental health issues, and motivation) were also influential in determining consumer's engagement in the digital mental health intervention. Third, environmental factors, such as availability of support, community awareness, stigma, culturally relevant graphics and content, and local production, were identified as areas related to consumer use of digital mental health apps.

Chan and Honey (2021) conducted a review of the literature to examine the acceptability and usability of digital mental health interventions. Results suggested that many consumers chose to use digital interventions as supplements for other traditional mental health interventions but were accepting and open to using the technology to varying degrees. Many participants reported that digital mental health interventions were helpful, especially when focusing on learning a new skill or knowledge or tracking symptoms. Consumers also rated digital mental health interventions as providing better access to care. Ease of use was essential to consumers, including being able to quickly learn how to use it, simple integration into daily life, and clarity of the directions. Engagement was also predicted by the degree of technical issues and fast addition of improvements or enhancements when needed.

User Contact

Preliminary results suggest that reminders can be useful in increasing client usage of digital mental health interventions (Hilvert-Bruce et al., 2012). Both phone and email reminders have demonstrated significant positive correlations with increased frequency of digital mental health intervention use (Brouwer et al., 2011; Robroek et al., 2012; Schneider et al., 2012b). Schneider and colleagues (2013) found that prompts sent early in the intervention (after two weeks of use) were more effective than prompts sent later in the intervention (after four or six weeks of use).

The role that frequency of contact with the practitioner guiding a digital intervention plays in the effectiveness of the intervention is not well understood (Andersson et al., 2007; Andersson & Titov, 2014). Results of studies examining the association between frequency of practitioner contact and outcome are conflicting. Klein et al. (2009) found no significant difference in treatment outcome based on level of therapist contact. Conversely, Johansson and Andersson (2012) found a significant positive correlation between frequency of contact and outcome. The conflicting results might be suggestive of disorder-specific factors moderating the association between frequency of contact and treatment outcome. As a result, more research is needed to help firmly establish if and how frequency of contact in a digital intervention is related to outcome.

Unguided, Guided, and Tailored Interventions

Research has consistently shown that both guided and unguided digital interventions can be efficacious for several mental health disorders (Andersson & Titov, 2014). Evidence would indicate that guided digital interventions produce greater treatment outcomes than unguided digital interventions (Andersson & Cuijpers, 2009; Andersson & Titov, 2014; Dülsen et al., 2020; Johansson & Andersson, 2012). However, greater treatment outcomes in guided digital interventions might be dependent upon the disorder being treated. For example, in a digital intervention for adults with ADHD only the unguided condition resulted in significant reductions in self-reported ADHD symptom severity (Pettersson et al., 2014).

A second explanation might be that only a limited number of factors in guided digital interventions are responsible for the increased treatment outcomes.

Specifically, the inclusion of more automated supportive factors in unguided digital interventions might increase treatment outcome. For instance, a meta-analysis of digital interventions for depression by Gellatly et al. (2007) found that although guided digital interventions were more effective than unguided digital interventions, when guided digital interventions were coded as either monitoring (i.e., monitoring material use and other non-therapeutic help) or supportive (i.e., offering therapeutic help such as advice or support), no increase in effectiveness was seen beyond monitoring.

There is also a shift that is occurring in mental health, one that is geared toward providing more personalized treatments to clients, to increase acceptability and treatment outcome (Titov et al., 2010). Tailoring digital interventions is the process of adapting different factors including treatment content, therapist factors, and delivery components to better suit the needs of each individual client (for an expansive review of different tailoring mechanisms see Lustria et al., 2009). Tailored digital interventions have the added benefit of avoiding the high exclusionary rates typically seen in non-tailored, manualized digital interventions which often focus on a specific disorder (Nordgren et al., 2014). For instance, tailored digital interventions could be created that have many therapeutic modules, each designed to treat a different disorder, such as depression, agoraphobia, and panic disorder; based on an individual's presenting issue, the digital interventions could then be tailored to include one or more modules specific to the issues the individual currently faces (Nordgren et al., 2012). Consequently, tailoring digital interventions allow for the treatment of other comorbidities beyond just the primary diagnosis. Moreover, tailoring factors such as personal relevance and content novelty are both positively related to acceptability and use of a digital intervention (Oenema et al., 2001), and information architecture (e.g., giving clients a choice of treatment components rather than assigning all modules) is an important factor in consumer judgment of digital intervention credibility (Danaher & Seeley, 2009).

Another possible way in which the tailoring of digital interventions might occur is using automated Internet-based assessments. Internet-based assessments can be a useful tool for referring potential clients to effective digital interventions, without the need for a firm diagnosis (Mason & Andrews, 2014). Moreover, according to Mason and Andrews (2014), automated self-report assessments may also eventually provide the best results compared with in person assessments by a clinician.

FUTURE RESEARCH DIRECTIONS

Further research is needed to elucidate under what settings digital mental health interventions would prove most effective. For instance, research has demonstrated that guided digital mental health interventions have been effective in ameliorating presenting symptoms when prescribed in several different settings including clinical (Andersson & Hedman, 2013), psychiatric (Bergström et al., 2009; Bergström et al., 2010), and general practitioner settings (Nordgren et al., 2014; Shandley et al., 2008). However, as noted by Andersson and Hedman (2013) in a review of guided digital interventions for many common mental health disorders, several issues remain regarding the setting in which a digital intervention is administered. There exists a need to determine outcome predictors for digital interventions in community samples. A second and more general issue noted was that there is no standard by which to follow for describing or reporting digital interventions. This further complicated the task of trying to determine the efficacy and effectiveness of digital interventions.

Future research should also examine the role of the therapist in digital mental health intervention outcomes. Andersson and Hedman (2013) suggest that guided digital interventions are efficacious in a few areas, including PTSD, depression, seasonal affective disorder, generalized anxiety disorder, and panic disorder; however, there is far less research on effectiveness. Amstadter et al. (2009) acknowledge that research is needed to better understand the dose-response relationship between clinician contact and treatment outcome. The existing literature does suggest that unguided digital interventions can be effective (Boettcher et al., 2014; Spek et al., 2007). However, there is still a significant need to better understand if certain factors affect whom would be best suited to use an unguided, guided, or tailored digital intervention (Andersson, 2014). Better understanding what the target population of unguided digital interventions should be is important because unguided digital interventions have the added benefit of expanding the reach of treatment and potentially helping those who do not have other alternatives or would not otherwise seek assistance.

CONCLUSION

Typically, mental health needs across the nation outpace the resources available to address them. By conducting additional research on digital mental health interventions, we will gain insight into people's current use of, or potential future uses of technology to assist in addressing their mental health needs. With a better understanding of areas of mental health strength and weakness, we can work to remediate areas of weakness that may exist. Producing digital mental health products would provide additional avenues for people to access mental health resources and potentially help reduce the discrepancy between the increasing need for mental health services and the resource constraints that typically exist. Ultimately, this work has the potential to help broader populations of people across the world.

REFERENCES

Amstadter, A. B., Broman-Fulks, J., Zinzow, H., Ruggiero, K. J., & Cercone, J. (2009). Internet-based interventions for traumatic stress-related mental health problems: A review and suggestion for future research. *Clinical Psychology Review*, *29*(5), 410–420. doi:10.1016/j.cpr.2009.04.001 PMID:19403215

Andersson, G. (2014). Age may moderate response to different unguided Internet-delivered interventions for depression. *Evidence-Based Mental Health*, *17*(1), 29. doi:10.1136/eb-2013-101638 PMID:24477534

Andersson, G., Berg, M., Riper, H., Huppert, J. D., & Titov, N. (2020). The Possible Role of Internet-Delivered Psychological Interventions in Relation to the COVID-19 Pandemic. *Clinical Psychology in Europe*, *2*(3), 1–4. doi:10.32872/cpe.v2i3.3941

Andersson, G., Bergström, J., Carlbring, P., & Lindefors, N. (2005). The use of the Internet in the treatment of anxiety disorders. *Current Opinion in Psychiatry*, *18*(1), 73–77. PMID:16639187

Andersson, G., & Cuijpers, P. (2009). Internet-based and other computerized psychological treatments for adult depression: A meta-analysis. *Cognitive Behaviour Therapy*, *38*(4), 196–205. doi:10.1080/16506070903318960 PMID:20183695

Andersson, G., Cuijpers, P., Carlbring, P., & Lindefors, N. (2007). Effects of Internet-delivered cognitive behaviour therapy for anxiety and mood disorders. *Psychiatry*, *1*(2), 9–14.

Andersson, G., & Hedman, E. (2013). Effectiveness of guided internet-based cognitive behavior therapy in regular clinical settings. *Verhaltenstherapie*, *23*(3), 140–148. doi:10.1159/000354779

Andersson, G., & Titov, N. (2014). Advantages and limitations of Internet-based interventions for common mental disorders. *World Psychiatry; Official Journal of the World Psychiatric Association (WPA)*, *13*(1), 4–11. doi:10.1002/wps.20083 PMID:24497236

Andersson, G., Waara, J., Jonsson, U., Malmaeus, F., Carlbring, P., & Öst, L.-G. (2013). Internet-Based Exposure Treatment Versus One-Session Exposure Treatment of Snake Phobia: A Randomized Controlled Trial. *Cognitive Behaviour Therapy*, *42*(4), 284–291. doi:10.1080/16506073.2013.844202 PMID:24245707

Anthes, E. (2016). Mental health: There's an app for that. *NATNews*, *532*(7597), 20–23. doi:10.1038/532020a PMID:27078548

Arnberg, F. K., Linton, S. J., Hultcrantz, M., Heintz, E., & Jonsson, U. (2014). Internet-delivered psychological treatments for mood and anxiety disorders: A systematic review of their efficacy, safety, and cost-effectiveness. *PLoS One*, *9*(5), e98118. doi:10.1371/journal.pone.0098118 PMID:24844847

Australian National University. (2015). *MoodGYM*. Retrieved 2021, May 14, from http://www.moodgym.anu.edu.au

Barak, A., Hen, L., Boniel-Nissim, M., & Shapira, N. (2008). A comprehensive review and a meta-analysis of the effectiveness of internet-based psychotherapeutic interventions. *Journal of Technology in Human Services*, *26*(2-4), 109–160. doi:10.1080/15228830802094429

Barak, A., Klein, B., & Proudfoot, J. G. (2009). Defining internet-supported therapeutic interventions. *Annals of Behavioral Medicine*, *38*(1), 4–17. doi:10.100712160-009-9130-7 PMID:19787305

Bastieans, T. J., Wood, L. C., & Reiners, T. (2014). New landscapes and new eye: The role of virtual world design for supply chain education. *Ubiquitous Learning: An International Journal*, *6*(1), 37–49. doi:10.18848/1835-9795/CGP/v06i01/40388

Batterham, P. J., Calear, A. L., O'Dea, B., Larsen, M. E. J., Kavanagh, D., Titov, N., March, S., Hickie, I., Teesson, M., Deat, B. F., Reynolds, J., Lowinger, J., Thorton, L., & Gorman, P. (2019). Stakeholder perspectives on evidence for digital mental health interventions: Implications for accreditation systems. *Digital Health*, *5*, 2055207619878069. doi:10.1177/2055207619878069 PMID:31565238

Beck, A., Dimidjian, S., Boggs, J., Felder, J., & Segal, Z. (2014). PS2-43: Internet delivered mindfulness-based cognitive therapy for reducing residual depressive symptoms: An open trial and quasi-experimental comparison to propensity matched controls. *Clinical Medicine & Research*, *12*(1-2), 104. doi:10.3121/cmr.2014.1250. ps2-43

Ben-Zeev, D. (2020). The digital mental health genie is out of the bottle. *Psychiatric Services (Washington, D.C.)*, *71*(12), 1212–1213. doi:10.1176/appi.ps.202000306 PMID:32576123

Bennett, K., Bennett, A. J., & Griffiths, K. M. (2010). Security considerations for e-mental health interventions. *Journal of Medical Internet Research*, *12*(5), e61. doi:10.2196/jmir.1468 PMID:21169173

Bergström, J., Andersson, G., Karlsson, A., Andréewitch, S., Rück, C., Carlbring, P., & Lindefors, N. (2009). An open study of the effectiveness of Internet treatment for panic disorder delivered in a psychiatric setting. *Nordic Journal of Psychiatry*, *63*(1), 44–50. doi:10.1080/08039480802191132 PMID:18985514

Bergström, J., Andersson, G., Ljótsson, B., Rück, C., Andréewitch, S., Karlsson, A., Carlbring, O., Andersson, E., & Lindefors, N. (2010). Internet-versus group-administered cognitive behaviour therapy for panic disorder in a psychiatric setting: A randomised trial. *BMC Psychiatry*, *10*(1), 54. doi:10.1186/1471-244X-10-54 PMID:20598127

Blanchard, M. (2011). *Navigating the digital disconnect: understanding the use of information communication technologies by the youth health workforce to help improve young people's mental health and wellbeing* (Ph.D. Thesis). The University of Melbourne, Melbourne, Australia.

Boettcher, J., Aström, V., Påhlsson, D., Schenström, O., Andersson, G., & Carlbring, P. (2014). Internet-based mindfulness treatment for anxiety disorders: A randomized controlled trial. *Behavior Therapy*, *45*(2), 241–253. doi:10.1016/j.beth.2013.11.003 PMID:24491199

Boggs, J. M., Beck, A., Felder, J. N., Dimidjian, S., Metcalf, C. A., & Segal, Z. V. (2014). Web-Based Intervention in Mindfulness Meditation for Reducing Residual Depressive Symptoms and Relapse Prophylaxis: A Qualitative Study. *Journal of Medical Internet Research*, *16*(3), e87. doi:10.2196/jmir.3129 PMID:24662625

Böing, J. (2014). Effect- and process evaluation of an internet- based intervention of Acceptance & Commitment Therapy for chronic pain patients: a randomized controlled trial (Master of Science). University of Twente, Netherlands.

Borghouts, J., Eikey, E., Mark, G., De Leon, C., Schueller, S. M., Schneider, M., Stadnick, N., Zheng, K., Mukamel, D., & Sorkin, D. H. (2021). Barriers to and Facilitators of User Engagement With Digital Mental Health Interventions: Systematic Review. *Journal of Medical Internet Research*, *23*(3), e24387. doi:10.2196/24387 PMID:33759801

Bretón-López, J., Quero, S., Botella, C., García-Palacios, A., Baños, R. M., & Alcañiz, M. (2010). An augmented reality system validation for the treatment of cockroach phobia. *Cyberpsychology, Behavior, and Social Networking*, *13*(6), 705–710. doi:10.1089/cyber.2009.0170 PMID:21142997

Brouwer, W., Oenema, A., Crutzen, R., de Nooijer, J., de Vries, N. K., & Brug, J. (2008). An exploration of factors related to dissemination of and exposure to internet-delivered behavior change interventions aimed at adults: A Delphi study approach. *Journal of Medical Internet Research, 10*(2), e10. doi:10.2196/jmir.956 PMID:18417443

Bucci, S., Berry, N., Morris, R., Berry, K., Haddock, G., Lewis, S., & Edge, D. (2019). "They Are Not Hard-to-Reach Clients. We Have Just Got Hard-to-Reach Services." Staff Views of Digital Health Tools in Specialist Mental Health Services. *Frontiers in Psychiatry, 10*, 344. doi:10.3389/fpsyt.2019.00344 PMID:31133906

Carlbring, P., Hägglund, M., Luthström, A., Dahlin, M., Kadowaki, Å., Vernmark, K., & Andersson, G. (2013). Internet-based behavioral activation and acceptance-based treatment for depression: A randomized controlled trial. *Journal of Affective Disorders, 148*(2), 331–337. doi:10.1016/j.jad.2012.12.020 PMID:23357657

Chan, A. H. Y., & Honey, M. L. (2021). User perceptions of mobile digital apps for mental health: Acceptability and usability-An integrative review. *Journal of Psychiatric and Mental Health Nursing*, jpm.12744. Advance online publication. doi:10.1111/jpm.12744 PMID:33604946

Chantzi, A. E., Plessa, C., Chatziparadeisis Gkanas, I., Tsakalidis, A., & Tsolis, D. (2013, July). An innovative augmented reality educational platform using gamification to enhance lifelong learning and cultural education. *International Conference on Information.*

Childress, C. A. (2000). Ethical Issues in Providing Online Psychotherapeutic Interventions. *Journal of Medical Internet Research, 2*(1), e5. doi:10.2196/jmir.2.1.e5 PMID:11720924

Coventry, L., & Branley, D. (2018). Cybersecurity in healthcare: A narrative review of trends, threats and ways forward. *Maturitas, 113*, 48–52. doi:10.1016/j.maturitas.2018.04.008 PMID:29903648

Crutzen, R., Cyr, D., & de Vries, N. K. (2012). The role of user control in adherence to and knowledge gained from a website: Randomized comparison between a tunneled version and a freedom-of-choice version. *Journal of Medical Internet Research, 14*(2), e45. doi:10.2196/jmir.1922 PMID:22532074

Cugelman, B., Thelwall, M., & Dawes, P. (2011). Online interventions for social marketing health behavior change campaigns: A meta-analysis of psychological architectures and adherence factors. *Journal of Medical Internet Research, 13*(1), e17. doi:10.2196/jmir.1367 PMID:21320854

Dagööa, J., Asplund, R. P., Bsenko, H. A., Hjerling, S., Holmberg, A., Westh, S., Öberg, L., Ljótsson, B., Carlbring, P., Fumark, T., & Andersson, G. (2014). Cognitive behavior therapy versus interpersonal psychotherapy for social anxiety disorder delivered via smartphone and computer: A randomized controlled trial. *Journal of Anxiety Disorders, 28*(4), 410–417. doi:10.1016/j.janxdis.2014.02.003 PMID:24731441

Danaher, B. G., & Seeley, J. R. (2009). Methodological issues in research on web-based behavioral interventions. *Annals of Behavioral Medicine, 38*(1), 28–39. doi:10.100712160-009-9129-0 PMID:19806416

Deiman, M., & Bastiaens, T. (2010). Competency-based education in an electronic-supported environment: An example from a distance teaching university. *International Journal of Continuing Engineering Education and Lifelong Learning, 20*(3/4/5), 278–289. doi:10.1504/IJCEELL.2010.037046

Donker, T., Bennett, K., Bennett, A., Mackinnon, A., van Straten, A., Cuijpers, P., Christensen, H., & Griffiths, M. K. (2013). Internet-delivered interpersonal psychotherapy versus internet-delivered cognitive behavioral therapy for adults with depressive symptoms: Randomized controlled noninferiority trial. *Journal of Medical Internet Research, 15*(5), e82. doi:10.2196/jmir.2307 PMID:23669884

Dülsen, P., Bendig, E., Küchler, A. M., Christensen, H., & Baumeister, H. (2020). Digital interventions in adult mental healthcare settings: Recent evidence and future directions. *Current Opinion in Psychiatry, 33*(4), 422–431. doi:10.1097/YCO.0000000000000614 PMID:32427592

Farrell, S. P., & McKinnon, C. R. (2003). Technology and rural mental health. *Archives of Psychiatric Nursing, 17*(1), 20–26. doi:10.1053/apnu.2003.4 PMID:12642884

Firth, J., Torous, J., Nicholas, J., Carney, R., Pratap, A., Rosenbaum, S., & Sarris, J. (2017a). The efficacy of smartphone-based mental health interventions for depressive symptoms: A meta-analysis of randomized controlled trials. *World Psychiatry; Official Journal of the World Psychiatric Association (WPA), 16*(3), 287–298. doi:10.1002/wps.20472 PMID:28941113

Firth, J., Torous, J., Nicholas, J., Carney, R., Rosenbaum, S., & Sarris, J. (2017b). Can smartphone mental health interventions reduce symptoms of anxiety? A meta-analysis of randomized controlled trials. *Journal of Affective Disorders, 218*, 15–22. doi:10.1016/j.jad.2017.04.046 PMID:28456072

Fisher, C. B., & Fried, A. L. (2003). Internet-mediated psychological services and the American Psychological Association Ethics Code. *Psychotherapy (Chicago, Ill.), 40*(1-2), 103–111. doi:10.1037/0033-3204.40.1-2.103

Fitzgerald, T. D., Hunter, P. V., Hadjistavropoulos, T., & Koocher, G. P. (2010). Ethical and legal considerations for internet-based psychotherapy. *Cognitive Behaviour Therapy*, *39*(3), 173–187. doi:10.1080/16506071003636046 PMID:20485997

Freeman, D., Reeve, S., Robinson, A., Ehlers, A., Clark, D., Spanlang, B., & Slater, M. (2017). Virtual reality in the assessment, understanding, and treatment of mental health disorders. *Psychological Medicine*, *47*(14), 2393–2400. doi:10.1017/S003329171700040X PMID:28325167

GBD 2017 Disease and Injury Incidence and Prevalence Collaborators. (2018). Global, regional, and national incidence, prevalence, and years lived with disability for 354 diseases and injuries for 195 countries and territories, 1990-2017: a systematic analysis for the Global Burden of Disease Study 2017. *Lancet*, *392*(10159), 1789-1858. . doi:10.1016/S0140-6736(18)32279-7

Gellatly, J., Bower, P., Hennessy, S., Richards, D., Gilbody, S., & Lovell, K. (2007). What makes self-help interventions effective in the management of depressive symptoms? Meta-analysis and meta-regression. *Psychological Medicine*, *37*(9), 1217–1228. doi:10.1017/S0033291707000062 PMID:17306044

Geraets, C. N., van der Stouwe, E. C., Pot-Kolder, R., & Veling, W. (2021). Advances in immersive virtual reality interventions for mental disorders–a new reality? *Current Opinion in Psychology*, *41*, 40–45. doi:10.1016/j.copsyc.2021.02.004 PMID:33714892

Gloff, N. E., LeNoue, S. R., Novins, D. K., & Myers, K. (2015). Telemental health for children and adolescents. *International Review of Psychiatry (Abingdon, England)*, *27*(6), 513–524. doi:10.3109/09540261.2015.1086322 PMID:26540584

Guazzaroni, G. (Ed.). (2018). *Virtual and augmented reality in mental health treatment*. IGI Global.

Gulikers, J. T. M., Bastiaens, T. J., & Martens, R. L. (2005). The surplus value of an authentic learning environment. *Computers in Human Behavior*, *21*(3), 509–521. doi:10.1016/j.chb.2004.10.028

Gun, S. Y., Titov, N., & Andrews, G. (2011). Acceptability of Internet treatment of anxiety and depression. *Australasian Psychiatry*, *19*(3), 259–264. doi:10.3109/10398562.2011.562295 PMID:21682626

Hedman, E., Andersson, E., Ljotsson, B., Andersson, G., Ruck, C., & Lindefors, N. (2011). Cost-effectiveness of Internet-based cognitive behavior therapy vs. cognitive behavioral group therapy for social anxiety disorder: Results from a randomized controlled trial. *Behaviour Research and Therapy*, *49*(11), 729–736. doi:10.1016/j.brat.2011.07.009 PMID:21851929

Hedman, E., El Alaoui, S., Lindefors, N., Andersson, E., Rück, C., Ghaderi, A., Kaldo, V., Lekander, M., Andersson, G., & Ljótsson, B. (2014). Clinical effectiveness and cost-effectiveness of Internet- vs. group-based cognitive behavior therapy for social anxiety disorder: 4-year follow-up of a randomized trial. *Behaviour Research and Therapy*, *59*, 20–29. doi:10.1016/j.brat.2014.05.010 PMID:24949908

Hilvert-Bruce, Z., Rossouw, P. J., Wong, N., Sunderland, M., & Andrews, G. (2012). Adherence as a determinant of effectiveness of internet cognitive behavioural therapy for anxiety and depressive disorders. *Behaviour Research and Therapy*, *50*(7-8), 463–468. doi:10.1016/j.brat.2012.04.001 PMID:22659155

Hofmann, S., & Mosemghvdlishvili, L. (2014). Perceiving spaces through digital augmentation: An exploratory study of navigation augmented reality apps. *Mobile Media & Communication*, *2*(3), 265–280. doi:10.1177/2050157914530700

Huckvale, K., Nicholas, J., Torous, J., & Larsen, M. E. (2020). Smartphone apps for the treatment of mental health conditions: Status and considerations. *Current Opinion in Psychology*, *36*, 65–70. Advance online publication. doi:10.1016/j.copsyc.2020.04.008 PMID:32553848

Ivanova, E., Lindner, P., Ly, K. H., Dahlin, M., Vernmark, K., Andersson, G., & Carlbring, P. (2016). Guided and unguided Acceptance and Commitment Therapy for social anxiety disorder and/or panic disorder provided via the Internet and a smartphone application: A randomized controlled trial. *Journal of Anxiety Disorders*, *44*, 27–35. doi:10.1016/j.janxdis.2016.09.012 PMID:27721123

Johansson, R., & Andersson, G. (2012). Internet-based psychological treatments for depression. *Expert Review of Neurotherapeutics*, *12*(7), 861–869. doi:10.1586/ern.12.63 PMID:22853793

Johansson, R., Nyblom, A., Carlbring, P., Cuijpers, P., & Andersson, G. (2013). Choosing between Internet-based psychodynamic versus cognitive behavioral therapy for depression: A pilot preference study. *BMC Psychiatry*, *13*(1), 268. doi:10.1186/1471-244X-13-268 PMID:24139066

Juan, M. C., Alcaniz, M., Monserrat, C., Botella, C., Baños, R. M., & Guerrero, B. (2005). Using augmented reality to treat phobias. *IEEE Computer Graphics and Applications*, *25*(6), 31–37. doi:10.1109/MCG.2005.143 PMID:16315475

Kaltenthaler, E., Brazier, J., De Nigris, E., Tumur, I., Ferriter, M., Beverley, C., Parry, G., Rooney, G., & Sutcliffe, P. (2006). Computerised cognitive behaviour therapy for depression and anxiety update: A systematic review and economic evaluation. *Health Technology Assessment, 10*(33), 1–186. doi:10.3310/hta10330 PMID:16959169

Kaufmann, H., & Dünser, A. (2007, July). Summary of usability evaluations of an educational augmented reality application. In *International conference on virtual reality* (pp. 660-669). Springer. 10.1007/978-3-540-73335-5_71

Kazdin, A. E. (2017). Addressing the treatment gap: A key challenge for extending evidence-based psychosocial interventions. *Behaviour Research and Therapy, 88,* 7–18. doi:10.1016/j.brat.2016.06.004 PMID:28110678

Kelders, S. M., Kok, R. N., Ossebaard, H. C., & van Gemert-Pijnen, J. E. W. C. (2012). Persuasive system design does matter: A systematic review of adherence to web-based interventions. *Journal of Medical Internet Research, 14*(6), e152. doi:10.2196/jmir.2104 PMID:23151820

Kessler, R. C., Aguilar-Gaxiola, S., Alonso, J., Chatterji, S., Lee, S., Ormel, J., Üstün, T. B., & Wang, P. S. (2009). The global burden of mental disorders: An update from the WHO World Mental Health (WMH) surveys. *Epidemiologia e Psichiatria Sociale, 18*(1), 23–33. doi:10.1017/S1121189X00001421 PMID:19378696

Kim, T. Y. (2013). A Situational Training System for Developmentally Disabled People Based on Augmented Reality. *IEICE Transactions on Information and Systems, 96*(D), 1561–1564. doi:10.1587/transinf.E96.D.1561

King, R., Bambling, M., Lloyd, C., Gomurra, R., Smith, S., Reid, W., & Wegner, K. (2006). Online counselling: The motives and experiences of young people who choose the Internet instead of face to face or telephone counselling. *Counselling & Psychotherapy Research, 6*(3), 169–174. doi:10.1080/14733140600848179

Klein, B., Austin, D., Pier, C., Kiropoulos, L., Shandley, K., Mitchell, J., Gilson, K., & Ciechomski, L. (2009). Internet-based treatment for panic disorder: Does frequency of therapist contact make a difference? *Cognitive Behaviour Therapy, 38*(2), 100–113. doi:10.1080/16506070802561132 PMID:19306149

Klein, B., Mitchell, J., Gilson, K., Shandley, K., Austin, D., Kiropoulos, L., Abbott, J., & Cannard, G. (2009). A therapist-assisted internet-based cbt intervention for posttraumatic stress disorder: Preliminary results. *Cognitive Behaviour Therapy, 38*(2), 121–131. doi:10.1080/16506070902803483 PMID:20183691

Klein, B., Richards, J. C., & Austin, D. W. (2006). Efficacy of internet therapy for panic disorder. *Journal of Behavior Therapy and Experimental Psychiatry, 37*(3), 213–238. doi:10.1016/j.jbtep.2005.07.001 PMID:16126161

Kok, R. N., van Straten, A., Beekman, A. T. F., & Cuijpers, P. (2014). Short-term effectiveness of web-based guided self-help for phobic outpatients: Randomized controlled trial. *Journal of Medical Internet Research, 16*(9), e226. doi:10.2196/jmir.3429 PMID:25266929

Kotsiou, A., Juriasingani, E., Maromonte, M., Marsh, J., Shelton, C. R., Zhao, R., & Elliot, L. J. (2021). Interdisciplinary approach to a coping skills app: A case study. The Journal of Interactive Technology and Pedagogy, *19.*

Lagan, S., D'Mello, R., Vaidyam, A., Bilden, R., & Torous, J. (2021). Assessing mental health apps marketplaces with objective metrics from 29,190 data points from 278 apps. *Acta Psychiatrica Scandinavica.* Advance online publication. doi:10.1111/acps.13306

Larsen, M. E., Huckvale, K., Nicholas, J., Torous, J., Birrell, L., Li, E., & Reda, B. (2019). Using science to sell apps: Evaluation of mental health app store quality claims. *NPJ Digital Medicine, 2*(1), 1–6. doi:10.103841746-019-0093-1 PMID:31304366

Linardon, J., Cuijpers, P., Carlbring, P., Messer, M., & Fuller-Tyszkiewicz, M. (2019). The efficacy of app-supported smartphone interventions for mental health problems: A meta-analysis of randomized controlled trials. *World Psychiatry; Official Journal of the World Psychiatric Association (WPA), 18*(3), 325–336. doi:10.1002/wps.20673 PMID:31496095

Lintvedt, O. K., Griffiths, K. M., Sørensen, K., Østvik, A. R., Wang, C. E. A., Eisemann, M., & Waterloo, K. (2013). Evaluating the effectiveness and efficacy of unguided internet-based self-help intervention for the prevention of depression: A randomized controlled trial. *Clinical Psychology & Psychotherapy, 20*(1), 10–27. doi:10.1002/cpp.770 PMID:21887811

Longyear, R. L., & Kushlev, K. (2021). Can mental health apps be effective for depression, anxiety, and stress during a pandemic? *Practice Innovations (Washington, D.C.).* Advance online publication. doi:10.1037/pri0000142

Lustria, M. L. A., Cortese, J., Noar, S. M., & Glueckauf, R. L. (2009). Computer-tailored health interventions delivered over the Web: Review and analysis of key components. *Patient Education and Counseling, 74*(2), 156–173. doi:10.1016/j.pec.2008.08.023 PMID:18947966

Luxton, D. D., McCann, R. A., Bush, N. E., Mishkind, M. C., & Reger, G. M. (2011). mHealth for mental health: Integrating smartphone technology in behavioral healthcare. *Professional Psychology, Research and Practice, 42*(6), 505–512. doi:10.1037/a0024485

Ly, K. H., Trüschel, A., Jarl, L., Magnusson, S., Windahl, T., Johansson, R., Carlbring, P., & Andersson, G. (2014). Behavioural activation versus mindfulness-based guided self-help treatment administered through a smartphone application: A randomised controlled trial. *BMJ Open, 4*(1), e003440. doi:10.1136/bmjopen-2013-003440 PMID:24413342

Maheu, M. M., & Gordon, B. L. (2000). Counseling and therapy on the Internet. *Professional Psychology, Research and Practice, 31*(5), 484–489. doi:10.1037/0735-7028.31.5.484

Martinengo, L., Van Galen, L., Lum, E., Kowalski, M., Subramaniam, M., & Car, J. (2019). Suicide prevention and depression apps' suicide risk assessment and management: A systematic assessment of adherence to clinical guidelines. *BMC Medicine, 17*(1), 1–12. doi:10.118612916-019-1461-z PMID:31852455

Mason, E. C., & Andrews, G. (2014). The use of automated assessments in internet-based CBT: The computer will be with you shortly. *Internet Interventions: the Application of Information Technology in Mental and Behavioural Health, 1*(4), 216–224. doi:10.1016/j.invent.2014.10.003

McLeod, A., & Dolezel, D. (2018). Cyber-analytics: Modeling factors associated with healthcare data breaches. *Decision Support Systems, 108*, 57–68. doi:10.1016/j.dss.2018.02.007

Melcher, J., & Torous, J. (2020). Smartphone apps for college mental health: A concern for privacy and quality of current offerings. *Psychiatric Services (Washington, D.C.), 71*(11), 1114–1119. doi:10.1176/appi.ps.202000098 PMID:32664822

Meyer, B., Berger, T., Caspar, F., Beevers, C. G., Andersson, G., & Weiss, M. (2009). Effectiveness of a novel integrative online treatment for depression (Deprexis): Randomized controlled trial. *Journal of Medical Internet Research, 11*(2), e15. doi:10.2196/jmir.1151 PMID:19632969

Midkiff, D. M., & Joseph Wyatt, W. (2008). Ethical issues in the provision of online mental health services (Etherapy). *Journal of Technology in Human Services, 26*(2-4), 310–332. doi:10.1080/15228830802096994

Mohr, D. C., Schueller, S. M., Araya, R., Gureje, O., & Montague, E. (2014). Mental health technologies and the needs of cultural groups. *The Lancet. Psychiatry, 1*(5), 326–327. doi:10.1016/S2215-0366(14)70261-5 PMID:26360986

Mora, L., Nevid, J., & Chaplin, W. (2008). Psychologist treatment recommendations for Internet-based therapeutic interventions. *Computers in Human Behavior, 24*(6), 3052–3062. doi:10.1016/j.chb.2008.05.011

Mordecai, D., Histon, T., Neuwirth, E., Heisler, W. S., Kraft, A., Bang, Y., Franchino, K., Taillac, C., & Nixon, J. P. (2021). How Kaiser Permanente created a mental health and wellness digital ecosystem. *NEJM Catalyst Innovations in Care Delivery, 2*(1), CAT.20.0295. Advance online publication. doi:10.1056/CAT.20.0295

Morrison, A., Oulasvirta, A., Peltonen, P., Lemmela, S., Jacucci, G., Reitmayr, G., ... Juustila, A. (2009, April). Like bees around the hive: a comparative study of a mobile augmented reality map. In *Proceedings of the SIGCHI conference on human factors in computing systems* (pp. 1889-1898). 10.1145/1518701.1518991

Newby, J. M., Mewton, L., Williams, A. D., & Andrews, G. (2014). Effectiveness of transdiagnostic internet cognitive behavioural treatment for mixed anxiety and depression in primary care. *Journal of Affective Disorders, 165*(0), 45–52. doi:10.1016/j.jad.2014.04.037 PMID:24882176

Nordgren, L. B., Hedman, E., Etienne, J., Bodin, J., Kadowaki, Å., Eriksson, S., Lindkvist, E., Andersson, G., & Carlbring, P. (2014). Effectiveness and cost-effectiveness of individually tailored Internet-delivered cognitive behavior therapy for anxiety disorders in a primary care population: A randomized controlled trial. *Behaviour Research and Therapy, 59*(0), 1–11. doi:10.1016/j.brat.2014.05.007 PMID:24933451

O'Mahen, H. A., Woodford, J., McGinley, J., Warren, F. C., Richards, D. A., Lynch, T. R., & Taylor, R. S. (2013). Internet-based behavioral activation—treatment for postnatal depression (Netmums): A randomized controlled trial. *Journal of Affective Disorders, 150*(3), 814–822. doi:10.1016/j.jad.2013.03.005 PMID:23602514

Oenema, A., Brug, J., & Lechner, L. (2001). Web-based tailored nutrition education: Results of a randomized controlled trial. *Health Education Research, 16*(6), 647–660. doi:10.1093/her/16.6.647 PMID:11780705

Opriş, D., Pintea, S., García-Palacios, A., Botella, C., Szamosközi, Ş., & David, D. (2012). Virtual reality exposure therapy in anxiety disorders: A quantitative meta-analysis. *Depression and Anxiety, 29*(2), 85–93. doi:10.1002/da.20910 PMID:22065564

Osenbach, J. E., O'Brien, K. M., Mishkind, M., & Smolenski, D. J. (2013). Synchronous telehealth technologies in psychotherapy for depression: A meta-analysis. *Depression and Anxiety, 30*(11), 1058–1067. doi:10.1002/da.22165 PMID:23922191

Parker, L., Halter, V., Karliychuk, T., & Grundy, Q. (2019). How private is your mental health app data? An empirical study of mental health app privacy policies and practices. *International Journal of Law and Psychiatry, 64*, 198–204. doi:10.1016/j.ijlp.2019.04.002 PMID:31122630

Perle, J. G., Langsam, L. C., & Nierenberg, B. (2011). Controversy clarified: An updated review of clinical psychology and tele-health. *Clinical Psychology Review, 31*(8), 1247–1258. doi:10.1016/j.cpr.2011.08.003 PMID:21963670

Pettersson, R., Soderstrom, S., Edlund-Soderstrom, K., & Nilsson, K. W. (2014). Internet-based cognitive behavioral therapy for adults with ADHD in outpatient psychiatric care: A randomized trial. *Journal of Attention Disorders, 21*(6), 508–521. doi:10.1177/1087054714539998 PMID:24970720

Pew Research Center. (2017). *Internet/broadband fact sheet.* Pew Research Center: Internet, Science & Tech. Retrieved May 15, 2021, from https://www.pewinternet.org/fact-sheet/internet-broadband/

Pier, C., Austin, D. W., Klein, B., Mitchell, J., Schattner, P., Ciechomski, L., ... Wade, V. (2008). A controlled trial of internet-based cognitive-behavioural therapy for panic disorder with face-to-face support from a general practitioner or email support from a psychologist. *Mental Health in Family Medicine, 5*(1), 29–39. PMID:22477844

Postel, M. G., De Jong, C. A., & De Haan, H. A. (2005). Does e-therapy for problem drinking reach hidden populations? *The American Journal of Psychiatry, 162*(12), 2393–2393. doi:10.1176/appi.ajp.162.12.2393 PMID:16330613

Postel, M. G., De Jong, C. A., & De Haan, H. A. (2005). Does e-therapy for problem drinking reach hidden populations? *The American Journal of Psychiatry, 162*(12), 2393–2393. doi:10.1176/appi.ajp.162.12.2393 PMID:16330613

Povey, J., Mills, P. P. J. R., Dingwall, K. M., Lowell, A., Singer, J., Rotumah, D., Bennett-Levy, J., & Nagel, T. (2016). Acceptability of mental health apps for Aboriginal and Torres Strait Islander Australians: A qualitative study. *Journal of Medical Internet Research, 18*(3), e65. doi:10.2196/jmir.5314 PMID:26969043

Proudfoot, J., Klein, B., Barak, A., Carlbring, P., Cuijpers, P., Lange, A., Ritterband, L., & Andersson, G. (2011). Establishing guidelines for executing and reporting internet intervention research. *Cognitive Behaviour Therapy, 40*(2), 82–97. doi:10.1080/16506073.2011.573807 PMID:25155812

Proudfoot, J. G. (2004). Computer-based treatment for anxiety and depression: Is it feasible? Is it effective? *Neuroscience and Biobehavioral Reviews, 28*(3), 353–363. doi:10.1016/j.neubiorev.2004.03.008 PMID:15225977

Rini, C., Porter, L. S., Somers, T. J., McKee, D. C., & Keefe, F. J. (2014). Retaining critical therapeutic elements of behavioral interventions translated for delivery via the Internet: Recommendations and an example using pain coping skills training. *Journal of Medical Internet Research, 16*(12), e245. doi:10.2196/jmir.3374 PMID:25532216

Ritterband, L. M., Andersson, G., Christensen, H. M., Carlbring, P., & Cuijpers, P. (2006). Directions for the international society for research on internet interventions (ISRII). *Journal of Medical Internet Research, 8*(3), e23. doi:10.2196/jmir.8.3.e23 PMID:17032639

Ritterband, L. M., Thorndike, F. P., Cox, D. J., Kovatchev, B. P., & Gonder-Frederick, L. A. (2009). A behavior change model for internet interventions. *Annals of Behavioral Medicine, 38*(1), 18–27. doi:10.100712160-009-9133-4 PMID:19802647

Rizzo, A. S., & Kim, G. J. (2005). A SWOT analysis of the field of virtual reality rehabilitation and therapy. *Presence (Cambridge, Mass.), 14*(2), 119–146. doi:10.1162/1054746053967094

Robroek, S. J., Lindeboom, D. E., & Burdorf, A. (2012). Initial and sustained participation in an internet-delivered long-term worksite health promotion program on physical activity and nutrition. *Journal of Medical Internet Research, 14*(2), e43. doi:10.2196/jmir.1788 PMID:22390886

Roepke, A. M., Jaffee, S. R., Riffle, O. M., McGonigal, J., Broome, R., & Maxwell, B. (2015). Randomized controlled trial of SuperBetter, a smartphone-based/internet-based self-help tool to reduce depressive symptoms. *Games for Health Journal, 4*(3), 235–246. doi:10.1089/g4h.2014.0046 PMID:26182069

Rozental, A., Andersson, G., Boettcher, J., Ebert, D. D., Cuijpers, P., Knaevelsrud, C., Ljótsson, B., Kaldo, V., Titov, N., & Carlbring, P. (2014). Consensus statement on defining and measuring negative effects of Internet interventions. *Internet Interventions: the Application of Information Technology in Mental and Behavioural Health, 1*(1), 12–19. doi:10.1016/j.invent.2014.02.001

Rummell, C. M., & Joyce, N. R. (2010). "So wat do u want to wrk on 2day?": The ethical implications of online counseling. *Ethics & Behavior, 20*(6), 482–496. doi:10.1080/10508422.2010.521450

Ruwaard, J., Broeksteeg, J., Schrieken, B., Emmelkamp, P., & Lange, A. (2010). Web-based therapist-assisted cognitive behavioral treatment of panic symptoms: A randomized controlled trial with a three-year follow-up. *Journal of Anxiety Disorders*, *24*(4), 387–396. doi:10.1016/j.janxdis.2010.01.010 PMID:20227241

Ruwaard, J., Schrieken, B., Schrijver, M., Broeksteeg, J., Dekker, J., Vermeulen, H., & Lange, A. (2009). Standardized web-based cognitive behavioural therapy of mild to moderate depression: A randomized controlled trial with a long-term follow-up. *Cognitive Behaviour Therapy*, *38*(4), 206–221. doi:10.1080/16506070802408086 PMID:19221919

Schneider, F., de Vries, H., Candel, M., van de Kar, A., & van Osch, L. (2013). Periodic email prompts to re-use an internet-delivered computer-tailored lifestyle program: Influence of prompt content and timing. *Journal of Medical Internet Research*, *15*(1), e23. doi:10.2196/jmir.2151 PMID:23363466

Schneider, F., van Osch, L., & de Vries, H. (2012a). Identifying factors for optimal development of health-related websites: A Delphi study among experts and potential future users. *Journal of Medical Internet Research*, *14*(1), e18. doi:10.2196/jmir.1863 PMID:22357411

Schneider, F., van Osch, L., Schulz, D. N., Kremers, S. P. J., & de Vries, H. (2012b). The influence of user characteristics and a periodic email prompt on exposure to an internet-delivered computer-tailored lifestyle program. *Journal of Medical Internet Research*, *14*(2), e40. doi:10.2196/jmir.1939 PMID:22382037

Schueller, S. M., Hunter, J. F., Figueroa, C., & Aguilera, A. (2019). Use of digital mental health for marginalized and underserved populations. *Current Treatment Options in Psychiatry*, *6*(3), 243–255. doi:10.100740501-019-00181-z

Shandley, K., Austin, D. W., Klein, B., Pier, C., Schattner, P., Pierce, D., & Wade, V. (2008). Therapist-assisted, internet-based treatment for panic disorder: Can general practitioners achieve comparable patient outcomes to psychologists? *Journal of Medical Internet Research*, *10*(2), e14. doi:10.2196/jmir.1033 PMID:18487138

Singh, K., Drouin, K., Newmark, L. P., Lee, J., Faxvaag, A., Rozenblum, R., Pabo, E. A., Landman, A., Klinger, E., & Bates, D. W. (2016). Many mobile health apps target high-need, high-cost populations, but gaps remain. *Health Affairs*, *35*(12), 2310–2318. doi:10.1377/hlthaff.2016.0578 PMID:27920321

Spek, V., Cuijpers, P., Nyklicek, I., Riper, H., Keyzer, J., & Pop, V. (2007). Internet-based cognitive behaviour therapy for symptoms of depression and anxiety: A meta-analysis. *Psychological Medicine*, *37*(3), 319–328. doi:10.1017/S0033291706008944 PMID:17112400

Stallard, P., Richardson, T., & Velleman, S. (2010). Clinicians' attitudes towards the use of computerized cognitive behaviour therapy (cCBT) with children and adolescents. *Behavioural and Cognitive Psychotherapy*, *38*(5), 545–560. doi:10.1017/S1352465810000421 PMID:20615273

Substance Abuse and Mental Health Services Administration. (2017). *Key substance use and mental health indicators in the United States: Results from the 2016 National Survey on Drug Use and Health* (HHS Publication No. SMA 17-5044, NSDUH Series H-52). Rockville, MD: Center for Behavioral Health Statistics and Quality, Substance Abuse and Mental Health Services Administration. Retrieved from https://www. samhsa.gov/data/

Suso-Ribera, C., Fernández-Álvarez, J., García-Palacios, A., Hoffman, H. G., Bretón-López, J., Banos, R. M., Quero, S., & Botella, C. (2019). Virtual reality, augmented reality, and in vivo exposure therapy: A preliminary comparison of treatment efficacy in small animal phobia. *Cyberpsychology, Behavior, and Social Networking*, *22*(1), 31–38. doi:10.1089/cyber.2017.0672 PMID:30335525

Tang, A., Owen, C., Biocca, F., & Mou, W. (2003, April). Comparative effectiveness of augmented reality in object assembly. In *Proceedings of the SIGCHI conference on Human factors in computing systems* (pp. 73-80). 10.1145/642611.642626

Tate, D. F., Wing, R. R., & Winett, R. A. (2001). Using internet technology to deliver a behavioral weight loss program. *Journal of the American Medical Association*, *285*(9), 1172–1177. doi:10.1001/jama.285.9.1172 PMID:11231746

Titov, N. (2007). Status of computerized cognitive behavioural therapy for adults. *Australasian Psychiatry*, *41*(2), 95–114. PMID:17464688

Titov, N., Andrews, G., Davies, M., McIntyre, K., Robinson, E., & Solley, K. (2010). Internet treatment for depression: A randomized controlled trial comparing clinician vs. technician assistance. *PLoS One*, *5*(6), e10939. doi:10.1371/journal.pone.0010939 PMID:20544030

Titov, N., Dear, B. F., Schwencke, G., Andrews, G., Johnston, L., Craske, M. G., & McEvoy, P. (2011). Transdiagnostic internet treatment for anxiety and depression: A randomised controlled trial. *Behaviour Research and Therapy*, *49*(8), 441–452. doi:10.1016/j.brat.2011.03.007 PMID:21679925

Torous, J., Andersson, G., Bertagnoli, A., Christensen, H., Cuijpers, P., Firth, J., Haim, A., Hsin, H., Hollis, C., Lewis, S., Mohr, D. C., Pratap, A., Roux, S., Sherrill, J., & Arean, P. A. (2019). Towards a consensus around standards for smartphone apps and digital mental health. *World Psychiatry; Official Journal of the World Psychiatric Association (WPA)*, *18*(1), 97–98. doi:10.1002/wps.20592 PMID:30600619

Torous, J., Myrick, K. J., Rauseo-Ricupero, N., & Firth, J. (2020). Digital mental health and COVID-19: Using technology today to accelerate the curve on access and quality tomorrow. *JMIR Mental Health*, *7*(3), e18848. doi:10.2196/18848 PMID:32213476

Valmaggia, L. R., Latif, L., Kempton, M. J., & Rus-Calafell, M. (2016). Virtual reality in the psychological treatment for mental health problems: A systematic review of recent evidence. *Psychiatry Research*, *236*, 189–195. doi:10.1016/j.psychres.2016.01.015 PMID:26795129

Ventura, S., Baños, R. M., Botella, C., & Mohamudally, N. (2018). Virtual and augmented reality: New frontiers for clinical psychology. *State of the Art Virtual Reality and Augmented Reality Knowhow*, 99-118.

Vigerland, S., Ljótsson, B., Bergdahl Gustafsson, F., Hagert, S., Thulin, U., Andersson, G., & Serlachius, E. (2014). Attitudes towards the use of computerized cognitive behavior therapy (cCBT) with children and adolescents: A survey among Swedish mental health professionals. *Internet Interventions: the Application of Information Technology in Mental and Behavioural Health*, *1*(3), 111–117. doi:10.1016/j.invent.2014.06.002

Vincenzi, D. A., Valimont, B., Macchiarella, N., Opalenik, C., Gangadharan, S. N., & Majoros, A. E. (2003, October). The effectiveness of cognitive elaboration using augmented reality as a training and learning paradigm. *Proceedings of the Human Factors and Ergonomics Society Annual Meeting*, *47*(19), 2054–2058. doi:10.1177/154193120304701909

Wang, P. S., Aguilar-Gaxiola, S., Alonso, J., Angermeyer, M. C., Borges, G., Bromet, E. J., ... Wells, J. E. (2007). Worldwide Use of Mental Health Services for Anxiety, Mood, and Substance Disorders: Results from 17 Countries in the WHO World Mental Health (WMH) Surveys. *Lancet*, *370*(9590), 841–850. doi:10.1016/S0140-6736(07)61414-7 PMID:17826169

Wantland, D. J., Portillo, C. J., Holzemer, W. L., Slaughter, R., & McGhee, E. M. (2004). The effectiveness of Web-based vs. non-Web-based interventions: A meta-analysis of behavioral change outcomes. *Journal of Medical Internet Research*, *6*(4), e40. doi:10.2196/jmir.6.4.e40 PMID:15631964

Whitfield, G., & Williams, C. (2004). If the evidence is so good – why doesn't anyone use them? A national survey of the use of computerized cognitive behaviour therapy. *Behavioural and Cognitive Psychotherapy*, *32*(01), 57–65. doi:10.1017/S1352465804001031

Williams, A. D., & Andrews, G. (2013). The effectiveness of internet cognitive behavioural therapy (iCBT) for depression in primary care: A quality assurance study. *PLoS One, 8*(2), e57447. doi:10.1371/journal.pone.0057447 PMID:23451231

Wood, L. C. & Reefke, H. (2010, November). *Working with a diverse class: Reflections on the role of team teaching, teaching tools and technological support.* IADIS International Conference on International Higher Education, Perth, Australia.

Yellowlees, P., Marks, S., Hilty, D., & Shore, J. H. (2008). Using e-health to enable culturally appropriate mental healthcare in rural areas. *Telemedicine Journal and e-Health, 14*(5), 486–492. doi:10.1089/tmj.2007.0070 PMID:18578685

Zack, J. S. (2008). How sturdy is that digital couch? Legal considerations for mental health professionals who deliver clinical services via the internet. *Journal of Technology in Human Services, 26*(2-4), 333–359. doi:10.1080/15228830802097083

ADDITIONAL READING

Andersson, G., Berg, M., Riper, H., Huppert, J. D., & Titov, N. (2020). The Possible Role of Internet-Delivered Psychological Interventions in Relation to the COVID-19 Pandemic. *Clinical Psychology in Europe, 2*(3), 1–4. doi:10.32872/cpe.v2i3.3941

Freeman, D., Reeve, S., Robinson, A., Ehlers, A., Clark, D., Spanlang, B., & Slater, M. (2017). Virtual reality in the assessment, understanding, and treatment of mental health disorders. *Psychological Medicine, 47*(14), 2393–2400. doi:10.1017/S003329171700040X PMID:28325167

Geraets, C. N., van der Stouwe, E. C., Pot-Kolder, R., & Veling, W. (2021). Advances in immersive virtual reality interventions for mental disorders–a new reality? *Current Opinion in Psychology, 41*, 40–45. doi:10.1016/j.copsyc.2021.02.004 PMID:33714892

Guazzaroni, G. (Ed.). (2018). *Virtual and augmented reality in mental health treatment.* IGI Global.

Kazdin, A. E. (2017). Addressing the treatment gap: A key challenge for extending evidence-based psychosocial interventions. *Behaviour Research and Therapy, 88*, 7–18. doi:10.1016/j.brat.2016.06.004 PMID:28110678

Linardon, J., Cuijpers, P., Carlbring, P., Messer, M., & Fuller-Tyszkiewicz, M. (2019). The efficacy of app-supported smartphone interventions for mental health problems: A meta-analysis of randomized controlled trials. *World Psychiatry; Official Journal of the World Psychiatric Association (WPA)*, *18*(3), 325–336. doi:10.1002/wps.20673 PMID:31496095

Torous, J., Andersson, G., Bertagnoli, A., Christensen, H., Cuijpers, P., Firth, J., Haim, A., Hsin, H., Hollis, C., Lewis, S., Mohr, D. C., Pratap, A., Roux, S., Sherrill, J., & Arean, P. A. (2019). Towards a consensus around standards for smartphone apps and digital mental health. *World Psychiatry; Official Journal of the World Psychiatric Association (WPA)*, *18*(1), 97–98. doi:10.1002/wps.20592 PMID:30600619

KEY TERMS AND DEFINITIONS

Augmented Reality: A technology that superimposes a computer-generated image on a user's view of the real world, thus providing a composite view.

Exposure Therapy: A form of therapy, where psychologists create a safe environment in which they "expose" individuals to the things they fear and avoid. The exposure to the feared objects, activities or situations in a safe environment helps reduce fear and decrease avoidance.

Internet-Based Interventions: Treatments that are mainly delivered via the Internet with at least some therapeutic tasks delegated to the computer.

Tailored Digital Interventions: Digital intervention that have adapted different factors including treatment content, therapist factors, and delivery components to better suit the needs of each individual client.

Virtual Reality: Computer-generated simulation of a three-dimensional image or environment that can be interacted with in a seemingly real or physical way by a person using special electronic equipment, such as a helmet with a screen inside or gloves fitted with sensors.

Chapter 9
Mariners or Machines:
Who's at the Helm? Shifting Roles and Responsibilities on Navy Warships

Kimberly E. Culley
U.S. Submarine Force, USA

ABSTRACT

Building in layers of safety and sharpening the warfighting edge does not necessarily mean using technology more, but rather using it more effectively. Deftly applied automation can buy back time and cognitive resources for operators, decreasing the chances of human error, but technology also has the potential to become less of a tool and more of a crutch if operational fundamentals and basic seafaring skills are forsaken to automation. Operators must be able to rely on their own "sea sense," developed through experience and mentoring, and use technology to accomplish specific objectives rather than defer to automation as the default decision-maker. Maintaining the competitive warfighting edge requires cultivating skilled mariners who know how to fight a well-equipped ship; adding complexity to the system without accounting for the human element creates added risk and cutting-edge failure modes. Technology alone cannot make the ship safe, but when the operator lacks fundamental knowledge and experience, it can make the ship unsafe.

INTRODUCTION

The Navy mission is rich in inherent complexity due to the nature of operations and the extreme environments and conditions in which work is performed. High-stakes, high-demand, high-tempo operations in a challenging maritime environment

DOI: 10.4018/978-1-7998-6453-0.ch009

provide various opportunities for errors and undesirable outcomes, which can manifest themselves in many different ways—but the driving forces behind these incidents are rarely unique. We can think of error as a consequence—not a cause. This is a major reform in the conceptualization and treatment of human error in Naval operations. Error is a result of some causal factor, or more likely factors, which impeded human performance; these could be environmental, like fog that degraded visual perception or a noisy workspace that muddled communication; cultural, like informal watchstanding standards or a lack of regard for crew fatigue; or systems related, like poor ergonomics or ineffective implementation of technology (Reason, 1990). A confluence of factors produces an error, which in turn may have consequences in the form of a near miss event or major mishap.

In a well-defined and well-guarded system, most errors are likely to have a short-lived impact, though the outcome may be of some consequence. However, as the margin to safety degrades—due to factors such as ineffective operational fundamentals or poor implementation of technology—the results can be disastrous. This may not be evident immediately, however, which can create a false sense of security while unknowingly accumulating risk.

Leading up to some untoward events, some watchteams seemed comfortable allowing the upper levels of their chain of command to monopolize decision making, due in part to an inability to leverage high end technological systems. Watchteams demonstrated a tendency to cede critical thinking to the Commanding Officer or designated officer in charge, relieving themselves of the responsibility to provide sound recommendations and forceful backup to the team and team leaders even when reality did not meet expectations. This may be due in part to limited opportunities to develop a sense of expertise and a true feel for the sea, exacerbated at times by superficial understanding of and overreliance on automated or semi-automated systems (Parasuraman & Manzey, 2010).

The fundamentals of seafaring have not changed per se, but they have become blanketed under many layers of technology. The lost experiential knowledge in the areas of operational fundamentals and basic seafaring is compensated for with increased technology. However, this adds risk, as junior personnel cannot engage in recognition-primed decision making and lack the ability to act intuitively. There is not enough time in each job to "experience experience." This contributes to an over-reliance on automation or complex technology at the expense of disregarding one's own instincts and decision-making brain (Lee & See, 2004). It has been said that "Machines have many qualities, but common sense isn't one of them." The inherent limitations on junior personnel developing their own sea sense bounds their ability to operate independently from automation and fosters a dependence on technology in the absence of basic seafaring fundamentals.

Advancements in computer-assisted operations technologies for ship control, navigation, sonar, and fire control systems have added powerful tools, reduced repetitive operator actions, and simplified the coordinated operation of complex systems to straightforward operator commands. These automation advancements enable operators to achieve consistently high levels of system performance unachievable by manual operation alone, but also introduce unacceptable risk if these systems are not fully understood and employed with a high level of competence (Stephens et al., 2018). Operators retain a critical role as directors and supervisors of most automated systems. Automated systems shift watchstander roles and responsibilities. Instead of directly performing multiple steps to execute routine tasks, the human's job becomes directing, supervising, and monitoring performance of an automated system (Culley & Madhavan, 2013). The human has become a director and the machine the performer, which can contribute to a sense of feeling "out of the performance loop". If an operator ceases to effectively direct and supervise an automated system, the operator loses overall situational awareness (SA) of the areas under their responsibility (Kennedy et al., 2014). Technology does not, and was never intended to, replace watchstanders' knowledge and basic seafaring skill. Watchstanders must have a detailed understanding of their automated systems, just as they do for systems that require more manual interaction.

Many automated systems have numerous modes of operation, and they often require the human director to select the appropriate mode for conditions without prompting from the system (Sarter & Woods, 1995). Selecting the wrong mode often leads to the system operating in a suboptimal or unexpected way, and in some cases can result in actions which are completely inappropriate to the situation or environment. Likewise, failing to recognize a change in operational conditions that requires a mode shift, or improperly assuming the system is in one mode when it is actually in another, will likely cause incorrect system response. The watchstander must continuously maintain SA, evaluate conditions, and make decisions regarding which mode is best suited to each particular set of circumstances. He or she must always be aware of the automation mode selected and what underlying processes and capabilities that mode entails. Training and qualification programs must give watchstanders a detailed understanding of each mode, when each mode is appropriate for use, and what situation changes would require mode changes. The selection of required mode(s) for automated systems should be considered during operational planning.

An automated system, working as designed, can lull a watchstander into a state of complacency, dramatically reducing SA. Watchstanders must monitor automated system performance and recognize failures or improper system operation. Further, they must understand the implications of the failure and properly respond to maintain the operational function normally provided by the automation. For the current generation of automation, a failure will almost certainly require more manual system manipulation, and backup modes will be less intuitive--sometimes much less so--than automated ones. Warfighting readiness requires a detailed understanding of back-up and manual modes of operation for continued safe operation during times of automation failure. Training plans must ensure watchstanders can identify automation failures, gun-drill immediate response actions to a loss of an automated system, and ensure that the watchstander is able to sustain operations manually and in all available backup modes. Additionally, an unnoticed improper automated action can lead a ship into an unrecognized extremis situation. Watchstanders and watch leaders should condition themselves to recognize an irregular automated action, achieve a clear awareness of the situation, and take decisive actions to maintain safe and effective operation of the ship.

Automated systems are designed to operate within a given operating envelope. Some automated functions can operate effectively in largely variable environments while others are only capable of performing a task under a specific set of conditions. Operators must understand the design operating bands of the automated system and be alert for conditions that will render the automation ineffective and inappropriate. Similar to selecting the correct automation mode, some conditions simply require manual operations.

Ideally, technology should both provide information and reduce time pressure for the watchteam by reducing repetitive, manual. Since the automation is performing some of the system operations that would otherwise require human attention, the watchstander should have more time for analysis which should enhance SA, depressurize a situation, and improve clarity in information processing and decision making (e.g., help overcome human biases). Automation should allow operators to execute their watchstation duties with a higher level of thoughtfulness and deliberativeness.

The best-intentioned technological and automated systems provide flexibility to operators in the sense of increasing the number of functions and options for carrying out a given task in various conditions. However, this flexibility comes at a cost. Because the operator must make a decision regarding which mode is best suited for particular circumstances, he or she must have more knowledge and awareness about both the intricacies of the system and how to interface with the system. Additionally, the operator must allocate attention and monitoring resources to track what mode the automation is actually in at any given time and maintain an understanding of what underlying processes and capabilities that particular mode entails. Put more simply, this involves tracking what the automation is doing, why it is doing it, and what it will do next (Levels 1, 2, and 3 Situational Awareness of the automation).

Situational Awareness (SA) is defined as the perception of elements in the environment within a volume of time and space (Level 1 SA), the comprehension of their meaning (Level 2 SA), and the projection of their status in the near future (Level 3 SA) (Endsley, 1995). SA should be considered a continuous process whereby the operator makes a diagnosis of the state of the world, which can be measured against ground truth (i.e., the accuracy of SA can be assessed against the objective state of the world or the objective unfolding of events that are predicted). Accurate decisions will depend on good SA and level of knowledge, but good SA is not the same as good judgment or level of knowledge. Most breakdowns in SA occur during the early phases—noticing and perceiving—rather than the later phases of diagnosis and prediction. Failures in operating mode awareness frequently align with this paradigm.

Higher levels of SA are critical to enabling decision makers at all levels to function in a timely and effective manner. However, if not guarded against, separation of watchstanders from the manual performance of a task and elevation to a supervising and monitoring role can contribute to degraded SA and automation-induced complacency (inappropriately relying on technology to "take care of itself" and abdicating the responsibility to properly direct and monitor the functions of the watchstation). As a result, when supervising and monitoring an automated system, operators are frequently slow to detect a problem that has occurred and requires intervention (Kennedy et al., 2014). The result of this lag ranges from a brief delay in problem-correction with no apparent adverse effect to catastrophic failures with major consequences. Of particular concern are problems that occur in automated critical systems that normally exhibit high levels of reliability. These automated systems are often capable of performing sets of coordinated repetitive tasks at a performance level that exceeds what most human operators could manually achieve on their own. In these cases, when things go wrong, they often go wrong in a big way.

In hindsight, the limited development of experiential knowledge and sea sense was evident in watchstander actions leading up the collision between the USS John S. McCain and Motor Vessel Alnic MC. When technology failed to conform to the expectations of the bridge team, watchstanders lacked the fundamental seafaring knowledge to understand the forces acting upon the ship. Moreover, as a result of gaps in training and procedures for bridge watchstanders operating new consoles, operators struggled with navigation and ship control due to what they perceived to be unreliable, unfamiliar automation technology. This system lacked both adequate transparency for an operator to appropriately calibrate trust in the system and an adequate training package to mature operator understanding of the various operating modes.

There is a general inclination to automate anything that creates an economic benefit or gives a technological edge, and leave the operator to manage the resulting system. However, the traditional view that technological feasibility and cost should determine which system functions to automate is falling out of favor as research regarding human interaction with automation evolves. While it is assumed that human operators have the flexibility and adaptability to manage a heavily automated system, the complexity of such systems can lead to information or technology overload. System complexity and lack of transparency can also lead to automation misuse, disuse, and abuse, directly impacting how an operator perceives and uses that system. The relationship between system performance and an individual's trust in its automation is referred to as calibration. Calibration of trust in automation bears a strong relationship with the use, misuse, disuse, and abuse of automation.

In order for automation to provide a benefit to the operator and the macro-organizational system as a whole, it must be applied with discretion. In many cases, human operators remain better than automation at responding to changing or unforeseen conditions, and thus remain critical to system operation. It is important that automation be designed and applied in such a way as to prevent the human operator from losing these capabilities because of technology overload. Additionally, unreliable automation can add negative value, in that it not only adds "cognitive overhead" with regard to distinguishing false alarms, but also results in automation disuse (due to distrust), which would likely not have been accounted for in system design. This results in operators defaulting to manual modes or overrides in a system that designers optimized for automation use; essentially, operators are at a greater deficit than had the automation not been implemented in the first place and there remained a system optimized for manual human operation. This is evident in several technological systems resident in recent maritime mishap events.

Challenges associated with an overreliance on or inadequate understanding of automated critical functions are illustrated in the following examples:

USS JOHN S. MCCAIN (JSM) collision with M/V ALNIC (the full account is contained in the Comprehensive Review of Recent Surface Force Incidents - Tab B.) event timeline (United States Fleet Forces Command, 2017):

0436 Commanding Officer (CO) ordered steering shifted from automatic control to backup manual control due to perceived reliability issues with the ship control console.

0454 Gained radar contact on ALNIC nearly ahead of JSM on the port side, within 8 nautical miles.

0519 CO noticed helmsman struggling to operate both the rudder and throttles, and ordered dividing the controls without realizing the low state of qualification, training, and proficiency for this type of split operation. Note: the shifting of thrust control while in backup manual mode resulted in the inadvertent and unrecognized shift of steering control from the helm to the lee helm leading to a perceived loss of steering by the helmsman. There were multiple inadvertent transfers of steering control as the situation evolved. These shifts of steering control were facilitated by the ship control console being in backup manual mode, which created a condition where a shift of steering control to any console with computer assisted manual steering mode available would not require positive action from a console operator to accept steering control. Additionally, the shift of control caused an unintentional and unrecognized unganging of the thrust control (uncoupling of the throttles for the two shafts) as the result of limited understanding of system/automation mode features when rudder and throttle control were decoupled.

0520 Lee helm station took control of steering in computer assisted mode; this shift in steering locations caused the rudder to move amidships (from a right rudder previously applied to maintain course). Lee helm took control of the port shaft.

0521 Helm reported loss of steering to the OOD. The rudder is amidships. JSM is on course 228.7t, engines are all ahead full for 20 knots, making 18.6 knots over ground and turning to port at 0.26 degrees per second. ALNIC was on course 230t, speed 9.6 knots, and was bearing 164t at a range of approximately 582 yards from JSM. Note: JSM believed she was in a rudder casualty because steering had been inadvertently transferred to a different station (facilitated by the earlier change from auto to backup manual mode). further, upon orders to slow the ship to 10 knots and eventually to 5 knots, only the speed of the port shaft was reduced as the throttles were not coupled together (ganged) as a result of the earlier change in automation mode. The starboard shaft continued at nearly 20 knots for another 68 seconds before its speed was reduced. The combination of the wrong rudder direction and unequal thrust caused an un-commanded turn to port into the heavily congested traffic scheme in close proximity to multiple ships, including ALNIC. None of the watchstanders were aware of the mismatch in thrust and the effect on causing the ship's turn to port.

0522 JSM is on course 204.4t at 16.6 knots, turning to port.

0523:01 After steering takes control of steering in backup manual mode.

0523:06 Port shaft continues to slow while starboard shaft remains at high speed. JSM continues turning port at a rate of approximately 0.5 degrees per second.

0523:16 Helm takes control of steering at the helm station in backup manual mode.

0523:24 Throttles are finally matched at the lee helm station and both shafts are ahead at 5 knots. JSM is on course 182.8t, speed 13.8 knots, and turning to port.

0523:27 Aft steering helmsman takes control of steering. Note: this is the fifth unintended transfer of steering and the second time the aft steering unit had gained control in the previous two minutes.

0523:44 JSM is on course 177t, speed 11.8 knots, and nearly steady on course due to an ordered and applied right 15-degree rudder that checked JSM's swing to port.

0523:58 ALNIC's bulbous bow struck JSM between frame 308 and 345 and below the waterline.

SUBMARINE test depth exceeded during a controlled deep dive:

While conducting a controlled deep dive, an ordered course change caused the ship control system to apply a large rudder causing the ship to slow and, in conjunction with a previously existing heavy trim condition, caused a depth excursion. Watch team action arrested the ship's depth rate, but was not effective to prevent placing a large angle on the ship, resulting in the aft portion of the ship exceeding test depth for greater than one minute.

The ship's control party failed to anticipate the speed and trim effects of a large rudder angle due to auto data being in maximal. Auto data maximal is not the appropriate setting for slow speed operations near test depth, as it will cause inappropriately large rudder angles. The pilot and co-pilot were not effectively evaluating changes in the ship's operational conditions and failed to appropriately monitor and direct the mode of operation of their automated control system. Neither the OOD, the other two qualified officers in control, nor any other members of the watchteam were aware of the ship's auto data setting. Subsequent investigation identified that officers did not typically know the status of auto data, nor did they consider the effect this has on helm orders they issue.

The watchteam demonstrated an over-reliance on its highly reliable automated ship control system to "take care of itself", failing to recognize that the ship's operating conditions had crossed a threshold that required a change in automated system operating mode. Because their SA did not include a sufficient awareness of the implications of the automated system's operating mode, they also did not correctly predict the system's response to a "simple" course change order. As a result, the watch team could not process the full "meaning" of the developing situation that should have led them to take manual control of the system, enabling robust recovery actions. Instead a different automation mode was selected, and the team's actions were ultimately ineffective in maintaining the ship shallower than test depth.

The inherent flexibility touted as a benefit of automation is what drives the demand for mode awareness–the operator's ability to notice, perceive, track, and anticipate the behavior of the automated system. Mode awareness can be impeded by other design changes that leave the operator increasingly removed from mechanical aspects of the system, as previously available cues about the system behavior—such as moving throttles, vibration, or engine noise—may have been reduced or removed in the design process. Limiting auditory, visual, and kinesthetic cues indicating system status can aggravate the already difficult problem of maintaining mode awareness and may result in automation surprise—an impression that the system acts independent of operator intent. Automation surprise is tied to gaps or misconceptions in the operator's mental model that may prevent him or her from tracking current mode and understanding when each mode is appropriate for given conditions, and also having a routine to verify that the system is operating as designed and intended. A well-developed and informed mental model, on the other hand, will support an impression of system behavior as deterministic and transparent with regard to automation capabilities, behavior, and mode state.

Essentially, mode awareness failures have two primary drivers—inadequate mental models and ambiguous indications of the status and behavior of automation. Insufficient mental models result from the failure of designers to anticipate the new knowledge demands associated with automation implementation and to provide mechanisms via training or tactical aids to acquire, maintain, and operationalize the requisite knowledge. Further, training rarely provides opportunities for operators to explore and experiment with the various modes in the process of learning how the systems work and how to work the systems, which limits the degree to which operators can extrapolate information because of a limited mental model. The challenge of opaque, low-transparency user interfaces reflects a failure of designers to support the operator's cognitively demanding task of tracking the potentially dynamic state and behavior of the automation.

When system designers proliferate various modes without accounting for the accompanying cognitive demands, novel mode-related error and failure paths can emerge. These unique potential failure paths may be difficult to anticipate despite robust risk management processes, because they originate at system nodes believed to be infallible—those that are normally automated and thought to operate in a predictable manner. Operational risk management that fails to address human-machine interaction and other human performance factors results in a myopic view of potential hazards and human error traps. Luck becomes as important as skill in driving expected outcomes without a full understanding of risk gained through holistic assessment of technical, tactical, operational, and behavioral fundamentals.

By thinking of errors as consequences and digging deep for their roots, we can better develop and focus on direct and sustainable solutions to prevent future similar errors. Too often, many underperforming organizations treat the symptoms of problems vice getting to their root, making it impossible to effect lasting change. Moreover, having a solid grasp of causal factors that lead to suboptimal human performance is critical to establishing high reliability operators and teams. All throughout, senior leadership must recognize, accept, and embrace their responsibility to seek every opportunity to impart knowledge and perspective on juniors and foster opportunities for them to accumulate experiential knowledge, and not allow low-return administrative or managerial functions to deter them from doing so.

Lastly, given the insights derived from recent mishaps and evolving perspectives rooted in science, it is critical that automation is applied with discretion and a consideration of second and third order effects. In some cases, an insular approach to deciding what systems to automate and a poorly executed implementation of technology are creating periods of avoidable vulnerability to untoward events. We need to take advantage of our technological edge and harness the art of the possible, but not at the expense of perishable skills or unwarranted cognitive overhead for operators. A thoughtful implementation of technology can buy down risk and increase the margin to safety, a lesson we learned at a high cost that should not be forgotten nor repeated.

REFERENCES

Culley, K. E., & Madhavan, P. (2013). Trust in automation and automation designers: Implications for HCI and HMI. *Computers in Human Behavior*, *29*(6), 2208–2210. doi:10.1016/j.chb.2013.04.032

Endsley, M. (1995). Towards a theory of situation awareness in dynamic systems. *Human Factors*, *37*(1), 32–64. doi:10.1518/001872095779049543

Kennedy, K. D., Stephens, C. L., Williams, R. A., & Schutte, P. (2014). Automation and inattentional blindness in a simulated flight task. *Proceedings of the 58th Annual Meeting of the Human Factors and Ergonomics Society*, *58*(1), 2058-2062.

Lee, J. D., & See, K. A. (2004). Trust in automation: Designing for appropriate reliance. *Human Factors*, *46*(1), 50–80. doi:10.1518/hfes.46.1.50.30392 PMID:15151155

Parasuraman, R., & Manzey, D. H. (2010). Complacency and bias in human use of automation: An attentional integration. *Human Factors*, *52*(3), 381–410. doi:10.1177/0018720810376055 PMID:21077562

Reason, J. (1990). *Human error*. Cambridge University Press. doi:10.1017/CBO9781139062367

Sarter, N. B., & Woods, D. D. (1995). How in the world did we ever get into that mode? Mode error and awareness in supervisory control. *Human Factors*, *37*(1), 5–19. doi:10.1518/001872095779049516

Stephens, C., Dehais, F., Roy, R. N., Harrivel, A., Last, M. C., Kennedy, K., & Pope, A. (2018). Biocybernetic adaptation strategies: machine awareness of human engagement for improved operational performance. In *International Conference on Augmented Cognition* (pp. 89-98). 10.1007/978-3-319-91470-1_9

United States Fleet Forces Command. (2017). *Comprehensive Review of Recent Surface Force Incidents*. https://www.hsdl.org/?abstract&did=805423

Chapter 10
Exploring Technology Tendencies and Their Impact on Human– Human Interactions

Heather C. Lum
Embry-Riddle Aeronautical University, USA

ABSTRACT

Although traditionally researchers have focused on making robotics more user-friendly from a human perspective, a new theory has begun to take shape in which humans take on the perspective of a robotic entity. The following set of studies examined the concept of technomorphism defined as the attribution of technological characteristics to humans. This concept has been mentioned anecdotally and studied indirectly, but there is nothing currently available to tap into the various forms that technomorphism may take. Through the study of technomorphism, researchers have come slightly closer to the question of how technology is influencing our perceptions of what it means to be human. The findings from this work should help fuel the desire of others in the field to think about the potential influences of technomorphism during the design and implementation of new devices as well as in how technology may be related to how we perceive each other.

INTRODUCTION

What makes us human? That is a philosophical question with many intricate pieces. In this paper, there will be a focus on one of those small pieces. More specifically,

DOI: 10.4018/978-1-7998-6453-0.ch010

how has technology influenced our perceptions of what makes each other human or not? As Brian Christian exclaimed in his book The Most Human Human, "in the mid-twentieth century, a piece of cutting edge mathematical gadgetry was 'like a computer.' In the twenty-first century, it is the human math whiz that is 'like a computer.' An odd twist: we're like the thing that used to be like us" (p. 11). Christian later asks a question which is the crux of the current work: "Does the fact that computers are so good at mathematics take away an arena of human activity, or does it free us from having to do a nonhuman activity, liberating us into a more human life?" (p. 13). So again the question of what makes us human is raised and how technology has changed the definition of humanity and the perception of other humans comes to the forefront.

Recently, operators working on the Mars rover were asked about their interactions with the distant robot. One engineer described how she used her knowledge of the robot's vision to help move the rover by "cupping her hands around her face like the head of the Rover's mast" (Moroney, 2010, p. 23). The engineer goes on to say that "I have frequently tried to put myself in the Rover's head and say, what do I know about the world...?" (Vertesi, 2008, p. 281). Although traditionally researchers have focused on how to make robotics more user-friendly from a human perspective, a new theory has begun to take shape in which the human makes decisions based on how a robot would. This type of thinking has enabled those working on the Mars rover to use their knowledge of how the robot viewed this strange world to go beyond the limitations of what a human would see. This concept, termed technomorphism, is the focus of this paper and includes the theoretical underpinnings as well as a scale creation designed to measure this evolving construct.

DEFINING TECHNOMORPHISM

The concept of technomorphism (first termed mechanomorphism) was mentioned initially in passing by Caporael (1986) as a "schema (albeit an elaboration of anthropomorphism) used by the scientific community, especially by researchers in artificial intelligence and cognitive science" to explain their field and understand complex concepts (p. 216). This term has since been expanded upon to define the attribution of technological characteristics to humans. In considering and perceiving a problem, a typical inclination is to consider the situation in an anthropomorphic way (Nowak & Bloca, 2003). Anthropomorphism involves the attribution of human-like characteristics to non-human entities that may be organic such as an animal, or inorganic, such as a robot or other object (Aggarwal & McGill, 2007). Although it is common to anthropomorphize as a way to understand and relate to non-human entities, perhaps equally as important is an examination of how we use those non-human entities to understand more about ourselves as human beings. Yet, only a handful of studies have even mentioned technomorphism in any form. It has been seen in the science fiction genre with countless characters in movies and books that are described in terms of their mechanical nature. For example, a series of commercials have been produced for the Droid cell phone in which a human using the phone is transformed into a cyborg while using the device. From a scientific perspective, however, technomorphism is something that researchers have been slow to investigate.

It should be noted that technonomorphism may have been employed, at least anecdotally, for many years. As Caporeal mentioned, computer scientists and those in similar fields have used technomorphism to explain how the human brain works by breaking it down into computer terms. For example, in explaining how human memory works, it is common to describe the human memory system by using RAM as a symbol of working memory, whereas a computer hard drive can be considered a long-term memory structure. Thinking in technomorphic terms can help us understand a complex structure such as the brain in much simpler concrete and relatable ways. Because the construct of technonomorphism would not be present without the presence of technology, so next will be a discussion of how the world has changed in the wake of technology's presence.

TECHNOLOGY IN OUR SOCIETY

Technology has become ever more present in our society and has enabled such objects as computers and robots to be more relatable to the average person (Osborne, Simon, & Collins, 2003). People born between 1982 and 1998 have been surrounded by and use technology like no other generation in history, with college-aged students now experiencing their academic years more "wired in" than their predecessors (McBride & Nief, 2010). Similarly, technology and robotics companies are now beginning to utilize cutting edge equipment to turn humans into "super humans." For example, the Raytheon Sarcos has created an exoskeleton, which allows a human user to increase his or her strength beyond normal human limits with minimal effort (Jacobsen, 2010). Other researchers, like Kevin Warwick from the University of Reading, have gone one step further by implanting a RFI chip into the body. This chip has rewired his brain in a way that allows him to move robots and devices with his mere thoughts (Warwick et al., 2010). Exposure to this constant wave of technological devices may have caused a shift in our thinking from an organic view to a more technological one.

Technology shapes our society in a multitude of ways. It has changed how we communicate with each other, both face to face as well as remotely. Even human-

human relationships have been formed through online connections. In 2010, one in six people who got married began his or her relationship online. This is "more than twice the number of people who met at bars, clubs, and other social events combined" (Koford, 2010, p. 1). With regard to television usage, the Nielsen group reports that the average American watches approximately 153 hours of television every month at home and at least 131 million watch on their mobile devices (Nielsen Company, 2009). An even more astounding statistic relates to today's youth and their online usage. According to the New York Times (Lewin, 2010), those between the ages of eight and eighteen years spend more than seven and a half hours a day using a smart phone, computer, television or other electronic devices. According to one 14 year old, "I feel like my days would be boring without it" (Lewin, 2010, p. 1). Businesses have been impacted equally by technology. Where would we be without the instant access to information via the Internet? The ability to send and receive information via email (over 294 billion sent every day or 2.8 million every second) has forever changed how we work and play (Tschabitscher, 2011).

Given that modern Western society has instant access to nearly anything we can think of, even our perception of time is evolving. As one researcher at UC Berkeley explains, "Because of the ability to instantaneously respond to others, our perception of time has been altered. No longer do we feel like we have enough time in the day. Many find themselves spending their entire work time and even personal time replying to e-mails. Though data proves otherwise, we now feel like there is less than 24 hours in a day. When we are bored, we find ourselves spending our whole time chatting online. By the end of the day, we discover that we have spent hours on the internet" (Meng, 2009, p. 1). We also are facing certain threats that people less than 20 years ago seldom thought about: identity theft and computer viruses. Last year, the FTC estimates that as many as 9 million Americans had their identities stolen, and the primary way of gaining that information was through the internet (Federal Trade Commission, 2011). With this influx of technology in our personal and professional lives, it is clear that we are fundamentally altering what is important to us as well as well as how we interact with each other. For centuries, face to face communication was the only way to interact and learn about each other and the world. But, now we can talk to each other over the phone or online and gain access to any information we want. As stated before, it is all almost instantaneous. These characteristics may cause a shift in the way we think and concepts such as technomorphism and anthropomorphism are becoming ever more important areas to study in this regard.

TECHNOMORPHISM AND ANTHROPOMORPHISM INTERTWINED

Technomorphism and anthropomorphism are intertwined in both definition and concept. If technomorphism involves the attribution of machine-like characteristics of humans, anthropomorphism can be considered the opposite, such that it is the attribution of human-like characteristics to non-human entities (Aggarwal & McGill, 2007). Different theories exist for why it may be beneficial to view the world in an anthropomorphic way. Guthrie (1993) has postulated three explanations for this behavior. The first describes the comfort-based idea that when one views human-like characteristics in others, it is a way of providing or extending relationships or companionship. The second involves the idea that by anthropomorphizing, it allows people to make better sense of the world around them. In the first two explanations, there is a more practical standpoint, whereas the third may be considered more theoretical. It involves the assumption that a person has evolved to think this way because it has an evolutionary benefit that has outweighed any risks associated with it.

Additionally, anthropomorphism can be thought of in terms of three main types or forms in which anthropomorphism is exhibited. These forms include the literal, accidental, and partial (Guthrie, 2003). In literal anthropomorphism, individuals actually believe an object or animal is human-like. This is usually considered a result of mistaken perception such as the case of a child seeing a monster in a shadow or an individual perceiving an object that is dimly lit as a human. Accidental anthropomorphism may occur when someone sees some element of a human in an object but does not consider the object to be human at all. This may include seeing a human shape in the clouds and similar instances (Guthrie, 1993). The most common form of anthropomorphism, and the one that this work has focused on, concerns individuals seeing objects or events as having some human characteristics but not considering the entire object's form actually to be human. This is termed partial anthropomorphism and this form is the one most described in the literature and most experienced by many consumers (Guthrie, 2003). Indeed, many individuals have noted that they saw their pet smiling at them or yelled at their computer for defying or angering them. Although many speak of this in terms of the human characteristics involved, most realize that the object or being is not human in all respects and still holds its own inherent features.

The current body of literature has examined anthropomorphism in the context of what is and what is not usually classified in an anthropomorphic way. Many have looked at the physical features of the object, including its shape, color, form, size, and movement to name a few (Graham & Poulin-Dubois 1999; Morewedge, Preston, & Wegner 2007; Tremoulet, Leslie, & Hall, 2000). It is important also to look at anthropomorphism as it relates to technology and specifically to robotics.

Robots have been created that encompass many anthropomorphic features, either intentionally or not. For instance, Sony Aibo, a robotic dog, was created as a companion, and has many of the same physical characteristics and mannerisms as a live dog. Additionally, the design of Roomba, a personal robotic vacuum, is very appealing because it is rounded and returns to its "home" when it needs to charge. Rounded surfaces are more organic and found more readily in nature than straight lines and shapes (Riek, 2009). In considering perceptions of robotic heads, designers account for the shape and dimensions of key features like the eyes, nose, and mouth (DiSalvo, Gemperle, Forlizzi, & Kiedler, 2002; Goetz, Kiesler, & Powers, 2003).

Even something as simple as the color and position of a set of dots inside of a box can elicit different anthropomorphic perceptions. In a study by Sims et al. (2006) participants viewed different patterns of circles and squares inside of a square box and made attributions about the emotional tone of the figure. The participants rated the object "faces" on attributions of aggression, friendliness, intelligence, trustworthiness, and degree of animation. They found that object "faces" that had round features as well as eyes with discernable pupils were rated most positively. This suggests that objects with round features, even those with minimal features, evoke "humanness". The concept of anthropomorphism can be found in everyday life, from an American Express commercial that shows objects with "happy" or "sad" faces, to the local grocery store that has boxes of snacks with animals expressing a smiling face beckoning someone to buy them. The concepts of both technomorphism and anthropomorphism come down to the idea of how we perceive other humans, beings, and objects. This perception develops, in part, through the use of schemas, which will be discussed in the next section.

SCHEMAS AND TECHNOMORPHISM

When an individual technomorphizes, anthropomorphizes, or for that matter, makes a judgment about any object, they are likely doing so through the use of a schema. A schema is a mental structure that is used to organize and simplify knowledge and make better sense of novel objects and events (Baldwin, 1992). Through the use of schemas, individuals can use their past experiences to form opinions and make judgments of an unfamiliar object. Though traditionally looked at in the Psychology field, even those in the engineering world have utilized schemas as a way to represent motor function in robots (Arkin, 1989). In this example, researchers created a motor schema that they implemented into their robot. This schema allowed said robot to operate in a concurrent and independent manner, while at the same time communicating to produce paths that reflected the uncertainty in the detection of objects and cope with conflicting or changing information.

In order to for an individual to use a technomorphic schema, he or she must make use of knowledge from a well-known domain and make analogies to apply that knowledge to another domain (Clement & Gentner, 1991; Spellman & Holyoak, 1996). It is this ability to use analogical reasoning that is a core feature of human cognition (Holyoak & Thagard, 1997). Humans construct and convey understanding of things through the use of terms previously reserved for other things, on the basis of some perceived or conjectured similarity between them (Leary, 1992).

It is the use of these schemas that allow humans to quickly perceive and produce an action in response. The use of schemas is also present in the assessment of what makes us human or not. For example, the Turing Test is a theoretical and applied concept from the 1950s that requires a human to judge whether another being with whom they are interacting is human or if it is a computer program (Turing, 1950). The Turing Test also has a human component to it as well. In his book, The Most Human Human, Brian Christian talks about his experiences as a confederate in the Turing Test. In addition to awarding a prize for the programming team that can fool participants into thinking the entity on the other side is human, there is also a "side" reward called the Loebner Prize for the confederate that participants thought was the "most human-like." Mr. Christian goes on to describe how he was instructed to just "be himself" and that will be considered enough to be considered human. But given the complex nature of what it means to be human, he found it difficult not to prepare and do all he could to have the winning edge, especially given that many of the nature cues that humans use to interact with each other (such as nonverbal communication) would be stripped when interacting via computer screen.

Interestingly, we used a version of a reverse Turing Test on a regular basis. It has been created to allow a computer program to recognize whether the being on the other side of the screen is a human or another computer program. Many have experienced this "test" when trying to register for a new email account, commented on a website forum, or tried purchasing tickets at an online vendor. A computer program called "Completely Automated Public Turing Test to Tell Computers and Humans Apart" or "CAPTCHA" has created a "test" that prompts users to enter a series of numbers and letters in a distorted, wavy image (von Ahn, Blum, & Langford, 2004). By using these security features, websites are protected against bots by generating and grading tests that humans can pass, but current computer programs cannot. It protects both companies and users from comments, spam in blogs, website registration, and online polls from being "spammed," etc. Up to this point, most human users can answer this prompt with little difficulty, whereas most computer programs lack the capability to perform a "CAPTCHA."

Through the Turing Test and CAPTCHA examples above, we can see that there are certain inherent human and computer characteristics that can be put to the test. These and other programs are examples of organizations trying to utilize the distinctions between what humans can do and what computers can do. In order to bridge the gap between research that focuses on aspects of humans that can be designed in computers, and aspects of computers that can help us understand ourselves better as humans, the conceptualization of technomorphism needs to be fleshed out and understood better.

THEORETICAL AND EMPIRICAL EVIDENCE FOR TECHNOMORPHISM

Technomorphism has been studied, at least indirectly, in a small number of studies. In a recent study by Reiser, Parlit, and Klein (2009), technomorphism was examined in the design and implementation of a new robot butler. Although technomorphism in this context referred to designing a robot to look more "tech" like, the same basic principle can be applied to humans. As humans use more and more technological devices, they too can potentially look more "tech" like. The authors go on to mention the uncanny valley as one possible reason why a more technomorphic robot would be preferable to a human-like model. The uncanny valley can be thought of as the "strange" feeling that individuals get when viewing a robot or other non-human entity that looks and acts almost like an actual human. It also can be expanded to humans that look "too perfect" in appearance There is a point at which a human replica can look "too much like a human" (Mori, 2005). However, other research has summarized the opposite when it comes to the appearance of a robot. In the matching hypothesis, it is predicted that the most successful human-robot interaction will occur when the robot's appearance matches its role in the interaction (Goetz, Kiesler, & Powers, 2003). There is some evidence to support the idea that robots whose features, both visually and behaviorally, mimic our own are more comforting to us. Indeed, people may be turned off by a robot whose appearance does not match its purpose (Duffy, 2003). Duffy describes several examples of this idea, including robots in factories that humans prefer to look less human-like as well as service robots that humans prefer to look and act more like humans in general. Conversely, there are others that believe that we too are becoming more robotic-like, as we try to design robots that are more human-like. Those like Andy Clark (2004) believe that we are becoming more and more like natural-born cyborgs. Indeed, many people would fall under Clarks description of "human-technology symbionts: whose thinking and reasoning systems whose minds and selves are spread across biological brain and non-biological circuitry" (p. 230). The current work seeks to test Clark's theory in a more empirical fashion.

In a study by Shamp (1991), technomorphism was examined in conversations with communication partners on a computer. Researchers hypothesized that perceptions of communication partners would become more computer-like when little personal information was exchanged and when small amounts of communication took place between computer communication partners. Their results suggested that their first hypothesis was supported but the second was not. As the participants interacted with each other via a computer interface, the content and tone of their conversation became much less conversational, and much more rote and computer-like with short, direct questions and answers between the two humans. In this case, technomorphism was studied through communication and interaction between humans, instead of through the study of the physical appearance of an individual. Therefore, it is important to study many facets of technomorphism, which include, but are not limited to appearance, interactions with others, our process for understanding the world, and how we perceive each other.

Technomorphism as a concept has been around for over 50 years. Waters defined and described it (then termed mechanomorphism) back in 1948. He explains it through the mention of mechanical advances that were taking place and how that brought about questions of what it meant to be human. This is, of course, a tricky question that brings about more questions than answers. After all, human to human interaction is a complex web of communication cues, social norms, and previous experience, as well as many other cues. Indeed, at Stanley Stark (1963) stated in his work " even if Armageddon never comes, we may still never learn whether metal brains can do everything human brains can do; the reason being that scientists may never agree what human brains can do" (p. 160). There has been slow advancement in answering this question nearly half a century later. There has been a plethora of research within the past two decades relating to how robots and other entities may interact with humans including how the robot should look, sound, and act. However, there is a decided lack of empirical work on what it means to be a human and even less on how technology has impacted how the definition of "humanness" is changed. This work seeks to fill that gap through the design, validation, and implementation of a technomorphic scale to begin to examine these key questions.

MEASURING TECHNOMORPHISM

Through a series of empirical studies, the researcher created and validated a measure of technomorphism, also called the Technomorphic Tendencies Scale. As stated above, little is known about technomorphism from an empirical standpoint, so this work is meant to lay down the framework for this type of study. A large component of this includes the creation of a scale to measure the concept of technomorphism. It has been mentioned anecdotally and studied indirectly, but there is nothing currently available to tap into the various forms that technomorphism may take. Therefore, the scale that was created serves to fill that purpose. This scale includes two main types of technomorphism, as determined through the theoretical literature. The first is a set of items which are meant to capture the problem solving or schema driven form of technomorphism. So, as humans try to "figure out" the world, do we use more concrete and definable objects in order to understand it better? These questions were developed out of the basic premise that, as technology is becoming more and more accessible it also may be causing a shift in the way we think and solve about problems. For instance, using the computer to model how the brain works, as described above, would fall in to this question type. The second type of items to be developed pertain to perceptions of others that may be eliciting a technomorphic features. This is further broken down into features that may be physical in nature such as the use of a Bluetooth, prosthesis, or other device, as well as those internal or non-physical features such as the way an individual acts, reasons, or emotes. The process of creating and validating a scale of this kind is a multi-step process and is described in depth below.

A detailed version of the Technomorphic Tendencies Scale can be found in another article. The scale below is the result of the validation efforts (figure 1). It should be noted that a revised version of this scale is currently being validated and will be published in the next year. The Technomorphic Tendencies Scale has the potential for numerous scientific and applied uses. For example, it could be used to predict individual differences in interactions with other humans, avatars, robots, and many others. Similarly, the military, NASA, and many other government agencies could use this scale to determine who is qualified uniquely to think about problems in a technomorphic way or can work with and use robots and be able to take on the robot's point of view. These results suggest that individuals may perceive others more positively on a number of attributes when they fit expectations for what people naturally look like. When designing consumer and military products, consideration of how people perceive those wearing the products should be taken into account.

DISCUSSION

Future research will be needed to determine if there are additional technomorphic tendencies that are not measured by the TTS or if the two types found in the present research represent a full range of possible types of technomorphism. Also, a more heterogeneous pool of participants should be sampled in order to measure the validity of this measure within different populations. This includes different age groups, races, ethnicities, and cultures. There also should be special attention to those who do and do not work with technology on a regular basis and how this may influence how much and what types of technomorphism they utilize. Furthermore, factors that were not assessed in the current studies may be correlated with technomorphic tendencies. Use and acceptance of technology, anthropomorphism, and personality characteristics were all predictive of tendency to technomorphize. However, other individual differences such as exposure to technology at a certain age, socio-economic status, and other factors may play into a person's propensity to technomorphize.

Technomorphic tendencies appear to be measurable, and this individual difference, along with other variables, may be used to further understand humans' interactions with each other. This study may be the very first of its kind to look at how we perceive technomorphic attributes in humans rather than how to humanize a robot or computer. The results of this study may serve as a stepping stone into a more introspective view of ourselves as humans within the larger context of a technologically driven society. The findings from this and future work should allow robotics developers, computer scientists, military agencies, and even advertisers to better understand the underlying tendencies that exist within many individuals, in order to create better, more engaging products. It is through an understanding of how technology is fundamentally changing us as human beings through the viewpoint of techanomorphism, which can be important to the future of our interactions with and perceptions of other human beings.

Although it is difficult to measure every form of technology and the potential negative implications of it, there may still be some importance in researching the social implications of technology in our society. If the social context in which we use technology is fundamentally changing the way that we perceive each other, that is a philosophical as well as practical question that should be addressed now, as we continue to move forward with ever more complex and intricate machines designed to further augment us. This is particularly important in light of the ever-increasing amount of technology that is being utilized by everyone including soldiers, school teachers, and everyday consumers.

REFERENCES

Aggarwal, P., & McGill, A. L. (2007). Is that car smiling at me? Schema congruity as a basis for evaluating anthropomorphized products. *Journal of Consumer Research. Inc, 34*, 468–479.

Arkin, R. C. (1989). Motor schema-based mobile robot navigation. *The International Journal of Robotics Research, 8*(4), 92–112. doi:10.1177/027836498900800406

Baldwin, M. W. (1992). Relational schemas and the processing of social information. *Psychological Bulletin, 112*(3), 461–484. doi:10.1037/0033-2909.112.3.461

Barrick, M., & Mount, M. (1991). The big five personality dimensions and job performance: A meta-analysis. *Personnel Psychology*, 2(1), 58–71. doi:10.1111/j.1744-6570.1991.tb00688.x

Boersma, P., & Weenink, D. (2000). *Praat, a system for doing phonetics by computer*. http://www.praat.org

Caporael, L. R. (1981). The paralanguage of caregiving: Baby talk to the institutionalized aged. *Journal of Personality and Social Psychology*, 40(5), 876–884. doi:10.1037/0022-3514.40.5.876 PMID:7241341

Caporeal, L. R. (1986). Anthropomorphism and mechanomorphism: Two faces of the human machine. *Computers in Human Behavior*, 2(3), 215–234. doi:10.1016/0747-5632(86)90004-X

Chin, M. G., Sims, V. K., Clark, B., & Rivera Lopez, G. (2004). Measuring Individual Differences in Anthropomorphism Toward Machines and Animals. *Proceedings of the Human Factors and Ergonomics Society*, 46. 10.1177/154193120404801110

Chin, M. G., Sims, V. K., Ellis, L. U., Yordon, R. E., Clark, B. R., Ballion, T., Dolezal, M. J., Shumaker, R., & Finkelstein, N. (2005). Developing an Anthropomorphic Tendencies Scale. *Proceedings of the Human Factors and Ergonomics Society*, 47.

Clark, A. (2004). *Natural-Born Cyborgs: Minds, Technologies, and the Future of Human Intelligence*. Oxford University Press.

Clement, C. A., & Gentner, D. (1991). Systematicity as a selection constraint in analogical mapping. *Cognitive Science*, 15(1), 89–132. doi:10.120715516709cog1501_3

Crowne, D. P., & Marlowe, D. (n.d.). A new scale of social desirabihty independent of psychopathology. *Journal of Consulting Psychology*, 960(M), 349–354.

DeVellis, R. F. (1991). *Scale development: Theory and applications*. Sage.

DiSalvo, C. F., Gemperle, F., Forlizzi, J., & Kiesler, S. (2002). All robots are not created equal: The design and perception of humanoid robot heads. *Proceedings of the DIS Conference*, 321-326. 10.1145/778712.778756

DiStefano, C., & Motl, R. W. (2009). Personality correlates of method effects due to negatively worded items on the Rosenberg self-esteem scale. *Personality and Individual Differences*, 46(3), 309–313. doi:10.1016/j.paid.2008.10.020

Donnellan, M. B., Oswald, F. L., Baird, B. M., & Lucas, R. E. (2006). The Mini-IPIP scales: Tiny-yet-effective measures of the Big Five factors of personality. *Psychological Assessment*, *18*(2), 192–203. doi:10.1037/1040-3590.18.2.192 PMID:16768595

Duffy, B. R. (2003). Anthropomorphism and the social robot. *Robotics and Autonomous Systems*, *42*(3-4), 177–190. doi:10.1016/S0921-8890(02)00374-3

Federal Trade Commission. (2011). *About identity theft*. Retrieved on May 03, 2011 from https://www.ftc.gov/bcp/edu/microsites/idtheft/consumers/about-identity-theft.html

Fong, T., Nourbakhsh, I., & Dautenhahn, K. (2003). A survey of socially interactive robots. *Robotics and Autonomous Systems*, *42*(3-4), 143–166. doi:10.1016/S0921-8890(02)00372-X

Goetz, J., Kiesler, S., & Powers, A. (2003). *Matching robot appearance and behavior to tasks to improve human-robot cooperation*. In *The Twelfth IEEE International Workshop on Robots and Human Interactive Communication*, Lisbon, Portugal. 10.1109/ROMAN.2003.1251796

Gorsuch, R. L. (1983). *Factor analysis* (2nd ed.). Lawrence Erlbaum.

Graham, S. A., Poulin-Dubois, D., & Baker, R. K. (1998). Infants' disambiguation of novel object words. *First Language*, *18*(53), 149–164. doi:10.1177/014272379801805302

Guthrie, S. (1993). *Faces in the clouds: A new theory of religion*. Oxford University Press.

Halse, S. E., Lum, H. C., Sims, V. K., & Chin, M. G. (2011). *First impressions: Is it you or the things you're with?* Poster presented at the APS 23rd Annual Conference, Washington, DC.

Holyoak, K. J., & Thagard, P. (1997). The analogical mind. *The American Psychologist*, *52*(1), 35–44. doi:10.1037/0003-066X.52.1.35 PMID:9017931

Horan, P. M., DiStefano, C., & Motl, R. W. (2003). Wording effects in self esteem scales: Methodological artifact or response style? *Structural Equation Modeling*, *10*(3), 444–455. doi:10.1207/S15328007SEM1003_6

Howe, N., & Strauss, W. (2000). *Millennials rising: The next great generation*. Vintage.

Jacobsen, S. (2010). *The exoskeleton's super technology*. Retrieved on August 21, 2010 from: https://www.raytheon.com/newsroom/technology/rtn08_exoskeleton/

Kewin, T. (2010). *If your kids are awake, they're probably online*. Retrieved on April 21, 2011 from https://www.nytimes.com/2010/01/20/education/20wired.html

Knapp, H., & Kirk, S. A. (2003). Using pencil and paper, internet and touch-tone phones for self administered surveys: Does methodology matter? *Computers in Human Behavior, 19*(1), 117–134. doi:10.1016/S0747-5632(02)00008-0

Koford, B. (2010). *Match.com and Chadwick Martin Bailey 2009 - 2010 studies: recent trends: online dating*. Retrieved on April, 17, 2010 from http://cp.match.com/cppp/media/CMB_Study.pdf

LaPlante, D., & Ambady, N. (2002). Saying it like it isn't: Responding to mixed messages from men and women in the workplace. *Journal of Applied Social Psychology, 32*(12), 2435–2457. doi:10.1111/j.1559-1816.2002.tb02750.x

Leary, D. E. (1995). Naming and knowing: Giving form to things unknown. *Social Research, 62*, 267–298.

Lum, H. C., Sims, V. K., Chin, M. G., & Lagattuta, N. C. (2009). Perceptions of humans wearing technology. *Proceedings of the Human Factors and Ergonomics Society, 53*.

McBride, T., & Nief, R. (2010). *Beloit college mindset list, entering class on 2014*. Retrieved on August 21, 2010 from https://www.beloit.edu/mindset/

Meng, J. (2009). *Living in internet time*. Retrieved on May 04, 2011 from https://www.ocf.berkeley.edu/~jaimeng/techtime.html

Morewedge, C. K., Preston, J., & Wegner, D. M. (2007). Timescale bias in the attribution of mind. *Journal of Personality and Social Psychology, 93*(1), 1–11. doi:10.1037/0022-3514.93.1.1 PMID:17605584

Mori, M. (2005). On the Uncanny Valley. *Proceedings of the Humanoids-2005 workshop: Views of the Uncanny Valley*.

Motl, R. W., & DiStefano, C. (2002). Longitudinal invariance of self-esteem and method effects associated with negatively worded items. *Structural Equation Modeling, 9*(4), 562–578. doi:10.1207/S15328007SEM0904_6

Nielsen Group. (2009). *Americans watching more tv than ever; web and mobile video up too*. Retrieved on April 20, 2011 from http://blog.nielsen.com/nielsenwire/online_mobile/americans-watching-more-tv-than-ever/

Nomura, T., Suzuki, T., Kanda, T., & Kato, K. (2006). Altered attitudes of people toward robots: Investigation through the Negative Attitudes toward Robots Scale. *Proc. AAAI-06 Workshop on Human Implications of Human-Robot Interaction*, 29-35.

Nowak, K. L., & Blocca, F. (2003). The effect of the agency and anthropomorphism on users' sense of telepresence, copresence, and social presence in virtual environments. *Presence (Cambridge, Mass.)*, *12*(5), 481–494. doi:10.1162/105474603322761289

Osborne, J., Simon, S., & Collins, S. (2003). Attitudes towards science: A review of the literature and its implications. *International Journal of Science Education*, *25*(9), 1049–1079. doi:10.1080/0950069032000032199

Parasuraman, A. (2000). Technology Readiness Index (TRI): A Multiple-Item Scale to Measure Readiness to Embrace New Technologies. *Journal of Service Research*, *2*(4), 307–320. doi:10.1177/109467050024001

Reiser, U., Connette, C. P., Fischer, J., Kubacki, J., Bubeck, A., Weisshardt, J., Jacobs, T., Parlitz, C., Hagele, M., & Verl, A. (2009). Care-O-bot 3 - Creating a product vision for service robot applications by integrating design and technology. *2009 IEEE/RSJ International Conference on Intelligent Robots and Systems IROS*, 1992-1998. 10.1109/IROS.2009.5354526

Reynolds, W. M. (1982). Development of reliable and valid short-forms of the Marlowe-Crowne Social Desirability Scale. *Journal of Clinical Psychology*, *38*(1), 119–125. doi:10.1002/1097-4679(198201)38:1<119::AID-JCLP2270380118>3.0.CO;2-I

Riek, L. D., Rabinowitch, T., Chakrabarti, B., & Robinson, P. (2009). How anthropomorphism affects empathy toward robots. *Proceedings of the 4th ACM/IEEE international conference on Human robot interaction*. 10.1145/1514095.1514158

Roncone, K. (2004). Nanotechnology: What next-generation warriors will wear. *Journal of Military Psychology*, *21*, 31–33.

Shamp, S. A. (1991). Mechanomorphism in Perception of Computer Communication Partners. *Computers in Human Behavior*, *7*(3), 147–161. doi:10.1016/0747-5632(91)90004-K

Sims, V. K., Chin, M. G., Smith, H. S., Ballion, T., Sushil, D. J., Strand, M., Mendoza, S., Shumaker, R., & Finkelstein, N. (2006). Effects of eye structure and color on attributions for intelligent agents. *Proceedings of the Human Factors and Ergonomics Society*, *50*. 10.1177/154193120605001728

Spellman, B. A., & Holyoak, K. J. (1996). Pragmatics in analogical mapping. *Cognitive Psychology*, *31*(3), 307–346. doi:10.1006/cogp.1996.0019 PMID:8975685

Stark, S. (1963). Creative leadership: Human vs. metal brains. *Academy of Management Journal, 6*(2), 160–169.

Tomás, J. M., & Oliver, A. (1999). Rosenberg's self-esteem scale: Two factors or method effects. *Structural Equation Modeling, 6*(1), 84–98. doi:10.1080/10705519909540120

Tremoulet, P. D., Leslie, A. M., & Hall, G. (2000). Infant attention to the shape and color of objects: Individuation and identification. *Cognitive Development, 15*, 499–522. doi:10.1016/S0885-2014(01)00038-7

Tschabitscher, H. (2011). *How many emails are sent every day?* Retrieved on April 20, 2011 from http://www.radicati.com/

Turing, A. M. (1950). Computing machinery and intelligence. *Mind, 59*(236), 433–460. doi:10.1093/mind/LIX.236.433

Venkatesh, V., & Davis, F. D. (2000). A Theoretical Extension of the Technology Acceptance Model: Four Longitudinal Field Studies. *Management Science, 46*(2), 186–204. doi:10.1287/mnsc.46.2.186.11926

von Ahn, L., Blum, M., & Langford, J. (2004). Telling humans and computers apart automatically. *Communications of the ACM, 47*(2), 56–60. doi:10.1145/966389.966390

Warwick, K., Xydas, D., Nasuto, S. J., Becerra, V. M., Hammond, M. W., Downes, J. H., Marshall, S., & Whalley, B. J. (2010). Controlling a Mobile Robot with a Biological Brain. *Defence Science Journal, 1*(60), 5–14. doi:10.14429/dsj.60.11

Waters, R. H. (1948). Mechanomorphism: A new term for an old mode of thought. *Psychological Review, 55*(3), 139–142. doi:10.1037/h0058952 PMID:18865255

APPENDIX 1

Figure 1. Technomorphic tendencies scale

TTS

Please read each statement carefully. Indicate the strength of your agreement with each statement by clicking on the button which corresponds with your opinion on the following 5-point scale. There are no right or wrong answers to any of these statements. We are interested in your honest reactions and opinions.

1	2	3	4	5
Strongly Disagree	Disagree	Neutral	Agree	Strongly Agree

1. I think of a machine with moving parts working in conjunction with one another when looking at how people dance.

2. I think of food as fuel that my body converts to energy in order to work as an effective machine.

3. I think of a computer with moving parts working in conjunction with one another when looking at how the human body moves.

4. I think of food as fuel that my body converts to energy in order to work as an effective computer.

5. I think of a machine with moving parts working in conjunction with one another to understand a concept such as how love works.

6. I use an analogy about how a machine works to understand a concept such as tiredness.

7. I think of a computer with moving parts working in conjunction with one another to understand a concept such as hatred.

8. I think of a computer with moving parts working in conjunction with one another to understand a concept such as how love works.

9. I break down the concept into machine-like parts when I am trying to understand how memory works.

10. I break down the concept into machine-like parts when I am trying to understand how an ecosystem works.

11. I break down the concept into machine-like parts when I am trying to understand how a business works.

12. I break down the concept into computer-like parts when I am trying to understand how the human body operates.

13. I break down the concept into computer-like parts when I am trying to understand how a business works.

Compilation of References

Abbate, E. (2020, June 17). Here's How the NBA's Coronavirus-Fighting Ring Might Help. *GQ.* https://www.gq.com/story/oura-ring-nba

Abhari, K., Baxter, J. S. H., Chen, E. C. S., Khan, A. R., Peters, T. M., de Ribaupierre, S., & Eagleson, R. (2015). Training for Planning Tumour Resection: Augmented Reality and Human Factors. *IEEE Transactions on Biomedical Engineering, 62*(6), 1466–1477. doi:10.1109/TBME.2014.2385874 PMID:25546854

Abid, S., Ferjani, S., El Moussi, A., Ferjani, A., Nasr, M., Landolsi, I., ... Safer, M. (2020). Assessment of sample pooling for SARS-CoV-2 molecular testing for screening of asymptomatic persons in Tunisia. *Diagnostic Microbiology and Infectious Disease, 98*(3), 115125. doi:10.1016/j.diagmicrobio.2020.115125 PMID:32768876

Accenture. (2018). *It's learning. Just not as we know it: How to accelerate skills acquisition in the age of intelligent technologies.* G20 Young Entrepreneurs' Alliance. https://www.accenture.com/_acnmedia/thought-leadership-assets/pdf/accenture-education-and-technology-skills-research.pdf

Adcock, A. (2012). Cognitive dissonance in the learning processes. *Encycl. Sci. Learning,* 588–590.

Adedokun-Shittu, N. A., Ajani, A. H., Nuhu, K. M., & Shitu, A. J. K. (2020). Augmented reality instructional tool in enhancing geography learners' academic performance and retention in Osun state Nigeria. *Education and Information Technologies, 25*(4), 3021–3033. doi:10.100710639-020-10099-2

Agarwal, R., Chandrasekaran, S., & Sridhar, M. (2016, October). The digital future of construction. In *Voices.* McKinsey Global Institute. https://www.globalinfrastructureinitiative.com/sites/default/files/pdf/The-digital-future-of-construction-Oct-2016.pdf

Aggarwal, P., & McGill, A. L. (2007). Is that car smiling at me? Schema congruity as a basis for evaluating anthropomorphized products. *Journal of Consumer Research. Inc, 34,* 468–479.

Aggerholm, H. K., Anderson, S. E., & Thomsen, C. (2011). Conceptualising employer branding in sustainable organizations. *Corporate Communication: An International Journal, 16*(2), 105–123. doi:10.1108/13563281111141642

Aghajani, H. A., Samadi Mirakalei, H., & Samadi Myrkalei, H. (2015). The relationship between entrepreneurship and characteristics of a learning organization. *Management Efficiency, 35*(9), 39-64.

Aguilar, J. B., Faust, J. S., Westafer, L. M., & Gutierrez, J. B. (2020). Investigating the impact of asymptomatic carriers on COVID-19 transmission. medRxiv. doi:10.1101/2020.03.18.20037994

Ahadzadeh, A. S., Pahlevan Sharif, S., Ong, F. S., & Khong, K. W. (2015). Integrating Health Belief Model and Technology Acceptance Model: An Investigation of Health-Related Internet Use. *Journal of Medical Internet Research, 17*(2), e45. doi:10.2196/jmir.3564 PMID:25700481

Ajzen, I. (1991). The theory of planned behavior. *Organizational Behavior and Human Decision Processes, 50*(2), 179–211. doi:10.1016/0749-5978(91)90020-T

Akçayır, M., & Akçayır, G. (2017). Advantages and challenges associated with augmented reality for education: A systematic review of the literature. *Educational Research Review, 20*, 1–11. doi:10.1016/j.edurev.2016.11.002

Alalwan, A. A., Dwivedi, Y. K., Rana, N. P., & Williams, M. D. (2016). Consumer adoption ofmobile banking in Jordan: Examining the role of usefulness, ease of use, perceived risk and self-efficacy. *Journal of Enterprise Information Management, 29*(1), 118–139. doi:10.1108/JEIM-04-2015-0035

Alexander, I. F. (2005). A taxonomy of stakeholders: Human roles in system development. *International Journal of Technology and Human Interaction, 1*(1), 23–59. doi:10.4018/jthi.2005010102

Alhabeeb, A., & Rowley, J. (2017). Critical success factors for eLearning in Saudi Arabian universities. *International Journal of Educational Management, 31*(2), 131–147. doi:10.1108/IJEM-01-2016-0006

Aliprantis, J., Konstantakis, M., Nikopoulou, R., Mylonas, P., & Caridakis, G. (2019). Natural Interaction in Augmented Reality Context. VIPERC@IRCDL 2019.

Allison, A. (2018, March 20). *Virtually view Lowe's spring collection in your backyard*. Lowe's Corporate. https://corporate.lowes.com/newsroom/stories/fresh-thinking/virtually-view-lowes-spring-collection-your-backyard

Alsabbagh, M., & Khalil, A. H. (2016). The impact of leadership styles on organizationallearning (an empirical study on the education sector in Damascus city). *International Journal of Academic Research in Business & Social Sciences, 6*(5), 197–217. doi:10.6007/IJARBSS/v6-i5/2126

Alt, D. (2015). Assessing the contribution of a constructivist learning environment to academic self-efficacy in higher education. *Learning Environments Research, 18*(1), 47–67. doi:10.100710984-015-9174-5

Alvani, S. M. (2008). *Public Administration*. Ney Publications.

Amstadter, A. B., Broman-Fulks, J., Zinzow, H., Ruggiero, K. J., & Cercone, J. (2009). Internet-based interventions for traumatic stress-related mental health problems: A review and suggestion for future research. *Clinical Psychology Review*, *29*(5), 410–420. doi:10.1016/j.cpr.2009.04.001 PMID:19403215

Andersson, G. (2014). Age may moderate response to different unguided Internet-delivered interventions for depression. *Evidence-Based Mental Health*, *17*(1), 29. doi:10.1136/eb-2013-101638 PMID:24477534

Andersson, G., Berg, M., Riper, H., Huppert, J. D., & Titov, N. (2020). The Possible Role of Internet-Delivered Psychological Interventions in Relation to the COVID-19 Pandemic. *Clinical Psychology in Europe*, *2*(3), 1–4. doi:10.32872/cpe.v2i3.3941

Andersson, G., Bergström, J., Carlbring, P., & Lindefors, N. (2005). The use of the Internet in the treatment of anxiety disorders. *Current Opinion in Psychiatry*, *18*(1), 73–77. PMID:16639187

Andersson, G., & Cuijpers, P. (2009). Internet-based and other computerized psychological treatments for adult depression: A meta-analysis. *Cognitive Behaviour Therapy*, *38*(4), 196–205. doi:10.1080/16506070903318960 PMID:20183695

Andersson, G., Cuijpers, P., Carlbring, P., & Lindefors, N. (2007). Effects of Internet-delivered cognitive behaviour therapy for anxiety and mood disorders. *Psychiatry*, *1*(2), 9–14.

Andersson, G., & Hedman, E. (2013). Effectiveness of guided internet-based cognitive behavior therapy in regular clinical settings. *Verhaltenstherapie*, *23*(3), 140–148. doi:10.1159/000354779

Andersson, G., & Titov, N. (2014). Advantages and limitations of Internet-based interventions for common mental disorders. *World Psychiatry; Official Journal of the World Psychiatric Association (WPA)*, *13*(1), 4–11. doi:10.1002/wps.20083 PMID:24497236

Andersson, G., Waara, J., Jonsson, U., Malmaeus, F., Carlbring, P., & Öst, L.-G. (2013). Internet-Based Exposure Treatment Versus One-Session Exposure Treatment of Snake Phobia: A Randomized Controlled Trial. *Cognitive Behaviour Therapy*, *42*(4), 284–291. doi:10.1080/16506073.2013.844202 PMID:24245707

Anen, C. (2007). *Neural correlates of economic and moral decision-making* (Tesis doctoral).

Angelis, C. T. (2016). The impact of national culture and knowledge management on governmental intelligence. *Journal of Modelling in Management*, *11*(1), 240–268. doi:10.1108/JM2-08-2014-0069

Anthes, E. (2016). Mental health: There's an app for that. *NATNews*, *532*(7597), 20–23. doi:10.1038/532020a PMID:27078548

Aranda, J. H., & Baig, S. (2018). Toward "JOMO": The joy of missing out and the freedom of disconnecting. In *Proceedings of the 20th International Conference on Human–Computer Interaction with Mobile Devices and Services*. Association for Computing Machinery. 10.1145/3229434.3229468

Argyris, C. (1998). Organizational behavior: Production of knowledge for action in the world of practice. In J. McKelvey & M. Neufeld (Eds.), *Industrial relations at the dawn of the new millennium* (pp. 54–61). New York State School of Industrial and Labor Relations.

Arkin, R. C. (1989). Motor schema-based mobile robot navigation. *The International Journal of Robotics Research, 8*(4), 92–112. doi:10.1177/027836498900800406

Arnberg, F. K., Linton, S. J., Hultcrantz, M., Heintz, E., & Jonsson, U. (2014). Internet-delivered psychological treatments for mood and anxiety disorders: A systematic review of their efficacy, safety, and cost-effectiveness. *PLoS One, 9*(5), e98118. doi:10.1371/journal.pone.0098118 PMID:24844847

Association, X. R. (2019). *XR primer 1.0: A starter guide for developers.* https://xra.org/wp-content/uploads/rs-xr-primer-1.0-01.pdf

Attwell, G. (2010). Work-based mobile learning environments: Contributing to a socio-cultural ecology of mobile learning. *International Journal of Mobile and Blended Learning, 2*(4), 19–34. doi:10.4018/jmbl.2010100102

Atwood, M. A., Mora, J. W., & Kaplan, A. W. (2010). Learning to lead: Evaluating leadershipand organizational learning. *Leadership and Organization Development Journal, 31*(7), 576–595. doi:10.1108/01437731011079637

Australian National University. (2015). *MoodGYM.* Retrieved 2021, May 14, from http://www.moodgym.anu.edu.au

Baber, C. (2001). Wearable computers: A human factors review. *International Journal of Human-Computer Interaction, 13*(2), 123–145. doi:10.1207/S15327590IJHC1302_3

Bacca, J., Baldiris, S., Fabregat, R., & Graf, S. (2014). Augmented reality trends in education: A systematic review of research and applications. *Journal of Educational Technology & Society, 17*(4), 133–149.

Bächle, K., & Gregorzik, S. (2019). Digital twins in industrial applications: Requirements to a comprehensive data model. *Industrial Internet Consortium Journal of Innovation.* https://www.iiconsortium.org/news/joi-articles/2019-November-JoI-Digital-Twins-in-Industrial-Applications.pdf

Balaji, S., Babu, M. M., & Aravind, L. (2007). Interplay between network structures, regulatory modes and sensing mechanisms of transcription factors in the transcriptional regulatory network of E. coli. *Journal of Molecular Biology, 372*(4), 1108–1122. doi:10.1016/j.jmb.2007.06.084 PMID:17706247

Baldwin, M. W. (1992). Relational schemas and the processing of social information. *Psychological Bulletin, 112*(3), 461–484. doi:10.1037/0033-2909.112.3.461

Baltes, P. B., & Baltes, M. M. (1990). Psychological perspectives on successful aging: The model of selective optimization with compensation. In P. B. Baltes & M. M. Baltes (Eds.), *Successful Aging* (pp. 1–34). Cambridge University Press. doi:10.1017/CBO9780511665684.003

Bandura, A. (2002). Social cognitive theory in cultural context. *Applied Psychology*, *51*(2), 269–290. doi:10.1111/1464-0597.00092

Baptista, P., Fernández, C., & Hernández, R. (2006). *Metodología de la investigación* (6th ed.). Editorial McGraw Hill.

Barak, A., Hen, L., Boniel-Nissim, M., & Shapira, N. (2008). A comprehensive review and a meta-analysis of the effectiveness of internet-based psychotherapeutic interventions. *Journal of Technology in Human Services*, *26*(2-4), 109–160. doi:10.1080/15228830802094429

Barak, A., Klein, B., & Proudfoot, J. G. (2009). Defining internet-supported therapeutic interventions. *Annals of Behavioral Medicine*, *38*(1), 4–17. doi:10.100712160-009-9130-7 PMID:19787305

Barney, J. (1991). Firm resources and sustained competitive advantage. *Journal of Management*, *17*(1), 99–120. doi:10.1177/014920639101700108

Barrick, M., & Mount, M. (1991). The big five personality dimensions and job performance: A meta-analysis. *Personnel Psychology*, *2*(1), 58–71. doi:10.1111/j.1744-6570.1991.tb00688.x

Barry, J. M. (2020). *The great influenza: The story of the deadliest pandemic in history*. Penguin UK.

Bastieans, T. J., Wood, L. C., & Reiners, T. (2014). New landscapes and new eye: The role of virtual world design for supply chain education. *Ubiquitous Learning: An International Journal*, *6*(1), 37–49. doi:10.18848/1835-9795/CGP/v06i01/40388

Batterham, P. J., Calear, A. L., O'Dea, B., Larsen, M. E. J., Kavanagh, D., Titov, N., March, S., Hickie, I., Teesson, M., Deat, B. F., Reynolds, J., Lowinger, J., Thorton, L., & Gorman, P. (2019). Stakeholder perspectives on evidence for digital mental health interventions: Implications for accreditation systems. *Digital Health*, *5*, 2055207619878069. doi:10.1177/2055207619878069 PMID:31565238

Baumeister, R. F., & Leary, M. R. (1995). The need to belong: Desire for interpersonal attachments as a fundamental human motivation. *Psychological Bulletin*, *117*(3), 497–529. doi:10.1037/0033-2909.117.3.497 PMID:7777651

Baumgartner, R. J., & Korhonen, J. (2010). Strategic thinking for sustainable development. International Sustainable Development Research Society, 18, 71-75.

Beck, A., Dimidjian, S., Boggs, J., Felder, J., & Segal, Z. (2014). PS2-43: Internet delivered mindfulness-based cognitive therapy for reducing residual depressive symptoms: An open trial and quasi-experimental comparison to propensity matched controls. *Clinical Medicine & Research*, *12*(1-2), 104. doi:10.3121/cmr.2014.1250.ps2-43

Becker, J. (2010). Use of backcasting to integrate indicators with principles of sustainability. *International Journal of Sustainable Development World*, *17*(3), 189–197. doi:10.1080/13504501003726974

Beer, T. (2020, Oct 20). Report: NBA's Bubble Prevented $1.5 Billion In Losses. *Forbes*. https://www.forbes.com/sites/tommybeer/2020/10/20/report-nbas-bubble-prevented-15-billion-in-losses/?sh=3215e3793823

Beer, M., Eisenstat, R. A., & Spector, B. (1990). *The Critical Path to Corporate Renewal*. Harvard Business School Press.

Behzadan, A. H., Dong, S., & Kamat, V. R. (2015). Augmented reality visualization: A review of civil infrastructure system applications. *Advanced Engineering Informatics*, *29*(2), 252–267. doi:10.1016/j.aei.2015.03.005

Belle, S. (2016). Organizational Learning? Look Again. *The Learning Organization*, *23*(5), 332–341. doi:10.1108/TLO-01-2016-0007

Bennett, K., Bennett, A. J., & Griffiths, K. M. (2010). Security considerations for e-mental health interventions. *Journal of Medical Internet Research*, *12*(5), e61. doi:10.2196/jmir.1468 PMID:21169173

Bennett, W. L., & Segerberg, A. (2012). The logic of connective action: Digital media and the personalization of contentious politics. *Information Communication and Society*, *15*(5), 739–768. doi:10.1080/1369118X.2012.670661

Bennis, W., Benne, K., & Chin, R. (1985). *The Planning of Change*. International Thompson Publishing.

Ben-Zeev, D. (2020). The digital mental health genie is out of the bottle. *Psychiatric Services (Washington, D.C.)*, *71*(12), 1212–1213. doi:10.1176/appi.ps.202000306 PMID:32576123

Bergström, J., Andersson, G., Karlsson, A., Andréewitch, S., Rück, C., Carlbring, P., & Lindefors, N. (2009). An open study of the effectiveness of Internet treatment for panic disorder delivered in a psychiatric setting. *Nordic Journal of Psychiatry*, *63*(1), 44–50. doi:10.1080/08039480802191132 PMID:18985514

Bergström, J., Andersson, G., Ljótsson, B., Rück, C., Andréewitch, S., Karlsson, A., Carlbring, O., Andersson, E., & Lindefors, N. (2010). Internet-versus group-administered cognitive behaviour therapy for panic disorder in a psychiatric setting: A randomised trial. *BMC Psychiatry*, *10*(1), 54. doi:10.1186/1471-244X-10-54 PMID:20598127

Bhargava, V. R., & Velasquez, M. (2020). Ethics of the attention economy: The problem of social media addiction. *Business Ethics Quarterly*, 1–39. doi:10.1017/beq.2020.32

Bianchi, C. (2012). Enhancing performance management and sustainable organizational growth through system-dynamics modelling. In *Systemic management for intelligent organizations* (pp. 143–161). Springer Berlin Heidelberg. doi:10.1007/978-3-642-29244-6_8

Bianchi, C. (2016). Fostering Sustainable Organizational Development Through Dynamic Performance Management. In *Dynamic Performance Management. System Dynamics for Performance Management* (Vol. 1). Springer. doi:10.1007/978-3-319-31845-5_3

Bian, S., Zhou, B., Bello, H., & Lukowicz, P. (2020, September). A wearable magnetic field-based proximity sensing system for monitoring COVID-19 social distancing. In *Proceedings of the 2020 International Symposium on Wearable Computers* (pp. 22-26). 10.1145/3410531.3414313

Bickler, P. E., Feiner, J. R., & Severinghaus, J. W. (2005). Effects of skin pigmentation on pulse oximeter accuracy at low saturation. *Anesthesiology: The Journal of the American Society of Anesthesiologists, 102*(4), 715–719. doi:10.1097/00000542-200504000-00004 PMID:15791098

Bilyk, V. (2020). Augmented reality issues: What you need to know. *The App Solutions Development Blog.* https://theappsolutions.com/blog/development/augmented-reality-challenges/

Birmingham, U. o. (2015). *Learning Theories, Stages and Styles.* University of Birmingham.

Bitter, S., & Grabner-Kräuter, S. (2013). Customer engagement behavior: Interacting with companies and brands on Facebook. In S. Rosengren, M. Dahlén, & S. Okazaki (Eds.), Advances in advertising research (Vol. 4, pp. 3–17). Springer. doi:10.1007/978-3-658-02365-2_1

Blanchard, M. (2011). *Navigating the digital disconnect: understanding the use of information communication technologies by the youth health workforce to help improve young people's mental health and wellbeing* (Ph.D. Thesis). The University of Melbourne, Melbourne, Australia.

Bodenheimer, T., Lorig, K., Holman, H., & Grumbach, K. (2002). Patient self-management of chronic disease in primary care. *Journal of the American Medical Association, 288*(19), 2469–2475. doi:10.1001/jama.288.19.2469 PMID:12435261

Boersma, P., & Weenink, D. (2000). *Praat, a system for doing phonetics by computer.* http://www.praat.org

Boettcher, J., Aström, V., Påhlsson, D., Schenström, O., Andersson, G., & Carlbring, P. (2014). Internet-based mindfulness treatment for anxiety disorders: A randomized controlled trial. *Behavior Therapy, 45*(2), 241–253. doi:10.1016/j.beth.2013.11.003 PMID:24491199

Boggs, J. M., Beck, A., Felder, J. N., Dimidjian, S., Metcalf, C. A., & Segal, Z. V. (2014). Web-Based Intervention in Mindfulness Meditation for Reducing Residual Depressive Symptoms and Relapse Prophylaxis: A Qualitative Study. *Journal of Medical Internet Research, 16*(3), e87. doi:10.2196/jmir.3129 PMID:24662625

Böing, J. (2014). Effect- and process evaluation of an internet- based intervention of Acceptance & Commitment Therapy for chronic pain patients: a randomized controlled trial (Master of Science). University of Twente, Netherlands.

Bontemps, T. (2020, Jun 16). In documents, NBA details coronavirus testing protocols, including 2-week resting period for positive tests. *ESPN.* https://www.espn.com/nba/story/_/id/29321006/in-documents-nba-details-coronavirus-testing-process-orlando-campus-life

Boons, F., & Lüdeke-Freund, F. (2013). Business models for sustainable innovation: State-of-the-art and steps towards a research agenda. *Journal of Cleaner Production, 45*(April), 9–19. doi:10.1016/j.jclepro.2012.07.007

Boonstra, J. J., & Elving, W. J. L. (2009) Veranderen als kunstje, kunde of kunst. In Communicatiemanagement in praktisch perspectief. Assen: Van Gorcum. Blz.

Boot, W. R., Charness, N., Czaja, S. J., & Rogers, W. A. (2020). *Designing for Older Adults: Case Studies, Methods, and Tools* (1st ed.). CRC Press. doi:10.1201/b22187

Borghouts, J., Eikey, E., Mark, G., De Leon, C., Schueller, S. M., Schneider, M., Stadnick, N., Zheng, K., Mukamel, D., & Sorkin, D. H. (2021). Barriers to and Facilitators of User Engagement With Digital Mental Health Interventions: Systematic Review. *Journal of Medical Internet Research, 23*(3), e24387. doi:10.2196/24387 PMID:33759801

Botin, L., Bertelsen, P., & Nøhr, C. (2017). Sustainable and viable introduction of tele-technologies in healthcare: A partial two-sided market approach. In V. Vimarlund (Ed.), *E-health two-sided markets* (pp. 93–123). Elsevier., doi:10.1016/B978-0-12-805250-1.00008-3

Boumosleh, J. M., & Jaalouk, D. (2017). Depression, anxiety, and smartphone addiction in university students – A cross sectional study. *PLoS One, 12*(8), e0182239. Advance online publication. doi:10.1371/journal.pone.0182239 PMID:28777828

Bovaird, T. (2007). Beyond engagement and participation: User and community coproduction of public services. *Public Administration Review, 67*(5), 846–860. doi:10.1111/j.1540-6210.2007.00773.x

Bragdon, A., Nelson, E., Li, Y., & Hinckley, K. (2011). Experimental Analysis of Touch-Screen Gesture Designs in Mobile Environments. *CHI '11: Proceedings of the SIGCHI Conference on Human Factors in Computing Systems*, 403–412. 10.1145/1978942.1979000

Braginsky, D. E. (2012). *Sending notifications to users based on users' notification tolerance levels.* U.S. Patent No. 20120239507A1. U.S. Patent and Trademark Office.

Brandão, W. L., & Pinho, M. S. (2017). Using augmented reality to improve dismounted operators' situation awareness. *2017 IEEE Virtual Reality (VR)*, 297–298. doi:10.1109/VR.2017.7892294

Bransford, J. D., Brown, A. L., & Cocking, R. R. (2000). *How people learn* (Vol. 11). National Academy Press.

Breazeal, C. L. (2002). *Designing sociable robots.* MIT Press. doi:10.7551/mitpress/2376.001.0001

Bretón-López, J., Quero, S., Botella, C., García-Palacios, A., Baños, R. M., & Alcañiz, M. (2010). An augmented reality system validation for the treatment of cockroach phobia. *Cyberpsychology, Behavior, and Social Networking, 13*(6), 705–710. doi:10.1089/cyber.2009.0170 PMID:21142997

Broniarczyk, S. M., & Alba, J. W. (1994). The importance of the brand in brand extension. *JMR, Journal of Marketing Research, 31*(2), 214–228. doi:10.1177/002224379403100206

Brouwer, W., Oenema, A., Crutzen, R., de Nooijer, J., de Vries, N. K., & Brug, J. (2008). An exploration of factors related to dissemination of and exposure to internet-delivered behavior change interventions aimed at adults: A Delphi study approach. *Journal of Medical Internet Research, 10*(2), e10. doi:10.2196/jmir.956 PMID:18417443

Brulin, G., & Svensson, L. (2012). *Managing Sustainable Development Programmes: A Learning Approach to Change*. Gower Publishing.

Brumby, D. P., Cox, A. L., Back, J., & Gould, S. J. (2013). Recovering from an interruption: Investigating speed–accuracy trade-offs in task resumption behavior. *Journal of Experimental Psychology. Applied*, *19*(2), 95–107. doi:10.1037/a0032696 PMID:23795978

Brynjolfsson, E., Dick, A., & Smith, M. (2010). A nearly perfect market? *Quantitative Marketing and Economics*, *8*(1), 1-33.

Bryson, J., & Winfield, A. (2017). Standardizing ethical design for artificial intelligence and autonomous systems. *Computer*, *50*(5), 116–119. doi:10.1109/MC.2017.154

Bucci, S., Berry, N., Morris, R., Berry, K., Haddock, G., Lewis, S., & Edge, D. (2019). "They Are Not Hard-to-Reach Clients. We Have Just Got Hard-to-Reach Services." Staff Views of Digital Health Tools in Specialist Mental Health Services. *Frontiers in Psychiatry*, *10*, 344. doi:10.3389/fpsyt.2019.00344 PMID:31133906

Buhmann, A., Paßmann, J., & Fieseler, C. (2019). Managing algorithmic accountability: Balancing reputational concerns, engagement strategies, and the potential of rational discourse. *Journal of Business Ethics*, *163*(2), 265–280. doi:10.100710551-019-04226-4

Bujak, K. R., Radu, I., Catrambone, R., MacIntyre, B., Zheng, R., & Golubski, G. (2013). A psychological perspective on augmented reality in the mathematics classroom. *Computers & Education*, *68*, 536–544. doi:10.1016/j.compedu.2013.02.017

Cabero, J., & Barroso, J. (2016). The educational possibilities of Augmented Reality. *New Approaches in Educational Research*, *5*(1), 44–50. doi:10.7821/naer.2016.1.140

Camacho, D., Luzón, M. V., & Cambria, E. (2020). New research methods & algorithms in social network analysis. *Future Generation Computer Systems*, *114*, 290–293. doi:10.1016/j.future.2020.08.006

Cambier, R., Van Laethem, M., & Vlerick, P. (2020). Private life telepressure and workplace cognitive failure among hospital nurses: The moderating role of mobile phone presence. *Journal of Advanced Nursing*, *76*(10), 2618–2626. doi:10.1111/jan.14496 PMID:32803902

Campbell-Kelly, M., Garcia-Swartz, D., Lam, R., & Yang, Y. (2015). Economic and business perspectives on smartphones as multi-sided platforms. *Telecommunications Policy*, *39*(8), 717–734. doi:10.1016/j.telpol.2014.11.001

Canale, N., Vieno, A., Doro, M., Rosa Mineo, E., Marino, C., & Billieux, J. (2019). Emotion-related impulsivity moderates the cognitive interference effect of smartphone availability on working memory. *Scientific Reports*, *9*(1), 1–10. doi:10.103841598-019-54911-7 PMID:31811205

Caporael, L. R. (1981). The paralanguage of caregiving: Baby talk to the institutionalized aged. *Journal of Personality and Social Psychology*, *40*(5), 876–884. doi:10.1037/0022-3514.40.5.876 PMID:7241341

Caporeal, L. R. (1986). Anthropomorphism and mechanomorphism: Two faces of the human machine. *Computers in Human Behavior, 2*(3), 215–234. doi:10.1016/0747-5632(86)90004-X

Carlbring, P., Hägglund, M., Luthström, A., Dahlin, M., Kadowaki, Å., Vernmark, K., & Andersson, G. (2013). Internet-based behavioral activation and acceptance-based treatment for depression: A randomized controlled trial. *Journal of Affective Disorders, 148*(2), 331–337. doi:10.1016/j.jad.2012.12.020 PMID:23357657

Carstensen, L., Isaacowitz, D., & Charles, S. (1999). Taking time seriously: A theory of socioemotional selectivity. *The American Psychologist, 54*(3), 165–181. doi:10.1037/0003-066X.54.3.165 PMID:10199217

Casaló, L. V., Flavián, C., & Ibáñez-Sánchez, S. (2018). Influencers on Instagram: Antecedents and consequences of opinion leadership. *Journal of Business Research, 117*, 510–519. doi:10.1016/j.jbusres.2018.07.005

Cellier, J.-M., & Eyrolle, H. (1992). Interference between switched tasks. *Ergonomics, 35*(1), 25–36. doi:10.1080/00140139208967795

Center for Humane Technology. (2020, October 8). *Potential policy reforms.* The Center for Humane Technology. https://www.humanetech.com/policy-reforms

Centers for Disease Control and Prevention. (2020). *About Chronic Diseases.* https://www.cdc.gov/chronicdisease/about/index.htm#:~:text=Chronic%20diseases%20are%20defined%20broadly,disability%20in%20the%20United%20States

CEPAL. (2004). Novena conferencia regional sobre la mujer de América Latina y El Caribe. *Consenso de México.*

Chan, A. M., Selvaraj, N., Ferdosi, N., & Narasimhan, R. (2013, July). Wireless patch sensor for remote monitoring of heart rate, respiration, activity, and falls. In *2013 35th Annual international conference of the IEEE engineering in medicine and biology society (EMBC)* (pp. 6115-6118). IEEE. 10.1109/EMBC.2013.6610948

Chan, A. H. Y., & Honey, M. L. (2021). User perceptions of mobile digital apps for mental health: Acceptability and usability-An integrative review. *Journal of Psychiatric and Mental Health Nursing,* jpm.12744. Advance online publication. doi:10.1111/jpm.12744 PMID:33604946

Chantzi, A. E., Plessa, C., Chatziparadeisis Gkanas, I., Tsakalidis, A., & Tsolis, D. (2013, July). An innovative augmented reality educational platform using gamification to enhance lifelong learning and cultural education. *International Conference on Information.*

Chen, C.-H. (2020). Impacts of augmented reality and a digital game on students' science learning with reflection prompts in multimedia learning. *Educational Technology Research and Development, 68*(6), 3057–3076. doi:10.100711423-020-09834-w

Chen, K., & Chan, A. H. S. (2014). Gerontechnology acceptance by elderly Hong Kong Chinese: A senior technology acceptance model (STAM). *Ergonomics, 57*(5), 635–652. doi:10.1080/00140139.2014.895855 PMID:24655221

Chen, T., Drennan, J., & Andrews, L. (2012). Experience sharing. *Journal of Marketing Management, 28*(13-14), 1535–1552. doi:10.1080/0267257X.2012.736876

Cheung, J. (2015). *Exploring Consumers' Experiential Responses and Shopping Intentions toward Visual User-Generated Content in Online Shopping Environments* (PhD Thesis). The University of Manchester, Manchester, UK.

Childress, C. A. (2000). Ethical Issues in Providing Online Psychotherapeutic Interventions. *Journal of Medical Internet Research, 2*(1), e5. doi:10.2196/jmir.2.1.e5 PMID:11720924

Chin, M. G., Sims, V. K., Clark, B., & Rivera Lopez, G. (2004). Measuring Individual Differences in Anthropomorphism Toward Machines and Animals. *Proceedings of the Human Factors and Ergonomics Society, 46.* 10.1177/154193120404801110

Chin, M. G., Sims, V. K., Ellis, L. U., Yordon, R. E., Clark, B. R., Ballion, T., Dolezal, M. J., Shumaker, R., & Finkelstein, N. (2005). Developing an Anthropomorphic Tendencies Scale. *Proceedings of the Human Factors and Ergonomics Society, 47.*

Chinta, R., & Kloppenborg, T. J. (2010). Projects and processes for sustainable organizational growth. *S.A.M. Advanced Management Journal, 75*(2), 22.

Chiou, J. (2000). Antecedents and Moderators of Behavioral Intention:Differences between US and Taiwanese Students. *Genetic, Social, and General Psychology Monographs, 126*(1), 105–124. PMID:10713903

Choo, Chun Wei (2001). Knowing Organization as Learning Organization. *Education + Training, 43*(4/5), 197-205.

Chowhan, J. (2016). Unpacking the black box: Understanding the relation-ship between strategy, HRM practices, innovation and organizational performance. *Human Resource Management Journal, 26*(2), 112–133. doi:10.1111/1748-8583.12097

Churchill, L. (2020, March 9*). The nightmare after Christmas: 'Tis the season for augmented reality for retailers*. TechSee: Intelligent Visual Assistance. https://techsee.me/blog/augmented-reality-for-retailers/

Clapp, M. (2020, Jun 18). NBA players can wear this Oura smart ring to monitor potential COVID-19 symptoms in Orlando. *The Comeback.* https://thecomeback.com/nba/nba-players-can-wear-this-oura-smart-ring-to-monitor-potential-covid-19-symptoms-in-orlando.html

Clark, A. (2004). *Natural-Born Cyborgs: Minds, Technologies, and the Future of Human Intelligence.* Oxford University Press.

Claypoole, V. L., Killingsworth, C. D., Hodges, C. A., Riley, J. M., & Stanney, K. M. (2020, in preparation). Multimodal interactions within augmented reality operational support tools for shipboard maintenance. In V. G. Duffy, M. R. Lehto, Y. Yih, & R. W. Proctor (Eds.), Human-Automation Interaction: Manufacturing, Services and UX. Springer ACES Book Series (ACES-Automation, Collaboration and E-Services).

Claypoole, V. L., Stanney, K. M., Padron, C. K., & Perez, R. (2020). Enhancing Naval enterprise readiness through augmented reality knowledge extraction. *Proceedings of the Interservice/ Industry Training, Simulation, and Education Conference (I/ITSEC) Annual Meeting*.

Claypoole, V., Brawand, N. P., Padron, C. K., Miller, C. A., Archer, J. L., Hughes, C. L., Horner, C. K., Riley, J. M., Fidopiastis, C. M., & Stanney, K. M. (2020). Unified Pedagogical FRamework ON Training in eXtended Reality (UPFRONT-XR). *International Journal of Artificial Intelligence in Education*.

Clement, C. A., & Gentner, D. (1991). Systematicity as a selection constraint in analogical mapping. *Cognitive Science*, *15*(1), 89–132. doi:10.120715516709cog1501_3

Coetzer, A., Kock, H., & Wallo, A. (2017). Distinctive characteristics of small businesses assites for informal learning. *Human Resource Development Review*, 18–32.

Cohen-McFarlane, M., Goubran, R., & Knoefel, F. (2020). Novel coronavirus cough database: Nococoda. *IEEE Access: Practical Innovations, Open Solutions*, *8*, 154087–154094. doi:10.1109/ACCESS.2020.3018028

Commission on Environment and Development. (1987). *World Commission on Environment and Development* (Brundtland Report). Available from: http://www.ace.mmu.ac.uk/eae/Sustainability/Older/Brundtland_Report.html

Constantinides, E. (2004) Influencing the online consumer's behavior: The Web experience. *Internet Research*, *14*(2), 111-126.

Cook, A. V., Ohri, L., Kusumoto, L., Reynolds, C., & Schwertzel, E. (2020, January 10). *Augmented shopping: the quiet revolution*. Deloitte Insights. https://www2.deloitte.com/us/en/insights/topics/emerging-technologies/augmented-shopping-3d-technology-retail.html

Coventry, L., & Branley, D. (2018). Cybersecurity in healthcare: A narrative review of trends, threats and ways forward. *Maturitas*, *113*, 48–52. doi:10.1016/j.maturitas.2018.04.008 PMID:29903648

Cowart, K. O., & Goldsmith, R. E. (2007). The influence of consumer decision-making styles on online apparel consumption by college students. *International Journal of Consumer Studies*, *31*(6), 639–647. doi:10.1111/j.1470-6431.2007.00615.x

Crossan, M. M., & Berdrow, I. (2011). Organizational learning and strategic renewal. *Strategic Management Journal*, *24*(11), 1087–1105. doi:10.1002mj.342

Crossan, M., Lane, H. W., & White, R. E. (1999). An organizational learning framework: From intuition to institution. *Academy of Management Review*, *24*(3), 522–537. doi:10.5465/amr.1999.2202135

Crowne, D. P., & Marlowe, D. (n.d.). A new scale of social desirabihty independent of psychopathology. *Journal of Consulting Psychology*, *960*(M), 349–354.

Crutzen, R., Cyr, D., & de Vries, N. K. (2012). The role of user control in adherence to and knowledge gained from a website: Randomized comparison between a tunneled version and a freedom-of-choice version. *Journal of Medical Internet Research, 14*(2), e45. doi:10.2196/jmir.1922 PMID:22532074

Csikszentmihalyi, M., (2015). Society, culture, and person: a systems view of creativity. *Syst. Model Creativity,* 47–61.

Csikszentmihalyi, M. (1990). *Flow: The psychology of optimal experience.* Harper & Row.

Cugelman, B., Thelwall, M., & Dawes, P. (2011). Online interventions for social marketing health behavior change campaigns: A meta-analysis of psychological architectures and adherence factors. *Journal of Medical Internet Research, 13*(1), e17. doi:10.2196/jmir.1367 PMID:21320854

Culley, K. E., & Madhavan, P. (2013). Trust in automation and automation designers: Implications for HCI and HMI. *Computers in Human Behavior, 29*(6), 2208–2210. doi:10.1016/j.chb.2013.04.032

Cummings, T. G., & Worley, C. G. (2014). *Organization development and change.* Cengage Learning.

Cutting, J. E., & Vishton, P. M. (1995). Perceiving layout and knowing distances: The integration, relative potency, and contextual use of different information about depth. In W. Epstein & S. Rogers (Eds.), Handbook of perception and cognition: Vol. 5. Perception of space and motion (pp. 69-117). Academic Press.

Czaja, S. J., Boot, W. R., Charness, N., & Rogers, W. A. (2019). *Designing for Older Adults: Principles and Creative Human Factors Approaches* (3rd ed.). CRC Press. doi:10.1201/b22189

D'Aurizio, N., Baldi, T. L., Paolocci, G., & Prattichizzo, D. (2020). Preventing Undesired Face-Touches with Wearable Devices and Haptic Feedback. *IEEE Access: Practical Innovations, Open Solutions, 8,* 139033–139043. doi:10.1109/ACCESS.2020.3012309

Dagööa, J., Asplund, R. P., Bsenko, H. A., Hjerling, S., Holmberg, A., Westh, S., Öberg, L., Ljótsson, B., Carlbring, P., Fumark, T., & Andersson, G. (2014). Cognitive behavior therapy versus interpersonal psychotherapy for social anxiety disorder delivered via smartphone and computer: A randomized controlled trial. *Journal of Anxiety Disorders, 28*(4), 410–417. doi:10.1016/j.janxdis.2014.02.003 PMID:24731441

Daily, B. F., Bishop, J. W., & Massoud, J. A. (2012). The role of training and empowerment in environmental performance: A study of the Mexican maquiladora industry. *International Journal of Operations & Production Management, 32*(5).

Damanpour, F. (1996). Organizational Complexity and Innovation Developing and Testing Multiple Contingency Models. *Management Science, 42,* 693–716.

Danaher, B. G., & Seeley, J. R. (2009). Methodological issues in research on web-based behavioral interventions. *Annals of Behavioral Medicine, 38*(1), 28–39. doi:10.100712160-009-9129-0 PMID:19806416

Danish, R. Q., Munir, Y., Kausar, A., Jabbar, M., & Munawar, N. (2015). Impact of change, culture and organizational politics on organizational learning. *Rev. Contemp. Bus.Res, 3*(1), 115–126.

Davidson, R. J., Jackson, D. C., & Kalin, N. H. (2000). Emotion, plasticity, context, and regulation: Perspectives from affective neuroscience. *Psychological Bulletin, Vol, 126*(6), 890–909. doi:10.1037/0033-2909.126.6.890 PMID:11107881

Davis, F. (1989). Perceived Usefulness, Perceived Ease of Use, and User Acceptance of Information Technology. *Management Information Systems Quarterly, 13*(3), 319–339. doi:10.2307/249008

Davis, F., Bagozzi, R., & Warshaw, P. (1989). User Acceptance of Computer Technology: A Comparison of Two Theoretical Models. *Management Science, 35*(8), 982–1003. doi:10.1287/mnsc.35.8.982

de Nooijer, J. A., van Gog, T., Paas, F., & Zwaan, R. A. (2013). Effects of imitating gestures during encoding or during retrieval of novel verbs on children's test performance. *Acta Psychologica, 144*(1), 173–179. doi:10.1016/j.actpsy.2013.05.013 PMID:23820099

De Reuver, M., Nikou, S., & Bouwman, H. (2016). Domestication of smartphones and mobile applications: A quantitative mixed-method study. *Mobile Media & Communication, 4*(3), 347–370. doi:10.1177/2050157916649989

Deac, C. N., Deac, G. C., Popa, C. L., Ghinea, M., & Cotet, C. E. (2017). Using augmented reality in smart manufacturing. In B. Katalinic (Ed.), *DAAAM Proceedings* (1st ed., Vol. 1, pp. 0727–0732). DAAAM International Vienna. 10.2507/28th.daaam.proceedings.102

Debarba, H. G., Boulic, R., Salomon, R., Blanke, O., & Herbelin, B. (2018). Self-attribution of distorted reaching movements in immersive virtual reality. *Computers & Graphics, 76*, 142–152. doi:10.1016/j.cag.2018.09.001

Deci, E. L., & Ryan, R. M. (1985). *Intrinsic motivation and self-determination in human behavior*. doi:10.1007/978-1-4899-2271-7

Deci, E. L., & Ryan, R. M. (2000). The "what" and "why" of goal pursuits: Human needs and the self-determination of behavior. *Psychological Inquiry, 11*(4), 227–268. doi:10.1207/S15327965PLI1104_01

Deiman, M., & Bastiaens, T. (2010). Competency-based education in an electronic-supported environment: An example from a distance teaching university. *International Journal of Continuing Engineering Education and Lifelong Learning, 20*(3/4/5), 278–289. doi:10.1504/IJCEELL.2010.037046

Delios, A. (2010). How can organizations be competitive but dare to care? *The Academy of Management Perspectives, 24*(3), 25–36. doi:10.5465/amp.24.3.25

DeVellis, R. F. (1991). *Scale development: Theory and applications*. Sage.

Di Gangi, P. M., & Wasko, M. M. (2016). Social media engagement theory: Exploring the influence of user engagement on social media usage. *Journal of Organizational and End User Computing, 28*(2), 53–73. doi:10.4018/JOEUC.2016040104

Dicle, Ü., & Okan, R.Y. (2015). The relationship between organizational structure and organizational learning in Turkish automotive R&D companies. *Int. J. Manag. Stud. Res.*, 62–71.

DiSalvo, C. F., Gemperle, F., Forlizzi, J., & Kiesler, S. (2002). All robots are not created equal: The design and perception of humanoid robot heads. *Proceedings of the DIS Conference*, 321-326. 10.1145/778712.778756

DiStefano, C., & Motl, R. W. (2009). Personality correlates of method effects due to negatively worded items on the Rosenberg self-esteem scale. *Personality and Individual Differences, 46*(3), 309–313. doi:10.1016/j.paid.2008.10.020

Docherty, P., Forslin, J., Shani, A. B., & Kira, M. (2002) Emerging Work Systems: From Intensive to Sustainable? In Creating Sustainable Work Systems: Perspectives and Practices. London: Routledge.

Dong, S., Feng, C., & Kamat, V. R. (2013). Sensitivity analysis of augmented reality-assisted building damage reconnaissance using virtual prototyping. *Automation in Construction, 33*, 24–36. doi:10.1016/j.autcon.2012.09.005

Donker, T., Bennett, K., Bennett, A., Mackinnon, A., van Straten, A., Cuijpers, P., Christensen, H., & Griffiths, M. K. (2013). Internet-delivered interpersonal psychotherapy versus internet-delivered cognitive behavioral therapy for adults with depressive symptoms: Randomized controlled noninferiority trial. *Journal of Medical Internet Research, 15*(5), e82. doi:10.2196/jmir.2307 PMID:23669884

Donnellan, M. B., Oswald, F. L., Baird, B. M., & Lucas, R. E. (2006). The Mini-IPIP scales: Tiny-yet-effective measures of the Big Five factors of personality. *Psychological Assessment, 18*(2), 192–203. doi:10.1037/1040-3590.18.2.192 PMID:16768595

Donovan, J. (2020). *Concrete Recommendations for Cutting Through Misinformation During the COVID-19 Pandemic*. Academic Press.

Dorst, K., & Stolterman, E. (2015). *Frame Innovation: Create New Thinking by Design*. MIT Press. doi:10.7551/mitpress/10096.001.0001

Duffy, B. R. (2003). Anthropomorphism and the social robot. *Robotics and Autonomous Systems, 42*(3-4), 177–190. doi:10.1016/S0921-8890(02)00374-3

Dul, J., Bruder, R., Buckle, P., Carayon, P., Falzon, P., Marras, W. S., Wilson, J. R., & van der Doelen, B. (2012). A strategy for human factors/ergonomics: Developing the discipline and profession. *Ergonomics, 55*(4), 377–395. doi:10.1080/00140139.2012.661087 PMID:22332611

Dülsen, P., Bendig, E., Küchler, A. M., Christensen, H., & Baumeister, H. (2020). Digital interventions in adult mental healthcare settings: Recent evidence and future directions. *Current Opinion in Psychiatry, 33*(4), 422–431. doi:10.1097/YCO.0000000000000614 PMID:32427592

Egbu, C. O. (2004). Managing knowledge and intellectual capital for improved organizational innovations in the construction industry: An examination of critical success factors. *Engineering, Construction, and Architectural Management, 11*(5), 301–315. doi:10.1108/09699980410558494

Ehrhardt, N., & Hirsch, I. B. (2020). The Impact of COVID-19 on CGM Use in the Hospital. *Diabetes Care, 43*(11), 2628–2630. doi:10.2337/dci20-0046 PMID:32978180

Ehsani Ghods, H., & Sayed Abbas Zadeh, M. M. (2012). Relationship between learning organization with creativity and innovation, a high school teacher and colleges. *Journal-Research New Approaches in Educational Administration. Islamic Azad University of Shiraz, 4*, 12–21.

Elander, K., & Cronje, J. (2016). Paradigms revisited: A quantitative investigation into a model to integrate objectivism and constructivism in instructional design. *Educational Technology Research and Development, 64*(3), 389–405. doi:10.100711423-016-9424-y

Ellström, P.-E. (2001). Integrating learning and work: Conceptual issues and critical conditions. *Human Resource Development Quarterly, 12*(4), 421–435.

Elving, W. J. (2005). The role of communication in organisational change. *Corporate Communications, 10*(2), 129–138. doi:10.1108/13563280510596943

Endsley, M. (1995). Towards a theory of situation awareness in dynamic systems. *Human Factors, 37*(1), 32–64. doi:10.1518/001872095779049543

Epstein, S. (1994). Integration of the cognitive and the psychodynamic unconscious. *The American Psychologist, 49*(8), 709–724. doi:10.1037/0003-066X.49.8.709 PMID:8092614

Erbas, C., & Demirer, V. (2019). The effects of augmented reality on students' academic achievement and motivation in a biology course. *Journal of Computer Assisted Learning, 35*(3), 450–458. doi:10.1111/jcal.12350

Etienne-Nugue, J. (2009). *Hablame de las artesanias*. UNESCO.

Evans, R. J. (2005). *Death in Hamburg: society and politics in the cholera years*. Penguin Group USA.

Farrell, S. P., & McKinnon, C. R. (2003). Technology and rural mental health. *Archives of Psychiatric Nursing, 17*(1), 20–26. doi:10.1053/apnu.2003.4 PMID:12642884

Federal Trade Commission. (2011). *About identity theft*. Retrieved on May 03, 2011 from https://www.ftc.gov/bcp/edu/microsites/idtheft/consumers/about-identity-theft.html

Fenais, A. S., Ariaratnam, S. T., Ayer, S. K., & Smilovsky, N. (2020). A review of augmented reality applied to underground construction. *Journal of Information Technology in Construction, 25*, 308–324. doi:10.36680/j.itcon.2020.018

Ferrer-Torregrosa, J., Jiménez-Rodríguez, M. Á., Torralba-Estelles, J., Garzón-Farinós, F., Pérez-Bermejo, M., & Fernández-Ehrling, N. (2016). Distance learning ects and flipped classroom in the anatomy learning: Comparative study of the use of augmented reality, video and notes. *BMC Medical Education, 16*(1), 230. doi:10.118612909-016-0757-3 PMID:27581521

Ferrer-Torregrosa, J., Torralba, J., Jimenez, M. A., García, S., & Barcia, J. M. (2015). ARBOOK: Development and Assessment of a Tool Based on Augmented Reality for Anatomy. *Journal of Science Education and Technology, 24*(1), 119–124. doi:10.100710956-014-9526-4

Fiorinelli, M., Di Mario, S., Surace, A., Mattei, M., Russo, C., Villa, G., Dionisi, S., Di Simone, E., Giannetta, N., & Di Muzio, M. (2021). Smartphone distraction during nursing care: Systematic literature review. *Applied Nursing Research, 151405*, 151405. Advance online publication. doi:10.1016/j.apnr.2021.151405 PMID:33745553

Firth, J., Torous, J., Nicholas, J., Carney, R., Pratap, A., Rosenbaum, S., & Sarris, J. (2017a). The efficacy of smartphone-based mental health interventions for depressive symptoms: A meta-analysis of randomized controlled trials. *World Psychiatry; Official Journal of the World Psychiatric Association (WPA), 16*(3), 287–298. doi:10.1002/wps.20472 PMID:28941113

Firth, J., Torous, J., Nicholas, J., Carney, R., Rosenbaum, S., & Sarris, J. (2017b). Can smartphone mental health interventions reduce symptoms of anxiety? A meta-analysis of randomized controlled trials. *Journal of Affective Disorders, 218*, 15–22. doi:10.1016/j.jad.2017.04.046 PMID:28456072

Fishbein, M., & Ajzen, I. (1977). *Belief, attitude, intention, and behavior: An introduction to theory and research.* Addison-Wesley.

Fisher, C. B., & Fried, A. L. (2003). Internet-mediated psychological services and the American Psychological Association Ethics Code. *Psychotherapy (Chicago, Ill.), 40*(1-2), 103–111. doi:10.1037/0033-3204.40.1-2.103

Fisher, E., & Mahajan, R. L. (2010). Embedding the humanities in engineering: Art, dialogue, and a laboratory. In M. E. Gorman (Ed.), *Trading zones and interactional expertise: Creating new kinds of collaboration* (pp. 209–230). MIT Press. doi:10.7551/mitpress/9780262014724.003.0010

Fitzgerald, T. D., Hunter, P. V., Hadjistavropoulos, T., & Koocher, G. P. (2010). Ethical and legal considerations for internet-based psychotherapy. *Cognitive Behaviour Therapy, 39*(3), 173–187. doi:10.1080/16506071003636046 PMID:20485997

Fitz, N., Kushlev, K., Jagannathan, R., Lewis, T., Paliwal, D., & Ariely, D. (2019). Batching smartphone notifications can improve well-being. *Computers in Human Behavior, 101*(July), 84–94. doi:10.1016/j.chb.2019.07.016

Flavián, C., Ibáñez-Sánchez, S., & Orús, C. (2019). The impact of virtual, augmented and mixed reality technologies on the customer experience. *Journal of Business Research, 100*, 547–560. doi:10.1016/j.jbusres.2018.10.050

Fleischmann, K. R. (2013). Information and human values. *Synthesis Lectures on Information Concepts, Retrieval, and Services, 5*(5), 1–99. doi:10.2200/S00545ED1V01Y201310ICR031

FONART. (2009). *Manual de Diferenciación entre Artesania y Manualidad.* Recovered from https://www.fonart.gob.mx/web/pdf/DO/mdma.pdf

Fong, T., Nourbakhsh, I., & Dautenhahn, K. (2003). A survey of socially interactive robots. *Robotics and Autonomous Systems, 42*(3-4), 143–166. doi:10.1016/S0921-8890(02)00372-X

Foote, W. (September 29, 2015). Tapping the potential of the artisan economy. *Forbes.* Recovered from https://www.forbes.com/sites/willyfoote/2015/09/29/tapping-the-potential-of-the- worlds-fourth-largest-economy/#3ea27e3f1aa2

Forgas, J. P. (Ed.). (2001). *Feeling and thinking: The role of affect in social cognition.* Cambridge University Press.

Foss, N. J., & Lyngsie, J. (2011). *The Emerging Strategic Entrepreneurship Field: Origins.* Academic Press.

Fowler, G. A. (2020 May 8). Wearable tech can spot coronavirus symptoms before you even realize you're sick. *The Washington Post.* https://www.washingtonpost.com/technology/2020/05/28/wearable-coronavirus-detect/

Freeman, D., Reeve, S., Robinson, A., Ehlers, A., Clark, D., Spanlang, B., & Slater, M. (2017). Virtual reality in the assessment, understanding, and treatment of mental health disorders. *Psychological Medicine, 47*(14), 2393–2400. doi:10.1017/S003329171700040X PMID:28325167

Friedman, B. (1996). Value-sensitive design. *Interaction, 3*(6), 16–23. doi:10.1145/242485.242493

Friedman, B., & Kahn, P. H. Jr. (2002). Human values, ethics, and design. In A. Sears & J. A. Jacko (Eds.), *The human–computer interaction handbook* (pp. 1209–1233). CRC Press. doi:10.1201/9781410606723-48

Friedman, S., Scholink, E., & Cocking, R. (1987). *Blue prints for thinking: The role of planning in cognitive development.* CambriDge Univ. Press.

Fruchard, B., Lecolinet, E., & Chapuis, O. (2020). Side-Crossing Menus: Enabling Large Sets of Gestures for Small Surfaces. *Proceedings of the ACM on Human-Computer Interaction, Association for Computing Machinery (ACM), 4,* 189:1 – 189:19. 10.1145/3427317

Furst, R. T., Evans, D. N., & Roderick, N. M. (2018). Frequency of college student smartphone use: Impact on classroom homework assignments. *Journal of Technology in Behavioral Science, 3*(2), 49–57. doi:10.100741347-017-0034-2

Gaioshko, D. (2017). *10 ways how augmented reality can help retailers.* Retail Dive. https://www.retaildive.com/ex/mobilecommercedaily/10-ways-how-augmented-reality-can-help-retailers

Garay-Cortes, J., & Uribe-Quevedo, A. (2016). Location-based augmented reality game to engage students in discovering institutional landmarks. *2016 7th International Conference on Information, Intelligence, Systems Applications (IISA),* 1–4. 10.1109/IISA.2016.7785433

Gazzaley, A., Rissman, J., Cooney, J., Rutman, A., Seibert, T., Clapp, W., & D'Esposito, M. (2007). Functional Interactions between Prefrontal and Visual Association Cortex Contribute to Top-Down Modulation of Visual Processing. *Cerebral Cortex (New York, N.Y.), 17*(suppl_1), i125–i135. doi:10.1093/cercor/bhm113 PMID:17725995

GBD 2017 Disease and Injury Incidence and Prevalence Collaborators. (2018). Global, regional, and national incidence, prevalence, and years lived with disability for 354 diseases and injuries for 195 countries and territories, 1990-2017: a systematic analysis for the Global Burden of Disease Study 2017. *Lancet, 392*(10159), 1789-1858. . doi:10.1016/S0140-6736(18)32279-7

Geertshuis, S., Holmes, M., Geertshuis, H., Clancy, D., & Bristol, A. (2002). Evaluation of workplace learning. *Journal of Workplace Learning, 14*(1), 11–18.

Gellatly, J., Bower, P., Hennessy, S., Richards, D., Gilbody, S., & Lovell, K. (2007). What makes self-help interventions effective in the management of depressive symptoms? Meta-analysis and meta-regression. *Psychological Medicine, 37*(9), 1217–1228. doi:10.1017/S0033291707000062 PMID:17306044

George, M. K., & Ball, K. (2019, July 2). Legal Risks Of Virtual And Augmented Reality On The Construction Site. *Mondaq.* https://www.mondaq.com/unitedstates/construction-planning/820886/legal-risks-of-virtual-and-augmented-reality-on-the-construction-site

Geraets, C. N., van der Stouwe, E. C., Pot-Kolder, R., & Veling, W. (2021). Advances in immersive virtual reality interventions for mental disorders—a new reality? *Current Opinion in Psychology, 41*, 40–45. doi:10.1016/j.copsyc.2021.02.004 PMID:33714892

Gerup, J., Soerensen, C. B., & Dieckmann, P. (2020). Augmented reality and mixed reality for healthcare education beyond surgery: An integrative review. *International Journal of Medical Education, 11*, 1–18. doi:10.5116/ijme.5e01.eb1a PMID:31955150

Giffi, C., Rodriguez, M. D., & Mondal, S. (2017). *A look ahead: How modern manufacturers can create positive perceptions with the US public.* Deloitte Center for Industry Insights. https://www2.deloitte.com/us/en/pages/manufacturing/articles/public-perception-of-the-manufacturing-industry.html

Girish, D. (2020, September 9). "The Social Dilemma" review: Unplug and run. *New York Times.* https://www.nytimes.com/2020/09/09/movies/the-social-dilemma-review.html

Glimcher, P. (2003). *Decisions, Uncertainty and the Brain: The Science of Neuroeconomics.* The MIT Press. doi:10.7551/mitpress/2302.001.0001

Glimcher, P. W., & Rustichini, A. (2004). Neuroeconomics: The Consilience of Brain and Decision. *Science, 306*(5695), 447–452. doi:10.1126cience.1102566 PMID:15486291

Glockner, H., Jannek, K., Mahn, J., & Theis, B. (2014). *Augmented Reality in Logistics: Changing the way we see logistics—A DHL perspective.* DHL Customer Solutions & Innovation. https://www.dhl.com/content/dam/downloads/g0/about_us/logistics_insights/csi_augmented_reality_report_290414.pdf

Gloff, N. E., LeNoue, S. R., Novins, D. K., & Myers, K. (2015). Telemental health for children and adolescents. *International Review of Psychiatry (Abingdon, England)*, *27*(6), 513–524. doi:10.3109/09540261.2015.1086322 PMID:26540584

Goetz, J., Kiesler, S., & Powers, A. (2003). *Matching robot appearance and behavior to tasks to improve human-robot cooperation*. In *The Twelfth IEEE International Workshop on Robots and Human Interactive Communication*, Lisbon, Portugal. 10.1109/ROMAN.2003.1251796

Goldberg, B., Davis, F., Riley, J. M., & Boyce, M. W. (2017). Adaptive Training Across Simulations in Support of a Crawl-Walk-Run Model of Interaction. In D. D. Schmorrow & C. M. Fidopiastis (Eds.), *Augmented Cognition. Enhancing Cognition and Behavior in Complex Human Environments* (pp. 116–130). Springer International Publishing. doi:10.1007/978-3-319-58625-0_8

Gomes, G., & Wojahn, R. M. (2017). Organizational learning capability, innovation and performance. *Revista ADM*, *52*, 163–175.

González, M. (2016). 31% del PIB nacional es aportado por mujeres empresarias. *Informa BTL*. Recovered from https://www.informabtl.com/31-del-pib-nacional-es-aportado-por-mujeres-empresarias/

Goodyear, M., Ames-Oliver, K., & Russell, K. (2014). *Organizational Strategies for Fostering a Culture of Learning*. University of Kansas.

Gorsuch, R. L. (1983). *Factor analysis* (2nd ed.). Lawrence Erlbaum.

Graham, S. A., Poulin-Dubois, D., & Baker, R. K. (1998). Infants' disambiguation of novel object words. *First Language*, *18*(53), 149–164. doi:10.1177/014272379801805302

Gray, C. M., & Chivukula, S. S. (2019). Ethical mediation in UX practice. In *Proceedings of the 2019 CHI Conference on Human Factors in Computing Systems*. Association for Computing Machinery. 10.1145/3290605.3300408

Griggs, M. B. (2020, Oct 31). A Swiss cheese approach to pandemic safety. *The Verge*. https://www.theverge.com/2020/10/31/21542207/swiss-cheese-infection-control-covid-19-antivirus

Guazzaroni, G. (Ed.). (2018). *Virtual and augmented reality in mental health treatment*. IGI Global.

Gulikers, J. T. M., Bastiaens, T. J., & Martens, R. L. (2005). The surplus value of an authentic learning environment. *Computers in Human Behavior*, *21*(3), 509–521. doi:10.1016/j.chb.2004.10.028

Gulikers, J. T., Bastiaens, T. J., & Kirschner, P. A. (2004). A five-dimensional framework for authentic assessment. *Educational Technology Research and Development*, *52*(3), 67–86. doi:10.1007/BF02504676

Gun, S. Y., Titov, N., & Andrews, G. (2011). Acceptability of Internet treatment of anxiety and depression. *Australasian Psychiatry*, *19*(3), 259–264. doi:10.3109/10398562.2011.562295 PMID:21682626

Gupta, A. (2008). Earth on fire: Implications for corporate responsibility. *American Journal of Business, 23*(1), 3–4.

Guston, D. H., & Sarewitz, D. (2002). Real-time technology assessment. *Technology in Society, 24*(1–2), 93–109. doi:10.1016/S0160-791X(01)00047-1

Guthrie, S. (1993). *Faces in the clouds: A new theory of religion.* Oxford University Press.

Gutnik, L., Forogh, A., Yoskowitz, N., & Patel, V. (2006). The role of emotions in decision making: a cognitive neuroeconomic approach towards understanding sexual risk behavior. *Journal of Biomedical Information.* doi:10.1016/j.jbi.2006.03.002

Halse, S. E., Lum, H. C., Sims, V. K., & Chin, M. G. (2011). *First impressions: Is it you or the things you're with?* Poster presented at the APS 23rd Annual Conference, Washington, DC.

Hancock, P. A., Pepe, A. A., & Murphy, L. L. (2005). Hedonomics: The power of positive and pleasurable ergonomics. *Ergonomics in Design, 13*(1), 8–14. doi:10.1177/106480460501300104

Han, S. H., Kim, D. Y., Jang, H. S., & Choi, S. (2010). Strategies for contractors to sustain growth in the global construction market. *Habitat International, 34*(1), 1–10. doi:10.1016/j.habitatint.2009.04.003

Han, Y. J., Nunes, J. C., & Dreze, X. (2010). Signaling status *with* luxury goods*: The* role *of* brand prominence. *Journal of Marketing, 74*(4), 15–30. doi:10.1509/jmkg.74.4.015

Hartanto, A., & Yang, H. (2016). Is the smartphone a smart choice? The effect of smartphone separation on executive functions. *Computers in Human Behavior, 64*, 329–336. doi:10.1016/j.chb.2016.07.002

Hartson, R., & Pyla, P. S. (2012). *The UX book: Process and guidelines for ensuring a quality user experience.* Morgan Kaufman.

Haslam, S. A. (1997). Stereotyping and social influence: Foundations of stereotype consensus. In R. Spears, P. J. Oakes, N. Ellemers, & S. A. Haslam (Eds.), *The social psychology of stereotyping and group life* (pp. 119–143). Blackwell.

Hausman, A., & Siekpe, J. (2009). The effect of web interface features on consumer online purchase intentions. *Journal of Business Research, 62*(1), 5–13. doi:10.1016/j.jbusres.2008.01.018

Heater, B. (2019, Feb 12). Sixteen percent of US adults own a smartwatch. *TechCrunch.* https://techcrunch.com/2019/02/12/sixteen-percent-of-u-s-adults-own-a-smartwatch/

Heckscher, Ch. (1994). *Defining the post-bureaucratic type.* Sage.

Hedman, E., Andersson, E., Ljotsson, B., Andersson, G., Ruck, C., & Lindefors, N. (2011). Cost-effectiveness of Internet-based cognitive behavior therapy vs. cognitive behavioral group therapy for social anxiety disorder: Results from a randomized controlled trial. *Behaviour Research and Therapy, 49*(11), 729–736. doi:10.1016/j.brat.2011.07.009 PMID:21851929

Hedman, E., El Alaoui, S., Lindefors, N., Andersson, E., Rück, C., Ghaderi, A., Kaldo, V., Lekander, M., Andersson, G., & Ljótsson, B. (2014). Clinical effectiveness and cost-effectiveness of Internet- vs. group-based cognitive behavior therapy for social anxiety disorder: 4-year follow-up of a randomized trial. *Behaviour Research and Therapy*, *59*, 20–29. doi:10.1016/j. brat.2014.05.010 PMID:24949908

Heller, L. (2010). Mujeres emprendedoras en América Latina y el Caribe: realidades, obstáculos y desafíos. Santiago de Chile: United Nations.

Hernández-Girón, J., Yexcas, M., & Domínguez-Hernández, M. (2007). Factores de éxito en los negocios de artesanía en México. *Estudios Gerenciales*, *23*(104), 77–99. doi:10.1016/S0123-5923(07)70018-9

Hill, R. C., & Bowen, P. A. (1997). Sustainable construction: Principles and a framework for attainment. *Construction Management and Economics*, *15*(3), 223–239. doi:10.1080/014461997372971

Hilvert-Bruce, Z., Rossouw, P. J., Wong, N., Sunderland, M., & Andrews, G. (2012). Adherence as a determinant of effectiveness of internet cognitive behavioural therapy for anxiety and depressive disorders. *Behaviour Research and Therapy*, *50*(7-8), 463–468. doi:10.1016/j.brat.2012.04.001 PMID:22659155

Hirschhorn, L. (1988). *The workplace within: Psychodynamics of organizational life*. The Mit Press. doi:10.7551/mitpress/7306.001.0001

Hofmann, S., & Mosemghvdlishvili, L. (2014). Perceiving spaces through digital augmentation: An exploratory study of navigation augmented reality apps. *Mobile Media & Communication*, *2*(3), 265–280. doi:10.1177/2050157914530700

Holbrook, M. B., & Hirschman, E. C. (1982). The experiential aspects of consumption: Consumer fantasies, feelings, and fun. *The Journal of Consumer Research*, *9*(2), 132–140. doi:10.1086/208906

Hollis, R. B., & Was, C. A. (2016). Mind wandering, control failures, and social media distractions in online learning. *Learning and Instruction*, *42*, 104–112. doi:10.1016/j.learninstruc.2016.01.007

Holyoak, K. J., & Thagard, P. (1997). The analogical mind. *The American Psychologist*, *52*(1), 35–44. doi:10.1037/0003-066X.52.1.35 PMID:9017931

Homer, M. J., D'Orsi, C. J., & Sitzman, S. B. (1994). Dermal calcifications in fixed orientation: The tattoo sign. *Radiology*, *192*(1), 161–163. doi:10.1148/radiology.192.1.8208930 PMID:8208930

Horan, P. M., DiStefano, C., & Motl, R. W. (2003). Wording effects in self esteem scales: Methodological artifact or response style? *Structural Equation Modeling*, *10*(3), 444–455. doi:10.1207/S15328007SEM1003_6

Horberry, T., Osborne, R., & Young, K. (2019). Pedestrian smartphone distraction: Prevalence and potential severity. *Transportation Research Part F: Traffic Psychology and Behaviour*, *60*, 515–523. doi:10.1016/j.trf.2018.11.011

Horvath, J., Mundinger, C., Schmitgen, M. M., Wolf, N. D., Sambataro, F., Hirjak, D., Kubera, K. M., Koenig, J., & Christian Wolf, R. (2020). Structural and functional correlates of smartphone addiction. *Addictive Behaviors, 105*(January), 106334. doi:10.1016/j.addbeh.2020.106334 PMID:32062336

Hotho, J.J., & Lyles, M.A. (2015). The mutual impact of global strategy and organizational learning: current themes and future directions. *Glob. Strat. J.*, 85–112.

Hou, L., Wang, X., & Truijens, M. (2013). Using Augmented Reality to Facilitate Piping Assembly: An Experiment-Based Evaluation. *Journal of Computing in Civil Engineering, 29*(1), 05014007. Advance online publication. doi:10.1061/(ASCE)CP.1943-5487.0000344

Hoveida, R. (2007). *Investigating the relationship between learning the components of the organization and improving the quality of education the door* (Master's thesis). Governmental Universities of Isfahan Province and Presentation of Student University Model, University of Isfahan.

Hoverstadt, P., & Bowling, D. (2005). Organisational Viability as a factor in Sustainable. *International Journal of Technology Management and Sustainable Development, 4*(2), 131–146.

Howe, N., & Strauss, W. (2000). *Millennials rising: The next great generation.* Vintage.

Huckvale, K., Nicholas, J., Torous, J., & Larsen, M. E. (2020). Smartphone apps for the treatment of mental health conditions: Status and considerations. *Current Opinion in Psychology, 36*, 65–70. Advance online publication. doi:10.1016/j.copsyc.2020.04.008 PMID:32553848

Hughes, C. L., Bailey, P. S., Ruiz, E., Fidopiastis, C. M., Taranta, N. R., & Stanney, K. M. (2020). (Manuscript submitted for publication). The psychometrics of cybersickness in augmented reality. *Frontiers in Virtual Reality: Virtual Reality in Industry*.

Huq, A., & Gilbert, D. (2017). All the world's a stage: Transforming entrepreneurship education through design thinking. *Education + Training, 59*(2), 155–170. doi:10.1108/ET-12-2015-0111

Hussain, A. (2013). El potencial del comercio electrónico: oportunidades para las PYME de los países en desarrollo. *Revista del centro de comercio internacional.* Recovered from http://www10.iadb.org/intal/intalcdi/PE/2014/14253.pdf

Ibáñez, M. B., Di Serio, Á., Villarán, D., & Kloos, C. D. (2014). Experimenting with electromagnetism using augmented reality: Impact on flow student experience and educational effectiveness. *Computers & Education, 71*, 1–13. doi:10.1016/j.compedu.2013.09.004

Indego Africa. (2016). How the artisan sector can change the world. *ONE.* Recovered from https://www.one.org/us/2016/05/13/how-the-artisan-sector-can-change-the-world/

INEGI. (2009). *Censo Económico.* Micro, pequeña, mediana y gran empresa. Recovered from https://www.inegi.org.mx/est/contenidos/espanol/proyectos/censos/ce2009/default.asp?s=est&c=14220

INEGI. (2012). *Conociendo México*. Análisis de la demografía de los establecimientos 2012. Recovered from http://buscador.inegi.org.mx/search?tx=analisis+de+la+demografia+de+los +establecimientos&q=analisis+de+la+demografia+de+los +establecimientos&site=sitioIN EGI_collection&client=INEGI_Default&proxystylesheet=INEGI_Default&getfield

International Ergonomics Association. (2020). *What is ergonomics?* https://iea.cc/what-is-ergonomics/

International Telecommunication Union. (2015). Measuring the Information Society Report. Ginebra: ITU.

Ivanova, E., Lindner, P., Ly, K. H., Dahlin, M., Vernmark, K., Andersson, G., & Carlbring, P. (2016). Guided and unguided Acceptance and Commitment Therapy for social anxiety disorder and/or panic disorder provided via the Internet and a smartphone application: A randomized controlled trial. *Journal of Anxiety Disorders*, *44*, 27–35. doi:10.1016/j.janxdis.2016.09.012 PMID:27721123

Jackson, T., Dawson, R., & Wilson, D. (2003). Reducing the effect of email interruptions on employees. *International Journal of Information Management*, *23*(1), 55–65. doi:10.1016/ S0268-4012(02)00068-3

Jacobsen, S. (2010). *The exoskeleton's super technology*. Retrieved on August 21, 2010 from: https://www.raytheon.com/newsroom/technology/rtn08_exoskeleton/

Jahmurataj, V. (2015). Impact of Culture on Organizational Development: Case Study Kosovo. *Academic Journal of Interdisciplinary Studies*, *4*(2), 206–210. doi:10.5901/ajis.2015.v4n2s1p206

Järvinen, A., & Poikela, E. (2001). Modelling Reflective and Contextual Learning at Work. *Journal of Workplace Learning*, *13*(7/8), 282-289.

Jenner, E. (1801). *An inquiry into the causes and effects of the variolae vaccinae: a disease discovered in some of the western counties of England, particularly Gloucestershire, and known by the name of the cow pox*. Academic Press.

Jeong, H., Rogers, J., & Xu, S. (2020, July). Continuous on-body sensing for the COVID-19 pandemic: Gaps and opportunities. *Science Advances*. https://advances.sciencemag.org/content/ early/2020/06/30/sciadv.abd4794

Jeon, Y., Choi, S., & Kim, H. (2014). Evaluation of a simplified augmented reality device for ultrasound-guided vascular access in a vascular phantom. *Journal of Clinical Anesthesia*, *26*(6), 485–489. doi:10.1016/j.jclinane.2014.02.010 PMID:25204510

Jesty, R., & Williams, G. (2011). Who invented vaccination? *Malta Medical Journal*, *23*(2), 29–32.

Ji, L., Huang, J., Liu, Z., Zhu, H., & Cai, Z. (2011). The effects of employee training on the relationship between environmental attitude and firms' performance in sustainable development. *International Journal of Human Resource Management*, *23*(14), 2995–3008. doi:10.1080/095 85192.2011.637072

Johannes, N., Veling, H., Dora, J., Meier, A., Reinecke, L., & Buijzen, M. (2018). Mind-wandering and mindfulness as mediators of the relationship between online vigilance and well-being. *Cyberpsychology, Behavior, and Social Networking, 21*(12), 761–767. doi:10.1089/cyber.2018.0373 PMID:30499683

Johansson, R., & Andersson, G. (2012). Internet-based psychological treatments for depression. *Expert Review of Neurotherapeutics, 12*(7), 861–869. doi:10.1586/ern.12.63 PMID:22853793

Johansson, R., Nyblom, A., Carlbring, P., Cuijpers, P., & Andersson, G. (2013). Choosing between Internet-based psychodynamic versus cognitive behavioral therapy for depression: A pilot preference study. *BMC Psychiatry, 13*(1), 268. doi:10.1186/1471-244X-13-268 PMID:24139066

Johns Hopkins Medicine. (2020, June 10). COVID-19 false negative test results if used too early. *ScienceDaily.* www.sciencedaily.com/releases/2020/06/200610094112.htm

Johns Hopkins. (2020). *Johns Hopkins Coronavirus Resource Center.* https://coronavirus.jhu.edu/

Johnson-Glenberg, M. C., Birchfield, D. A., Tolentino, L., & Koziupa, T. (2014). Collaborative embodied learning in mixed reality motion-capture environments: Two science studies. *Journal of Educational Psychology, 106*(1), 86–104. doi:10.1037/a0034008

Johnson-Glenberg, M. C., Megowan-Romanowicz, C., Birchfield, D. A., & Savio-Ramos, C. (2016). Effects of embodied learning and digital platform on the retention of physics content: Centripetal force. *Frontiers in Psychology, 7,* 1819. doi:10.3389/fpsyg.2016.01819 PMID:27933009

Johnson, J. (2014). *Designing with the mind in mind: Simple guide to understanding user interface design guidelines.* Elsevier Science & Technology.

Jonassen, D. H. (1991). Objectivism versus constructivism: Do we need a new philosophical paradigm? *Educational Technology Research and Development, 39*(3), 5–14. doi:10.1007/BF02296434

Jonassen, D. H., Peck, K. L., & Wilson, B. G. (1999). *Learning with technology: A constructivist perspective.* Prentice Hall.

Juan, M. C., Alcaniz, M., Monserrat, C., Botella, C., Baños, R. M., & Guerrero, B. (2005). Using augmented reality to treat phobias. *IEEE Computer Graphics and Applications, 25*(6), 31–37. doi:10.1109/MCG.2005.143 PMID:16315475

Kaltenthaler, E., Brazier, J., De Nigris, E., Tumur, I., Ferriter, M., Beverley, C., Parry, G., Rooney, G., & Sutcliffe, P. (2006). Computerised cognitive behaviour therapy for depression and anxiety update: A systematic review and economic evaluation. *Health Technology Assessment, 10*(33), 1–186. doi:10.3310/hta10330 PMID:16959169

Kamat, V. R., & El-Tawil, S. (2007). Evaluation of Augmented Reality for Rapid Assessment of Earthquake-Induced Building Damage. *Journal of Computing in Civil Engineering, 21*(5), 303–310. doi:10.1061/(ASCE)0887-3801(2007)21:5(303)

Kanter, R. M. (2008). *Men and women of the corporation: New edition.* Basic Books.

Karimi, S. (2013). *A purchase decision-making process model of online consumers and its influential factor a cross sector analysis* (PhD thesis). Manchester Business School.

Karlsson, M. (2015). *Challenges of designing augmented reality for military use.* https://www.diva-portal.org/smash/get/diva2:823544/FULLTEXT01.pdf

Kaufmann, H., & Dünser, A. (2007, July). Summary of usability evaluations of an educational augmented reality application. In *International conference on virtual reality* (pp. 660-669). Springer. 10.1007/978-3-540-73335-5_71

Kazdin, A. E. (2017). Addressing the treatment gap: A key challenge for extending evidence-based psychosocial interventions. *Behaviour Research and Therapy, 88*, 7–18. doi:10.1016/j.brat.2016.06.004 PMID:28110678

Kelders, S. M., Kok, R. N., Ossebaard, H. C., & van Gemert-Pijnen, J. E. W. C. (2012). Persuasive system design does matter: A systematic review of adherence to web-based interventions. *Journal of Medical Internet Research, 14*(6), e152. doi:10.2196/jmir.2104 PMID:23151820

Keller, K. L. (1987). Memory factors in advertising: The effect of advertising retrieval cues on brand evaluations. *The Journal of Consumer Research, 14*(3), 316–333. doi:10.1086/209116

Kennedy, K. D., Stephens, C. L., Williams, R. A., & Schutte, P. (2014). Automation and inattentional blindness in a simulated flight task. *Proceedings of the 58th Annual Meeting of the Human Factors and Ergonomics Society, 58*(1), 2058-2062.

Keri, Z., Sydor, D., Ungi, T., Holden, M. S., McGraw, R., Mousavi, P., Borschneck, D. P., Fichtinger, G., & Jaeger, M. (2015). Computerized training system for ultrasound-guided lumbar puncture on abnormal spine models: A randomized controlled trial. *Canadian Journal of Anaesthesia / Journal Canadien D'anesthesie, 62*(7), 777–784. doi:10.100712630-015-0367-2

Kerr, I.R. (2006). Leadership strategies for sustainable SME operation. *Business Strategy and the Environment, 15*(1), 30-39.

Kersten-Oertel, M., Jannin, P., & Collins, D. L. (2013). The state of the art of visualization in mixed reality image guided surgery. *Computerized Medical Imaging and Graphics, 37*(2), 98–112. doi:10.1016/j.compmedimag.2013.01.009 PMID:23490236

Kessler, R. C., Aguilar-Gaxiola, S., Alonso, J., Chatterji, S., Lee, S., Ormel, J., Üstün, T. B., & Wang, P. S. (2009). The global burden of mental disorders: An update from the WHO World Mental Health (WMH) surveys. *Epidemiologia e Psichiatria Sociale, 18*(1), 23–33. doi:10.1017/S1121189X00001421 PMID:19378696

Kewin, T. (2010). *If your kids are awake, they're probably online.* Retrieved on April 21, 2011 from https://www.nytimes.com/2010/01/20/education/20wired.html

Khan, T., Johnston, K., & Ophoff, J. (2019). The Impact of an Augmented Reality Application on Learning Motivation of Students. *Advances in Human-Computer Interaction, 2019*, 1–14. doi:10.1155/2019/7208494

Kim, G. U., Kim, M. J., Ra, S. H., Lee, J., Bae, S., Jung, J., & Kim, S. H. (2020). Clinical characteristics of asymptomatic and symptomatic patients with mild COVID-19. *Clinical Microbiology and Infection*, 26(7), 948.e1–948.e3. doi:10.1016/j.cmi.2020.04.040 PMID:32360780

Kim, H. K., Choe, M., Choi, Y., & Park, J. (2019). Does the Hand Anthropometric Dimension Influence Touch Interaction? *Journal of Computer Information Systems*, 59(1), 85–96. doi:10.1080/08874417.2017.1305876

Kim, H., Suh, K., & Lee, U. (2013). Effects of collaborative online shopping on shopping experience through social and relational perspectives. *Information & Management*, 50(4), 169–180. doi:10.1016/j.im.2013.02.003

Kim, J., Park, J., Kim, J., & Park, J. (2005). A consumer shopping channel extension model: Attitude shift toward the online store. *Journal of Fashion Marketing and Management*, 9(1), 106–121. doi:10.1108/13612020510586433

Kim, T. Y. (2013). A Situational Training System for Developmentally Disabled People Based on Augmented Reality. *IEICE Transactions on Information and Systems*, 96(D), 1561–1564. doi:10.1587/transinf.E96.D.1561

Kim, Y., Kim, D. J., & Wachter, K. (2013). A study of mobile user engagement (MoEN): Engagement motivations, perceived value, satisfaction, and continued engagement intention. *Decision Support Systems*, 56, 361–370. doi:10.1016/j.dss.2013.07.002

Kim, Y., Wang, Y., & Oh, J. (2016). Digital media use and social engagement: How social media and smartphone use influence social activities of college students. *Cyberpsychology, Behavior, and Social Networking*, 19(4), 264–269. doi:10.1089/cyber.2015.0408 PMID:26991638

King, J. A., Whitten, T. A., Bakal, J. A., & McAlister, F. A. (2020). Symptoms associated with a positive result for a swab for SARS-CoV-2 infection among children in Alberta. *Canadian Medical Association Journal*, 193(1), E1–E9. doi:10.1503/cmaj.202065 PMID:33234533

King, R., Bambling, M., Lloyd, C., Gomurra, R., Smith, S., Reid, W., & Wegner, K. (2006). Online counselling: The motives and experiences of young people who choose the Internet instead of face to face or telephone counselling. *Counselling & Psychotherapy Research*, 6(3), 169–174. doi:10.1080/14733140600848179

Kinnunen, H., Laakkonen, H., Kivela, K., Colley, A., Lahtela, P., Koskela, M., & Jurvelin, H. (2016, Feb 23). *Method and system for assessing a readiness score of a user.* US patent 201562121425. https://patents.google.com/patent/WO2016135382A1

Klein, B., Austin, D., Pier, C., Kiropoulos, L., Shandley, K., Mitchell, J., Gilson, K., & Ciechomski, L. (2009). Internet-based treatment for panic disorder: Does frequency of therapist contact make a difference? *Cognitive Behaviour Therapy*, 38(2), 100–113. doi:10.1080/16506070802561132 PMID:19306149

Klein, B., Mitchell, J., Gilson, K., Shandley, K., Austin, D., Kiropoulos, L., Abbott, J., & Cannard, G. (2009). A therapist-assisted internet-based cbt intervention for posttraumatic stress disorder: Preliminary results. *Cognitive Behaviour Therapy*, *38*(2), 121–131. doi:10.1080/16506070902803483 PMID:20183691

Klein, B., Richards, J. C., & Austin, D. W. (2006). Efficacy of internet therapy for panic disorder. *Journal of Behavior Therapy and Experimental Psychiatry*, *37*(3), 213–238. doi:10.1016/j.jbtep.2005.07.001 PMID:16126161

Klimmt, C., Hefner, D., Reinecke, L., Rieger, D., & Vorderer, P. (2017). The permanently online and permanently connected mind: Mapping the cognitive structures behind mobile internet use. In P. Vorderer, D. Hefner, L. Reinecke, & C. Klimmt (Eds.), *Permanently online, permanently connected* (pp. 18–28). Routledge. doi:10.4324/9781315276472-3

Knapp, H., & Kirk, S. A. (2003). Using pencil and paper, internet and touch-tone phones for self administered surveys: Does methodology matter? *Computers in Human Behavior*, *19*(1), 117–134. doi:10.1016/S0747-5632(02)00008-0

Koford, B. (2010). *Match.com and Chadwick Martin Bailey 2009 - 2010 studies: recent trends: online dating.* Retrieved on April, 17, 2010 from http://cp.match.com/cppp/media/CMB_Study.pdf

Kok, R. N., van Straten, A., Beekman, A. T. F., & Cuijpers, P. (2014). Short-term effectiveness of web-based guided self-help for phobic outpatients: Randomized controlled trial. *Journal of Medical Internet Research*, *16*(9), e226. doi:10.2196/jmir.3429 PMID:25266929

Koskimäki, H., Kinnunen, H., Rönkä, S., & Smarr, B. (2019, September). Following the heart: what does variation of resting heart rate tell about us as individuals and as a population. In *Adjunct Proceedings of the 2019 ACM International Joint Conference on Pervasive and Ubiquitous Computing and Proceedings of the 2019 ACM International Symposium on Wearable Computers* (pp. 1178-1181). 10.1145/3341162.3344836

Kotsiou, A., Juriasingani, E., Maromonte, M., Marsh, J., Shelton, C. R., Zhao, R., & Elliot, L. J. (2021). Interdisciplinary approach to a coping skills app: A case study. The Journal of Interactive Technology and Pedagogy, *19*.

Kouhkan, A., & Mousavi, S. A. (2015). Review the relationship between the components of the organization Learner and Organizational innovation) Case study: (FreeUniversity of Mazandaran) *First International Conference on Economics, Management, Accounting, Social Sciences.*

Kronbichler, A., Kresse, D., Yoon, S., Lee, K. H., Effenberger, M., & Shin, J. I. (2020). Asymptomatic patients as a source of COVID-19 infections: A systematic review and meta-analysis. *International Journal of Infectious Diseases*, *98*, 180–186. doi:10.1016/j.ijid.2020.06.052 PMID:32562846

Kucirka, L. M., Lauer, S. A., Laeyendecker, O., Boon, D., & Lessler, J. (2020). Variation in false-negative rate of reverse transcriptase polymerase chain reaction–based SARS-CoV-2 tests by time since exposure. *Annals of Internal Medicine*, *173*(4), 262–267. doi:10.7326/M20-1495 PMID:32422057

Küçük, S., Kapakin, S., & Göktaş, Y. (2016). Learning anatomy via mobile augmented reality: Effects on achievement and cognitive load. *Anatomical Sciences Education*, 9(5), 411–421. doi:10.1002/ase.1603 PMID:26950521

Lagan, S., D'Mello, R., Vaidyam, A., Bilden, R., & Torous, J. (2021). Assessing mental health apps marketplaces with objective metrics from 29,190 data points from 278 apps. *Acta Psychiatrica Scandinavica*. Advance online publication. doi:10.1111/acps.13306

Lally, P., & Gardner, B. (2013). Promoting habit formation. *Health Psychology Review*, 7(sup1), S137–S158. doi:10.1080/17437199.2011.603640

LaPlante, D., & Ambady, N. (2002). Saying it like it isn't: Responding to mixed messages from men and women in the workplace. *Journal of Applied Social Psychology*, 32(12), 2435–2457. doi:10.1111/j.1559-1816.2002.tb02750.x

Larsen, M. E., Huckvale, K., Nicholas, J., Torous, J., Birrell, L., Li, E., & Reda, B. (2019). Using science to sell apps: Evaluation of mental health app store quality claims. *NPJ Digital Medicine*, 2(1), 1–6. doi:10.103841746-019-0093-1 PMID:31304366

Lawrence, A. D., Kinney, T. B., O'Connell, M. S., & Delgado, K. M. (2017). Stop interrupting me! Examining the relationship between interruptions, test performance and reactions. *Personnel Assessment and Decisions*, 3(1), 2. doi:10.25035/pad.2017.002

Leary, D. E. (1995). Naming and knowing: Giving form to things unknown. *Social Research*, 62, 267–298.

Lee, E., & Hannafin, M. J. (2016). A design framework for enhancing engagement in student-centered learning: Own it, learn it, and share it. *Educational Technology Research and Development*, 64(4), 707–234. doi:10.100711423-015-9422-5

Lee, J. D., & See, K. A. (2004). Trust in automation: Designing for appropriate reliance. *Human Factors*, 46(1), 50–80. doi:10.1518/hfes.46.1.50.30392 PMID:15151155

Lee, K. (2012). Augmented Reality in Education and Training. *TechTrends*, 56(2), 13–21. doi:10.100711528-012-0559-3

Leelayouthayotin, L. (2004). *Factors influencing online purchase intention: the case of health food consumers in Thailand* (PhD thesis). Universidad Southern Queensland, Australia.

Léger, É., Drouin, S., Collins, D. L., Popa, T., & Kersten-Oertel, M. (2017). Quantifying attention shifts in augmented reality image-guided neurosurgery. *Healthcare Technology Letters*, 4(5), 188–192. doi:10.1049/htl.2017.0062 PMID:29184663

Léger, É., Reyes, J., Drouin, S., Collins, D. L., Popa, T., & Kersten-Oertel, M. (2018). Gesture-based registration correction using a mobile augmented reality image-guided neurosurgery system. *Healthcare Technology Letters*, 5(5), 137–142. doi:10.1049/htl.2018.5063 PMID:30800320

Leitritz, M. A., Ziemssen, F., Suesskind, D., Partsch, M., Voykov, B., Bartz-Schmidt, K. U., & Szurman, G. B. (2014). Critical evaluation of the usability of augmented reality ophthalmoscopy for the training of inexperienced examiners. *Retina (Philadelphia, Pa.)*, *34*(4), 785–791. doi:10.1097/IAE.0b013e3182a2e75d PMID:24670999

Leiva, L. A., Bohmer, M., Gehring, S., & Kruger, A. (2012). Back to the app: The costs of mobile application interruptions. In *Proceedings of the 14th International Conference on Human Computer Interaction with Mobile Devices and Services*. Association for Computing Machinery. 10.1145/2371574.2371617

Levy, B. R., & Myers, L. M. (2004). Preventive health behaviors influenced by self-perceptions of aging. *Preventive Medicine*, *39*(3), 625–629. doi:10.1016/j.ypmed.2004.02.029 PMID:15313104

Liebowitz, J. (2010). The role of HR in achieving a sustainability culture. *Journal of Sustainable Development*, *3*(4), 50-57.

Linardon, J., Cuijpers, P., Carlbring, P., Messer, M., & Fuller-Tyszkiewicz, M. (2019). The efficacy of app-supported smartphone interventions for mental health problems: A meta-analysis of randomized controlled trials. *World Psychiatry; Official Journal of the World Psychiatric Association (WPA)*, *18*(3), 325–336. doi:10.1002/wps.20673 PMID:31496095

Lindgren, R., Tscholl, M., Wang, S., & Johnson, E. (2016). Enhancing learning and engagement through embodied interaction within a mixed reality simulation. *Computers & Education*, *95*, 174–187. doi:10.1016/j.compedu.2016.01.001

Lintvedt, O. K., Griffiths, K. M., Sørensen, K., Østvik, A. R., Wang, C. E. A., Eisemann, M., & Waterloo, K. (2013). Evaluating the effectiveness and efficacy of unguided internet-based self-help intervention for the prevention of depression: A randomized controlled trial. *Clinical Psychology & Psychotherapy*, *20*(1), 10–27. doi:10.1002/cpp.770 PMID:21887811

Lin, Y. H., Chen, C. Y., Li, P., & Lin, S. H. (2013). A dimensional approach to the phantom vibration and ringing syndrome during medical internship. *Journal of Psychiatric Research*, *47*(9), 1254–1258. doi:10.1016/j.jpsychires.2013.05.023 PMID:23786911

Liu, Y. (2003). The aesthetic and the ethic dimensions of human factors and design. *Ergonomics*, *46*(13–14), 1293–1305. doi:10.1080/00140130310001610838 PMID:14612320

Livingston, M. A., Rosenblum, L. J., Brown, D. G., Schmidt, G. S., Julier, S. J., Baillot, Y., & Maassel, P. (2011). Military applications of augmented reality. In *Handbook of Augmented Reality* (pp. 671–706). Springer. doi:10.1007/978-1-4614-0064-6_31

Li, X., Yi, W., Chi, H.-L., Wang, X., & Chan, A. P. C. (2018). A critical review of virtual and augmented reality (VR/AR) applications in construction safety. *Automation in Construction*, *86*, 150–162. doi:10.1016/j.autcon.2017.11.003

Longyear, R. L., & Kushlev, K. (2021). Can mental health apps be effective for depression, anxiety, and stress during a pandemic? *Practice Innovations (Washington, D.C.)*. Advance online publication. doi:10.1037/pri0000142

Compilation of References

Lopez-Cabrales, A., Pérez-Luño, A., & Cabrera, R.V. (2009). Knowledge as amediator between HRM practices and innovative activity. *Hum Resour Manage.*, *48*(4), 485–503. doi: 48:4113 doi:10.1002/hrm.v

Love, A. (1991). *Internal evaluation. Building organizations from within.* Sage.

Lukas, H., Xu, C., Yu, Y., & Gao, W. (2020). Emerging Telemedicine Tools for Remote COVID-19 Diagnosis, Monitoring, and Management. *ACS nano.*

Lum, H. C., Sims, V. K., Chin, M. G., & Lagattuta, N. C. (2009). Perceptions of humans wearing technology. *Proceedings of the Human Factors and Ergonomics Society*, 53.

Lustria, M. L. A., Cortese, J., Noar, S. M., & Glueckauf, R. L. (2009). Computer-tailored health interventions delivered over the Web: Review and analysis of key components. *Patient Education and Counseling*, *74*(2), 156–173. doi:10.1016/j.pec.2008.08.023 PMID:18947966

Luxton, D. D., McCann, R. A., Bush, N. E., Mishkind, M. C., & Reger, G. M. (2011). mHealth for mental health: Integrating smartphone technology in behavioral healthcare. *Professional Psychology, Research and Practice*, *42*(6), 505–512. doi:10.1037/a0024485

Ly, K. H., Trüschel, A., Jarl, L., Magnusson, S., Windahl, T., Johansson, R., Carlbring, P., & Andersson, G. (2014). Behavioural activation versus mindfulness-based guided self-help treatment administered through a smartphone application: A randomised controlled trial. *BMJ Open*, *4*(1), e003440. doi:10.1136/bmjopen-2013-003440 PMID:24413342

Magsamen-Conrad, K., & Dillon, J. M. (2020). Mobile technology adoption across the lifespan: A mixed methods investigation to clarify adoption stages, and the influence of diffusion attributes. *Computers in Human Behavior*, *112*(106456), 106456. Advance online publication. doi:10.1016/j.chb.2020.106456 PMID:32834465

Maheu, M. M., & Gordon, B. L. (2000). Counseling and therapy on the Internet. *Professional Psychology, Research and Practice*, *31*(5), 484–489. doi:10.1037/0735-7028.31.5.484

Maier, T., Donghia, V., Chen, C., Menold, J., & McComb, C. (2019). Assessing the impact of cognitive assistants on mental workload in simple tasks. In *International Design Engineering Technical Conferences and Computers and Information in Engineering Conference* (Vol. 59278). American Society of Mechanical Engineers. 10.1115/DETC2019-97543

Mancas, M. (2016). What is attention? In M. Mancas, V. P. Ferrera, N. Riche, & J. G. Taylor (Eds.), *From human attention to computational attention: A multidisciplinary approach* (pp. 9–20). Springer. doi:10.1007/978-1-4939-3435-5_2

Mandrola, J. (2020). CoViD-19 and PPE: Some of us will die because of the shortage. *Recenti Progressi in Medicina*, *111*(4), 183. PMID:32319434

Manser, M. (2017). 7 mobile engagement statistics that show push notification ROI. *Medium.* https://airship.medium.com/7-mobile-engagement-statistics-that-show-push-notification-roi-f664409943a2

Mao, C.-C., & Chen, F.-Y. (2020). Augmented Reality and 3-D Visualization Effects to Enhance Battlefield Situational Awareness. In T. Ahram, R. Taiar, S. Colson, & A. Choplin (Eds.), *Human Interaction and Emerging Technologies* (pp. 303–309). Springer International Publishing. doi:10.1007/978-3-030-25629-6_47

March, J. G. (1981). Footnotes to organizational change. *Administrative Science Quarterly, 26*(4), 563–577. doi:10.2307/2392340

Marra, R., Jonassen, D. H., Palmer, B., & Luft, S. (2014). Why problem-based learning works: Theoretical foundations. *Journal on Excellence in College Teaching, 25*(3&4), 221–238.

Marshall, N. (2007). Cognitive and practice-based theories of organisational knowing and learning: incompatible or complementary? In *Proceedings of OLKC Learning Fusion*. University of Brighton.

Martinengo, L., Van Galen, L., Lum, E., Kowalski, M., Subramaniam, M., & Car, J. (2019). Suicide prevention and depression apps' suicide risk assessment and management: A systematic assessment of adherence to clinical guidelines. *BMC Medicine, 17*(1), 1–12. doi:10.118612916-019-1461-z PMID:31852455

Martínez-Leon, I. M., & Martínez-García, J. A. (2011). The influence of organizational structure on organizational learning. *International Journal of Manpower, 32*(5), 537–566. doi:10.1108/01437721111158198

Mason, E. C., & Andrews, G. (2014). The use of automated assessments in internet-based CBT: The computer will be with you shortly. *Internet Interventions: the Application of Information Technology in Mental and Behavioural Health, 1*(4), 216–224. doi:10.1016/j.invent.2014.10.003

McBride, T., & Nief, R. (2010). *Beloit college mindset list, entering class on 2014*. Retrieved on August 21, 2010 from https://www.beloit.edu/mindset/

McGaughey, R., & Mason, K. (1998). The Internet as a marketing tool. *Journal of Marketing Theory and Practice, 6*(6), 1–11. doi:10.1080/10696679.1998.11501800

McKinnon, T. (2020, May 8). *10 of the Best Augmented Reality (AR) Shopping Apps to Try Today*. Indigo9Digital. https://www.indigo9digital.com/blog/how-six-leading-retailers-use-augmented-reality-apps-to-disrupt-the-shopping-experience

McLaughlin, A. C., & Pak, R. (2020). *Designing displays for older adults* (2nd ed.). CRC Press., doi:10.1201/9780429439674

McLeod, A., & Dolezel, D. (2018). Cyber-analytics: Modeling factors associated with healthcare data breaches. *Decision Support Systems, 108*, 57–68. doi:10.1016/j.dss.2018.02.007

McMichael, T. M., Currie, D. W., Clark, S., Pogosjans, S., Kay, M., Schwartz, N. G., Lewis, J., Baer, A., Kawakami, V., Lukoff, M. D., Ferro, J., Brostrom-Smith, C., Rea, T. D., Sayre, M. R., Riedo, F. X., Russell, D., Hiatt, B., Montgomery, P., Rao, A. K., ... Duchin, J. S. (2020). Epidemiology of Covid-19 in a long-term care facility in King County, Washington. *The New England Journal of Medicine, 382*(21), 2005–2011. doi:10.1056/NEJMoa2005412 PMID:32220208

Medicine, U. A. B. (n.d.). All About Continuous Glucose Monitors for People with Diabetes. *UAB Medicine News.* https://www.uabmedicine.org/-/all-about-continuous-glucose-monitors-for-people-with-diabetes

Mehrabi, J., Soltani, I., Alemzadeh, M., & Jadidi, M. (2013). Explaining the relationship between organizational structure and dimensions of learning organizations (case study: Education organization in Boroojerd county and the related departments). *International Journal of Academic Research in Business & Social Sciences,* 116–129.

Melcher, J., & Torous, J. (2020). Smartphone apps for college mental health: A concern for privacy and quality of current offerings. *Psychiatric Services (Washington, D.C.),* 71(11), 1114–1119. doi:10.1176/appi.ps.202000098 PMID:32664822

Memarzadeh, M., & Golparvar-Fard, M. (2012). *Monitoring and Visualization of Building Construction Embodied Carbon Footprint Using DnAR-N-Dimensional Augmented Reality Models.* doi:10.1061/9780784412329.134

Meng, J. (2009). *Living in internet time.* Retrieved on May 04, 2011 from https://www.ocf.berkeley.edu/~jaimeng/techtime.html

Meyer, B., Berger, T., Caspar, F., Beevers, C. G., Andersson, G., & Weiss, M. (2009). Effectiveness of a novel integrative online treatment for depression (Deprexis): Randomized controlled trial. *Journal of Medical Internet Research,* 11(2), e15. doi:10.2196/jmir.1151 PMID:19632969

Midkiff, D. M., & Joseph Wyatt, W. (2008). Ethical issues in the provision of online mental health services (Etherapy). *Journal of Technology in Human Services,* 26(2-4), 310–332. doi:10.1080/15228830802096994

Milgram, P., & Kishino, F. (1994). A taxonomy of mixed reality visual displays. *IEICE Transactions on Information and Systems,* 77(12), 1321–1329.

Mintzberg, H. (1994). *The Rise and Fall of Strategic Planning: Reconceiving Roles for Planning, Plans, Planners.* The Free Press.

Misra, S., Cheng, L., Genevie, J., & Yuan, M. (2016). The iPhone effect: The quality of in-person social interactions in the presence of mobile devices. *Environment and Behavior,* 48(2), 275–298. doi:10.1177/0013916514539755

Mitzner, T. L., Boron, J. B., Fausset, C. B., Adams, A. E., Charness, N., Czaja, S. J., Dijkstra, K., Fisk, A. D., Rogers, W. A., & Sharit, J. (2010). Older adults talk technology: Technology usage and attitudes. *Computers in Human Behavior,* 26(6), 1710–1721. doi:10.1016/j.chb.2010.06.020 PMID:20967133

Mohan, P. M., Nagarajan, V., & Das, S. R. (2016, April). Stress measurement from wearable photoplethysmographic sensor using heart rate variability data. In *2016 International Conference on Communication and Signal Processing (ICCSP)* (pp. 1141-1144). IEEE. 10.1109/ICCSP.2016.7754331

Mohr, D. C., Schueller, S. M., Araya, R., Gureje, O., & Montague, E. (2014). Mental health technologies and the needs of cultural groups. *The Lancet. Psychiatry, 1*(5), 326–327. doi:10.1016/S2215-0366(14)70261-5 PMID:26360986

Mohr, D. C., Schueller, S. M., Montague, E., Burns, M. N., & Rashidi, P. (2014). The behavioral intervention technology model: An integrated conceptual and technological framework for eHealth and mHealth interventions. *Journal of Medical Internet Research, 16*(6), e146. doi:10.2196/jmir.3077 PMID:24905070

Monk, C. A. (2004). The effect of frequent versus infrequent interruptions on primary task resumption. *Proceedings of the Human Factors and Ergonomics Society Annual Meeting, 48*(3), 295–299. doi:10.1177/154193120404800304

Moon, B.J. (2004). Consumer adoption of the internet as an information search and product purchase channel: some research hypotheses. *International Journal of Internet Marketing and Advertising, 1*(1), 104-118.

Moon, H., Ruona, W., & Valentine, T. (2017). Organizational strategic learning capability: Exploring the dimensions. *European Journal of Training and Development, 41*(3), 222–240. doi:10.1108/EJTD-08-2016-0061

Moore, S. B., & Manring, S. L. (2009). Strategy development in small and medium sized enterprises for sustainability and increased value creation. *Journal of Cleaner Production, 17*(2), 276–282. doi:10.1016/j.jclepro.2008.06.004

Morais-Storz, M., & Nguyen, N. (2017). The role of unlearning in metamorphosis and strategic resilience. *The Learning Organization, 24*(2), 93–106. doi:10.1108/TLO-12-2016-0091

Mora, L., Nevid, J., & Chaplin, W. (2008). Psychologist treatment recommendations for Internet-based therapeutic interventions. *Computers in Human Behavior, 24*(6), 3052–3062. doi:10.1016/j.chb.2008.05.011

Mordecai, D., Histon, T., Neuwirth, E., Heisler, W. S., Kraft, A., Bang, Y., Franchino, K., Taillac, C., & Nixon, J. P. (2021). How Kaiser Permanente created a mental health and wellness digital ecosystem. *NEJM Catalyst Innovations in Care Delivery, 2*(1), CAT.20.0295. Advance online publication. doi:10.1056/CAT.20.0295

Morewedge, C. K., Preston, J., & Wegner, D. M. (2007). Timescale bias in the attribution of mind. *Journal of Personality and Social Psychology, 93*(1), 1–11. doi:10.1037/0022-3514.93.1.1 PMID:17605584

Mori, M. (2005). On the Uncanny Valley. *Proceedings of the Humanoids-2005 workshop: Views of the Uncanny Valley.*

Morrison, A., Oulasvirta, A., Peltonen, P., Lemmela, S., Jacucci, G., Reitmayr, G., ... Juustila, A. (2009, April). Like bees around the hive: a comparative study of a mobile augmented reality map. In *Proceedings of the SIGCHI conference on human factors in computing systems* (pp. 1889-1898). 10.1145/1518701.1518991

Motl, R. W., & DiStefano, C. (2002). Longitudinal invariance of self-esteem and method effects associated with negatively worded items. *Structural Equation Modeling*, *9*(4), 562–578. doi:10.1207/S15328007SEM0904_6

Mumford, M. D., Michelle, E., Higgs, T. C., & McIntosh, T. (2017). Cognitive skills and leadership performance: The nine critical skills. *The Leadership Quarterly*, *28*(1), 24–39. doi:10.1016/j.leaqua.2016.10.012

Nasermoadeli, A., Ling, K. C., & Severi, E. (2013). Exploring the Relationship between Social Environment and Customer Experience. *Asian Social Science*, *9*(1), 130–141.

National Council on Aging. (n.d.). *Healthy Aging Facts*. https://www.ncoa.org/news/resources-for-reporters/get-the-facts/healthy-aging-facts/

NBA. (2020, Dec 2). *NBA and NBPA announce COVID-19 test results*. https://www.nba.com/news/nba-and-nbpa-announce-covid-19-test-results

Newby, J. M., Mewton, L., Williams, A. D., & Andrews, G. (2014). Effectiveness of transdiagnostic internet cognitive behavioural treatment for mixed anxiety and depression in primary care. *Journal of Affective Disorders*, *165*(0), 45–52. doi:10.1016/j.jad.2014.04.037 PMID:24882176

Newman, A., Round, H., Bhattacharya, S., & Roy, A. (2017). Ethical climates in organizations: A review and research agenda. *Business Ethics Quarterly*, *27*(4), 475–512. doi:10.1017/beq.2017.23

Nielsen Group. (2009). *Americans watching more tv than ever; web and mobile video up too*. Retrieved on April 20, 2011 from http://blog.nielsen.com/nielsenwire/online_mobile/americans-watching-more-tv-than-ever/

Nielsen, R. K., Fletcher, R., Kalogeropoulos, A., & Simon, F. (2020). *Communications in the coronavirus crisis: lessons for the second wave. In Communications in the Coronavirus Crisis: Lessons for the Second Wave.* Reuters Institute for the Study of Journalism.

Nieuwenhuijse, D. F., Munnink, B. B. O., Phan, M. V., Munk, P., Venkatakrishnan, S., Aarestrup, F. M., ... Koopmans, M. P. (2020). Setting a baseline for global urban virome surveillance in sewage. *Scientific Reports*, *10*(1), 1–13. doi:10.103841598-020-69869-0 PMID:32792677

Nilsson, N. C. (2018). Perceptual Illusions and Distortions in Virtual Reality. In N. Lee (Ed.), *Encyclopedia of Computer Graphics and Games*. Springer. doi:10.1007/978-3-319-08234-9_245-1

Nomura, T., Suzuki, T., Kanda, T., & Kato, K. (2006). Altered attitudes of people toward robots: Investigation through the Negative Attitudes toward Robots Scale. *Proc. AAAI-06 Workshop on Human Implications of Human-Robot Interaction*, 29-35.

Nordgren, L. B., Hedman, E., Etienne, J., Bodin, J., Kadowaki, Å., Eriksson, S., Lindkvist, E., Andersson, G., & Carlbring, P. (2014). Effectiveness and cost-effectiveness of individually tailored Internet-delivered cognitive behavior therapy for anxiety disorders in a primary care population: A randomized controlled trial. *Behaviour Research and Therapy*, *59*(0), 1–11. doi:10.1016/j.brat.2014.05.007 PMID:24933451

Norman, D. (2002). *The Design of Everyday Things*. Basic Books.

Nowak, K. L., & Blocca, F. (2003). The effect of the agency and anthropomorphism on users' sense of telepresence, copresence, and social presence in virtual environments. *Presence (Cambridge, Mass.)*, *12*(5), 481–494. doi:10.1162/105474603322761289

Nowlis, S., & McCabe, D. (2000). The effect of the inability to touch merchandise on the likelihood of choosing products online. In *American Marketing Association. Conference Proceedings.* (Vol. 11, p. 308). American Marketing Association.

O'Brien, H., & Toms, E. G. (2008). What is user engagement? A conceptual framework for defining user engagement with technology. *Journal of the American Society for Information Science and Technology*, *59*(6), 938–955. doi:10.1002/asi.20801

O'Mahen, H. A., Woodford, J., McGinley, J., Warren, F. C., Richards, D. A., Lynch, T. R., & Taylor, R. S. (2013). Internet-based behavioral activation—treatment for postnatal depression (Netmums): A randomized controlled trial. *Journal of Affective Disorders*, *150*(3), 814–822. doi:10.1016/j.jad.2013.03.005 PMID:23602514

Oenema, A., Brug, J., & Lechner, L. (2001). Web-based tailored nutrition education: Results of a randomized controlled trial. *Health Education Research*, *16*(6), 647–660. doi:10.1093/her/16.6.647 PMID:11780705

Okoshi, T., Ramos, J., Nozaki, H., Nakazawa, J., Dey, A. K., & Tokuda, H. (2015). Reducing users' perceived mental effort due to interruptive notifications in multi-device mobile environments. In *Proceedings of the 2015 ACM International Joint Conference on Pervasive and Ubiquitous Computing*. Association for Computing Machinery. 10.1145/2750858.2807517

Olson, N., Nolin, J., & Nelhans, G. (2015). Semantic web, ubiquitous computing, or internet of things? A macro-analysis of scholarly publications. *The Journal of Documentation*, *71*(5), 884–916. doi:10.1108/JD-03-2013-0033

Omamo, A. O., Rodrigues, A. J., & Muliaro, W. J. (2020). A system dynamics model of technology and society: In the context of a developing nation. *International Journal of System Dynamics Applications*, *9*(2), 42–63. doi:10.4018/IJSDA.2020040103

Opriş, D., Pintea, S., García-Palacios, A., Botella, C., Szamosközi, Ş., & David, D. (2012). Virtual reality exposure therapy in anxiety disorders: A quantitative meta-analysis. *Depression and Anxiety*, *29*(2), 85–93. doi:10.1002/da.20910 PMID:22065564

Oran, D. P., & Topol, E. J. (2020). Prevalence of Asymptomatic SARS-CoV-2 Infection: A Narrative Review. *Annals of Internal Medicine*.

Oren, T. (1990). Designing a new medium. In B. Laurel (Ed.), *The Art of Human-Computer Interface Design* (pp. 467–479). Addison-Wesley.

Osborne, J., Simon, S., & Collins, S. (2003). Attitudes towards science: A review of the literature and its implications. *International Journal of Science Education*, *25*(9), 1049–1079. doi:10.1080/0950069032000032199

Osenbach, J. E., O'Brien, K. M., Mishkind, M., & Smolenski, D. J. (2013). Synchronous telehealth technologies in psychotherapy for depression: A meta-analysis. *Depression and Anxiety, 30*(11), 1058–1067. doi:10.1002/da.22165 PMID:23922191

Osterholm, M. T., Kelley, N. S., Sommer, A., & Belongia, E. A. (2012). Efficacy and effectiveness of influenza vaccines: A systematic review and meta-analysis. *The Lancet. Infectious Diseases, 12*(1), 36–44. doi:10.1016/S1473-3099(11)70295-X PMID:22032844

Osterloh, M., & Frey, B. S. (2000). Motivation, knowledge transfer, and organizational forms. *Organization Science, 11*(5), 538–550. doi:10.1287/orsc.11.5.538.15204

Parasuraman, A. (2000). Technology Readiness Index (TRI): A Multiple-Item Scale to Measure Readiness to Embrace New Technologies. *Journal of Service Research, 2*(4), 307–320. doi:10.1177/109467050024001

Parasuraman, R., & Manzey, D. H. (2010). Complacency and bias in human use of automation: An attentional integration. *Human Factors, 52*(3), 381–410. doi:10.1177/0018720810376055 PMID:21077562

Park, C. S., & Kaye, B. K. (2019). Smartphone and self-extension: Functionally, anthropomorphically, and ontologically extending self via the smartphone. *Mobile Media & Communication, 7*(2), 215–231. doi:10.1177/2050157918808327

Parker, L., Halter, V., Karliychuk, T., & Grundy, Q. (2019). How private is your mental health app data? An empirical study of mental health app privacy policies and practices. *International Journal of Law and Psychiatry, 64*, 198–204. doi:10.1016/j.ijlp.2019.04.002 PMID:31122630

Pasteur, L. (2013). *Características y diferencias de la investigación documental, de campo y experimental*. Formación de competencias para la investigación.

Patra, R. (2008). Vaastu Shastra: Towards sustainable development. *Sustainable Development Journal, 17*(4), 244–256. doi:10.1002d.388

Patton, M. (1998). Discovering Process Use. *Evaluation, 4*(2), 225-233.

Patton, M. (1997). *Utilization-focused Evaluation*. Sage.

Pegher, K. (2020, Oct 12). Coronavirus Today: The NBA's bubble worked. *Los Angeles Times.* https://www.latimes.com/science/newsletter/2020-10-12/coronavirus-today-nba-bubble-success-covid-lakers-coronavirus-today

Pelanis, E., Kumar, R. P., Aghayan, D. L., Palomar, R., Fretland, Å. A., Brun, H., Elle, O. J., & Edwin, B. (2020). Use of mixed reality for improved spatial understanding of liver anatomy. *Minimally Invasive Therapy & Allied Technologies, 29*(3), 154–160. doi:10.1080/13645706.2019.1616558 PMID:31116053

Penz, E., & Hogg, M. (2011). The role of mixed emotions in consumer behaviour: Investigating ambivalence in consumers' experiences of approach-avoidance conflicts in online and offline settings. *European Journal of Marketing, 45*(1/2), 104–132. doi:10.1108/03090561111095612

Pereira, A., Prada, R., & Paiva, A. (2014). Improving social presence in human–agent interaction. In *Proceedings of the SIGCHI Conference on Human Factors in Computing Systems*. Association for Computing Machinery. 10.1145/2556288.2557180

Perle, J. G., Langsam, L. C., & Nierenberg, B. (2011). Controversy clarified: An updated review of clinical psychology and tele-health. *Clinical Psychology Review, 31*(8), 1247–1258. doi:10.1016/j.cpr.2011.08.003 PMID:21963670

Pettersson, R., Soderstrom, S., Edlund-Soderstrom, K., & Nilsson, K. W. (2014). Internet-based cognitive behavioral therapy for adults with ADHD in outpatient psychiatric care: A randomized trial. *Journal of Attention Disorders, 21*(6), 508–521. doi:10.1177/1087054714539998 PMID:24970720

Pew Research Center. (2017). *Internet/broadband fact sheet*. Pew Research Center: Internet, Science & Tech. Retrieved May 15, 2021, from https://www.pewinternet.org/fact-sheet/internet-broadband/

Pew Research Center. (2019). *Demographics of Mobile Device Ownership and Adoption in the United States*. https://www.pewresearch.org/internet/fact-sheet/mobile/

Pfeffer, J. (2010). Building sustainable organizations: The human factor. *The Academy of Management Perspectives, 24*(1), 34–45.

Phau, I., & Poon, S. (2000). Factors influencing the types of products and services purchased over the Internet. *Internet Research, 10*(2), 102–113. doi:10.1108/10662240010322894

Phillips, L. (2007). Go green to gain the edge over rivals. *People Management*, p. 9. Available at: www2.cipd.co.uk/pm/peoplemanagement/b/weblog/archive/2013/01/29/gogreentogaintheedgeoverrivals-2007-08.aspx

Pickens, A. W., & Benden, M. E. (2013). Curriculum Development for HF/E Graduate Students: Lessons Learned in an Ongoing Effort to Educate and Meet Industry Demands. *Proceedings of the Human Factors and Ergonomics Society Annual Meeting, 57*(1), 452–456. doi:10.1177/1541931213571098

Pier, C., Austin, D. W., Klein, B., Mitchell, J., Schattner, P., Ciechomski, L., ... Wade, V. (2008). A controlled trial of internet-based cognitive-behavioural therapy for panic disorder with face-to-face support from a general practitioner or email support from a psychologist. *Mental Health in Family Medicine, 5*(1), 29–39. PMID:22477844

Pietrzak, M., & Paliszkiewicz, J. (2013). *Framework of Strategic Learning: the PDCA Cycle*. Warsaw University of Life Sciences.

Piroozfar, D. P. (2018, July). *The application of Augmented Reality (AR) in the Architecture Engineering and Construction (AEC) industry*. International Conference on Construction in the 21st Century (CITC-10), Colombo, Sri Lanka.

Porter, P., Claxton, S., Brisbane, J., Bear, N., Wood, J., Peltonen, V., Della, P., Purdie, F., Smith, C., & Abeyratne, U. (2020). Diagnosing Chronic Obstructive Airway Disease on a Smartphone Using Patient-Reported Symptoms and Cough Analysis: Diagnostic Accuracy Study. *JMIR Formative Research*, *4*(11), e24587. doi:10.2196/24587 PMID:33170129

Postel, M. G., De Jong, C. A., & De Haan, H. A. (2005). Does e-therapy for problem drinking reach hidden populations? *The American Journal of Psychiatry*, *162*(12), 2393–2393. doi:10.1176/appi.ajp.162.12.2393 PMID:16330613

Postmes, T. (2003). A social identity approach to communication in organizations. *Social Identity at Work: Developing Theory for Organizational Practice*, *81*, 191-203.

Povey, J., Mills, P. P. J. R., Dingwall, K. M., Lowell, A., Singer, J., Rotumah, D., Bennett-Levy, J., & Nagel, T. (2016). Acceptability of mental health apps for Aboriginal and Torres Strait Islander Australians: A qualitative study. *Journal of Medical Internet Research*, *18*(3), e65. doi:10.2196/jmir.5314 PMID:26969043

Powers, J., & Magnoni, B. (2010). *Dueña de tu propia empresa: identificación, análisis y superación de las limitaciones a las pequeñas empresas de las mujeres en América Latina y el Caribe*. Fondo Multilateral de Inversiones, BID.

Prochaska, J. O., & Velicer, W. F. (1997). The transtheoretical model of health behavior change. *American Journal of Health Promotion*, *12*(1), 38–48. doi:10.4278/0890-1171-12.1.38 PMID:10170434

Proctor, R. W., & Vu, K.-P. L. (2016). Principles for Designing Interfaces Compatible With Human Information Processing. *International Journal of Human-Computer Interaction*, *32*(1), 2–22. doi:10.1080/10447318.2016.1105009

Proudfoot, J. G. (2004). Computer-based treatment for anxiety and depression: Is it feasible? Is it effective? *Neuroscience and Biobehavioral Reviews*, *28*(3), 353–363. doi:10.1016/j.neubiorev.2004.03.008 PMID:15225977

Proudfoot, J., Klein, B., Barak, A., Carlbring, P., Cuijpers, P., Lange, A., Ritterband, L., & Andersson, G. (2011). Establishing guidelines for executing and reporting internet intervention research. *Cognitive Behaviour Therapy*, *40*(2), 82–97. doi:10.1080/16506073.2011.573807 PMID:25155812

Qermane, K., & Mancha, R. (2020). WHOOP, Inc.: Digital Entrepreneurship During the Covid-19 Pandemic. *Entrepreneurship Education and Pedagogy*, 2515127420975181.

Quijada, M. D. R. B., Arriaga, J. L. D. O., & Domingo, D. A. (2020). Insights into user engagement on social media. Findings from two fashion retailers. *Electronic Markets*. Advance online publication. doi:10.100712525-020-00429-0

Radianti, J., Majchrzak, T. A., Fromm, J., & Wohlgenannt, I. (2020). A systematic review of immersive virtual reality applications for higher education: Design elements, lessons learned, and research agenda. *Computers & Education*, *147*, 103778. doi:10.1016/j.compedu.2019.103778

Radu, I. (2012). Why should my students use AR? A comparative review of the educational impacts of augmented-reality. *IEEE International Symposium on Mixed and Augmented Reality (ISMAR)*, 313–314. 10.1109/ISMAR.2012.6402590

Radu, I., & Antle, A. (2017). Embodied learning mechanics and their relationship to usability of handheld augmented reality. *IEEE Virtual Reality Workshop on K-12 Embodied Learning through Virtual Augmented Reality (KELVAR)*, 1–5. 10.1109/KELVAR.2017.7961561

Ragan, E. D., Sowndararajan, A., Kopper, R., & Bowman, D. A. (2010). The effects of higher levels of immersion on procedure memorization performance and implications for educational virtual environments. *Presence (Cambridge, Mass.)*, *19*(6), 527–543. doi:10.1162/pres_a_00016

Rahimian, H., Zamaneh, M. P., Ahmadpour, M., & Piri, M. (2014). A study of the relationship between empowerment and organizational learning among employees of gas transmission company. *J. Life Sci. Biomed*, *4*(6), 550–556.

Rai, A. S., Rai, A. S., Mavrikakis, E., & Lam, W. C. (2017). Teaching binocular indirect ophthalmoscopy to novice residents using an augmented reality simulator. *Canadian Journal of Ophthalmology, Journal Canadien D'ophtalmologie*, *52*(5), 430–434. doi:10.1016/j.jcjo.2017.02.015 PMID:28985799

Rantanen, E. M., Colombo, D. J., Miller, S. M., Alexander, A. L., Lacson, F. C., & Andre, A. D. (2013). Practicing Relevant Skills in the Classroom: Advice From Experts in the Industry to Professors. *Proceedings of the Human Factors and Ergonomics Society Annual Meeting*, *57*(1), 443–446. doi:10.1177/1541931213571096

Rantanen, E. M., & Moroney, W. F. (2012). Employers' Expectations for Education and Skills of New Human Factors/Ergonomics Professionals. *Proceedings of the Human Factors and Ergonomics Society Annual Meeting*, *56*(1), 581–585. doi:10.1177/1071181312561121

Reason, J. (1990). *Human error*. Cambridge University Press. doi:10.1017/CBO9781139062367

Reason, J. (2000). Human error: Models and management. *BMJ (Clinical Research Ed.)*, *320*(7237), 768–770. doi:10.1136/bmj.320.7237.768 PMID:10720363

Reidl, L., Cuevas, C., & López, R. (2010). *Métodos de Investigación en Psicología*. Universidad Nacional Autónoma de México. Recovered from https://www.rua.unam.mx/objeto/7987/metodos-de-investigacion-en-psicologia

Reiser, U., Connette, C. P., Fischer, J., Kubacki, J., Bubeck, A., Weisshardt, J., Jacobs, T., Parlitz, C., Hagele, M., & Verl, A. (2009). Care-O-bot 3 - Creating a product vision for service robot applications by integrating design and technology. *2009 IEEE/RSJ International Conference on Intelligent Robots and Systems IROS*, 1992-1998. 10.1109/IROS.2009.5354526

Renwick, D., Redman, T., & Maguire, S. (2013). Green human resource management: A review, process model, and research agenda. *International Journal of Management Reviews*, *15*(1), 1–14. doi:10.1111/j.1468-2370.2011.00328.x

Reynolds, W. M. (1982). Development of reliable and valid short-forms of the Marlowe-Crowne Social Desirability Scale. *Journal of Clinical Psychology, 38*(1), 119–125. doi:10.1002/1097-4679(198201)38:1<119::AID-JCLP2270380118>3.0.CO;2-I

Rickwood, C., and White, L. (2009). Pre-purchase decision-making for a complex service: retirement planning. *Journal of Services Marketing, 23*(3), 145-153.

Riek, L. D., Rabinowitch, T., Chakrabarti, B., & Robinson, P. (2009). How anthropomorphism affects empathy toward robots. *Proceedings of the 4th ACM/IEEE international conference on Human robot interaction.* 10.1145/1514095.1514158

Rigby, S., & Ryan, R. M. (2011). *Glued to games: How video games draw us in and hold us spellbound.* Praeger.

Rimanoczy, I., & Pearson, T. (2010). Role of HR in the new world of sustainability. *Industrial and Commercial Training, 42*(1), 11–17. doi:10.1108/00197851011013661

Rini, C., Porter, L. S., Somers, T. J., McKee, D. C., & Keefe, F. J. (2014). Retaining critical therapeutic elements of behavioral interventions translated for delivery via the Internet: Recommendations and an example using pain coping skills training. *Journal of Medical Internet Research, 16*(12), e245. doi:10.2196/jmir.3374 PMID:25532216

Ritterband, L. M., Andersson, G., Christensen, H. M., Carlbring, P., & Cuijpers, P. (2006). Directions for the international society for research on internet interventions (ISRII). *Journal of Medical Internet Research, 8*(3), e23. doi:10.2196/jmir.8.3.e23 PMID:17032639

Ritterband, L. M., Thorndike, F. P., Cox, D. J., Kovatchev, B. P., & Gonder-Frederick, L. A. (2009). A behavior change model for internet interventions. *Annals of Behavioral Medicine, 38*(1), 18–27. doi:10.100712160-009-9133-4 PMID:19802647

Riva, G., Baños, R. M., Botella, C., Mantovani, F., & Gaggioli, A. (2016). Transforming Experience: The Potential of Augmented Reality and Virtual Reality for Enhancing Personal and Clinical Change. *Frontiers in Psychiatry, 7*, 164. doi:10.3389/fpsyt.2016.00164 PMID:27746747

Rizzo, A. S., & Kim, G. J. (2005). A SWOT analysis of the field of virtual reality rehabilitation and therapy. *Presence (Cambridge, Mass.), 14*(2), 119–146. doi:10.1162/1054746053967094

Roberts, S. (2020, Dec 5). The Swiss Cheese Model of Pandemic Defense. *New York Times.* https://www.nytimes.com/2020/12/05/health/coronavirus-swiss-cheese-infection-mackay.html

Roberts, K. H., & O'Reilly, C. A. (1974). Failures in upward communication in organizations: Three possible culprits. *Academy of Management Journal, 17*(2), 205–215.

Robinson, A. R., Gravenstein, N., Cooper, L. A., Lizdas, D., Luria, I., & Lampotang, S. (2014). A mixed-reality part-task trainer for subclavian venous access. *Simulation in Healthcare: Journal of the Society for Simulation in Healthcare, 9*(1), 56–64. doi:10.1097/SIH.0b013e31829b3fb3 PMID:24310163

Robroek, S. J., Lindeboom, D. E., & Burdorf, A. (2012). Initial and sustained participation in an internet-delivered long-term worksite health promotion program on physical activity and nutrition. *Journal of Medical Internet Research*, *14*(2), e43. doi:10.2196/jmir.1788 PMID:22390886

Roepke, A. M., Jaffee, S. R., Riffle, O. M., McGonigal, J., Broome, R., & Maxwell, B. (2015). Randomized controlled trial of SuperBetter, a smartphone-based/internet-based self-help tool to reduce depressive symptoms. *Games for Health Journal*, *4*(3), 235–246. doi:10.1089/g4h.2014.0046 PMID:26182069

Rogers, K., Funke, J., Frommel, J., Stamm, S., & Weber, M. (2019). Exploring Interaction Fidelity in Virtual Reality: Object Manipulation and Whole-Body Movements. *Proceedings of the 2019 CHI Conference on Human Factors in Computing Systems*, 1–14. 10.1145/3290605.3300644

Rohan, D. (2013). *Neuroeconomic Studies on Personality and Decision-Making* (Tesis doctoral). The University of Minnesota.

Roncone, K. (2004). Nanotechnology: What next-generation warriors will wear. *Journal of Military Psychology*, *21*, 31–33.

Ronquillo, Y., Meyers, A., & Korvek, S. J. (2020). Digital health. In *StatPearls*. StatPearls Publishing. https://www.ncbi.nlm.nih.gov/books/NBK470260/

Rosenstock, I. M. (1974). The health belief model and preventive health behavior. *Health Education Monographs*, *2*(4), 354–386. doi:10.1177/109019817400200405

Rose, S., Clark, M., Samouel, P., & Hair, N. (2012). Online Customer Experience in e-Retailing: An empirical model of Antecedents and Outcomes. *Journal of Retailing*, *88*(2), 308–322. doi:10.1016/j.jretai.2012.03.001

Rozental, A., Andersson, G., Boettcher, J., Ebert, D. D., Cuijpers, P., Knaevelsrud, C., Ljótsson, B., Kaldo, V., Titov, N., & Carlbring, P. (2014). Consensus statement on defining and measuring negative effects of Internet interventions. *Internet Interventions: the Application of Information Technology in Mental and Behavioural Health*, *1*(1), 12–19. doi:10.1016/j.invent.2014.02.001

Rozgonjuk, D., Elhai, J. D., Ryan, T., & Scott, G. G. (2019). Fear of missing out is associated with disrupted activities from receiving smartphone notifications and surface learning in college students. *Computers & Education*, *140*, 103590. doi:10.1016/j.compedu.2019.05.016

Rozgonjuk, D., Kattago, M., & Täht, K. (2018). Social media use in lectures mediates the relationship between procrastination and problematic smartphone use. *Computers in Human Behavior*, *89*, 191–198. doi:10.1016/j.chb.2018.08.003

Rummell, C. M., & Joyce, N. R. (2010). "So wat do u want to wrk on 2day?": The ethical implications of online counseling. *Ethics & Behavior*, *20*(6), 482–496. doi:10.1080/10508422.2010.521450

Ruwaard, J., Broeksteeg, J., Schrieken, B., Emmelkamp, P., & Lange, A. (2010). Web-based therapist-assisted cognitive behavioral treatment of panic symptoms: A randomized controlled trial with a three-year follow-up. *Journal of Anxiety Disorders*, 24(4), 387–396. doi:10.1016/j. janxdis.2010.01.010 PMID:20227241

Ruwaard, J., Schrieken, B., Schrijver, M., Broeksteeg, J., Dekker, J., Vermeulen, H., & Lange, A. (2009). Standardized web-based cognitive behavioural therapy of mild to moderate depression: A randomized controlled trial with a long-term follow-up. *Cognitive Behaviour Therapy*, 38(4), 206–221. doi:10.1080/16506070802408086 PMID:19221919

Ryan, R. M., & Deci, E. L. (2000). Self-determination theory and the facilitation of intrinsic motivation, social development, and well-being. *The American Psychologist*, 55(1), 68–78. doi:10.1037/0003-066X.55.1.68 PMID:11392867

Ryan, R. M., & Rigby, C. S. (2018). *MIT handbook of gamification*. MIT Press.

Ryan, R. M., Rigby, C. S., & Przybylski, A. (2006). The motivational pull of video games: A self-determination theory approach. *Motivation and Emotion*, 30(4), 344–360. doi:10.100711031-006-9051-8

Saadat, V., & Saadat, Z. (2016). Organizational learning as a key role of organizational success. *Procedia: Social and Behavioral Sciences*, 230(12), 219–225. doi:10.1016/j.sbspro.2016.09.028

Saadon, N. F. S. M., Ahmad, I., Hanapi, A. N. C. P., & Che, H. (2020). The Implementation of Augmented Reality in Increasing Student Motivation: Systematic Literature Review. *IOP Conference Series. Materials Science and Engineering*, 854, 012043. doi:10.1088/1757-899X/854/1/012043

Sacristan, J. (2013). La pyme tiene problema para lanzar su e-commerce. *El economista*. Recovered from https://www.eleconomista.es/catalunya/noticias/4766122/04/13/La-pyme-tiene-problemas-para-lanzar-su-ecommerce.html

Saltan, F., & Arslan, O. (2016). The use of augmented reality in formal education: A scoping review. *Eurasia Journal of Mathematics, Science and Technology Education*, 13(2), 503–520. doi:10.12973/eurasia.2017.00628a

Sandoval, E., & Guerra, E. (2010). *Migrantes e indígenas: acceso a la información en comunidades virtuales interculturales*. Recuperado de www.eumed.net/libros/2010b/684/

Santos, M. E. C., Chen, A., Taketomi, T., Yamamoto, G., Miyazaki, J., & Kato, H. (2014). Augmented reality learning experiences: Survey of prototype design and evaluation. *IEEE Transactions on Learning Technologies*, 7(1), 38–56. doi:10.1109/TLT.2013.37

Sarter, N. B., & Woods, D. D. (1995). How in the world did we ever get into that mode? Mode error and awareness in supervisory control. *Human Factors*, 37(1), 5–19. doi:10.1518/001872095779049516

Schaik, P. (2016). Chapter. In P. Barker (Ed.), Electronic Performance Support: Using Digital Technology to Enhance Human Ability (pp. 3–29). Taylor & Francis Group. doi:10.4324/9781315579047

Schein, E. (1996). Kurt Lewin's Change Theory in the field and in the classroom: Notes toward a model of managed learning. *Systems Practice, 9*(1), 27–47. doi:10.1007/BF02173417

Schmiedinger, B., Valentin, K., & Stephan, E. (2005). Competence based business development-organizational competencies as basis for successful companies. *Journal of Universal Knowledge Management, 1*, 13–20.

Schneider, F., de Vries, H., Candel, M., van de Kar, A., & van Osch, L. (2013). Periodic email prompts to re-use an internet-delivered computer-tailored lifestyle program: Influence of prompt content and timing. *Journal of Medical Internet Research, 15*(1), e23. doi:10.2196/jmir.2151 PMID:23363466

Schneider, F., van Osch, L., & de Vries, H. (2012a). Identifying factors for optimal development of health-related websites: A Delphi study among experts and potential future users. *Journal of Medical Internet Research, 14*(1), e18. doi:10.2196/jmir.1863 PMID:22357411

Schneider, F., van Osch, L., Schulz, D. N., Kremers, S. P. J., & de Vries, H. (2012b). The influence of user characteristics and a periodic email prompt on exposure to an internet-delivered computer-tailored lifestyle program. *Journal of Medical Internet Research, 14*(2), e40. doi:10.2196/jmir.1939 PMID:22382037

Schueller, S. M., Hunter, J. F., Figueroa, C., & Aguilera, A. (2019). Use of digital mental health for marginalized and underserved populations. *Current Treatment Options in Psychiatry, 6*(3), 243–255. doi:10.100740501-019-00181-z

Schultz, C. D. (2016). Insights from consumer interactions on a social networking site: Findings from six apparel retail brands. *Electronic Markets, 26*(3), 203–217. doi:10.100712525-015-0209-7

Schwartz, M., Oppold, P., & Hancock, P. A. (2019). Wearables and Workload. In Critical Issues Impacting Science, Technology, Society (STS), and Our Future (pp. 145-170). IGI Global. doi:10.4018/978-1-5225-7949-6.ch007

Schwarzer, R. (1999). Self-regulatory processes in the adoption and maintenance of health behaviors. *Journal of Health Psychology, 4*(2), 115–127. doi:10.1177/135910539900400208 PMID:22021474

Schwarzer, R. (2011). *Health Behavior Change.* Oxford University Press., doi:10.1093/oxfordhb/9780195342819.013.0024

Schwarzer, R., & Luszczynska, A. (2008). How to Overcome Health-Compromising Behaviors: The Health Action Process Approach. *European Psychologist, 13*(2), 141–151. doi:10.1027/1016-9040.13.2.141

Scott, H., Biello, S. M., & Woods, H. C. (2019). Identifying drivers for bedtime social media use despite sleep costs: The adolescent perspective. *Sleep Health, 5*(6), 539–545. . doi:10.1016/j.sleh.2019.07.006 PMID:31523005

Sedighi, M. (2016). Application of word co-occurrence analysis method in mapping of the scientific fields (case study: The field of Informetrics). *Computer Science. Library Review.* Advance online publication. doi:10.1108/LR-07-2015-0075

Seshadri, D. R., Davies, E. V., Harlow, E. R., Hsu, J. J., Knighton, S. C., Walker, T. A., Voos, J. E., & Drummond, C. K. (2020). Wearable sensors for COVID-19: A call to action to harness our digital infrastructure for remote patient monitoring and virtual assessments. *Frontiers in Digital Health, 2,* 8. doi:10.3389/fdgth.2020.00008

Shaham, H. (2020). *Augmented reality instruction manual: The perfect user manual?* TechSee: Intelligent Virtual Assistance. https://techsee.me/blog/augmented-reality-instruction-manual/

Shakiba, M., Nazemipour, M., Heidarzadeh, A., & Mansournia, M. A. (2020). Prevalence of asymptomatic COVID-19 infection using a seroepidemiological survey. *Epidemiology and Infection, 148,* 1–7. doi:10.1017/S0950268820002745 PMID:33183367

Shames, S., Bello, N. A., Schwartz, A., Homma, S., Patel, N., Garza, J., Kim, J. H., Goolsby, M., DiFiori, J. P., & Engel, D. J. (2020). Echocardiographic characterization of female professional basketball players in the US. *JAMA Cardiology, 5*(9), 991–998. doi:10.1001/jamacardio.2020.0988 PMID:32936269

Shamp, S. A. (1991). Mechanomorphism in Perception of Computer Communication Partners. *Computers in Human Behavior, 7*(3), 147–161. doi:10.1016/0747-5632(91)90004-K

Shandley, K., Austin, D. W., Klein, B., Pier, C., Schattner, P., Pierce, D., & Wade, V. (2008). Therapist-assisted, internet-based treatment for panic disorder: Can general practitioners achieve comparable patient outcomes to psychologists? *Journal of Medical Internet Research, 10*(2), e14. doi:10.2196/jmir.1033 PMID:18487138

Shapiro, L. (Ed.). (2014). *The Routledge handbook of embodied cognition.* Routledge. doi:10.4324/9781315775845

Sharp, C. (2001). *Evaluation of Organizational learning intervention and Communities of Practice.* Paper presented in Australasian Evaluation Society Conference, Canberra.

Sharp, H., Rogers, Y., & Preece, J. (2019). *Interaction Design: Beyond Human-Computer Interaction.* John Wiley & Sons, Inc.

Shcherbina, A., Mattsson, C. M., Waggott, D., Salisbury, H., Christle, J. W., Hastie, T., Wheeler, M., & Ashley, E. A. (2017). Accuracy in wrist-worn, sensor-based measurements of heart rate and energy expenditure in a diverse cohort. *Journal of Personalized Medicine, 7*(2), 3. doi:10.3390/jpm7020003 PMID:28538708

Shereen, M. A., Khan, S., Kazmi, A., Bashir, N., & Siddique, R. (2020). COVID-19 infection: Origin, transmission, and characteristics of human coronaviruses. *Journal of Advanced Research, 24,* 91–98. doi:10.1016/j.jare.2020.03.005 PMID:32257431

Shilton, K. (2013). Values levers: Building ethics into design. *Science, Technology & Human Values, 38*(3), 374–397. doi:10.1177/0162243912436985

Shilton, K. (2018). Values and ethics in human-computer interaction. *Foundations and Trends in Human–Computer Interaction, 12*(2), 1–53. doi:10.1561/1100000073

Shilton, K., & Anderson, S. (2017). Blended, not bossy: Ethics roles, responsibilities and expertise in design. *Interacting with Computers, 29*(1), 71–79. doi:10.1093/iwc/iww002

Shneiderman, B. (2000). Universal usability. *Communications of the ACM, 43*(5), 84–91. doi:10.1145/332833.332843

Short, S. E., & Mollborn, S. (2015). Social determinants and health behaviors: Conceptual frames and empirical advances. *Current Opinion in Psychology, 5*, 78–84. doi:10.1016/j.copsyc.2015.05.002 PMID:26213711

Shukla, M. (2011). *Entrepreneurship and small business management.* Kitab Mahal.

Siebenhüner, B., & Arnold, M. (2007). Organizational learning to manage sustainable development. *Business Strategy and the Environment, 16*(5), 339–353. doi:10.1002/bse.579

Sierra, E. A., Benne, M., & Fisk, A. D. (2002). It's a Zoo Out there: Teaching Human Factors in a Real—World Context. *Ergonomics in Design, 10*(3), 6–10. doi:10.1177/106480460201000303

Siew, C. Y., Ong, S. K., & Nee, A. Y. C. (2019). A practical augmented reality-assisted maintenance system framework for adaptive user support. *Robotics and Computer-integrated Manufacturing, 59*, 115–129. doi:10.1016/j.rcim.2019.03.010

Simao, L. B. (2016). External relationships in the organizational innovation. *RAI Revista de Administração e Inovação, 13*(3), 156–165. doi:10.1016/j.rai.2016.06.002

Sims, V. K., Chin, M. G., Smith, H. S., Ballion, T., Sushil, D. J., Strand, M., Mendoza, S., Shumaker, R., & Finkelstein, N. (2006). Effects of eye structure and color on attributions for intelligent agents. *Proceedings of the Human Factors and Ergonomics Society, 50.* 10.1177/154193120605001728

Singh, K., Drouin, K., Newmark, L. P., Lee, J., Faxvaag, A., Rozenblum, R., Pabo, E. A., Landman, A., Klinger, E., & Bates, D. W. (2016). Many mobile health apps target high-need, high-cost populations, but gaps remain. *Health Affairs, 35*(12), 2310–2318. doi:10.1377/hlthaff.2016.0578 PMID:27920321

Sivak, M., & Schoettle, B. (2015). Road safety with self-driving vehicles: General limitations and road sharing with conventional vehicles. University of Michigan, Ann Arbor, Transportation Research Institute.

Sjoding, M. W., Dickson, R. P., Iwashyna, T. J., Gay, S. E., & Valley, T. S. (2020). Racial bias in pulse oximetry measurement. *The New England Journal of Medicine, 383*(25), 2477–2478. doi:10.1056/NEJMc2029240 PMID:33326721

Skulmowski, A., & Rey, G. D. (2018). Embodied learning: Introducing a taxonomy based on bodily engagement and task integration. *Cognitive Research: Principles and Implications, 3*(1), 6. doi:10.118641235-018-0092-9 PMID:29541685

Slovic, P., Finucane, M. L., Peters, E., & MacGregor, D. G. (2004). Risk as analysis and risk as feelings: Some thoughts about affect, reason, risk, and rationality. *Risk Analysis, 24*(2), 311–322. doi:10.1111/j.0272-4332.2004.00433.x PMID:15078302

Smarr, B. L., Aschbacher, K., Fisher, S. M., Chowdhary, A., Dilchert, S., Puldon, K., Rao, A., Hecht, F. M., & Mason, A. E. (2020). Feasibility of continuous fever monitoring using wearable devices. *Scientific Reports, 10*(1), 1–11. doi:10.103841598-020-78355-6 PMID:33318528

Sohn, S., Rees, P., Wildridge, B., Kalk, N. J., & Carter, B. (2019). Prevalence of problematic smartphone usage and associated mental health outcomes amongst children and young people: A systematic review, meta-analysis and GRADE of the evidence. *BMC Psychiatry, 19*(1), 1–10. doi:10.118612888-019-2350-x PMID:30606141

Sonnichsen, R. (2000). *High Impact Internal Evaluation. A Practitioner's Guide to Evaluating and Consulting Inside Organizations.* Sage. doi:10.4135/9781483328485

Spectar. (2019). *Optimizing construction with augmented reality: how augmented reality is shaping the smart job site of tomorrow.* https://cdn2.hubspot.net/hubfs/4905971/SpectarWhitepaper.pdf

Spek, V., Cuijpers, P., Nyklicek, I., Riper, H., Keyzer, J., & Pop, V. (2007). Internet-based cognitive behaviour therapy for symptoms of depression and anxiety: A meta-analysis. *Psychological Medicine, 37*(3), 319–328. doi:10.1017/S0033291706008944 PMID:17112400

Spellman, B. A., & Holyoak, K. J. (1996). Pragmatics in analogical mapping. *Cognitive Psychology, 31*(3), 307–346. doi:10.1006/cogp.1996.0019 PMID:8975685

Spiekermann, S. (2015). *Ethical IT innovation: A value-based system design approach.* CRC Press. doi:10.1201/b19060

Stallard, P., Richardson, T., & Velleman, S. (2010). Clinicians' attitudes towards the use of computerized cognitive behaviour therapy (cCBT) with children and adolescents. *Behavioural and Cognitive Psychotherapy, 38*(5), 545–560. doi:10.1017/S1352465810000421 PMID:20615273

Stanney, K. M., Nye, H., Haddad, S., Padron, C. K., Hale, K. S., & Cohn, J. V. (2020, in press). eXtended reality environments. In G. Salvendy & W. Karwowski (Eds.), Handbook of human factors and ergonomics (5th ed.). New York: John Wiley.

Stanney, K. M., Hale, K. S., Nahmens, I., & Kennedy, R. S. (2003). What to expect from immersive virtual environment exposure: Influences of gender, body mass index, and past experience. *Human Factors, 45*(3), 504–520. doi:10.1518/hfes.45.3.504.27254 PMID:14702999

Stanney, K. M., Lawson, B. D., Rokers, B., Dennison, M., Fidopiastis, C., Stoffregen, T., Weech, S., & Fulvio, J. M. (2020). Identifying causes of and solutions for cybersickness in immersive technology: Reformulation of a research and development agenda. *International Journal of Human-Computer Interaction, 36*(19), 1783–1803. doi:10.1080/10447318.2020.1828535

Stanney, K. M., Moralez, L., Archer, J., Brawand, N. P., Martin, E., & Fidopiastis, C. M. (2020). (Manuscript submitted for publication). Performance gains from adaptive extended reality training fueled by artificial intelligence. *Journal of Defense Modeling and Simulation.*

Stark, S. (1963). Creative leadership: Human vs. metal brains. *Academy of Management Journal, 6*(2), 160–169.

Statista. (2018). *E-commerce share of total global retail sales in 2016, by region*. The Statistics Portal. Recovered from https://www.statista.com/statistics/239300/number-of-online-buyers-in-selected-countries/

Statista. (2018). *Number of digital buyers worldwide from 2014 to 2021 (in billions)*. The Statistics Portal. Recovered from https://www.statista.com/statistics/251666/number-of-digital-buyers-worldwide/

Statista. (2018). *Retail e-commerce sales worldwide from 2014 to 2021 (in billions US dollars)*. The Statistics Portal. Recovered from https://www.statista.com/statistics/379046/worldwide-retail-e-commerce-sales/

Stephens, C., Dehais, F., Roy, R. N., Harrivel, A., Last, M. C., Kennedy, K., & Pope, A. (2018). Biocybernetic adaptation strategies: machine awareness of human engagement for improved operational performance. In *International Conference on Augmented Cognition* (pp. 89-98). 10.1007/978-3-319-91470-1_9

Stieff, M., Lira, M. E., & Scopelitis, S. A. (2016). Gesture supports spatial thinking in STEM. *Cognition and Instruction, 34*(2), 80–99. doi:10.1080/07370008.2016.1145122

Stolovitch, H. D., & Keeps, E. (2011). *Telling ain't training*. American Society for Training and Development.

Stone, N., Chaparro, A., Keebler, J., Chaparro, B., & McConnell, D. (2018). *Introduction to Human Factors*. CRC Press., doi:10.1201/9781315153704

Storms, R. L. (2002). Auditory-visual cross-modality interaction and illusions. In K. M. Stanney (Ed.), *Handbook of Virtual Environments: Design, Implementation, and Applications* (pp. 455–470). Lawrence Erlbaum Associates.

Stothart, C., Mitchum, A., & Yehnert, C. (2015). Supplemental material for the attentional cost of receiving a cell phone notification. *Journal of Experimental Psychology. Human Perception and Performance, 41*(4), 893–897. doi:10.1037/xhp0000100 PMID:26121498

Strange, A. (2017, December 6). *BMW Uses ARKit to Let You Customize Your New Car in iOS*. Next Reality. https://mobile-ar.reality.news/news/bmw-uses-arkit-let-you-customize-your-new-car-ios-0181532/

Stroud, N. J., Peacock, C., & Curry, A. L. (2020). The effects of mobile push notifications on news consumption and learning. *Digital Journalism, 8*(1), 32–48. doi:10.1080/21670811.2019.1655462

Substance Abuse and Mental Health Services Administration. (2017). *Key substance use and mental health indicators in the United States: Results from the 2016 National Survey on Drug Use and Health* (HHS Publication No. SMA 17-5044, NSDUH Series H-52). Rockville, MD: Center for Behavioral Health Statistics and Quality, Substance Abuse and Mental Health Services Administration. Retrieved from https://www. samhsa.gov/data/

Suso-Ribera, C., Fernández-Álvarez, J., García-Palacios, A., Hoffman, H. G., Bretón-López, J., Banos, R. M., Quero, S., & Botella, C. (2019). Virtual reality, augmented reality, and in vivo exposure therapy: A preliminary comparison of treatment efficacy in small animal phobia. *Cyberpsychology, Behavior, and Social Networking, 22*(1), 31–38. doi:10.1089/cyber.2017.0672 PMID:30335525

Taj, F., Klein, M. C. A., & van Halteren, A. (2019). Digital health behavior change technology: Bibliometric and scoping review of two decades of research. *JMIR mHealth and uHealth, 7*(12), e13311. doi:10.2196/13311 PMID:31833836

Talmaki, S. A., Dong, S., & Kamat, V. R. (2010). *Geospatial Databases and Augmented Reality Visualization for Improving Safety in Urban Excavation Operations.* doi:10.1061/41109(373)10

Tandon, A., Kaur, P., Dhir, A., & Mäntymäki, M. (2020). Sleepless due to social media? Investigating problematic sleep due to social media and social media sleep hygiene. *Computers in Human Behavior, 113*, 106487. doi:10.1016/j.chb.2020.106487

Tang, A., Owen, C., Biocca, F., & Mou, W. (2003, April). Comparative effectiveness of augmented reality in object assembly. In *Proceedings of the SIGCHI conference on Human factors in computing systems* (pp. 73-80). 10.1145/642611.642626

TAR. (2020). Tactical augmented reality. http://www.tacticalaugmentedreality.com

Tate, D. F., Wing, R. R., & Winett, R. A. (2001). Using internet technology to deliver a behavioral weight loss program. *Journal of the American Medical Association, 285*(9), 1172–1177. doi:10.1001/jama.285.9.1172 PMID:11231746

Tauber, E. M. (1981). Brand franchise extension: New product benefits from existing brand names. *Business Horizons, 24*(2), 36–41. doi:10.1016/0007-6813(81)90144-0

Taylor, K., & Silver, L. (2019). *Smartphone ownership is growing rapidly around the world, but not always equally.* Pew Research Center. https://www.pewresearch.org/global/2019/02/05/smartphone-ownership-is-growing-rapidly-around-the-world-but-not-always-equally/

Technologies, U. (2020). *Unity Manual: Colliders.* Retrieved October 28, 2020, from https://docs.unity3d.com/Manual/CollidersOverview.html

Teixeira, A. A., Jabbour, C. J. C., & de Sousa Jabbour, A. B. L. (2012). Relationship between green management and environmental training in companies located in Brazil: A theoretical framework and case studies. *International Journal of Production Economics, 140*(1), 318–329. doi:10.1016/j.ijpe.2012.01.009

Tene, O., & Polonetsky, J. (2014). A theory of creepy: Technology, privacy and shifting social norms. *Yale Journal of Law and Technology, 16*(1), 59–102. https://yjolt.org/sites/default/files/theory_of_creepy_1_0.pdf

Thakker, D. R. (2011). Culture and cognitive theory: Toward a reformulation. *Cult.Cog. Psychopathol, 3*, 53–71.

Thakur, N., Lovinsky-Desir, S., Bime, C., Wisnivesky, J. P., & Celedón, J. C. (2020). The Structural and Social Determinants of the Racial/Ethnic Disparities in the US COVID-19 Pandemic. What's Our Role? *American Journal of Respiratory and Critical Care Medicine*, *202*(7), 943–949. doi:10.1164/rccm.202005-1523PP PMID:32677842

Thomas, R., Bhat, R., Khan, A., & Devan, P. (2018). Deloitte and The Manufacturing Institute skills gap and future of work study. *Deloitte Insights*. https://www.themanufacturinginstitute.org/wp-content/uploads/2020/03/MI-Deloitte-skills-gap-Future-of-Workforce-study-2018.pdf

Thomas, K. W., & Velthouse, B. A. (1990). Cognitive elements of empowerment: An "interpretive" model of intrinsic task motivation. *Academy of Management Review*, *15*(4), 666–681.

Titov, N. (2007). Status of computerized cognitive behavioural therapy for adults. *Australasian Psychiatry*, *41*(2), 95–114. PMID:17464688

Titov, N., Andrews, G., Davies, M., McIntyre, K., Robinson, E., & Solley, K. (2010). Internet treatment for depression: A randomized controlled trial comparing clinician vs. technician assistance. *PLoS One*, *5*(6), e10939. doi:10.1371/journal.pone.0010939 PMID:20544030

Titov, N., Dear, B. F., Schwencke, G., Andrews, G., Johnston, L., Craske, M. G., & McEvoy, P. (2011). Transdiagnostic internet treatment for anxiety and depression: A randomised controlled trial. *Behaviour Research and Therapy*, *49*(8), 441–452. doi:10.1016/j.brat.2011.03.007 PMID:21679925

Tomasello, M. (2010). *Culture and Cognitive Development*. Institute of Evolutionary Anthropology.

Tomás, J. M., & Oliver, A. (1999). Rosenberg's self-esteem scale: Two factors or method effects. *Structural Equation Modeling*, *6*(1), 84–98. doi:10.1080/10705519909540120

Torous, J., Andersson, G., Bertagnoli, A., Christensen, H., Cuijpers, P., Firth, J., Haim, A., Hsin, H., Hollis, C., Lewis, S., Mohr, D. C., Pratap, A., Roux, S., Sherrill, J., & Arean, P. A. (2019). Towards a consensus around standards for smartphone apps and digital mental health. *World Psychiatry; Official Journal of the World Psychiatric Association (WPA)*, *18*(1), 97–98. doi:10.1002/wps.20592 PMID:30600619

Torous, J., Myrick, K. J., Rauseo-Ricupero, N., & Firth, J. (2020). Digital mental health and COVID-19: Using technology today to accelerate the curve on access and quality tomorrow. *JMIR Mental Health*, *7*(3), e18848. doi:10.2196/18848 PMID:32213476

Toumpaniari, K., Loyens, S., Mavilidi, M.-F., & Paas, F. (2015). Preschool Children's Foreign Language Vocabulary Learning by Embodying Words Through Physical Activity and Gesturing. *Educational Psychology Review*, *27*(3), 445–456. doi:10.100710648-015-9316-4

Tower, N. (2018, Dec 12). In an ethnic breakdown of sports, NBA takes lead for most diverse. *Global Sport Matters*. https://globalsportmatters.com/culture/2018/12/12/in-an-ethnic-breakdown-of-sports-nba-takes-lead-for-most-diverse/

Tran, Q., & Tian, Y. (2013). Organizational structure: Influencing factors and impact on afirm. *Am. J. Ind. Bus. Manag*, *3*(02), 229–236. doi:10.4236/ajibm.2013.32028

Tremoulet, P. D., Leslie, A. M., & Hall, G. (2000). Infant attention to the shape and color of objects: Individuation and identification. *Cognitive Development, 15,* 499–522. doi:10.1016/S0885-2014(01)00038-7

Tschabitscher, H. (2011). *How many emails are sent every day?* Retrieved on April 20, 2011 from http://www.radicati.com/

Tucker, M. L., Meyer, G. D., & Westerman, J. W. (1996). Organizational communication: Development of internal strategic competitive advantage. *The Journal of Business Communication, 33*(1), 51-69.

Turing, A. M. (1950). Computing machinery and intelligence. *Mind, 59*(236), 433–460. doi:10.1093/mind/LIX.236.433

Turner, L. D., Allen, S. M., & Whitaker, R. M. (2017). Reachable but not receptive: Enhancing smartphone interruptibility prediction by modelling the extent of user engagement with notifications. *Pervasive and Mobile Computing, 40,* 480–494. doi:10.1016/j.pmcj.2017.01.011

Ullo, S. L., Piedimonte, P., Leccese, F., & De Francesco, E. (2019). A step toward the standardization of maintenance and training services in C4I military systems with Mixed Reality application. *Measurement, 138,* 149–156. doi:10.1016/j.measurement.2019.02.036

Uncapher, M. R., & Wagner, A. D. (2018). Minds and brains of media multitaskers: Current findings and future directions. *Proceedings of the National Academy of Sciences of the United States of America, 115*(40), 9889–9896. doi:10.1073/pnas.1611612115 PMID:30275312

Underwood, K. (2020, April 1). Augmented reality goes airborne. *Signal.* https://www.afcea.org/content/augmented-reality-goes-airborne

UNESCO. (2001). *Artesanías creadoras.* París: Unesco, Sección de Artesanías y Diseño.

United Nations Industrial Development Organisation (UNIDO). (2001). *Women Entrepreneurship Development in Selected African Countries.* Working Paper No. 7, United Nations Industrial Development Organisation.

United Nations, Department of Economic and Social Affairs, Population Division. (2019). *World Population Ageing 2019: Highlights* (ST/ESA/SER.A/430). Author.

United States Fleet Forces Command. (2017). *Comprehensive Review of Recent Surface Force Incidents.* https://www.hsdl.org/?abstract&did=805423

Vallée-Tourangeau, F., Sirota, M., & Vallée-Tourangeau, G. (2016). Interactivity mitigates the impact of working memory depletion on mental arithmetic performance. *Cognitive Research: Principles and Implications, 1*(1), 26. doi:10.118641235-016-0027-2 PMID:28180177

Valmaggia, L. R., Latif, L., Kempton, M. J., & Rus-Calafell, M. (2016). Virtual reality in the psychological treatment for mental health problems: A systematic review of recent evidence. *Psychiatry Research, 236,* 189–195. doi:10.1016/j.psychres.2016.01.015 PMID:26795129

Van de Ven, A. H., Angle, H. L., & Poole, M. S. (Eds.). (2000). *Research on the Management of Innovation: The Minnesota Studies*. Oxford University Press.

Vandenberg, O., Martiny, D., Rochas, O., van Belkum, A., & Kozlakidis, Z. (2020). Considerations for diagnostic COVID-19 tests. *Nature Reviews. Microbiology*, 1–13. PMID:33057203

VanderMeer, D., Dutta, K., & Datta, A. (2012). A Cost-Based Database Request Distribution Technique for Online e-Commerce Applications. *Management Information Systems Quarterly*, *36*(2), 479–507. doi:10.2307/41703464

Vansina, L. (1988). The general manager and organizational leadership. In M. Lambrechts (Ed.), *Corporate revival: Managing into the nineties*. University Press.

Venero, P., Rowe, A., & Boyer, J. (2012). Using Augmented Reality to Help Maintain Persistent Stare of a Moving Target inn an Urban Environment. *Proceedings of the Human Factors and Ergonomics Society Annual Meeting*, *56*(1), 2575–2579. doi:10.1177/1071181312561535

Venkatesh, V., Morris, M. G., Davis, G. B., & Davis, F. D. (2003). User acceptance of information technology: Toward a unified view. *MIS Quarterly*, *27*(3), 425–478. doi:10.2307/30036540

Venkatesh, V., Thong, J. Y. L., & Xu, X. (2012). Consumer acceptance and use of information technology: Extending the unified theory of acceptance and use of technology. *MIS Quarterly*, *36*(1), 157–178. doi:10.2307/41410412

Venkatesh, V., & Davis, F. D. (2000). A Theoretical Extension of the Technology Acceptance Model: Four Longitudinal Field Studies. *Management Science*, *46*(2), 186–204. doi:10.1287/mnsc.46.2.186.11926

Ventura, S., Baños, R. M., Botella, C., & Mohamudally, N. (2018). Virtual and augmented reality: New frontiers for clinical psychology. *State of the Art Virtual Reality and Augmented Reality Knowhow*, 99-118.

Vigerland, S., Ljótsson, B., Bergdahl Gustafsson, F., Hagert, S., Thulin, U., Andersson, G., & Serlachius, E. (2014). Attitudes towards the use of computerized cognitive behavior therapy (cCBT) with children and adolescents: A survey among Swedish mental health professionals. *Internet Interventions: the Application of Information Technology in Mental and Behavioural Health*, *1*(3), 111–117. doi:10.1016/j.invent.2014.06.002

Vincenzi, D. A., Valimont, B., Macchiarella, N., Opalenik, C., Gangadharan, S. N., & Majoros, A. E. (2003, October). The effectiveness of cognitive elaboration using augmented reality as a training and learning paradigm. *Proceedings of the Human Factors and Ergonomics Society Annual Meeting*, *47*(19), 2054–2058. doi:10.1177/154193120304701909

Vogels, E. A. (2019). *Millennials stand out for their technology use, but older generations also embrace digital life*. https://www.pewresearch.org/fact-tank/2019/09/09/us-generations-technology-use/

Volberda, H. W., Van Den Bosch, F. A., & Heij, C. V. (2013). Management innova-tion: Management as fertile ground for innovation. *European Management Review*, *10*(1), 1–15. doi:10.1111/emre.12007

von Ahn, L., Blum, M., & Langford, J. (2004). Telling humans and computers apart automatically. *Communications of the ACM*, *47*(2), 56–60. doi:10.1145/966389.966390

Wanberg, J., Caston, M., & Berthold, D. (2019). Ergonomics in Alternative Vehicle Design: Educating Students on the Practical Application of Anthropometric Data. *Ergonomics in Design*, *27*(3), 24–29. doi:10.1177/1064804618782615

Wang, P. S., Aguilar-Gaxiola, S., Alonso, J., Angermeyer, M. C., Borges, G., Bromet, E. J., ... Wells, J. E. (2007). Worldwide Use of Mental Health Services for Anxiety, Mood, and Substance Disorders: Results from 17 Countries in the WHO World Mental Health (WMH) Surveys. *Lancet*, *370*(9590), 841–850. doi:10.1016/S0140-6736(07)61414-7 PMID:17826169

Wang, X., Love, P. E. D., Kim, M. J., Park, C.-S., Sing, C.-P., & Hou, L. (2013). A conceptual framework for integrating building information modeling with augmented reality. *Automation in Construction*, *34*, 37–44. doi:10.1016/j.autcon.2012.10.012

Wang, Y., Minor, M., & Wei, J. (2011). Aesthetics and the online shopping environment: Understanding consumer responses. *Journal of Retailing*, *87*(1), 46–58. doi:10.1016/j.jretai.2010.09.002

Wantland, D. J., Portillo, C. J., Holzemer, W. L., Slaughter, R., & McGhee, E. M. (2004). The effectiveness of Web-based vs. non-Web-based interventions: A meta-analysis of behavioral change outcomes. *Journal of Medical Internet Research*, *6*(4), e40. doi:10.2196/jmir.6.4.e40 PMID:15631964

Ward, A. F., Duke, K., Gneezy, A., & Bos, M. W. (2017). Brain drain: The mere presence of one's own smartphone reduces available cognitive capacity. *Journal of the Association for Consumer Research*, *2*(2), 140–154. doi:10.1086/691462

Ware, C. (2003). Design as Applied Perception. In J. M. Carroll (Ed.), *Carroll, J. M. (2003). HCI Models, Theories, and Frameworks: Toward a Multidisciplinary Science* (pp. 11–26). Morgan Kaufmann Publishers. doi:10.1016/B978-155860808-5/50002-2

Warren, T. (2017, March 17). *Microsoft is infesting Windows 10 with annoying ads*. The Verge. https://www.theverge.com/2017/3/17/14956540/microsoft-windows-10-ads-taskbar-file-explorer

Warwick, K., Xydas, D., Nasuto, S. J., Becerra, V. M., Hammond, M. W., Downes, J. H., Marshall, S., & Whalley, B. J. (2010). Controlling a Mobile Robot with a Biological Brain. *Defence Science Journal*, *1*(60), 5–14. doi:10.14429/dsj.60.11

Warzel, C. (2014, January 17). *How Google leapfrogged the creepy line*. Buzz Feed News. https://www.buzzfeednews.com/article/charliewarzel/how-google-leapfrogged-the-creepy-line

Waters, R. H. (1948). Mechanomorphism: A new term for an old mode of thought. *Psychological Review*, *55*(3), 139–142. doi:10.1037/h0058952 PMID:18865255

WeConnect International. (n.d.). *Prospere como mujer empresaria*. Recovered from https://weconnectinternational.org

Weinbach, M. (2020, July 4). *Ads are taking over Samsung's Galaxy smartphones—And it needs to stop*. Android Police. https://www.androidpolice.com/2020/07/04/ads-are-taking-over-samsungs-galaxy-smartphones-and-im-fed-up/

Wei, R. (2014). Texting, tweeting, and talking: Effects of smartphone use on engagement in civic discourse in China. *Mobile Media & Communication, 2*(1), 3–19. doi:10.1177/2050157913500668

Wen, Y., & Looi, C.-K. (2019). Review of Augmented Reality in Education: Situated Learning with Digital and Non-digital Resources. In P. Díaz, A. Ioannou, K. K. Bhagat, & J. M. Spector (Eds.), *Learning in a Digital World: Perspective on Interactive Technologies for Formal and Informal Education* (pp. 179–193). Springer. doi:10.1007/978-981-13-8265-9_9

Wheeler, J. R., Janz, N. K., & Dodge, J. A. (2003). Can a disease self-management program reduce healthcare costs? The case of older women with heart disease. *Medical Care, 41*, 706–715. doi:10.1097/01.MLR.0000065128.72148.D7 PMID:12773836

Whitfield, G., & Williams, C. (2004). If the evidence is so good – why doesn't anyone use them? A national survey of the use of computerized cognitive behaviour therapy. *Behavioural and Cognitive Psychotherapy, 32*(01), 57–65. doi:10.1017/S1352465804001031

Wiener, N. (1953). The machines as threat and promise. In P. Masani (Ed.), *Norbert Wiener: Collected works and commentaries* (Vol. 4, pp. 673–678). MIT Press.

Wiig, K. (2002). Knowledge management in Public Administration. *Journal of Knowledge Management, 6*(3), 224-239.

Williams, A. D., & Andrews, G. (2013). The effectiveness of internet cognitive behavioural therapy (iCBT) for depression in primary care: A quality assurance study. *PLoS One, 8*(2), e57447. doi:10.1371/journal.pone.0057447 PMID:23451231

Winfield, A. (2019). Ethical standards in robotics and AI. *Nature Electronics, 2*(2), 46–48. doi:10.103841928-019-0213-6

Winnick, M. (2016). *Putting a finger on our phone obsession. Mobile touches: A study on how humans use technology*. Dscout. https://blog.dscout.com/mobile-touches

Witmer, B., & Singer, M. (1998). Measuring presence in virtual environments: A presence questionnaire. *Presence (Cambridge, Mass.), 7*(3), 225–240. doi:10.1162/105474698565686

Won Jeong, S., Fiore, A., Niehm, L., & Lorenz, F. (2009). The role of experiential value in online shopping: The impacts of product presentation on consumer responses towards an apparel web site. *Internet Research, 19*(1), 105–124. doi:10.1108/10662240910927858

Wong, P. C., Zhu, K., Yang, X., & Fu, H. (2020). Exploring Eyes-Free Bezel-Initiated Swipe on Round Smartwatches. In *Proceedings of the 2020 CHI Conference on Human Factors in Computing Systems (CHI '20)*. Association for Computing Machinery. 10.1145/3313831.3376393

Wong, P. S. (2012). *Drucker's Knowledge-Worker Productivity Theory: A Practitioner's Approach to Integrating Organisational Work Processes with Drucker's Six Major Factors Determining Knowledge-Worker Productivity*. Southern Cross University.

Wood, L. C. & Reefke, H. (2010, November). *Working with a diverse class: Reflections on the role of team teaching, teaching tools and technological support*. IADIS International Conference on International Higher Education, Perth, Australia.

Woods, D., & Dekker, S. (2000). Anticipating the effects of technological change: A new era of dynamics for human factors. *Theoretical Issues in Ergonomics Science, 1*(3), 272–282. doi:10.1080/14639220110037452

Wood, W., & Neal, D. T. (2016). Healthy through habit: Interventions for initiating & maintaining health behavior change. *Behavioral Science & Policy, 2*(1), 71–83. doi:10.1353/bsp.2016.0008

Wu, H.-K., Lee, S. W.-Y., Chang, H.-Y., & Liang, J.-C. (2013). Current status, opportunities and challenges of augmented reality in education. *Computers & Education, 62*, 41–49. doi:10.1016/j.compedu.2012.10.024

WVU Medicine News. (2020, May 28). WVU Rockefeller Neuroscience Institute announces capability to predict COVID-19 related symptoms up to three days in advance. *WVU Medicine.* https://wvumedicine.org/news/article/wvu-rockefeller-neuroscience-institute-announces-capability-to-predict-covid-19-related-symptoms-up-/

Xiaomi, A., & Wang, W. (2010). Knowledge management technologies and applications: a literature review. IEEE, 138–144.

Yang, Z., Kasprzyk-Hordern, B., Frost, C. G., Estrela, P., & Thomas, K. V. (2015). *Community sewage sensors for monitoring public health*. Academic Press.

Yang, Q., & Gong, X. (2021). The engagement–addiction dilemma: An empirical evaluation of mobile user interface and mobile game affordance. *Internet Research.* Advance online publication. doi:10.1108/INTR-11-2020-0622

Yeh, K.-C., Tsai, M.-H., & Kang, S.-C. (2012). On-Site Building Information Retrieval by Using Projection-Based Augmented Reality. *Journal of Computing in Civil Engineering, 26*(3), 342–355. doi:10.1061/(ASCE)CP.1943-5487.0000156

Yeh, M., & Wickens, C. D. (2001). Display signaling in augmented reality: Effects of cue reliability and image realism on attention allocation and trust calibration. *Human Factors, 43*(3), 355–365. doi:10.1518/001872001775898269 PMID:11866192

Yellowlees, P., Marks, S., Hilty, D., & Shore, J. H. (2008). Using e-health to enable culturally appropriate mental healthcare in rural areas. *Telemedicine Journal and e-Health, 14*(5), 486–492. doi:10.1089/tmj.2007.0070 PMID:18578685

Yoon, S. A., Elinich, K., Wang, J., Steinmeier, C., & Tucker, S. (2012). Using augmented reality and knowledge-building scaffolds to improve learning in a science museum. *Computer-Supported Collaborative Learning, 7*(4), 519–541. doi:10.100711412-012-9156-x

Yunis, H. (Ed.). (2011). *Plato: Phaedrus*. Cambridge University Press.

Zack, J. S. (2008). How sturdy is that digital couch? Legal considerations for mental health professionals who deliver clinical services via the internet. *Journal of Technology in Human Services*, *26*(2-4), 333–359. doi:10.1080/15228830802097083

Zarandona, J., Cariñanos-Ayala, S., Cristóbal-Domínguez, E., Martín-Bezos, J., Yoldi-Mitxelena, A., & Cillero, I. H. (2019). With a smartphone in one's pocket: A descriptive cross-sectional study on smartphone use, distraction and restriction policies in nursing students. *Nurse Education Today*, *82*, 67–73. doi:10.1016/j.nedt.2019.08.001 PMID:31445465

Zehir, C., Üzmez, A., & Yıldız, H. (2016). The effect of SHRM practices on innovation performance: The mediating role of global capabilities. *Procedia: Social and Behavioral Sciences*, *235*, 797–806. doi:10.1016/j.sbspro.2016.11.088

Zhang, F., Zhang, Y., Quin, L., Zhang, W., & Lin, X. (2018). Efficiently reinforcing social networks over user engagement and tie strength. In *IEEE 34th International Conference on Data Engineering (ICDE)*. IEEE. 10.1109/ICDE.2018.00057

Zhang, T., Agarwal, R., & Lucas, H. (2011). The value of IT-enabled retailer learning: personalized product recommendations and customer store loyalty in electronic markets. *MIS Quarterly*, *35*(4), 859.

Ziegelmann, J. P., & Knoll, N. (2015). Future directions in the study of health behavior among older adults. *Gerontology*, *61*(5), 469–476. doi:10.1159/000369857 PMID:25660128

Zoogah, D. B. (2011). The dynamics of green HRM behaviors: a cognitive social information processing approach, *Zeitschrift Für Personalforschung/German Journal of Research in Human Resource Management, 25*(2), 117-139.

Related References

To continue our tradition of advancing media and communications research, we have compiled a list of recommended IGI Global readings. These references will provide additional information and guidance to further enrich your knowledge and assist you with your own research and future publications.

Abashian, N., & Fisher, S. (2018). Intercultural Effectiveness in Libraries: Supporting Success Through Collaboration With Co-Curricular Programs. In B. Blummer, J. Kenton, & M. Wiatrowski (Eds.), *Promoting Ethnic Diversity and Multiculturalism in Higher Education* (pp. 219–236). Hershey, PA: IGI Global. doi:10.4018/978-1-5225-4097-7.ch012

Adebayo, O., Fagbohun, M. O., Esse, U. C., & Nwokeoma, N. M. (2018). Change Management in the Academic Library: Transition From Print to Digital Collections. In R. Bhardwaj (Ed.), *Digitizing the Modern Library and the Transition From Print to Electronic* (pp. 1–28). Hershey, PA: IGI Global. doi:10.4018/978-1-5225-2119-8.ch001

Adegbore, A. M., Quadri, M. O., & Oyewo, O. R. (2018). A Theoretical Approach to the Adoption of Electronic Resource Management Systems (ERMS) in Nigerian University Libraries. In A. Tella & T. Kwanya (Eds.), *Handbook of Research on Managing Intellectual Property in Digital Libraries* (pp. 292–311). Hershey, PA: IGI Global. doi:10.4018/978-1-5225-3093-0.ch015

Adesola, A. P., & Olla, G. O. (2018). Unlocking the Unlimited Potentials of Koha OSS/ILS for Library House-Keeping Functions: A Global View. In M. Khosrow-Pour (Ed.), *Optimizing Contemporary Application and Processes in Open Source Software* (pp. 124–163). Hershey, PA: IGI Global. doi:10.4018/978-1-5225-5314-4.ch006

Adigun, G. O., Sobalaje, A. J., & Salau, S. A. (2018). Social Media and Copyright in Digital Libraries. In A. Tella & T. Kwanya (Eds.), *Handbook of Research on Managing Intellectual Property in Digital Libraries* (pp. 19–36). Hershey, PA: IGI Global. doi:10.4018/978-1-5225-3093-0.ch002

Adomi, E. E., Eriki, J. A., Tiemo, P. A., & Akpojotor, L. O. (2016). Incidents of Cyberbullying Among Library and Information Science (LIS) Students at Delta State University, Abraka, Nigeria. *International Journal of Digital Literacy and Digital Competence*, 7(4), 52–63. doi:10.4018/IJDLDC.2016100104

Afolabi, O. A. (2018). Myths and Challenges of Building an Effective Digital Library in Developing Nations: An African Perspective. In A. Tella & T. Kwanya (Eds.), *Handbook of Research on Managing Intellectual Property in Digital Libraries* (pp. 51–79). Hershey, PA: IGI Global. doi:10.4018/978-1-5225-3093-0.ch004

Agrawal, P. R. (2016). Google Search: Digging into the Culture of Information Retrieval. In E. de Smet & S. Dhamdhere (Eds.), *E-Discovery Tools and Applications in Modern Libraries* (pp. 210–239). Hershey, PA: IGI Global. doi:10.4018/978-1-5225-0474-0.ch012

Ahuja, Y., & Kumar, P. (2017). Web 2.0 Tools and Application: Knowledge Management and Sharing in Libraries. In B. Gunjal (Ed.), *Managing Knowledge and Scholarly Assets in Academic Libraries* (pp. 218–234). Hershey, PA: IGI Global. doi:10.4018/978-1-5225-1741-2.ch010

Ajmi, A. (2018). Developing In-House Digital Tools: Case Studies From the UMKC School of Law Library. In L. Costello & M. Powers (Eds.), *Developing In-House Digital Tools in Library Spaces* (pp. 117–139). Hershey, PA: IGI Global. doi:10.4018/978-1-5225-2676-6.ch006

Akakandelwa, A. (2016). A Glimpse of the Information Seeking Behaviour Literature on the Web: A Bibliometric Approach. In A. Tella (Ed.), *Information Seeking Behavior and Challenges in Digital Libraries* (pp. 127–155). Hershey, PA: IGI Global. doi:10.4018/978-1-5225-0296-8.ch007

Akande, F. T., & Adewojo, A. A. (2016). Information Need and Seeking Behavior of Farmers in Laduba Community of Kwara State, Nigeria. In A. Tella (Ed.), *Information Seeking Behavior and Challenges in Digital Libraries* (pp. 238–271). Hershey, PA: IGI Global. doi:10.4018/978-1-5225-0296-8.ch012

Related References

Al-Kharousi, R., Al-Harrasi, N. H., Jabur, N. H., & Bouazza, A. (2018). Soft Systems Methodology (SSM) as an Interdisciplinary Approach: Reflection on the Use of SSM in Adoption of Web 2.0 Applications in Omani Academic Libraries. In M. Al-Suqri, A. Al-Kindi, S. AlKindi, & N. Saleem (Eds.), *Promoting Interdisciplinarity in Knowledge Generation and Problem Solving* (pp. 243–257). Hershey, PA: IGI Global. doi:10.4018/978-1-5225-3878-3.ch016

Alenzuela, R. (2017). Research, Leadership, and Resource-Sharing Initiatives: The Role of Local Library Consortia in Access to Medical Information. In S. Ram (Ed.), *Library and Information Services for Bioinformatics Education and Research* (pp. 199–211). Hershey, PA: IGI Global. doi:10.4018/978-1-5225-1871-6.ch012

Allison, D. (2017). When Sales Talk Meets Reality: Implementing a Self-Checkout Kiosk. In E. Iglesias (Ed.), *Library Technology Funding, Planning, and Deployment* (pp. 36–54). Hershey, PA: IGI Global. doi:10.4018/978-1-5225-1735-1.ch003

Anglim, C. T., & Rusk, F. (2018). Empowering DC's Future Through Information Access. In A. Burtin, J. Fleming, & P. Hampton-Garland (Eds.), *Changing Urban Landscapes Through Public Higher Education* (pp. 57–77). Hershey, PA: IGI Global. doi:10.4018/978-1-5225-3454-9.ch003

Asmi, N. A. (2017). Social Media and Library Services. *International Journal of Library and Information Services*, 6(2), 23–36. doi:10.4018/IJLIS.2017070103

Awoyemi, R. A. (2018). Adoption and Use of Innovative Mobile Technologies in Nigerian Academic Libraries. In J. Keengwe (Ed.), *Handbook of Research on Digital Content, Mobile Learning, and Technology Integration Models in Teacher Education* (pp. 354–389). Hershey, PA: IGI Global. doi:10.4018/978-1-5225-2953-8.ch019

Awoyemi, R. A. (2018). Adoption and Use of Innovative Mobile Technologies in Nigerian Academic Libraries. In J. Keengwe (Ed.), *Handbook of Research on Digital Content, Mobile Learning, and Technology Integration Models in Teacher Education* (pp. 354–389). Hershey, PA: IGI Global. doi:10.4018/978-1-5225-2953-8.ch019

Ayson, M. C. (2016). Maximizing Social Media Tools: Planning and Evaluating Social Media Strategies for Special Libraries. In J. Yap, M. Perez, M. Ayson, & G. Entico (Eds.), *Special Library Administration, Standardization and Technological Integration* (pp. 166–179). Hershey, PA: IGI Global. doi:10.4018/978-1-4666-9542-9.ch007

Babatope, I. S. (2018). Social Media Applications as Effective Service Delivery Tools for Librarians. In M. Khosrow-Pour, D.B.A. (Ed.), Encyclopedia of Information Science and Technology, Fourth Edition (pp. 5252-5261). Hershey, PA: IGI Global. doi:10.4018/978-1-5225-2255-3.ch456

Bakare, A. A. (2018). Digital Libraries and Copyright of Intellectual Property: An Ethical Practice Management. In A. Tella & T. Kwanya (Eds.), *Handbook of Research on Managing Intellectual Property in Digital Libraries* (pp. 377–395). Hershey, PA: IGI Global. doi:10.4018/978-1-5225-3093-0.ch019

Baker, W. (2016). Responding to High-Volume Water Disasters in the Research Library Context. In E. Decker & J. Townes (Eds.), *Handbook of Research on Disaster Management and Contingency Planning in Modern Libraries* (pp. 282–310). Hershey, PA: IGI Global. doi:10.4018/978-1-4666-8624-3.ch013

Baker-Gardner, R., & Smart, C. (2017). Ignorance or Intent?: A Case Study of Plagiarism in Higher Education among LIS Students in the Caribbean. In D. Velliaris (Ed.), *Handbook of Research on Academic Misconduct in Higher Education* (pp. 182–205). Hershey, PA: IGI Global. doi:10.4018/978-1-5225-1610-1.ch008

Baker-Gardner, R., & Stewart, P. (2018). Educating Caribbean Librarians to Provide Library Education in a Dynamic Information Environment. In S. Bhattacharyya & K. Patnaik (Eds.), *Changing the Scope of Library Instruction in the Digital Age* (pp. 187–226). Hershey, PA: IGI Global. doi:10.4018/978-1-5225-2802-9.ch008

Bassuener, L. (2016). Knowledge in the Shrinking Commons: Libraries and Open Access in a Market-Driven World. In E. Railean, G. Walker, A. Elçi, & L. Jackson (Eds.), *Handbook of Research on Applied Learning Theory and Design in Modern Education* (pp. 358–379). Hershey, PA: IGI Global. doi:10.4018/978-1-4666-9634-1.ch017

Baylen, D. M., & Cooper, O. P. (2016). Social Media and Special Collections: Exploring Presence, Prevalence, and Practices in Academic Libraries. In J. Yap, M. Perez, M. Ayson, & G. Entico (Eds.), *Special Library Administration, Standardization and Technological Integration* (pp. 180–201). Hershey, PA: IGI Global. doi:10.4018/978-1-4666-9542-9.ch008

Belden, D., Phillips, M. E., Carlisle, T., & Hartman, C. N. (2016). The Portal to Texas History: Building a Partnership Model for a Statewide Digital Library. In B. Doherty (Ed.), *Space and Organizational Considerations in Academic Library Partnerships and Collaborations* (pp. 182–204). Hershey, PA: IGI Global. doi:10.4018/978-1-5225-0326-2.ch009

Bengtson, J. (2017). Funding a Gamification Machine. In E. Iglesias (Ed.), *Library Technology Funding, Planning, and Deployment* (pp. 99–112). Hershey, PA: IGI Global. doi:10.4018/978-1-5225-1735-1.ch006

Bhebhe, S., & Ngwenya, S. (2016). Adoption and Use of Discovery Tools by Selected Academic Libraries in Zimbabwe. In E. de Smet & S. Dhamdhere (Eds.), *E-Discovery Tools and Applications in Modern Libraries* (pp. 168–180). Hershey, PA: IGI Global. doi:10.4018/978-1-5225-0474-0.ch009

Blummer, B., & Kenton, J. M. (2017). Access and Accessibility of Academic Libraries' Electronic Resources and Services: Identifying Themes in the Literature From 2000 to the Present. In H. Alphin Jr, J. Lavine, & R. Chan (Eds.), *Disability and Equity in Higher Education Accessibility* (pp. 242–267). Hershey, PA: IGI Global. doi:10.4018/978-1-5225-2665-0.ch011

Blummer, B., & Kenton, J. M. (2018). Academic and Research Libraries' Portals: A Literature Review From 2003 to the Present. In R. Bhardwaj (Ed.), *Digitizing the Modern Library and the Transition From Print to Electronic* (pp. 29–63). Hershey, PA: IGI Global. doi:10.4018/978-1-5225-2119-8.ch002

Blummer, B., & Kenton, J. M. (2018). International Students and Academic Libraries: Identifying Themes in the Literature From 2001 to the Present. In B. Blummer, J. Kenton, & M. Wiatrowski (Eds.), *Promoting Ethnic Diversity and Multiculturalism in Higher Education* (pp. 237–263). Hershey, PA: IGI Global. doi:10.4018/978-1-5225-4097-7.ch013

Bodolay, R., Frye, S., Kruse, C., & Luke, D. (2016). Moving from Co-Location to Cooperation to Collaboration: Redefining a Library's Role within the University. In B. Doherty (Ed.), *Space and Organizational Considerations in Academic Library Partnerships and Collaborations* (pp. 230–254). Hershey, PA: IGI Global. doi:10.4018/978-1-5225-0326-2.ch011

Boom, D. (2017). The Embedded Librarian: Do More With less. In B. Gunjal (Ed.), *Managing Knowledge and Scholarly Assets in Academic Libraries* (pp. 76–97). Hershey, PA: IGI Global. doi:10.4018/978-1-5225-1741-2.ch004

Bosire-Ogechi, E. (2018). Social Media, Social Networking, Copyright, and Digital Libraries. In A. Tella & T. Kwanya (Eds.), *Handbook of Research on Managing Intellectual Property in Digital Libraries* (pp. 37–50). Hershey, PA: IGI Global. doi:10.4018/978-1-5225-3093-0.ch003

Bradley-Sanders, C., & Rudshteyn, A. (2018). MyLibrary at Brooklyn College: Developing a Suite of Digital Tools. In L. Costello & M. Powers (Eds.), *Developing In-House Digital Tools in Library Spaces* (pp. 140–167). Hershey, PA: IGI Global. doi:10.4018/978-1-5225-2676-6.ch007

Brisk, A. T., Pittman, K., & Rosendahl, M. (2016). Collaborating Off Campus: Creating Communities of Practice with New Partners. In B. Doherty (Ed.), *Technology-Centered Academic Library Partnerships and Collaborations* (pp. 245–274). Hershey, PA: IGI Global. doi:10.4018/978-1-5225-0323-1.ch009

Brown, V. (2018). Technology Access Gap for Postsecondary Education: A Statewide Case Study. In M. Yildiz, S. Funk, & B. De Abreu (Eds.), *Promoting Global Competencies Through Media Literacy* (pp. 20–40). Hershey, PA: IGI Global. doi:10.4018/978-1-5225-3082-4.ch002

Carroll, V. (2016). Conservation Since 2000. In E. Decker & J. Townes (Eds.), *Handbook of Research on Disaster Management and Contingency Planning in Modern Libraries* (pp. 467–493). Hershey, PA: IGI Global. doi:10.4018/978-1-4666-8624-3.ch020

Chaiyasoonthorn, W., & Suksa-ngiam, W. (2018). Users' Acceptance of Online Literature Databases in a Thai University: A Test of UTAUT2. *International Journal of Information Systems in the Service Sector, 10*(1), 54–70. doi:10.4018/IJISSS.2018010104

Chandler, D. R. (2016). Prepared for Anything and Everything: Libraries, Archives, and Unexpected Small Scale Disasters. In E. Decker & J. Townes (Eds.), *Handbook of Research on Disaster Management and Contingency Planning in Modern Libraries* (pp. 240–256). Hershey, PA: IGI Global. doi:10.4018/978-1-4666-8624-3.ch011

Chaudron, G. (2016). After the Flood: Lessons Learned from Small-Scale Disasters. In E. Decker & J. Townes (Eds.), *Handbook of Research on Disaster Management and Contingency Planning in Modern Libraries* (pp. 389–411). Hershey, PA: IGI Global. doi:10.4018/978-1-4666-8624-3.ch017

Chaudron, G. (2016). Managing the Commonplace: Small Water Emergencies in Libraries. *International Journal of Risk and Contingency Management, 5*(1), 42–61. doi:10.4018/IJRCM.2016010104

Chaudron, G. (2018). Burst Pipes and Leaky Roofs: Small Emergencies Are a Challenge for Libraries. In K. Strang, M. Korstanje, & N. Vajjhala (Eds.), *Research, Practices, and Innovations in Global Risk and Contingency Management* (pp. 211–231). Hershey, PA: IGI Global. doi:10.4018/978-1-5225-4754-9.ch012

Chemulwo, M. J. (2018). Managing Intellectual Property in Digital Libraries and Copyright Challenges. In A. Tella & T. Kwanya (Eds.), *Handbook of Research on Managing Intellectual Property in Digital Libraries* (pp. 165–183). Hershey, PA: IGI Global. doi:10.4018/978-1-5225-3093-0.ch009

Chen, J., Lan, X., Huang, Q., Dong, J., & Chen, C. (2017). Scholarly Learning Commons. In L. Ruan, Q. Zhu, & Y. Ye (Eds.), *Academic Library Development and Administration in China* (pp. 90–109). Hershey, PA: IGI Global. doi:10.4018/978-1-5225-0550-1.ch006

Chigwada, J. P. (2018). Adoption of Open Source Software in Libraries in Developing Countries. *International Journal of Library and Information Services*, 7(1), 15–29. doi:10.4018/IJLIS.2018010102

Chisita, C. T., & Chinyemba, F. (2017). Utilising ICTs for Resource Sharing Initiatives in Academic Institutions in Zimbabwe: Towards a New Trajectory. In B. Gunjal (Ed.), *Managing Knowledge and Scholarly Assets in Academic Libraries* (pp. 174–187). Hershey, PA: IGI Global. doi:10.4018/978-1-5225-1741-2.ch008

Colmenero-Ruiz, M. (2016). Discussion on Digital Inclusion Good Practices at Europe's Libraries. In B. Passarelli, J. Straubhaar, & A. Cuevas-Cerveró (Eds.), *Handbook of Research on Comparative Approaches to the Digital Age Revolution in Europe and the Americas* (pp. 352–369). Hershey, PA: IGI Global. doi:10.4018/978-1-4666-8740-0.ch021

Costello, B. (2016). Academic Libraries in Partnership with the Government Publishing Office: A Changing Paradigm. In B. Doherty (Ed.), *Space and Organizational Considerations in Academic Library Partnerships and Collaborations* (pp. 87–110). Hershey, PA: IGI Global. doi:10.4018/978-1-5225-0326-2.ch005

Costello, L., & Fazal, S. (2018). Developing Unique Study Room Reservation Systems: Examples From Teachers College and Stony Brook University. In L. Costello & M. Powers (Eds.), *Developing In-House Digital Tools in Library Spaces* (pp. 168–176). Hershey, PA: IGI Global. doi:10.4018/978-1-5225-2676-6.ch008

Cowick, C., & Cowick, J. (2016). Planning for a Disaster: Effective Emergency Management in the 21st Century. In E. Decker & J. Townes (Eds.), *Handbook of Research on Disaster Management and Contingency Planning in Modern Libraries* (pp. 49–69). Hershey, PA: IGI Global. doi:10.4018/978-1-4666-8624-3.ch003

Cui, Y. (2017). Research Data Management: Models, Challenges, and Actions. In L. Ruan, Q. Zhu, & Y. Ye (Eds.), *Academic Library Development and Administration in China* (pp. 184–195). Hershey, PA: IGI Global. doi:10.4018/978-1-5225-0550-1.ch011

Das, T. (2016). Academic Library Collaborations to Strengthen Open Government Data and Expand Librarianship. In B. Doherty (Ed.), *Technology-Centered Academic Library Partnerships and Collaborations* (pp. 167–193). Hershey, PA: IGI Global. doi:10.4018/978-1-5225-0323-1.ch006 de Smet, E. (2016). E-Discovery with the ABCD Information Management System. In E. de Smet & S. Dhamdhere (Eds.), *E-Discovery Tools and Applications in Modern Libraries* (pp. 332–357). Hershey, PA: IGI Global. doi:10.4018/978-1-5225-0474-0.ch017

Decker, E. N., & Odom, R. Y. (2016). Publish or Perish: Librarians Collaborating to Support Junior Faculty to Publish within the Academic Environment. In B. Doherty (Ed.), *Space and Organizational Considerations in Academic Library Partnerships and Collaborations* (pp. 298–316). Hershey, PA: IGI Global. doi:10.4018/978-1-5225-0326-2.ch014

Desilets, M. R., DeJonghe, J., & Filkins, M. (2016). Better Together: The Successful Public/Academic Joint Use Library. In B. Doherty (Ed.), *Space and Organizational Considerations in Academic Library Partnerships and Collaborations* (pp. 1–21). Hershey, PA: IGI Global. doi:10.4018/978-1-5225-0326-2.ch001

Dhamdhere, S. N., De Smet, E., & Lihitkar, R. (2017). Web-Based Bibliographic Services Offered by Top World and Indian University Libraries: A Comparative Study. *International Journal of Library and Information Services*, 6(1), 53–72. doi:10.4018/IJLIS.2017010104

Dhamdhere, S. N., & Lihitkar, R. (2016). Commercial and Open Access Integrated Information Search Tools in Indian Libraries. In E. de Smet & S. Dhamdhere (Eds.), *E-Discovery Tools and Applications in Modern Libraries* (pp. 41–55). Hershey, PA: IGI Global. doi:10.4018/978-1-5225-0474-0.ch002

Dixon, J., & Abashian, N. (2016). Beyond the Collection: Emergency Planning for Public and Staff Safety. In E. Decker & J. Townes (Eds.), *Handbook of Research on Disaster Management and Contingency Planning in Modern Libraries* (pp. 120–140). Hershey, PA: IGI Global. doi:10.4018/978-1-4666-8624-3.ch006

Doherty, B. (2016). Marriage after Divorce: The Challenges and Opportunities of a Shared Library after Institutions Separate. In B. Doherty (Ed.), *Space and Organizational Considerations in Academic Library Partnerships and Collaborations* (pp. 22–44). Hershey, PA: IGI Global. doi:10.4018/978-1-5225-0326-2.ch002

Dongardive, P. (2016). Digital Libraries as Information Superhighway. In A. Tella (Ed.), *Information Seeking Behavior and Challenges in Digital Libraries* (pp. 304–315). Hershey, PA: IGI Global. doi:10.4018/978-1-5225-0296-8.ch015

Dougan, K. (2016). Music Information Seeking Opportunities and Behavior Then and Now. In P. Kostagiolas, K. Martzoukou, & C. Lavranos (Eds.), *Trends in Music Information Seeking, Behavior, and Retrieval for Creativity* (pp. 42–57). Hershey, PA: IGI Global. doi:10.4018/978-1-5225-0270-8.ch003

Related References

Eiriemiokhale, K. A. (2018). Copyright Issues in a Digital Library Environment. In A. Tella & T. Kwanya (Eds.), *Handbook of Research on Managing Intellectual Property in Digital Libraries* (pp. 142–164). Hershey, PA: IGI Global. doi:10.4018/978-1-5225-3093-0.ch008

El Mimouni, H., Anderson, J., Tempelman-Kluit, N. F., & Dolan-Mescal, A. (2018). UX Work in Libraries: How (and Why) to Do It. In L. Costello & M. Powers (Eds.), *Developing In-House Digital Tools in Library Spaces* (pp. 1–36). Hershey, PA: IGI Global. doi:10.4018/978-1-5225-2676-6.ch001

Emiri, O. T. (2017). Digital Literacy Skills Among Librarians in University Libraries In the 21st Century in Edo And Delta States, Nigeria. *International Journal of Library and Information Services*, 6(1), 37–52. doi:10.4018/IJLIS.2017010103

Entico, G. J. (2016). Knowledge Management and the Medical Health Librarians: A Perception Study. In J. Yap, M. Perez, M. Ayson, & G. Entico (Eds.), *Special Library Administration, Standardization and Technological Integration* (pp. 52–77). Hershey, PA: IGI Global. doi:10.4018/978-1-4666-9542-9.ch003

Esposito, T. (2018). Exploring Opportunities in Health Science Information Instructional Outreach: A Case Study Highlighting One Academic Library's Experience. In S. Bhattacharyya & K. Patnaik (Eds.), *Changing the Scope of Library Instruction in the Digital Age* (pp. 118–135). Hershey, PA: IGI Global. doi:10.4018/978-1-5225-2802-9.ch005

Esse, U. C., & Ohaegbulam, H. (2016). Library and Information Services for Open and Distance Learning: Assessing the Role of Mobile Technologies and Distance Learning in Higher Education. In G. Eby, T. Yuzer, & S. Atay (Eds.), *Developing Successful Strategies for Global Policies and Cyber Transparency in E-Learning* (pp. 29–45). Hershey, PA: IGI Global. doi:10.4018/978-1-4666-8844-5.ch003

Fagbohun, M. O., Nwokocha, N. M., Itsekor, V., & Adebayo, O. (2016). Responsive Library Website Design and Adoption of Federated Search Tools for Library Services in Developing Countries. In E. de Smet & S. Dhamdhere (Eds.), *E-Discovery Tools and Applications in Modern Libraries* (pp. 76–108). Hershey, PA: IGI Global. doi:10.4018/978-1-5225-0474-0.ch005

Fagbola, O. O. (2016). Indexing and Abstracting as Tools for Information Retrieval in Digital Libraries: A Review of Literature. In A. Tella (Ed.), *Information Seeking Behavior and Challenges in Digital Libraries* (pp. 156–178). Hershey, PA: IGI Global. doi:10.4018/978-1-5225-0296-8.ch008

Fan, Y., Zhang, X., & Li, G. (2017). Research Initiatives and Projects in Academic Libraries. In L. Ruan, Q. Zhu, & Y. Ye (Eds.), *Academic Library Development and Administration in China* (pp. 230–252). Hershey, PA: IGI Global. doi:10.4018/978-1-5225-0550-1.ch014

Farmer, L. S. (2017). ICT Literacy Integration: Issues and Sample Efforts. In J. Keengwe & P. Bull (Eds.), *Handbook of Research on Transformative Digital Content and Learning Technologies* (pp. 59–80). Hershey, PA: IGI Global. doi:10.4018/978-1-5225-2000-9.ch004

Farmer, L. S. (2017). Data Analytics for Strategic Management: Getting the Right Data. In V. Wang (Ed.), *Encyclopedia of Strategic Leadership and Management* (pp. 810–822). Hershey, PA: IGI Global. doi:10.4018/978-1-5225-1049-9.ch056

Farmer, L. S. (2017). Managing Portable Technologies for Special Education. In V. Wang (Ed.), *Encyclopedia of Strategic Leadership and Management* (pp. 977–987). Hershey, PA: IGI Global. doi:10.4018/978-1-5225-1049-9.ch068

Fujishima, D., & Kamada, T. (2017). Collective Relocation for Associative Distributed Collections of Objects. *International Journal of Software Innovation*, 5(2), 55–69. doi:10.4018/IJSI.2017040104

Gaetz, I. (2016). Processes, Opportunities, and Challenges Creating and Managing a Scholarly Open Access Journal: An Investigation of "Collaborative Librarianship". In B. Doherty (Ed.), *Space and Organizational Considerations in Academic Library Partnerships and Collaborations* (pp. 205–229). Hershey, PA: IGI Global. doi:10.4018/978-1-5225-0326-2.ch010

Galloup, A. (2016). One Plan, Four Libraries: A Case Study in Disaster Planning for a Four-Campus Academic Institution. In E. Decker & J. Townes (Eds.), *Handbook of Research on Disaster Management and Contingency Planning in Modern Libraries* (pp. 166–183). Hershey, PA: IGI Global. doi:10.4018/978-1-4666-8624-3.ch008

Gamtso, C. W., Vogt, R. B., Donahue, A., Donovan, K., & Jefferson, J. (2016). Librarian and Peer Research Mentor Partnerships that Promote Student Success. In B. Doherty (Ed.), *Space and Organizational Considerations in Academic Library Partnerships and Collaborations* (pp. 255–279). Hershey, PA: IGI Global. doi:10.4018/978-1-5225-0326-2.ch012

Ghani, S. R. (2017). Ontology: Advancing Flawless Library Services. In T. Ashraf & N. Kumar (Eds.), *Interdisciplinary Digital Preservation Tools and Technologies* (pp. 79–102). Hershey, PA: IGI Global. doi:10.4018/978-1-5225-1653-8.ch005

Gibbons, P. (2016). Disaster Management and Exhibition Loans: Contingency Planning for Items on Display. In E. Decker & J. Townes (Eds.), *Handbook of Research on Disaster Management and Contingency Planning in Modern Libraries* (pp. 141–165). Hershey, PA: IGI Global. doi:10.4018/978-1-4666-8624-3.ch007

Gibbons, P. (2016). Assessing Risk and Safeguarding Rare Library Materials During Exhibition Loans. *International Journal of Risk and Contingency Management*, 5(1), 15–25. doi:10.4018/IJRCM.2016010102

Gibson, R. (2016). Wearable Technologies in Academic Information Search. In J. Holland (Ed.), *Wearable Technology and Mobile Innovations for Next-Generation Education* (pp. 122–146). Hershey, PA: IGI Global. doi:10.4018/978-1-5225-0069-8.ch007

Goldman, B. (2016). Two Fires and a Flood: Lasting Impact on a Public Library, Its Staff, and Community. In E. Decker & J. Townes (Eds.), *Handbook of Research on Disaster Management and Contingency Planning in Modern Libraries* (pp. 560–581). Hershey, PA: IGI Global. doi:10.4018/978-1-4666-8624-3.ch024

Goovaerts, M., Nieuwenhuysen, P., & Dhamdhere, S. N. (2016). VLIR-UOS Workshop 'E-Info Discovery and Management for Institutes in the South': Presentations and Conclusions, Antwerp, 8-19 December, 2014. In E. de Smet, & S. Dhamdhere (Eds.), E-Discovery Tools and Applications in Modern Libraries (pp. 1-40). Hershey, PA: IGI Global. doi:10.4018/978-1-5225-0474-0.ch001

Gu, J. (2017). Library Buildings on New Campuses. In L. Ruan, Q. Zhu, & Y. Ye (Eds.), *Academic Library Development and Administration in China* (pp. 110–124). Hershey, PA: IGI Global. doi:10.4018/978-1-5225-0550-1.ch007

Guan, Z., & Wang, J. (2017). The China Academic Social Sciences and Humanities Library (CASHL). In L. Ruan, Q. Zhu, & Y. Ye (Eds.), *Academic Library Development and Administration in China* (pp. 31–54). Hershey, PA: IGI Global. doi:10.4018/978-1-5225-0550-1.ch003

Gul, S., & Shueb, S. (2018). Confronting/Managing the Crisis of Indian Libraries: E-Consortia Initiatives in India - A Way Forward. In R. Bhardwaj (Ed.), *Digitizing the Modern Library and the Transition From Print to Electronic* (pp. 129–163). Hershey, PA: IGI Global. doi:10.4018/978-1-5225-2119-8.ch006

Gunjal, B. (2017). Managing Knowledge and Scholarly Assets in Academic Libraries: Issues and Challenges. In B. Gunjal (Ed.), *Managing Knowledge and Scholarly Assets in Academic Libraries* (pp. 270–279). Hershey, PA: IGI Global. doi:10.4018/978-1-5225-1741-2.ch013

Guo, J., Zhang, H., & Zong, Y. (2017). Leadership Development and Career Planning. In L. Ruan, Q. Zhu, & Y. Ye (Eds.), *Academic Library Development and Administration in China* (pp. 264–279). Hershey, PA: IGI Global. doi:10.4018/978-1-5225-0550-1.ch016

Hallis, R. (2018). Leveraging Library Instruction in a Digital Age. In S. Bhattacharyya & K. Patnaik (Eds.), *Changing the Scope of Library Instruction in the Digital Age* (pp. 1–23). Hershey, PA: IGI Global. doi:10.4018/978-1-5225-2802-9.ch001

Hamilton, R., & Brown, D. (2016). Disaster Management and Continuity Planning in Libraries: Changes since the Year 2000. In E. Decker & J. Townes (Eds.), *Handbook of Research on Disaster Management and Contingency Planning in Modern Libraries* (pp. 1–24). Hershey, PA: IGI Global. doi:10.4018/978-1-4666-8624-3.ch001

Hamilton, R., & Brown, D. (2016). Disaster Management and Continuity Planning in Libraries: Literature Review. *International Journal of Risk and Contingency Management*, 5(1), 26–41. doi:10.4018/IJRCM.2016010103

Hartsock, R., & Alemneh, D. G. (2018). Electronic Theses and Dissertations (ETDs). In M. Khosrow-Pour, D.B.A. (Ed.), Encyclopedia of Information Science and Technology, Fourth Edition (pp. 6748-6755). Hershey, PA: IGI Global. doi:10.4018/978-1-5225-2255-3.ch584

Haugh, D. (2018). Mobile Applications for Libraries. In L. Costello & M. Powers (Eds.), *Developing In-House Digital Tools in Library Spaces* (pp. 76–90). Hershey, PA: IGI Global. doi:10.4018/978-1-5225-2676-6.ch004

Hill, V. (2017). Digital Citizens as Writers: New Literacies and New Responsibilities. In E. Monske & K. Blair (Eds.), *Handbook of Research on Writing and Composing in the Age of MOOCs* (pp. 56–74). Hershey, PA: IGI Global. doi:10.4018/978-1-5225-1718-4.ch004

Horne-Popp, L. M., Tessone, E. B., & Welker, J. (2018). If You Build It, They Will Come: Creating a Library Statistics Dashboard for Decision-Making. In L. Costello & M. Powers (Eds.), *Developing In-House Digital Tools in Library Spaces* (pp. 177–203). Hershey, PA: IGI Global. doi:10.4018/978-1-5225-2676-6.ch009

Huang, C., & Xue, H. F. (2017). The China Academic Digital Associative Library (CADAL). In L. Ruan, Q. Zhu, & Y. Ye (Eds.), *Academic Library Development and Administration in China* (pp. 20–30). Hershey, PA: IGI Global. doi:10.4018/978-1-5225-0550-1.ch002

Related References

Hunsaker, A. J., Majewski, N., & Rocke, L. E. (2018). Pulling Content out the Back Door: Creating an Interactive Digital Collections Experience. In L. Costello & M. Powers (Eds.), *Developing In-House Digital Tools in Library Spaces* (pp. 205–226). Hershey, PA: IGI Global. doi:10.4018/978-1-5225-2676-6.ch010

Ibrahim, H., Mustapa, R., Edzan, N., & Yahya, W. A. (2016). Profiling Prominent Malaysians in Bernama Library and Infolink Service. In J. Yap, M. Perez, M. Ayson, & G. Entico (Eds.), *Special Library Administration, Standardization and Technological Integration* (pp. 315–336). Hershey, PA: IGI Global. doi:10.4018/978-1-4666-9542-9.ch014

Idiegbeyan-Ose, J., Ifijeh, G., Iwu-James, J., & Ilogho, J. (2016). Management of Institutional Repositories (IR) in Developing Countries. In E. de Smet & S. Dhamdhere (Eds.), *E-Discovery Tools and Applications in Modern Libraries* (pp. 306–331). Hershey, PA: IGI Global. doi:10.4018/978-1-5225-0474-0.ch016

Idiegbeyan-ose, J., Nkiko, C., Idahosa, M., & Nwokocha, N. (2016). Digital Divide: Issues and Strategies for Intervention in Nigerian Libraries. *Journal of Cases on Information Technology*, *18*(3), 29–39. doi:10.4018/JCIT.2016070103

Ifijeh, G., Adebayo, O., Izuagbe, R., & Olawoyin, O. (2018). Institutional Repositories and Libraries in Nigeria: Interrogating the Nexus. *Journal of Cases on Information Technology*, *20*(2), 16–29. doi:10.4018/JCIT.2018040102

Ifijeh, G., Idiegbeyan-ose, J., Segun-Adeniran, C., & Ilogho, J. (2016). Disaster Management in Digital Libraries: Issues and Strategies in Developing Countries. *International Journal of Risk and Contingency Management*, *5*(1), 1–14. doi:10.4018/IJRCM.2016010101

Iglesias, E. (2017). Insourcing and Outsourcing of Library Technology. In E. Iglesias (Ed.), *Library Technology Funding, Planning, and Deployment* (pp. 113–123). Hershey, PA: IGI Global. doi:10.4018/978-1-5225-1735-1.ch007

Ikolo, V. E. (2018). Transformational Leadership for Academic Libraries in Nigeria. In M. Khosrow-Pour, D.B.A. (Ed.), Encyclopedia of Information Science and Technology, Fourth Edition (pp. 5726-5735). Hershey, PA: IGI Global. doi:10.4018/978-1-5225-2255-3.ch497

Jaafar, T. M. (2016). Law Library Consortium in Metro Manila: A Proposed Model and the Management of Law Libraries. In J. Yap, M. Perez, M. Ayson, & G. Entico (Eds.), *Special Library Administration, Standardization and Technological Integration* (pp. 134–164). Hershey, PA: IGI Global. doi:10.4018/978-1-4666-9542-9.ch006

Joe, J. A. (2018). Changing Expectations of Academic Libraries. In M. Khosrow-Pour, D.B.A. (Ed.), Encyclopedia of Information Science and Technology, Fourth Edition (pp. 5204-5212). Hershey, PA: IGI Global. doi:10.4018/978-1-5225-2255-3.ch452

Johnson, H., & Simms, S. (2016). Concept, Conversion, Cultivation, and Consequence: The Four Cs of Successful Collaboration. In B. Doherty (Ed.), *Space and Organizational Considerations in Academic Library Partnerships and Collaborations* (pp. 280–297). Hershey, PA: IGI Global. doi:10.4018/978-1-5225-0326-2.ch013

Jones, A. (2016). Shortcomings and Successes: A Small-Scale Disaster Case Study. In E. Decker & J. Townes (Eds.), *Handbook of Research on Disaster Management and Contingency Planning in Modern Libraries* (pp. 412–435). Hershey, PA: IGI Global. doi:10.4018/978-1-4666-8624-3.ch018

Juliana, I., Izuagbe, R., Itsekor, V., Fagbohun, M. O., Asaolu, A., & Nwokeoma, M. N. (2018). The Role of the School Library in Empowering Visually Impaired Children With Lifelong Information Literacy Skills. In P. Epler (Ed.), *Instructional Strategies in General Education and Putting the Individuals With Disabilities Act (IDEA) Into Practice* (pp. 245–271). Hershey, PA: IGI Global. doi:10.4018/978-1-5225-3111-1.ch009

Kalusopa, T. (2018). Preservation and Access to Digital Materials: Strategic Policy Options for Africa. In P. Ngulube (Ed.), *Handbook of Research on Heritage Management and Preservation* (pp. 150–174). Hershey, PA: IGI Global. doi:10.4018/978-1-5225-3137-1.ch008

Kamau, G. W. (2018). Copyright Challenges in Digital Libraries in Kenya From the Lens of a Librarian. In A. Tella & T. Kwanya (Eds.), *Handbook of Research on Managing Intellectual Property in Digital Libraries* (pp. 312–336). Hershey, PA: IGI Global. doi:10.4018/978-1-5225-3093-0.ch016

Karbach, L. (2016). Public Libraries: Analysis of Services for Immigrant Populations and Suggestions to Improve Outreach. In K. González & R. Frumkin (Eds.), *Handbook of Research on Effective Communication in Culturally Diverse Classrooms* (pp. 153–182). Hershey, PA: IGI Global. doi:10.4018/978-1-4666-9953-3.ch008

Karmakar, R. (2018). Development and Management of Digital Libraries in the Regime of IPR Paradigm. *International Journal of Library and Information Services*, 7(1), 44–57. doi:10.4018/IJLIS.2018010104

Kasemsap, K. (2016). Mastering Digital Libraries in the Digital Age. In E. de Smet & S. Dhamdhere (Eds.), *E-Discovery Tools and Applications in Modern Libraries* (pp. 275–305). Hershey, PA: IGI Global. doi:10.4018/978-1-5225-0474-0.ch015

Kasemsap, K. (2017). Mastering Knowledge Management in Academic Libraries. In B. Gunjal (Ed.), *Managing Knowledge and Scholarly Assets in Academic Libraries* (pp. 27–55). Hershey, PA: IGI Global. doi:10.4018/978-1-5225-1741-2.ch002

Kehinde, A. (2018). Digital Libraries and the Role of Digital Librarians. In A. Tella & T. Kwanya (Eds.), *Handbook of Research on Managing Intellectual Property in Digital Libraries* (pp. 98–119). Hershey, PA: IGI Global. doi:10.4018/978-1-5225-3093-0.ch006

Kenausis, V., & Herman, D. (2017). Don't Make Us Use the "Get Along Shirt": Communication and Consensus Building in an RFP Process. In E. Iglesias (Ed.), *Library Technology Funding, Planning, and Deployment* (pp. 1–22). Hershey, PA: IGI Global. doi:10.4018/978-1-5225-1735-1.ch001

Kohl, L. E., Lombardi, P., & Moroney, M. (2017). Moving from Local to Global via the Integrated Library System: Cost-Savings, ILS Management, Teams, and End-Users. In E. Iglesias (Ed.), *Library Technology Funding, Planning, and Deployment* (pp. 23–35). Hershey, PA: IGI Global. doi:10.4018/978-1-5225-1735-1.ch002

Kowalsky, M. (2016). Analysis of Initial Involvement of Librarians in the Online Virtual World of Second Life. In B. Baggio (Ed.), *Analyzing Digital Discourse and Human Behavior in Modern Virtual Environments* (pp. 126–148). Hershey, PA: IGI Global. doi:10.4018/978-1-4666-9899-4.ch007

Kumar, K. (2018). Library in Your Pocket Delivery of Instruction Service Through Library Mobile Apps: A World in Your Pocket. In S. Bhattacharyya & K. Patnaik (Eds.), *Changing the Scope of Library Instruction in the Digital Age* (pp. 228–249). Hershey, PA: IGI Global. doi:10.4018/978-1-5225-2802-9.ch009

Kwanya, T. (2016). Information Seeking Behaviour in Digital Library Contexts. In A. Tella (Ed.), *Information Seeking Behavior and Challenges in Digital Libraries* (pp. 1–25). Hershey, PA: IGI Global. doi:10.4018/978-1-5225-0296-8.ch001

Kwanya, T. (2018). Social Bookmarking in Digital Libraries: Intellectual Property Rights Implications. In A. Tella & T. Kwanya (Eds.), *Handbook of Research on Managing Intellectual Property in Digital Libraries* (pp. 1–18). Hershey, PA: IGI Global. doi:10.4018/978-1-5225-3093-0.ch001

LaMoreaux, N. E. (2016). Collaborating to Create a Fashionable Event: A Guide for Creating a Library-Sponsored Conference. In B. Doherty (Ed.), *Space and Organizational Considerations in Academic Library Partnerships and Collaborations* (pp. 317–334). Hershey, PA: IGI Global. doi:10.4018/978-1-5225-0326-2.ch015

Lewis, J. K. (2018). Change Leadership Styles and Behaviors in Academic Libraries. In M. Khosrow-Pour, D.B.A. (Ed.), Encyclopedia of Information Science and Technology, Fourth Edition (pp. 5194-5203). Hershey, PA: IGI Global. doi:10.4018/978-1-5225-2255-3.ch451

Lillard, L. L. (2018). Is Interdisciplinary Collaboration in Academia an Elusive Dream?: Can the Institutional Barriers Be Broken Down? A Review of the Literature and the Case of Library Science. In M. Al-Suqri, A. Al-Kindi, S. AlKindi, & N. Saleem (Eds.), *Promoting Interdisciplinarity in Knowledge Generation and Problem Solving* (pp. 139–147). Hershey, PA: IGI Global. doi:10.4018/978-1-5225-3878-3. ch010

Lock, M. B., Fansler, C., & Webb, M. (2016). (R)Evolutionary Emergency Planning: Adding Resilience through Continuous Review. *International Journal of Risk and Contingency Management, 5*(2), 47–65. doi:10.4018/IJRCM.2016040103

Long, X., & Yao, B. (2017). The Construction and Development of the Academic Digital Library of Chinese Ancient Collections. In L. Ruan, Q. Zhu, & Y. Ye (Eds.), *Academic Library Development and Administration in China* (pp. 126–135). Hershey, PA: IGI Global. doi:10.4018/978-1-5225-0550-1.ch008

Lowe, M., & Reno, L. M. (2018). Academic Librarianship and Burnout. In *Examining the Emotional Dimensions of Academic Librarianship: Emerging Research and Opportunities* (pp. 72–89). Hershey, PA: IGI Global. doi:10.4018/978-1-5225-3761-8.ch005

Lowe, M., & Reno, L. M. (2018). Emotional Dimensions of Academic Librarianship. In *Examining the Emotional Dimensions of Academic Librarianship: Emerging Research and Opportunities* (pp. 54–71). Hershey, PA: IGI Global. doi:10.4018/978-1-5225-3761-8.ch004

Lowe, M., & Reno, L. M. (2018). Why Isn't This Being Studied? In *Examining the Emotional Dimensions of Academic Librarianship: Emerging Research and Opportunities* (pp. 90–108). Hershey, PA: IGI Global. doi:10.4018/978-1-5225-3761-8.ch006

Lowe, M., & Reno, L. M. (2018). Research Agenda: Research Ideas and Recommendations. In *Examining the Emotional Dimensions of Academic Librarianship: Emerging Research and Opportunities* (pp. 109–125). Hershey, PA: IGI Global. doi:10.4018/978-1-5225-3761-8.ch007

Luyombya, D., Kiyingi, G. W., & Naluwooza, M. (2018). The Nature and Utilisation of Archival Records Deposited in Makerere University Library, Uganda. In P. Ngulube (Ed.), *Handbook of Research on Heritage Management and Preservation* (pp. 96–113). Hershey, PA: IGI Global. doi:10.4018/978-1-5225-3137-1.ch005

Mabe, M., & Ashley, E. A. (2017). The Natural Role of the Public Library. In *The Developing Role of Public Libraries in Emergency Management: Emerging Research and Opportunities* (pp. 25–43). Hershey, PA: IGI Global. doi:10.4018/978-1-5225-2196-9.ch003

Mabe, M., & Ashley, E. A. (2017). I'm Trained, Now What? In *The Developing Role of Public Libraries in Emergency Management: Emerging Research and Opportunities* (pp. 87–95). Hershey, PA: IGI Global. doi:10.4018/978-1-5225-2196-9.ch007

Mabe, M., & Ashley, E. A. (2017). Emergency Preparation for the Library and Librarian. In *The Developing Role of Public Libraries in Emergency Management: Emerging Research and Opportunities* (pp. 61–78). Hershey, PA: IGI Global. doi:10.4018/978-1-5225-2196-9.ch005

Mabe, M., & Ashley, E. A. (2017). The CCPL Model. In *The Developing Role of Public Libraries in Emergency Management: Emerging Research and Opportunities* (pp. 15–24). Hershey, PA: IGI Global. doi:10.4018/978-1-5225-2196-9.ch002

Mabe, M., & Ashley, E. A. (2017). The Local Command Structure and How the Library Fits. In *In The Developing Role of Public Libraries in Emergency Management: Emerging Research and Opportunities* (pp. 44–60). Hershey, PA: IGI Global. doi:10.4018/978-1-5225-2196-9.ch004

Mabe, M. R. (2016). Libraries to the Rescue. *International Journal of Risk and Contingency Management, 5*(1), 62–81. doi:10.4018/IJRCM.2016010105

Mabe, M. R. (2016). The Library as Lifeboat. In E. Decker & J. Townes (Eds.), *Handbook of Research on Disaster Management and Contingency Planning in Modern Libraries* (pp. 494–515). Hershey, PA: IGI Global. doi:10.4018/978-1-4666-8624-3.ch021

Manzoor, A. (2018). Social Media: A Librarian's Tool for Instant and Direct Interaction With Library Users. In R. Bhardwaj (Ed.), *Digitizing the Modern Library and the Transition From Print to Electronic* (pp. 112–128). Hershey, PA: IGI Global. doi:10.4018/978-1-5225-2119-8.ch005

Maringanti, H. (2018). A Decision Making Paradigm for Software Development in Libraries. In L. Costello & M. Powers (Eds.), *Developing In-House Digital Tools in Library Spaces* (pp. 59–75). Hershey, PA: IGI Global. doi:10.4018/978-1-5225-2676-6.ch003

Markman, K. M., Ferrarini, M., & Deschenes, A. H. (2018). User Testing and Iterative Design in the Academic Library: A Case Study. In R. Roscoe, S. Craig, & I. Douglas (Eds.), *End-User Considerations in Educational Technology Design* (pp. 160–183). Hershey, PA: IGI Global. doi:10.4018/978-1-5225-2639-1.ch008

Marks, A. B., & Owen, E. (2016). It Is Everywhere: Handling a Mold Outbreak in a Library's High-Density Storage Collection. In E. Decker & J. Townes (Eds.), *Handbook of Research on Disaster Management and Contingency Planning in Modern Libraries* (pp. 311–339). Hershey, PA: IGI Global. doi:10.4018/978-1-4666-8624-3.ch014

Mavodza, J. (2016). Relationship between Knowledge Management and Academic Integrity in a Middle Eastern University. In A. Goel & P. Singhal (Eds.), *Product Innovation through Knowledge Management and Social Media Strategies* (pp. 241–264). Hershey, PA: IGI Global. doi:10.4018/978-1-4666-9607-5.ch011

Maynor, A. (2016). Response to the Unthinkable: Collecting and Archiving Condolence and Temporary Memorial Materials following Public Tragedies. In E. Decker & J. Townes (Eds.), *Handbook of Research on Disaster Management and Contingency Planning in Modern Libraries* (pp. 582–624). Hershey, PA: IGI Global. doi:10.4018/978-1-4666-8624-3.ch025

McFall, L. M., Simons, J. T., Lord, G., MacDonald, P. J., Nieves, A. D., & Young, S. (2016). Collaborations in Liberal Arts Colleges in Support of Digital Humanities. In B. Doherty (Ed.), *Technology-Centered Academic Library Partnerships and Collaborations* (pp. 31–60). Hershey, PA: IGI Global. doi:10.4018/978-1-5225-0323-1.ch002

Na, L. (2017). Library and Information Science Education and Graduate Programs in Academic Libraries. In L. Ruan, Q. Zhu, & Y. Ye (Eds.), *Academic Library Development and Administration in China* (pp. 218–229). Hershey, PA: IGI Global. doi:10.4018/978-1-5225-0550-1.ch013

Nagarkar, S. P. (2017). Biomedical Librarianship in the Post-Genomic Era. In S. Ram (Ed.), *Library and Information Services for Bioinformatics Education and Research* (pp. 1–17). Hershey, PA: IGI Global. doi:10.4018/978-1-5225-1871-6.ch001

Natarajan, M. (2016). Exploring the E-Discovery Tools on the Use of Library Collections by Users. In E. de Smet & S. Dhamdhere (Eds.), *E-Discovery Tools and Applications in Modern Libraries* (pp. 122–137). Hershey, PA: IGI Global. doi:10.4018/978-1-5225-0474-0.ch007

Natarajan, M. (2017). Exploring Knowledge Sharing over Social Media. In R. Chugh (Ed.), *Harnessing Social Media as a Knowledge Management Tool* (pp. 55–73). Hershey, PA: IGI Global. doi:10.4018/978-1-5225-0495-5.ch003

Nazir, T. (2017). Preservation Initiatives in E-Environment to Protect Information Assets. In T. Ashraf & N. Kumar (Eds.), *Interdisciplinary Digital Preservation Tools and Technologies* (pp. 193–208). Hershey, PA: IGI Global. doi:10.4018/978-1-5225-1653-8.ch010

Ngulube, P. (2017). Embedding Indigenous Knowledge in Library and Information Science Education in Anglophone Eastern and Southern Africa. In P. Ngulube (Ed.), *Handbook of Research on Social, Cultural, and Educational Considerations of Indigenous Knowledge in Developing Countries* (pp. 92–115). Hershey, PA: IGI Global. doi:10.4018/978-1-5225-0838-0.ch006

Nicolajsen, H. W., Sørensen, F., & Scupola, A. (2016). The Potential of Workshops vs Blogs for User Involvement in Service Innovation. *International Journal of E-Services and Mobile Applications*, 8(4), 1–19. doi:10.4018/IJESMA.2016100101

Nicolajsen, H. W., Sorensen, F., & Scupola, A. (2018). User Involvement in Service Innovation Processes. In M. Khosrow-Pour (Ed.), *Optimizing Current Practices in E-Services and Mobile Applications* (pp. 42–61). Hershey, PA: IGI Global. doi:10.4018/978-1-5225-5026-6.ch003

Nixon, M. L. (2016). Safety Doesn't Happen by Accident: Disaster Planning at the University of Pittsburgh. In E. Decker & J. Townes (Eds.), *Handbook of Research on Disaster Management and Contingency Planning in Modern Libraries* (pp. 184–206). Hershey, PA: IGI Global. doi:10.4018/978-1-4666-8624-3.ch009

Nwabueze, A. U., & Ibeh, B. O. (2016). Extent of ICT Literacy Possessed by Librarians in Federal University Libraries in South East Nigeria. *International Journal of Digital Literacy and Digital Competence*, 7(3), 13–22. doi:10.4018/IJDLDC.2016070102

O'Grady, A. R. (2016). The Boston Library Consortium and RapidR: Partnering to Develop an Unmediated Book Sharing Module. In B. Doherty (Ed.), *Technology-Centered Academic Library Partnerships and Collaborations* (pp. 194–219). Hershey, PA: IGI Global. doi:10.4018/978-1-5225-0323-1.ch007

Ochonogor, W. C., & Okite-Amughoro, F. A. (2018). Building an Effective Digital Library in a University Teaching Hospital (UTH) in Nigeria. In A. Tella & T. Kwanya (Eds.), *Handbook of Research on Managing Intellectual Property in Digital Libraries* (pp. 184–204). Hershey, PA: IGI Global. doi:10.4018/978-1-5225-3093-0.ch010

Oladapo, Y. O. (2018). Open Access to Knowledge and Challenges in Digital Libraries. In A. Tella & T. Kwanya (Eds.), *Handbook of Research on Managing Intellectual Property in Digital Libraries* (pp. 260–291). Hershey, PA: IGI Global. doi:10.4018/978-1-5225-3093-0.ch014

Oladokun, O., & Zulu, S. F. (2017). Document Description and Coding as Key Elements in Knowledge, Records, and Information Management. In P. Jain & N. Mnjama (Eds.), *Managing Knowledge Resources and Records in Modern Organizations* (pp. 179–197). Hershey, PA: IGI Global. doi:10.4018/978-1-5225-1965-2.ch011

Olin, J. R. (2016). Libraries and Digital Media. In B. Guzzetti & M. Lesley (Eds.), *Handbook of Research on the Societal Impact of Digital Media* (pp. 163–177). Hershey, PA: IGI Global. doi:10.4018/978-1-4666-8310-5.ch007

Oluwaseun, A. A. (2016). Barriers to Information Seeking in the Digital Libraries. In A. Tella (Ed.), *Information Seeking Behavior and Challenges in Digital Libraries* (pp. 291–303). Hershey, PA: IGI Global. doi:10.4018/978-1-5225-0296-8.ch014

Omeluzor, S. U., Abayomi, I., & Gbemi-Ogunleye, P. (2018). Contemporary Media for Library Users' Instruction in Academic Libraries in South-West Nigeria: Contemporary Library Instruction in the Digital Age. In S. Bhattacharyya & K. Patnaik (Eds.), *Changing the Scope of Library Instruction in the Digital Age* (pp. 162–185). Hershey, PA: IGI Global. doi:10.4018/978-1-5225-2802-9.ch007

Ondari-Okemwa, E. (2016). Information-Seeking Behaviour of Users in the Digital Libraries' Environment in Sub-Saharan Africa. In A. Tella (Ed.), *Information Seeking Behavior and Challenges in Digital Libraries* (pp. 26–56). Hershey, PA: IGI Global. doi:10.4018/978-1-5225-0296-8.ch002

Oshilalu, A. H., & Ogochukwu, E. T. (2017). Modeling a Software for Library and Information Centers. *International Journal of Library and Information Services*, 6(2), 1–10. doi:10.4018/IJLIS.2017070101

Osterman, A. C., O'Gara, G., & Armstrong, A. M. (2016). The Evolution of Collaborative Collection Development within a Library Consortium: Data Analysis Applied in a Cultural Context. In B. Doherty (Ed.), *Space and Organizational Considerations in Academic Library Partnerships and Collaborations* (pp. 157–181). Hershey, PA: IGI Global. doi:10.4018/978-1-5225-0326-2.ch008

Related References

Oswal, S. K. (2017). Institutional, Legal, and Attitudinal Barriers to the Accessibility of University Digital Libraries: Implications for Retention of Disabled Students. In H. Alphin Jr, J. Lavine, & R. Chan (Eds.), *Disability and Equity in Higher Education Accessibility* (pp. 223–241). Hershey, PA: IGI Global. doi:10.4018/978-1-5225-2665-0.ch010

Otike, J. (2016). Legal Considerations of Providing Information in Support of Distance Learning by Digital Libraries in Universities in Kenya. In A. Tella (Ed.), *Information Seeking Behavior and Challenges in Digital Libraries* (pp. 57–69). Hershey, PA: IGI Global. doi:10.4018/978-1-5225-0296-8.ch003

Oukrich, J., & Bouikhalene, B. (2017). A Survey of Users' Satisfaction in the University Library by Using a Pareto Analysis and the Automatic Classification Methods. *International Journal of Library and Information Services*, 6(1), 17–36. doi:10.4018/IJLIS.2017010102

Özel, N. (2018). Developing Visual Literacy Skills Through Library Instructions. In V. Osinska & G. Osinski (Eds.), *Information Visualization Techniques in the Social Sciences and Humanities* (pp. 32–48). Hershey, PA: IGI Global. doi:10.4018/978-1-5225-4990-1.ch003

Patel, D., & Thakur, D. (2017). Managing Open Access (OA) Scholarly Information Resources in a University. In A. Munigal (Ed.), *Scholarly Communication and the Publish or Perish Pressures of Academia* (pp. 224–255). Hershey, PA: IGI Global. doi:10.4018/978-1-5225-1697-2.ch011

Patnaik, K. R. (2018). Crafting a Framework for Copyright Literacy and Licensed Content: A Case Study at an Advanced Management Education and Research Library. In S. Bhattacharyya & K. Patnaik (Eds.), *Changing the Scope of Library Instruction in the Digital Age* (pp. 136–160). Hershey, PA: IGI Global. doi:10.4018/978-1-5225-2802-9.ch006

Paynter, K. (2017). Elementary Library Media Specialists' Roles in the Implementation of the Common Core State Standards. In M. Grassetti & S. Brookby (Eds.), *Advancing Next-Generation Teacher Education through Digital Tools and Applications* (pp. 262–283). Hershey, PA: IGI Global. doi:10.4018/978-1-5225-0965-3.ch014

Perez, M. J. (2016). Local Studies Centers in the Philippines: An Introductory Text. In J. Yap, M. Perez, M. Ayson, & G. Entico (Eds.), *Special Library Administration, Standardization and Technological Integration* (pp. 249–266). Hershey, PA: IGI Global. doi:10.4018/978-1-4666-9542-9.ch011

Perry, S. C., & Waggoner, J. (2018). Processes for User-Centered Design and Development: The Omeka Curator Dashboard Project. In L. Costello & M. Powers (Eds.), *Developing In-House Digital Tools in Library Spaces* (pp. 37–58). Hershey, PA: IGI Global. doi:10.4018/978-1-5225-2676-6.ch002

Phuritsabam, B., & Devi, A. B. (2017). Information Seeking Behavior of Medical Scientists at Jawaharlal Nehru Institute of Medical Science: A Study. In S. Ram (Ed.), *Library and Information Services for Bioinformatics Education and Research* (pp. 177–187). Hershey, PA: IGI Global. doi:10.4018/978-1-5225-1871-6.ch010

Pina, P. (2016). Copyright Issues in the Context of the Digital Library. In A. Tella (Ed.), *Information Seeking Behavior and Challenges in Digital Libraries* (pp. 70–83). Hershey, PA: IGI Global. doi:10.4018/978-1-5225-0296-8.ch004

Pionke, J. (2016). Disaster is in the Eye of the Beholder. In E. Decker & J. Townes (Eds.), *Handbook of Research on Disaster Management and Contingency Planning in Modern Libraries* (pp. 516–533). Hershey, PA: IGI Global. doi:10.4018/978-1-4666-8624-3.ch022

Quadri, R. F., & Sodiq, O. A. (2018). Managing Intellectual Property in Digital Libraries: The Roles of Digital Librarians. In A. Tella & T. Kwanya (Eds.), *Handbook of Research on Managing Intellectual Property in Digital Libraries* (pp. 337–355). Hershey, PA: IGI Global. doi:10.4018/978-1-5225-3093-0.ch017

Ram, S. (2017). Library Services for Bioinformatics: Establishing Synergy Data Information and Knowledge. In S. Ram (Ed.), *Library and Information Services for Bioinformatics Education and Research* (pp. 18–33). Hershey, PA: IGI Global. doi:10.4018/978-1-5225-1871-6.ch002

Rao, M. (2017). Use of Institutional Repository for Information Dissemination and Knowledge Management. In B. Gunjal (Ed.), *Managing Knowledge and Scholarly Assets in Academic Libraries* (pp. 156–173). Hershey, PA: IGI Global. doi:10.4018/978-1-5225-1741-2.ch007

Rao, Y., & Zhang, Y. (2017). The Construction and Development of Academic Library Digital Special Subject Databases. In L. Ruan, Q. Zhu, & Y. Ye (Eds.), *Academic Library Development and Administration in China* (pp. 163–183). Hershey, PA: IGI Global. doi:10.4018/978-1-5225-0550-1.ch010

Razip, S. N., Kadir, S. F., Saim, S. N., Dolhan, F. N., Jarmil, N., Salleh, N. H., & Rajin, G. (2017). Predicting Users' Intention towards Using Library Self-Issue and Return Systems. In N. Suki (Ed.), *Handbook of Research on Leveraging Consumer Psychology for Effective Customer Engagement* (pp. 102–115). Hershey, PA: IGI Global. doi:10.4018/978-1-5225-0746-8.ch007

Related References

Ress, A. D., McLaughlin, J. A., & Bertuca, C. (2016). Online Video Tutorials and Interlibrary Resource Sharing: A Model for Understanding the Role of Internet Video in Library Science and Education. In B. Doherty (Ed.), *Technology-Centered Academic Library Partnerships and Collaborations* (pp. 61–88). Hershey, PA: IGI Global. doi:10.4018/978-1-5225-0323-1.ch003

Rothwell, S. L. (2018). Librarians and Instructional Design Challenges: Concepts, Examples, and a Flexible Design Framework. In S. Bhattacharyya & K. Patnaik (Eds.), *Changing the Scope of Library Instruction in the Digital Age* (pp. 24–59). Hershey, PA: IGI Global. doi:10.4018/978-1-5225-2802-9.ch002

Roy, L., & Frydman, A. (2018). Community Outreach. In M. Khosrow-Pour, D.B.A. (Ed.), Encyclopedia of Information Science and Technology, Fourth Edition (pp. 6685-6694). Hershey, PA: IGI Global. doi:10.4018/978-1-5225-2255-3.ch579

Rutto, D., & Yudah, O. (2018). E-Books in University Libraries in Kenya: Trends, Usage, and Intellectual Property Issues. In A. Tella & T. Kwanya (Eds.), *Handbook of Research on Managing Intellectual Property in Digital Libraries* (pp. 120–141). Hershey, PA: IGI Global. doi:10.4018/978-1-5225-3093-0.ch007

Ryan, S. M., & Grubbs, W. T. (2016). Curricular Collaborations: Using Emerging Technologies to Foster Innovative Partnerships. In B. Doherty (Ed.), *Technology-Centered Academic Library Partnerships and Collaborations* (pp. 89–125). Hershey, PA: IGI Global. doi:10.4018/978-1-5225-0323-1.ch004

Sabharwal, A. (2017). The Transformative Role of Institutional Repositories in Academic Knowledge Management. In B. Gunjal (Ed.), *Managing Knowledge and Scholarly Assets in Academic Libraries* (pp. 127–155). Hershey, PA: IGI Global. doi:10.4018/978-1-5225-1741-2.ch006

Sadiku, S. A., Kpakiko, M. M., & Tsafe, A. G. (2018). Institutional Digital Repository and the Challenges of Global Visibility in Nigeria. In A. Tella & T. Kwanya (Eds.), *Handbook of Research on Managing Intellectual Property in Digital Libraries* (pp. 356–376). Hershey, PA: IGI Global. doi:10.4018/978-1-5225-3093-0.ch018

Sahu, M. K. (2018). Web-Scale Discovery Service in Academic Library Environment: A Birds Eye View. *International Journal of Library and Information Services*, 7(1), 1–14. doi:10.4018/IJLIS.2018010101

Salim, F., Saigar, B., Armoham, P. K., Gobalakrishnan, S., Jap, M. Y., & Lim, N. A. (2017). Students' Information-Seeking Intention in Academic Digital Libraries. In N. Suki (Ed.), *Handbook of Research on Leveraging Consumer Psychology for Effective Customer Engagement* (pp. 259–273). Hershey, PA: IGI Global. doi:10.4018/978-1-5225-0746-8.ch017

San Kong, E. W., Chiu, D. K., & Ho, K. K. (2016). Applications of Social Media in Academic Library Services: A Case of the Hong Kong Polytechnic University Library. *International Journal of Systems and Service-Oriented Engineering*, 6(2), 53–65. doi:10.4018/IJSSOE.2016040103

Saroja, G. (2017). Changing Face of Scholarly Communication and Its Impact on Library and Information Centres. In A. Munigal (Ed.), *Scholarly Communication and the Publish or Perish Pressures of Academia* (pp. 100–117). Hershey, PA: IGI Global. doi:10.4018/978-1-5225-1697-2.ch006

Sawant, S. (2016). Collaborative Online Learning Tools and Types: Few Perspectives of Its Use in Academic Library. In H. Rahman (Ed.), *Human Development and Interaction in the Age of Ubiquitous Technology* (pp. 94–119). Hershey, PA: IGI Global. doi:10.4018/978-1-5225-0556-3.ch005

Sawsaa, A. F., & Lu, J. (2017). Research Background on Ontology. In J. Lu & Q. Xu (Eds.), *Ontologies and Big Data Considerations for Effective Intelligence* (pp. 443–509). Hershey, PA: IGI Global. doi:10.4018/978-1-5225-2058-0.ch011

Schuster, D. W. (2017). Selection Process for Free Open Source Software. In E. Iglesias (Ed.), *Library Technology Funding, Planning, and Deployment* (pp. 55–71). Hershey, PA: IGI Global. doi:10.4018/978-1-5225-1735-1.ch004

Segaetsho, T. (2018). Environmental Consideration in the Preservation of Paper Materials in Heritage Institutions in the East and Southern African Region. In P. Ngulube (Ed.), *Handbook of Research on Heritage Management and Preservation* (pp. 183–212). Hershey, PA: IGI Global. doi:10.4018/978-1-5225-3137-1.ch010

Shakhsi, L. (2017). Cataloging Images in Library, Archive, and Museum. In T. Ashraf & N. Kumar (Eds.), *Interdisciplinary Digital Preservation Tools and Technologies* (pp. 119–141). Hershey, PA: IGI Global. doi:10.4018/978-1-5225-1653-8.ch007

Sharma, C. (2017). Digital Initiatives of the Indian Council of World Affairs' Library. In T. Ashraf & N. Kumar (Eds.), *Interdisciplinary Digital Preservation Tools and Technologies* (pp. 231–241). Hershey, PA: IGI Global. doi:10.4018/978-1-5225-1653-8.ch012

Shaw, M. D. (2016). Navigating Campus Disasters from Within the Library: Lessons and Implications from Gulf Coast Institutions. In E. Decker & J. Townes (Eds.), *Handbook of Research on Disaster Management and Contingency Planning in Modern Libraries* (pp. 340–365). Hershey, PA: IGI Global. doi:10.4018/978-1-4666-8624-3.ch015

Shawish, A., & Salama, M. (2016). Cloud-Based Digital Library Era. In J. Yap, M. Perez, M. Ayson, & G. Entico (Eds.), *Special Library Administration, Standardization and Technological Integration* (pp. 226–247). Hershey, PA: IGI Global. doi:10.4018/978-1-4666-9542-9.ch010

Siddaiah, D. K. (2018). Commonwealth Professional Fellowship: A Gateway for the Strategic Development of Libraries in India. In R. Bhardwaj (Ed.), *Digitizing the Modern Library and the Transition From Print to Electronic* (pp. 270–286). Hershey, PA: IGI Global. doi:10.4018/978-1-5225-2119-8.ch012

Silvana de Rosa, A. (2018). Mission, Tools, and Ongoing Developments in the So.Re. Com. "A.S. de Rosa" @-library. In M. Khosrow-Pour, D.B.A. (Ed.), Encyclopedia of Information Science and Technology, Fourth Edition (pp. 5237-5251). Hershey, PA: IGI Global. doi:10.4018/978-1-5225-2255-3.ch455

Silverman, R., Nakashima, T., Hunt, J. M., & Tuia, J. (2016). A Stitch in Time: Disaster Mitigation Strategies for Cultural Heritage Collections. In E. Decker & J. Townes (Eds.), *Handbook of Research on Disaster Management and Contingency Planning in Modern Libraries* (pp. 208–239). Hershey, PA: IGI Global. doi:10.4018/978-1-4666-8624-3.ch010

Smart, C. (2016). The Public Library's Role in Enabling E-Government: A View of Two Countries in the English-Speaking Caribbean. *International Journal of Public Administration in the Digital Age, 3*(3), 18–32. doi:10.4018/IJPADA.2016070102

Smolenski, N., Kostic, M., & Sofronijevic, A. M. (2018). Intrapreneurship and Enterprise 2.0 as Grounds for Developing In-House Digital Tools for Handling METS/ALTO Files at the University Library Belgrade. In L. Costello & M. Powers (Eds.), *Developing In-House Digital Tools in Library Spaces* (pp. 92–116). Hershey, PA: IGI Global. doi:10.4018/978-1-5225-2676-6.ch005

Sochay, L., & Junus, R. (2017). From Summon to SearchPlus: The RFP Process for a Discovery Tool at the MSU Libraries. In E. Iglesias (Ed.), *Library Technology Funding, Planning, and Deployment* (pp. 72–98). Hershey, PA: IGI Global. doi:10.4018/978-1-5225-1735-1.ch005

Sonawane, C. S. (2018). Library Catalogue in the Internet Age. In R. Bhardwaj (Ed.), *Digitizing the Modern Library and the Transition From Print to Electronic* (pp. 204–223). Hershey, PA: IGI Global. doi:10.4018/978-1-5225-2119-8.ch009

Sonawane, M. (2016). Creating an Agile Library. In E. de Smet & S. Dhamdhere (Eds.), *E-Discovery Tools and Applications in Modern Libraries* (pp. 109–121). Hershey, PA: IGI Global. doi:10.4018/978-1-5225-0474-0.ch006

Staley, C., Kenyon, R. S., & Marcovitz, D. M. (2018). Embedded Services: Going Beyond the Field of Dreams Model for Online Programs. In D. Polly, M. Putman, T. Petty, & A. Good (Eds.), *Innovative Practices in Teacher Preparation and Graduate-Level Teacher Education Programs* (pp. 368–381). Hershey, PA: IGI Global. doi:10.4018/978-1-5225-3068-8.ch020

Stavridi, S. V., & Hamada, D. R. (2016). Children and Youth Librarians: Competencies Required in Technology-Based Environment. In J. Yap, M. Perez, M. Ayson, & G. Entico (Eds.), *Special Library Administration, Standardization and Technological Integration* (pp. 25–50). Hershey, PA: IGI Global. doi:10.4018/978-1-4666-9542-9.ch002

Stewart, M. C., Atilano, M., & Arnold, C. L. (2017). Improving Customer Relations with Social Listening: A Case Study of an American Academic Library. *International Journal of Customer Relationship Marketing and Management*, 8(1), 49–63. doi:10.4018/IJCRMM.2017010104

Sukula, S. K., & Bhardwaj, R. K. (2018). An Extensive Discussion on Transition of Libraries: The Panoramic View of Library Resources, Services, and Evolved Librarianship. In R. Bhardwaj (Ed.), *Digitizing the Modern Library and the Transition From Print to Electronic* (pp. 255–269). Hershey, PA: IGI Global. doi:10.4018/978-1-5225-2119-8.ch011

Taylor, L. N., Alteri, S. A., Minson, V. I., Walker, B., Hawley, E. H., Dinsmore, C. S., & Jefferson, R. J. (2016). Library Collaborative Networks Forging Scholarly Cyberinfrastructure and Radical Collaboration. In B. Doherty (Ed.), *Technology-Centered Academic Library Partnerships and Collaborations* (pp. 1–30). Hershey, PA: IGI Global. doi:10.4018/978-1-5225-0323-1.ch001

Tella, A., & Babatunde, B. J. (2017). Determinants of Continuance Intention of Facebook Usage Among Library and Information Science Female Undergraduates in Selected Nigerian Universities. *International Journal of E-Adoption*, 9(2), 59–76. doi:10.4018/IJEA.2017070104

Tella, A., Okojie, V., & Olaniyi, O. T. (2018). Social Bookmarking Tools and Digital Libraries. In A. Tella & T. Kwanya (Eds.), *Handbook of Research on Managing Intellectual Property in Digital Libraries* (pp. 396–409). Hershey, PA: IGI Global. doi:10.4018/978-1-5225-3093-0.ch020

Tella, A., Oyeniran, S., & Ojo, O. J. (2016). Digital Libraries and Copyright Issues. In A. Tella (Ed.), *Information Seeking Behavior and Challenges in Digital Libraries* (pp. 108–126). Hershey, PA: IGI Global. doi:10.4018/978-1-5225-0296-8.ch006

Thull, J. J. (2018). Librarians and the Evolving Research Needs of Distance Students. In I. Oncioiu (Ed.), *Ethics and Decision-Making for Sustainable Business Practices* (pp. 203–216). Hershey, PA: IGI Global. doi:10.4018/978-1-5225-3773-1.ch012

Titilope, A. O. (2017). Ethical Issues in Library and Information Science Profession in Nigeria: An Appraisal. *International Journal of Library and Information Services*, 6(2), 11–22. doi:10.4018/IJLIS.2017070102

Tutu, J. M. (2018). Intellectual Property Challenges in Digital Library Environments. In A. Tella & T. Kwanya (Eds.), *Handbook of Research on Managing Intellectual Property in Digital Libraries* (pp. 225–240). Hershey, PA: IGI Global. doi:10.4018/978-1-5225-3093-0.ch012

Upev, M. T., Beetseh, K., & Idachaba, J. A. (2016). Usability of Digital Resources: A Study of Francis Sulemanu Idachaba Library University of Agriculture Makurdi. In A. Tella (Ed.), *Information Seeking Behavior and Challenges in Digital Libraries* (pp. 224–237). Hershey, PA: IGI Global. doi:10.4018/978-1-5225-0296-8.ch011

Verplaetse, A., Mascareñas, P., & O'Neill, K. (2016). Zen and the Art of Disaster Planning: Collaboration Challenges in Library Disaster Plan Design and Execution. In E. Decker & J. Townes (Eds.), *Handbook of Research on Disaster Management and Contingency Planning in Modern Libraries* (pp. 96–119). Hershey, PA: IGI Global. doi:10.4018/978-1-4666-8624-3.ch005

Walker, B., & Pursley, T. (2016). A Statewide Collaborative Storage and Print Repository Model: The Florida Academic Repository (FLARE). In B. Doherty (Ed.), *Space and Organizational Considerations in Academic Library Partnerships and Collaborations* (pp. 111–129). Hershey, PA: IGI Global. doi:10.4018/978-1-5225-0326-2.ch006

Wallace, D., & Hemment, M. (2018). Enabling Scholarship in the Digital Age: A Case for Libraries Creating Value at HBS. In S. Bhattacharyya & K. Patnaik (Eds.), *Changing the Scope of Library Instruction in the Digital Age* (pp. 86–117). Hershey, PA: IGI Global. doi:10.4018/978-1-5225-2802-9.ch004

Wani, Z. A., Zainab, T., & Hussain, S. (2018). Web 2.0 From Evolution to Revolutionary Impact in Library and Information Centers. In M. Khosrow-Pour, D.B.A. (Ed.), Encyclopedia of Information Science and Technology, Fourth Edition (pp. 5262-5271). Hershey, PA: IGI Global. doi:10.4018/978-1-5225-2255-3.ch457

Waring, S. M. (2016). Teaching with Primary Sources: Moving from Professional Development to a Model of Professional Learning. In T. Petty, A. Good, & S. Putman (Eds.), *Handbook of Research on Professional Development for Quality Teaching and Learning* (pp. 295–306). Hershey, PA: IGI Global. doi:10.4018/978-1-5225-0204-3.ch014

Weiss, A. P. (2018). Massive Digital Libraries (MDLs). In M. Khosrow-Pour, D.B.A. (Ed.), Encyclopedia of Information Science and Technology, Fourth Edition (pp. 5226-5236). Hershey, PA: IGI Global. doi:10.4018/978-1-5225-2255-3.ch454

Wentao, C., Jinyu, Z., & Zhonggen, Y. (2016). Learning Outcomes and Affective Factors of Blended Learning of English for Library Science. *International Journal of Information and Communication Technology Education, 12*(3), 13–25. doi:10.4018/IJICTE.2016070102

White, G. W. (2016). The Library as a Center for Innovation: A Collaboration at the University of Maryland. In B. Doherty (Ed.), *Space and Organizational Considerations in Academic Library Partnerships and Collaborations* (pp. 68–86). Hershey, PA: IGI Global. doi:10.4018/978-1-5225-0326-2.ch004

Wu, S. K., Bess, M., & Price, B. R. (2018). Digitizing Library Outreach: Leveraging Bluetooth Beacons and Mobile Applications to Expand Library Outreach. In R. Bhardwaj (Ed.), *Digitizing the Modern Library and the Transition From Print to Electronic* (pp. 193–203). Hershey, PA: IGI Global. doi:10.4018/978-1-5225-2119-8.ch008

Wulff, E. (2018). Evaluation of Digital Collections and Political Visibility of the Library. In R. Bhardwaj (Ed.), *Digitizing the Modern Library and the Transition From Print to Electronic* (pp. 64–89). Hershey, PA: IGI Global. doi:10.4018/978-1-5225-2119-8.ch003

Xiao, L., & Liu, Y. (2017). Development of Innovative User Services. In L. Ruan, Q. Zhu, & Y. Ye (Eds.), *Academic Library Development and Administration in China* (pp. 56–73). Hershey, PA: IGI Global. doi:10.4018/978-1-5225-0550-1.ch004

Xin, X., & Wu, X. (2017). The Practice of Outreach Services in Chinese Special Libraries. In L. Ruan, Q. Zhu, & Y. Ye (Eds.), *Academic Library Development and Administration in China* (pp. 74–89). Hershey, PA: IGI Global. doi:10.4018/978-1-5225-0550-1.ch005

Yao, X., Zhu, Q., & Liu, J. (2017). The China Academic Library and Information System (CALIS). In L. Ruan, Q. Zhu, & Y. Ye (Eds.), *Academic Library Development and Administration in China* (pp. 1–19). Hershey, PA: IGI Global. doi:10.4018/978-1-5225-0550-1.ch001

Related References

Yap, J. M. (2016). Social Media Literacy of Agricultural Librarians in the Philippines. In J. Yap, M. Perez, M. Ayson, & G. Entico (Eds.), *Special Library Administration, Standardization and Technological Integration* (pp. 202–224). Hershey, PA: IGI Global. doi:10.4018/978-1-4666-9542-9.ch009

Yasue, A. (2016). Preservation Management in Company Libraries. In J. Yap, M. Perez, M. Ayson, & G. Entico (Eds.), *Special Library Administration, Standardization and Technological Integration* (pp. 305–314). Hershey, PA: IGI Global. doi:10.4018/978-1-4666-9542-9.ch013

Yin, Q., Yingying, W., Yan, Z., & Xiaojia, M. (2017). Resource Sharing and Mutually Beneficial Cooperation: A Look at the New United Model in Public and College Libraries. In L. Ruan, Q. Zhu, & Y. Ye (Eds.), *Academic Library Development and Administration in China* (pp. 334–352). Hershey, PA: IGI Global. doi:10.4018/978-1-5225-0550-1.ch019

Yuhua, F. (2018). Computer Information Library Clusters. In M. Khosrow-Pour, D.B.A. (Ed.), Encyclopedia of Information Science and Technology, Fourth Edition (pp. 4399-4403). Hershey, PA: IGI Global. doi:10.4018/978-1-5225-2255-3.ch382

Yusuf, F., Owolabi, S., Aregbesola, A., Oguntayo, S., Okocha, F., & Eyiolorunse, T. (2016). Demographics, Socio-Economic and Cognitive Skills as Barriers to Information Seeking in a Digital Library Environment. In A. Tella (Ed.), *Information Seeking Behavior and Challenges in Digital Libraries* (pp. 179–202). Hershey, PA: IGI Global. doi:10.4018/978-1-5225-0296-8.ch009

Yusuf, F., & Owolabi, S. E. (2018). Open Access to Knowledge and Challenges in Digital Libraries: Nigeria's Peculiarity. In A. Tella & T. Kwanya (Eds.), *Handbook of Research on Managing Intellectual Property in Digital Libraries* (pp. 241–259). Hershey, PA: IGI Global. doi:10.4018/978-1-5225-3093-0.ch013

Yuvaraj, M. (2016). Impact of Discovery Layers on Accessing E-Resources in Academic Libraries: A Case Study of Central University of Bihar. In E. de Smet & S. Dhamdhere (Eds.), *E-Discovery Tools and Applications in Modern Libraries* (pp. 181–200). Hershey, PA: IGI Global. doi:10.4018/978-1-5225-0474-0.ch010

Zaremohzzabieh, Z., Ahrari, S., Abu Samah, B., & Bolong, J. (2016). Researching Information Seeking in Digital Libraries through Information-Seeking Models. In A. Tella (Ed.), *Information Seeking Behavior and Challenges in Digital Libraries* (pp. 84–107). Hershey, PA: IGI Global. doi:10.4018/978-1-5225-0296-8.ch005

Zhu, S., & Shi, W. (2017). A Bibliometric Analysis of Research and Services in Chinese Academic Libraries. In L. Ruan, Q. Zhu, & Y. Ye (Eds.), *Academic Library Development and Administration in China* (pp. 253–262). Hershey, PA: IGI Global. doi:10.4018/978-1-5225-0550-1.ch015

Zimeras, S., Kostagiolas, P., & Lavranos, C. (2016). Dealing with the Uncertainty of Satisfaction Surveys in Organizations That Employ Interactive Multimedia: An Analysis of False Answers Statistical Models through a Digital Music Library Case Study. In I. Deliyannis, P. Kostagiolas, & C. Banou (Eds.), *Experimental Multimedia Systems for Interactivity and Strategic Innovation* (pp. 160–175). Hershey, PA: IGI Global. doi:10.4018/978-1-4666-8659-5.ch008

About the Contributors

Victoria L. Claypoole is a Research Associate III with Design Interactive, Inc. With previous experience at the Air Force Research Lab and her current work with the United States Navy, Dr. Claypoole's research interest lies at the intersection of increasing warfighter readiness and advancing scientific knowledge. Her previous work has examined how individual differences and social cues can improve attention and enhance enemy threat detection. Currently, her work is centered on leveraging emerging technology to develop next-generation training and operational support for the warfighter. Dr. Claypoole has earned numerous professional awards, including the University of Florida's 40 under 40, the University of Central Florida's 30 under 30, and several Best Paper awards at various conferences. She received a Ph.D. in Human Factors and Cognitive Psychology and a Master's in Modeling and Simulation from the University of Central Florida.

Kimberly E. Culley has an earned Ph.D. in Human Factors with a specialization in Cognitive Engineering and Applied Decision Making. She is a Board of Certification in Professional Ergonomics (BCPE) Certified Human Factors Professional (CHFP), INCOSE Certified Systems Engineering Professional (CSEP), and holds DAWIA Level III Certification in both Engineering and Science and Technology Management. She currently serves as the Chief Human Factors Engineer for the U.S. Submarine Force. Her Human Factors and Decision Science program includes the development of data-driven decision making tools for senior leadership regarding technical, organizational, and behavioral indicators (TOBI) of command-level risk; analysis of causal factors in near miss events and incidents to steer force improvement initiatives; development of formal doctrine and training materials relating to human factors, decision science, and risk based analysis; and providing Human Factors and Decision Science support to various DoD partners. Dr. Culley was the sole Human Factors SME member of the CNO-directed, USFF-led Comprehensive Review of Surface Force Incidents, and provided a unique Human Factors review of systemic cultural issues that contributed to the FTZ and JSM collisions. This led to a reinvigoration of focus at high levels of Navy leadership on human performance factors that impact human-machine systems. Dr. Culley lives on a small farm in Virginia with her significant other and their German Shepherd Heidi. Disclaimer: The views expressed are those of the author and do not necessarily reflect the official policy or position of the Department of the Navy, Department of Defense, nor the U.S. Government.

William J. Gibbs is an Associate Professor in the MEDIA Department at Duquesne University where he teaches courses in Digital Media, Interaction Design, Instructional Design, Human-Computer Interaction, and Interface Design. He received a Ph.D. in Instructional Systems from The Pennsylvania State University. His research interests include technology-based learning environments, usability engineering and measures for observing human-computer interactions. His research has also examined learning and behavioral changes while people interact with computer interfaces.

Maurita T. Harris, M.S., is a doctoral student in Applied Health Sciences at the University of Illinois Urbana-Champaign. Her research interests include aging with disabilities, design for aging, technology-based health interventions, and technology acceptance.

Melanie D. Hetzel-Riggin, Ph.D., is a Professor of Psychology at Penn State Behrend. She is a licensed psychologist, Associate Director of the School of Humanities and Social Sciences and serves as a faculty research affiliate at the Susan Hirt Hagen Center for Community Outreach, Research, and Evaluation (CORE). Dr. Hetzel-Riggin's research focuses on the effectiveness of prevention education to reduce interpersonal violence and peer mistreatment, community-level prevention, and the relationship among interpersonal trauma, coping style, risk and resiliency, and mental health outcomes.

Catherine Hodges has seven years of design experience, including print, web, mobile, augmented reality, and virtual reality. She is experienced in all facets of User Experience and User Interface design including user research, user personas, storyboarding, journey mapping, user flows, wireframing, color theory, iconography, typography, prototyping, illustration, animation, and interaction design. She currently acts as design lead for for multiple cross-platform XR maintenance division projects.

Clay Killingsworth is an Applied Research Intern in the XR Division at Design Interactive and a graduate researcher and PhD candidate at the University of Central Florida. His experience includes learning and decision-making research, computational modeling, and usability assessment for diverse clients including the United

States Navy and Army, National Institutes of Health, and Crescent Moon Games. His current work focuses on the design and development of XR solutions for job training and performance aids. He holds a Master's in Applied Experimental and Human Factors Psychology from the University of Central Florida and a Bachelor's in Psychology from Harding University.

Antigoni Kotsiou received her MA in Applied Clinical Psychology from Pennsylvania State University, the Behrend College in 2020. She worked as a content creator in the development of the mental health application for smartphones Serene in the summer of 2020. She currently works as a therapist providing treatment to children, adolescents, and young adults with trauma history and/or other mental health and behavioral concerns. Her research interests include therapeutic processes, techniques, and models, and psychopathology. She is interested in qualitative research and the subjective experiences of those involved in psychotherapy and mental health services.

Michael Miuccio is a PhD student in the Human Factors and Cognitive Psychology program at the University of Central Florida. He received a Bachelor of Arts in Psychology at Rutgers University and is currently a member of the Attention and Memory lab. His research interests involve understanding how mental representations guide attention in visual search.

Fernando L. Montalvo received a B.S. in aeronautical science from Embry-Riddle Aeronautical University, as well as a B.S. in psychology and a B.A. in anthropology from the University of Central Florida (UCF). Additionally, he received an M.A. in applied experimental and human factors psychology from UCF. In the Technology and Aging Laboratory, his primary research interests include human-robot and human-computer interaction.

Larry Moralez is an experienced transdisciplinary researcher with a demonstrated history of working in academic and technological industries. Skilled in usability testing, design evaluation, rapid prototyping, experiment moderation, data analysis, data presentation, and machine learning. He is an adaptable research professional with graduate degrees focused in Cognitive Science and Modeling and Simulation from University of Central Florida.

Hannah Nye has seven years of experience with interaction and user-centered design which includes delivering to clients both in the commercial and government sector to deliver systems based on positive user experience. Her professional highlights include: (a) UI/UX design lead of an autonomous flying system created for helicopters that works as a co-pilot to deliver data-driven suggestions to handle contingencies and routes for the U.S. military; (b) designer for the Full Sail University online instructional portal, which included evaluation design, user testing, and interviews with professors to deliver student-driven content; (c) UI/UX designer and developer for RadKidz, a patient education application for Nemours Children Hospital featuring a multimedia interactive experience of radiology procedures; and (d) lead designer for a Chevron AR application – an instructional, location-based system that increases retention of maintenance for oil compressors and included integration with their manager tool.

Paul Oppold is a PhD student in the School of Modeling, Simulation and Training at the University of Central Florida. His research examines wearables and wearable applications, how distributed teams demonstrate and share knowledge, and Communities of Practice and Play.

Wendy A. Rogers, Ph.D., is Shahid and Ann Carlson Khan Professor of Applied Health Sciences at the University of Illinois Urbana-Champaign. She is the Director of the McKechnie Family LIFE Home; the Health Technology Education Program; Program Director of CHART(Collaborations in Health, Aging, Research, and Technology); and Director of the Human Factors and Aging Laboratory. Her research interests include design for aging; technology acceptance; human-automation interaction; aging-in-place; human-robot interaction; aging with disabilities; cognitive aging; skill acquisition; and training. Dr. Rogers' research is funded by the National Institutes of Health through the National Institute on Aging and through the National Institute of Nursing Research. In addition, her work is funded by the Department of health and Human Services through the National Institute on Disability, Independent Living, and Rehabilitation Research.

Ernesto Ruiz is a Research Associate I with Design Interactive, Inc. His previous work examined how socio-cultural, psychological, and political-economic factors impacted the distribution of human biological variation. He has studied patterns of child growth and development in the context of changing dietary patterns in Latin America, the role of stress and trauma in relation to chronic pain among African American adults, and health disparities in relation to globalization. Currently Ernesto works on understanding the physiological and psychological effects of immersive environments. Ernesto received a Masters in Public Health and a Ph.D. in Applied Biological Anthropology from the University of South Florida.

Michael Schwartz is the founder of Wearable Electronics Augmented Reality (WEAR) Lab. His research focuses on the design and usability of wearable devices and alternative interfaces for people with sensory impairments. Michael has a Masters in psychology from Stephen F Austin University and a Masters in modeling and simulation from the University of Central Florida. He is currently pursuing a PhD in human factors.

Emalee Sekely is a graduate student in the Media Arts and Technology Master of Science program at Duquesne University.

Christopher R. Shelton earned his Ph.D. in Clinical Psychology from the University of Wyoming in 2018. He completed an APA-accredited internship at the University of Miami. His dissertation focused on the feasibility and acceptability of a tailored Internet-based intervention for college students and adults with ADHD. Currently, he is an Assistant Professor of Clinical Psychology at Penn State Behrend and the Director of the Virtual/Augmented Reality Lab. His current research interests broadly fall within three areas: (1) examination of ADHD and Sluggish Cognitive Tempo, particularly within emerging adult (18-25) and adult (26+) populations; (2) development of digital mental health assessments and interventions to increase treatment availability; and (3) the use of immersive technologies across a range of domains.

Kay M. Stanney is CEO and Founder of Design Interactive (DI), Inc., a small women-owned company that has been focusing on empowering people through innovative solutions since 1998. In 2019, she was inducted into the National Academy of Engineering (NAE) for her contributions to "human factors engineering through virtual reality technology and strategic leadership." She works with the DoD and Fortune 500 companies to harness the power of interactive technology to help people realize their full potential. Stanney received the 2006 IEEE Virtual Reality Technical Achievement Award from the IEEE Computer Society, an award designed to honor individuals for their seminal technical achievement in virtual and augmented reality. She received a B.S. in Industrial Engineering from the State University of New York at Buffalo, after which time she worked as an engineer for Intel Corporation in Santa Clara, CA. She received her Masters and Ph.D. in Industrial Engineering, with a focus on Human Factors Engineering, from Purdue University, after which time she spent 15 years as an Industrial Engineering professor at the University of Central Florida (UCF).

José G. Vargas-Hernández, M.B.A., Ph.D., Member of the National System of Researchers of Mexico and a research professor at University Center for Economic and Managerial Sciences, University of Guadalajara. Professor Vargas-Hernández has a Ph. D. in Public Administration and a Ph.D. in Organizational Economics. He has undertaken studies in Organisational Behaviour and has a Master of Business

Administration, published four books and more than 200 papers in international journals and reviews (some translated to English, French, German, Portuguese, Farsi, Chinese, etc.) and more than 300 essays in national journals and reviews. He has obtained several international Awards and recognition.

Grace Waldfogle is a fourth-year doctoral student in the Human Factors and Cognitive Psychology program at The University of Central Florida. She earned her B.S. in Psychology, Human Factors and Design at The Pennsylvania State University, followed by her Master's degree at UCF. Her current research interests are training for vigilance as well as how individual differences contribute to variations in performance. Furthermore, Grace's dissertation topic focuses on the vigilance taxonomy through a remote work lens.

Index

A

Affordance 47, 67, 76
augmented reality 78-79, 84-85, 87-88, 90,
    92, 97-108, 180, 182, 185, 195-196,
    198-200, 203, 207-210
authentic learning 48-52, 68-70, 76, 198
automation 95, 99, 102, 107, 211-217,
    219-221

B

behavioral economics 140

C

Constructivists Learning Approaches 76
Continuous Control 76
Control Coding 61, 66-67, 76
COVID-19 1-12, 14-19, 181, 184, 193,
    208-209

D

decision making 8, 61, 63, 68, 87, 140,
    143-144, 150-151, 159, 212, 214
Defense 11, 13, 18, 106
design research 53, 59, 68
detection 1-2, 7-8, 10-13, 227
digital health technology 164-167, 171
Digital media 39, 43
digital mental health 180-182, 186, 188-
    192, 194-195, 206-208, 210
Discrete Controls 76

E

Education 2, 18, 34, 38, 45, 47-50, 74-75,
    78-79, 84-86, 97-105, 108, 113, 118,
    121, 130, 132, 134-135, 143, 174, 185,
    194, 196-197, 201, 203, 209, 235-236
Electronic Performance Support Systems
    (EPSS) 61, 77
embodied cognition 85, 105
error 18, 81-82, 211-212, 219, 221
ethical considerations 35, 188
ethical values 20-21, 38
expectations 12, 75, 123, 157, 212, 215, 231
exposure therapy 185-186, 203, 207, 210
eXtended reality 98, 106

H

health 2-3, 5, 7-13, 18-19, 22, 30, 45-46,
    50, 86, 116, 119, 125, 160, 164-175,
    180-186, 188-210
health behavior change 164, 166-172,
    174-175, 196
health self-management 165-166, 168, 172
higher education 48-49, 74, 104, 121, 209
human factors 4, 14, 21-22, 26-27, 29-32,
    34-36, 38, 41-45, 47-48, 50-51, 61,
    68, 70-72, 74-77, 97, 105-108, 164,
    166, 173, 203, 207-208, 220-221,
    233, 235-236
Human-Human Interactions 222
human-technology interactions 222

I

innovation 46, 49, 74, 97, 101, 109-110, 113-115, 119-129, 131-133, 135, 137-139, 147

interaction 14, 23, 27-28, 30, 34-35, 39, 41-43, 45, 48, 50-52, 61, 67-68, 70-72, 74-77, 85, 89-90, 92, 97-98, 101-103, 105-106, 149, 188, 213, 216, 219, 229-230, 236

interaction design 48, 50-52, 61, 68, 70, 76-77

interface 23, 25-26, 47-48, 51, 59, 63-65, 67-68, 74, 89-90, 103, 150, 159, 214, 230

Internet-based interventions 180, 182, 193, 210

K

knowledge transfer 95, 109, 129, 136, 139

L

learning organizations 109, 119, 122-124, 128-129, 135, 139

M

mental model 219
mitigation 1-2, 4-5, 7, 9, 150
mixed reality 100-103, 107
mode awareness 215, 219

N

Navy 211
neuroeconomics 140-141, 144, 157, 159

O

Objectivists Learning Approaches 77
organizational culture 109-114, 116, 120, 122, 128-129, 139

P

Pedagogy 18, 89, 201
Performance Aides 78
preprints 1-2, 7-10, 13
prevention 1, 6, 9, 11, 13, 82, 165, 173, 201-202
prototyping 55, 59, 70, 99

S

situational awareness 87-88, 103, 211, 213-214

smartphone apps 180, 182-185, 199, 202, 207, 210

social technology 20-23, 25-32, 34-38
strategy 24, 36, 41, 111, 113, 119-120, 127-128, 132, 134-137, 139

sustainable organizational development 110-117, 119-129, 131, 139

T

Tailored Digital Interventions 191, 210
teaching and learning 49, 74
technology 3, 8, 10, 12-13, 15, 18, 20-32, 34-40, 42, 44-45, 47, 49, 51-52, 61, 74-75, 78-79, 81-82, 84, 88-89, 93, 95, 97-100, 102-103, 105-106, 111, 120, 128-129, 134, 158, 164-167, 169-175, 181, 183, 185-187, 189, 192, 194, 197, 200-202, 205, 207-216, 220, 222-226, 230-232, 235-237

technology acceptance 164, 166, 169-173, 237

technology adoption 81, 164, 171, 173
technomorphism 222-227, 229-231
training 34, 38, 51, 74, 78-79, 82, 84-89, 93, 95, 97-99, 101-102, 106-107, 110-112, 116, 118, 120, 127, 129, 132, 134-137, 148, 183, 185, 200, 205, 208, 213-216, 219

Trust in automation 216, 220

U

usability 5, 30-31, 37-38, 46, 48, 51, 59,

70, 72, 91, 102, 104, 184, 189, 200
user engagement 20-27, 30-33, 35, 37-38, 41, 43-47, 103, 180, 189, 195
user experience 25, 31, 48, 51, 74, 89, 166
User Experience Design 48
user research 20, 34, 36, 38

V

validation 3, 7, 9-11, 195, 230-231

Virtual Reality 78-79, 83, 93, 98-99, 101, 103-105, 185, 198, 200, 203, 205, 207-210

W

Warfighting 211, 214
wearables 1-9, 11-13, 18, 68

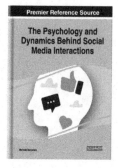

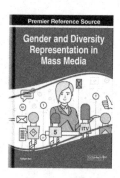

Printed in the United States
by Baker & Taylor Publisher Services